SCRIPTURAL TRACES: CRITICAL PERSPECTIVES ON
THE RECEPTION AND INFLUENCE OF THE BIBLE

5

Published under

LIBRARY OF HEBREW BIBLE/
OLD TESTAMENT STUDIES

614

Formerly Journal for the Study of the Old Testament Supplement Series

CHILDREN'S BIBLES IN AMERICA

A Reception History of the Story of Noah's Ark in US Children's Bibles

Russell W. Dalton

LONDON · NEW YORK · OXFORD · NEW DELHI · SYDNEY

T&T CLARK
Bloomsbury Publishing Plc
50 Bedford Square, London, WC1B 3DP, UK
1385 Broadway, New York, NY 10018, USA

BLOOMSBURY, T&T CLARK and the T&T Clark logo are
trademarks of Bloomsbury Publishing Plc

First published in Great Britain 2016
Paperback edition first published 2018

For legal purposes the Acknowledgements on p. xiii constitute
an extension of this copyright page.

A catalogue record for this book is available from the British Library.

Library of Congress Cataloging-in-Publication Data
Dalton, Russell W.
Children's Bibles in America : a reception history of the story of Noah's Ark in US children's
Bibles / Russell W. Dalton.
pages cm. – (The library of Hebrew Bible/Old Testament studies ; volume 614)
ISBN 978-0-567-66015-2 (hardback)
1. Noah's ark. 2. Bible stories. 3. Children's Bibles–United States–History.
4. United States–Religion. I. Title.
BS658.D28 2015
220.95'050973–dc23
2015018445

ISBN: HB: 978-0-56766-015-2
PB: 978-0-56768-392-2
ePDF: 978-0-56766-017-6
ePub: 978-0-56766-016-9

Series: Library of Hebrew Bible/Old Testament Studies, volume 614

Typeset by Fakenham Prepress Solutions, Fakenham, Norfolk NR21 8NN

To find out more about our authors and books visit
www.bloomsbury.com and sign up for our newsletters.

DISCLAIMER

This book is dedicated to Benjamin Thomas Dalton.
"I have set my bow in the clouds." Genesis 9.13

CONTENTS

ACKNOWLEDGMENTS

I have been working on this project in one form or another for a long time and many people have encouraged me and helped me along the way. Two decades ago, when I was a new doctoral student at the Presbyterian School of Christian Education, now a part of Presbyterian Theological Seminary, I wrote my first thesis paper on children's Bibles. My advisor, Dr. Pamela Mitchell-Legg, gave me invaluable guidance and feedback. Also, even before the publication of her groundbreaking book *The Bible for Children*, Ruth B. Bottigheimer gave me, a young scholar unknown to her, great encouragement and insights and provided me with some of her unpublished work.

Over the past decade I have presented papers on children's Bibles at annual meetings of the Religious Education Association, the American Academy of Religion, and the Society of Biblical Literature, as well as "The Bible in American Life Conference" sponsored by the Center for the Study of Religion and American Culture. In each case my colleagues in these various fields provided me with their enthusiastic encouragement for the project and helpful feedback.

I received an Association of Theological Schools Research Expense Grant, funded by the Lilly Foundation, which allowed me to conduct research for this book at the Library of Congress in Washington, DC and the American Antiquarian Society in Worcester, Massachusetts. I am especially indebted to Laura E. Wasowicz, Curator of Children's Literature at the American Antiquarian Society, and the very helpful staff there for all of their assistance.

The administration and faculty of Brite Divinity School granted me research leave to complete this project. Many of my colleagues offered their insights, but special mention must be made of Warren Carter, David Gunn, and Jeffrey Williams who read early drafts of sections of the book and provided keen and helpful insights and advice. My student assistants at Brite, Lisa Barnett, Nathan Russell, and James Webner, each provided invaluable aid in research and editing portions of the book. Loren Baxter, Brite Divinity School's Director of Technology Resources, helped me format and prepare the images in this book for publication.

I also wish to thank the editors of the "Scriptural Traces" series at T&T Clark, Claudia V. Camp, Andrew Mein, and W. J. Lyons along with Editorial Assistant Miriam Cantwell and Library of Biblical Studies Series Editor Dominic Mattos for all of their support.

My wife Lisa has been patient and kind with me, as always, as I wrote this book. Our children, Nathan, Anna, Maria, and Joseph, have each, at different times, asked me very thoughtful and provocative questions about Bible stories and the versions of those stories that appear in children's Bibles. They have been excellent dialogue partners for this project.

LIST OF FIGURES

The author and the publishers gratefully acknowledge the permission granted to reproduce the copyright material in this book. Every effort has been made to trace copyright holders and obtain their permission for the use of copyright material. The publisher apologizes for any errors or omissions in the following list and would be grateful if notified of any corrections that should be incorporated in future reprints or editions of this book.

INTRODUCTION: THE SIGNIFICANCE AND SCOPE OF THIS STUDY

I.1. A Reception History of Children's Bibles as the Source of Fruitful Academic Inquiry

For over 200 years, children's Bibles have been among the most popular and influential religious education publications in the United States. Through the ways in which they revise and adapt Bible stories, children's Bibles have both reflected and reinforced America's diverse and changing assumptions about the nature of childhood, the purpose of religious education, and the nature of the Bible and its role in religious instruction. Despite this, to date relatively few academic books have been published that examine children's Bibles in a serious manner.[1]

Why should one devote serious scholarly attention to something as seemingly trivial and juvenile as children's Bibles? Several reasons come to mind. First of all, children's Bibles have arguably been the most common type of religious education resource published in the United States other than the Bible itself. Since the beginning of the republic, when American publishers began republishing British children's Bibles, and especially since the explosion of American Christian book buying in the late nineteenth century, Americans have been purchasing and reading a large number and wide variety of children's Bibles. In recent decades, their popularity has only increased. *Publisher's Weekly* reported that in the year 1990 Americans spent over $40 million on children's Bibles,[2] and the demand for children's religious products continued throughout the decade.[3]

---

1. Among the significant studies of children's Bibles that have been published are Ruth B. Bottigheimer, *The Bible for Children: From the Age of Gutenberg to the Present* (New Haven: Yale University Press, 1996), Penny Schine Gold, *Making the Bible Modern: Children's Bibles and Jewish Education in Twentieth-Century America* (Ithaca, NY: Cornell University Press, 2003), and Caroline Vander Stichele and Hugh S. Pyper, eds, *Text, Image, and Otherness in Children's Bibles: What is in the Picture?*, Semeia Studies 56 (Atlanta, GA: Society of Biblical Literature, 2012).

2. Thomas S. Giles, "Pick a Bible – Any Bible," *Christianity Today* (October 26, 1992): 27.

3. Shannon Maughan, "In the Kids' Corner," *Publishers Weekly* 246:41 (October 11, 1999): 46.

According to a book buyer for Family Christian Stores, a popular chain of Christian bookstores, in 1999 children's Bible storybooks accounted for 10–12 percent of their total company sales and 28 percent of their children's book sales.[4] In her 2001 article, "Bible Stories: Facing a Floodtide," LaVonne Neff reported that "Today the flood of Bible-related products continues unabated, and many Bible story books are bankrolling their companies."[5] These children's Bibles range from colorful Bible picture books that abridge and simplify Bible stories for very young children to study Bibles for older children that contain a translation of the entire Bible.

In the twenty-first century, the demand for children's Bibles does not appear to be waning in the least. Another indication of their significant place in American culture is the recent appearance of several parodies of children's Bibles written for adults. *The Awkward Moments Children's Bible* by "Horus Gilgamesh," for example, features a cartoonish illustration of a cheerful Noah and his smiling animal friends looking out over the ark while the corpses of people and animals float in the water below them.[6] The American Atheist Press published another parody of a children's Bible, Paul Farrell's *Illustrated Stories from the Bible (That They Won't Tell You in Sunday School)*, in 2005.[7] Brendan Powell Smith's *The Brick Bible: A New Spin on the Old Testament*, offers adults photographs of graphic and violent scenes from the Bible that were created using Lego blocks.[8] The depiction of the story of the flood, for example, shows Noah's family and the animals walking through skeletons and corpses as they leave the ark.[9] These books expose the irony and limitations of children's Bibles. Since the humor of these books depends upon readers' familiarity with the genre, they also attest to children's Bibles' place in America's cultural consciousness.

In addition to their popularity, children's Bibles are also an influential phenomenon in American religious history precisely because they are written for children. Many Americans have received their first impressions of what the Bible is and why they should read it from children's Bibles. Should the faithful read Bible stories to learn about God, to learn about salvation, or is each Bible story a fable that provides a lesson in moral behavior? The texts of children's Bibles convey to readers basic assumptions about the nature and use of the Bible. At the same

---

4. Ibid., 46.

5. LaVonne Neff, "Bible Stories: Facing a Floodtide," *Publishers Weekly* 248:42 (October 15, 2001), 38.

6. Horus Gilgamesh, *The Awkward Moments Children's Bible* (Awkward Moments, 2013). The website for the book states that it was a #1 Amazon Bestseller in Amazon.com's Humor & Religion category a week before it was released. http://www.awkwardmoments-bible.com/about (accessed September 9, 2014).

7. Paul Farrell, *Illustrated Stories from the Bible (That They Won't Tell You in Sunday School)* (Austin, TX: American Atheist Press, 2005).

8. Brendan Powell Smith, *The Brick Bible: A New Spin on the Old Testament* (New York: Skyhorse Publishing, 2011).

9. Ibid., *The Brick Bible*, 27–9.

time, the illustrations in children's Bibles present children with powerful impressions of the tone and content of the faith. Many of these impressions last well into adulthood.

Children's Bibles also represent a sort of people's history of the interpretation of the Bible. They are among the few types of American religious literature written by approximately an equal number of women and men. They have been written by laity, clergy, and scholars, and by the faithful of a wide variety of faiths, denominations, and sects. Therefore, they provide illuminating examples of American religious expression written from a wide range of perspectives. That said, the children's Bibles examined in this study certainly do not tell the whole story of America's engagement with the Bible. Because children's Bibles are commercial products that require money to be produced and access to distribution, they primarily represent the history of privileged class thinking in America. Other communities, of course, told Bible stories to their children, but at the outset of this book it is important to recognize that throughout American history it has primarily been middle- and upper-class white people who have published and purchased children's Bibles.

Children's Bibles also provide unique insights into the religious and moral priorities and perspectives of their authors and the times in which they lived. In most cases, the retelling of Bible stories in children's Bibles appear to represent an earnest attempt by Americans to make plain their understanding of the Bible and the most basic teachings of their faith communities that they feel must be passed on to the next generation. Because of this, children's Bibles lend insight into which beliefs and values have made up the core of what these authors felt was essential for the religious education of America's youngest citizens. Even within particular denominations, these beliefs and lessons have changed significantly over the course of US history.

Many children's Bible authors claim that they are merely simplifying Bible stories for children and not changing the substance of the stories in any way. The wide variety of ways in which they consciously or unconsciously revise and adapt these stories, however, provides a striking illustration of the multivalence and malleability of these texts and reflects and reveals America's changing assumptions about the Bible, religion, the nature of childhood, and what beliefs and values must be passed on to the next generation. This study of Bible stories for American children offers a grassroots-level view of diverse movements in American culture and American religion in their most basic forms.

The story of Noah from the book of Genesis serves as a particularly helpful story to examine in children's Bibles. Not only is it the Bible story that is most commonly included in children's Bibles, often serving as the inspiration for the cover illustration, but the story of Noah also contains a vast plurality of potential meanings that have been mined in creative and wildly diverse ways throughout American history. A study of the ways in which the story of Noah, the flood, and the ark has been adapted, then, lends rewarding insights into American religion and culture.

This study is a focused exercise in the "reception history" of the story of Noah in the United States as it has been presented to children in children's Bibles. As David Gunn has pointed out, however, the term "reception" is an unfortunate phrase because the appropriation of texts is far from a passive act.[10] This is especially the case for sacred texts that carry with them their own level of opacity and surplus of meaning when being appropriated to teach religious orthodoxy and morality to children. The retellings of the story of Noah in this study often reflect what the authors believe are the most crucial values and beliefs to pass on to the next generation and they do not hesitate to abridge, expand, revise, or annotate the story in order to make their points.

I.2. The Scope of this Study

This study uses the term "children's Bible" in an inclusive and expansive sense. This book surveys "children's Bibles" created by adults for both children and teenagers (or "youth"). Many children's Bibles, especially those created for teenagers and older children, are full translations or comprehensive paraphrase editions of the entire Bible that have been created specifically for children. Others are children's editions of popular translations such as the King James Version, the New International Version, or the New Century Version that include devotional notes and illustrations. These children's Bibles are fascinating in their own right and could serve as the subject of their own book-length examination. This book, however, focuses on children's Bibles that are sometimes alternatively referred to as "Bible storybooks" and are collections of one or more Bible stories that are more freely retold and illustrated for children.

This work focuses on children's Bibles published in the United States.[11] Many children's Bibles published in the United States in the earliest decades of the republic were merely republications of British children's Bibles. Many other children's Bibles included in this study are written and illustrated by authors and illustrators from countries other than the United States. This study, then, is not limited to books that originated in the United States or books that were produced by American authors and illustrators, but is limited to children's Bibles published by American publishers and published to be read by American children. Also, while some children's Bibles have been published in the United States in Spanish, German, and other languages, this study focuses on those published in English.

---

10. David Gunn, "Cultural Criticism," in Gale A. Yee, ed., *Judges & Method: New Approaches in Biblical Studies*, 2nd edn (Minneapolis, MN: Fortress Press, 2007), 204.

11. This study is an extensive examination of children's Bibles that have been published in the United States and reflects upon what they reflect and reveal about American culture. It does not compare or contrast these findings to children's Bibles published in other countries—though such a study would be a fruitful project.

This study examines hundred of children's Bibles.[12] The bibliography includes approximately 400 children's Bibles, and hundreds more from the 1800s to the present have been consulted during the research for this study that are not listed in the bibliography. While this book represents the most extensive review of American children's Bibles to date, it is certainly not an exhaustive study of every children's Bible ever published in the United States.

A reception history of American children's Bibles calls for an interdisciplinary and multidisciplinary approach, drawing connections to the fields of biblical studies, the history of religion in America, religious education, childhood studies, moral education, and more. One purpose of this study has been to share primary research with scholars and students of various fields of inquiry so that they can make their own connections and raise their own questions. Portions of this research have been shared with scholars at the annual meetings of the Society of Biblical Literature, the American Academy of Religion, the Religious Education Association, and historians and Americanists at a conference on the Bible in American Life.[13] In each setting, scholars in attendance found fruitful ways to connect the study to their own research interests. It is beyond the scope of this book to pursue all relevant and fruitful avenues of inquiry. One of the reasons this study offers extended quotes from children's Bibles rather than just summaries of their contents is to allow the texts themselves to raise questions that others can explore from the perspectives of their own areas of expertise.

I.3. Summary of Chapters

The first chapter of this book examines some of the many ways in which Bible stories, and the story of Noah in particular, are embellished, abridged, annotated, and illustrated in the process of retelling the story for children. The chapters that follow it each consider a particular theme or approach to retelling Bible stories for children. Chapter 2 offers an extended examination of the variety of ways in which the story of Noah has been used in children's Bibles published in the United States to teach children about the character of God. The chapter traces the transformation of God in the story of Noah from a dangerous God whom children should fear in children's Bibles of the early years of the American republic to a

12. This study of children's Bibles from throughout US history is the result of years of research into hundreds of children's Bibles and was partially funded by a generous Association of Theological Schools Research Expense Grant provided by the Lilly Foundation. This grant allowed the author to conduct research at the American Antiquarian Society, the United States Library of Congress, and other libraries and to purchase modern and antiquarian children's Bibles that were unavailable from these libraries.

13. To be specific, "The Bible in American Life Conference" in Indianapolis, August 6–9, 2014, sponsored by the Center for the Study of Religion and American Culture at Indiana University—Purdue University in Indianapolis.

kind and friendly God who keeps children safe presented in most children's Bibles of the twenty-first century.

A primary concern for many American Christians has been that their children accept Jesus Christ as their savior: Chapter 3 examines the creative ways in which the story of Noah from the Hebrew Bible has been appropriated in Christian children's Bibles as a story that calls children to salvation in Christ.

Chapter 4 is another lengthy chapter that explores the most common way that children's Bibles use Bible stories, namely to teach children lessons on moral behavior. The story of Noah has been used most often in this regard to teach children the virtues of obedience and hard work, but the chapter traces the ways in which the story has been used throughout US history to teach a wide range of other virtues as well.

Chapter 5 takes a slightly different approach. It examines the ways in which children's Bible retellings of the story of Noah have presented the Bible to children alternatively as a sacred historical event or as the fun and amusing story of a boat ride with animal friends. In the process the chapter explores several aspects of the history of children's literature in the United States.

Finally, a conclusion consolidates some overarching themes and insights from the study, outlines four different approaches adults can take to presenting Bible stories to children, and offers some directions for further investigation.

Chapter 1

RETELLING BIBLE STORIES FOR CHILDREN: CHANGING AND REFRAMING THE STORY OF NOAH

Noah told the people that God was going to drown the world, and advised them to leave off their wickedness. But they would not mind. Still they went on eating and drinking, and not thinking of God, nor trying to please him.[1]

D. P. Kidder, *Bible Stories for Children*, 1851

Then Noah told them of the coming flood, and tried to get them to stop their bad ways, that they might live and not be drowned. But the neighbors only laughed at Noah, and said he must be crazy to build a boat on dry land, and so they went back to their wicked lives. Sometimes, when it rained, they thought of Noah, but the rain cleared away, and they laughed again, and were worse than ever.[2]

George Hodges, *The Garden of Eden*, 1909

The authors of many children's Bibles published throughout US history state in their introductions that their goal is simply to pass on to children the stories of the Bible in ways that make the stories clear and accessible. The ways in which they revise, adapt, and comment upon those stories, however, significantly reframe them in ways that reflect and reinforce certain assumptions, beliefs, and values. Since such retellings always make changes to the content the original text, it is informative to examine the particular ways in which children's Bibles alter the stories from the way they appear in the Bible itself.

The chapters that follow this one examine the ways in which American children's Bibles have appropriated the story of Noah to teach children a variety of perspectives on the character of God, salvation in Jesus Christ, the virtues they should live upon, or to engage the Bible either as historical events or entertaining stories. Before examining these particular ways in which the story of Noah has been appropriated for use with children, this chapter pauses to provide an

---

1. D. P. Kidder, *Bible Stories for Children*, Vol. I (New York: Lane & Scott, 1851), 36–7.

2. George Hodges, *The Garden of Eden: Stories from the First Nine Books of the Old Testament* (Boston, MA: Houghton Mifflin Company, 1909), 8.

overview of the sorts of changes and adaptations that children's Bible authors and illustrators make when they appropriate the story of Noah.

1.1. Biblical Literacy: Learning the Story of Noah for Its Own Sake

Before examining children's Bibles that change and reframe Bible stories through their retellings of them, it is important to note that many Bible resources created for children throughout US history have been designed primarily to do nothing more than aid in increasing children's knowledge of the words or events of the Bible. From the beginning of the republic to the present day, many American parents, grandparents, clergy, and others have demonstrated their belief that their children should be biblically literate by continually making children's Bibles among the most popular publications for children in the United States. Authors, illustrators, and publishers have found a wide variety of creative ways to entice children to open their Bibles and learn the words of Scripture, including Bible catechisms, hieroglyphical Bibles, thumb Bibles and short chapbooks for small hands, illustrated versions of the King James Version of the Bible, translations of the Bible created especially for children, and the brightly colored theme Bibles of the twenty-first century. While close analysis of these books may reveal that they serve particular theological and moral agendas, they also provide a stark contrast to the more thorough retelling and reshaping of Bible stories in the children's Bibles described in the chapters that follow. These resources, however, attest to America's early and persisting desire for children to learn the words and events of the Bible for their own sake, trusting that biblical literacy is beneficial in its own right.

During the colonial period, theological or doctrinal catechisms were the most popular Christian education resources in America.[3] The increasingly sectarian theology reflected in these catechisms, however, along with a growing desire for direct study of the Bible, led to the publication of Sunday School lessons and other resources focused on increasing children's knowledge of the Bible.[4]

During the nineteenth century, Bible catechisms became a mainstay of Christian education. These Bible catechisms would often contain passages of Scripture taken directly from the King James Version followed by a list of questions testing children's close reading of the passage, and answers that were taken directly from the passage itself. These Bible catechisms almost always included the story

---

3. Among the most popular of these, first published in England but reprinted many times and readily available in the United States, were John Cotton, *Milke for Babes. Drawn Out of the Breasts of both Testaments* (London: F. Coe, 1646) and Isaac Watts, *Dr. Watts's Plain and Easy Catechisms for Children: The Shorter Catechism* (Cambridge: Hillard & Metcalf, 1815).

4. See James C. Wilhoit, "The Bible Goes to Sunday School: An Historical Response to Pluralism," *Religious Education* 82 (Summer 1987): 390–8.

of Noah.[5] As Albert Barnes wrote in the introduction to his *Questions on the Historical Books of the New Testament*, the "one great design of these questions is to fix attention distinctly on the text."[6] For example, in 1838 the American Sunday-School Union published *The Child's Scripture Question Book* which contained the following questions and answers regarding Genesis chapter 6:

Q. Who brought the flood upon the earth?
A. God. *Gen.* vi. 17.
Q. Why?
A. Because the great wickedness of its inhabitants. *Gen.* vi. 13.
Q. Who found grace in the sight of the Lord at that time?
A. Noah. *Gen.* vi. 8.
Q. What was the character of Noah?
A. He was a just man, perfect in his generations, and walked with God. *Gen.* vi. 9.
Q. What was Noah instructed to build for his preservation from the flood?
A. An ark. *Gen.* vi. 14.[7]

Like most other Bible catechisms, these Union questions focused children's attention on certain aspects of the text, but refrained from having children draw theological or moral applications from the text.

In a similar manner, Rabbi Frederick de Sola Mendes's *The Child's First Bible*, first published in 1887, offered children an abridged version of the story of Noah that stayed close to the wording and events found in Genesis, and followed the story with questions such as "1. What kind of man was Noah? 2. What did God tell him to build? 3. Who were to be taken into the ark?"[8] While the biblical text was abridged, the questions were designed to help children recall facts about the story rather than to make theological or moral applications based upon the text.

Another creative way that adults encouraged children to learn and remember the words of Scripture was through hieroglyphical Bibles that used a combination of words and pictures on each page to present a Bible verse or two. These

---

5. For example, Isaac Watts, *Scripture History* (New York: George Routledge and Sons, 1820), 11; *Union Questions on Select Portions of Scripture*, Vol. 1, *Containing the History of the Life of Jesus Christ* (Philadelphia, PA: American Sunday School Union, 1828), 3; *The Child's Scripture Question Book* (Philadelphia, PA: American Sunday-School Union, 1836, 1858), 8–9; B. K. Peirce, *Child's Lesson-Book on the Bible* (New York: Carlton & Porter, 1851), 19; and "Noah Saved in the Ark," *Little Bible Lesson Pictures* 18:3, Part 3 (July 21, 1901).

6. Albert Barnes, *Questions on the Historical Books of the New Testament*, Vol. 1, *Matthew* (New York: Harper & Brothers, 1830), vi.

7. *The Child's Scripture Question Book*, 8–9.

8. F. De Sola Mendes, *The Child's First Bible: Mainly in Words of One and Two Syllables, for Younger Children with Questions*, 14th edn (New York: To Be Had of the Author, 1915), 6.

hieroglyphical Bibles are among the first Bible education resources published for children in the United States and represent another innovative tool that was designed, according to the authors, to focus children's careful attention on the words of Scripture.[9] These books occasionally devoted a page to the destruction of humankind in the flood, but more often the story of Noah was represented by the episode in which Noah sends forth the dove.[10] The anonymous author of *A New Hieroglyphical Bible*, published in Boston around 1796, begins the preface by stating, "To imprint on the memory of Youth, by lively and sensible images, the sacred and important truths of Holy Writ, is the object of the following Work."[11] The story of Noah and the dove, then, begins with the words "But the" followed by an illustration of a dove, then the words "found no rest for the sole of her," followed by the illustration of a bird's foot, then the words "and she returned unto him into the," followed by a small illustration of an ark, and so on (See Figure 1.1).[12] Again, one can speculate upon various assumptions and agendas behind the presentation of these passages, but the goal of hieroglyphical Bibles was to get children to pay careful attention to the words of the Bible itself.

Another group of children's Bibles designed to improve the biblical literacy of children were tiny books that offered brief overviews of what their authors deemed to be the most significant people and events of the Bible. These publications, popular in the nineteenth century, were often so small, both in the size and number of their pages, that they did not have the space to add embellishments to the stories or to include lessons or explanations at the end of the stories. Instead, they seem to have been primarily designed to pass on to children a basic biblical literacy.[13] Many of these collections of Bible stories were published in the small

9. Several authors explicitly state this goal in their introductions, including *A Curious Heiroglyphick Bible; or Select Passages in the Old and New Testaments, Represented with Emblematic Figures for the Amusement of Youth* (Worcester, MA: Isaiah Thomas, 1788), vii; *A New Hieroglyphical Bible* (Boston, MA: Norman, c. 1796), n.p.; and Frank Beard et al., *Picture Puzzles or How to Read the Bible by Symbols (Designed Especially for the Boys and Girls to Stimulate a Greater Interest in the Holy Bible)* (Naperville, IL: J. L. Nichols & Co., 1899), 3.

10. See, for example, *A Curious Heiroglyphick Bible*, 19; *The Hieroglyphick Bible*, 2d edn (Boston, MA: Buckingham for Thomas, 1814); *A New Hieroglyphical Bible* (c. 1796), 10; *A New Hieroglyphical Bible. With Four Hundred Embellishments on Wood*, 11th edn (New York: American Heritage Press, 1836), 9; Beard et al., *Picture Puzzles*, 64.

11. *A New Hieroglyphical Bible* (c. 1796).

12. Ibid., 9.

13. For an interesting variation to this pattern, see William Turner, *An Abstract of the Bible History* (Boston, MA: Bowles & Dearborn, 1828). Turner's book is over 200 pages long, but still allots only a paragraph or two to each Bible story and at times takes minor liberties with the text. The book is so much longer than most because Turner includes in the book nearly every story from the Bible, instead of selecting just a few, as most of these overviews do.

GENESIS VIII. 9. 9

But the 🕊 found no rest for the sole of her 🦶 and she returned unto him into the 🏠 for the waters were on the 👤 of the whole earth. Then he put forth his ✋ and took her, and pulled her in unto him into the ark.

But the *dove* found no rest for the sole of her *foot*, and she returned unto him into the *ark*: for the waters were upon the *face* of the whole earth. Then he put forth his *hand*, and took her, and pulled her in unto him into the ark.

Figure 1.1. The story of Noah and the dove from *A New Hieroglyphical Bible* (Boston, MA: Norman, c. 1796), 9.

pamphlet-style publications known as chapbooks. These chapbook Bibles were often just three and a half to five inches tall and consisted of as little as eight to as many as thirty pages and were bound with a colored and slightly thicker stock of paper.[14] They were therefore inexpensive to produce, allowing Sunday School teachers to give them out as prizes and evangelistic societies to pass them out to less fortunate children. Organizations such as the American Bible Society, founded in 1816, and the influential American Tract Society, founded in 1825, both published a number of these inexpensive chapbooks that briefly retold one or more Bible stories in order to get the bare facts of the Bible into the minds of America's children.[15] Thumb Bibles were another style of publication that served this purpose. These tiny Bibles, perhaps named after the diminutive Tom Thumb, were hardcover books that often measured only two or three inches in height (see Figure 1.2). Though the small type and fragile bindings of these texts made them of questionable practical value,[16] they proved quite popular.[17]

Most of these chapbook Bibles and thumb Bibles devoted more space to the story of Noah than any other story of the Bible.[18] The *History of the Holy Bible* from around 1816, for example, uses only fifty-eight words to retell the story of Noah, but even at that length the relatively large font used on the small pages means the story spreads over three of the book's sixteen pages. The story of Noah in its entirety reads,

> As the earth progressed in population, sin became more and more apparent, until for the dreadful wickedness of man, the Lord destroyed every living

14. For example *Bible Stories with Engravings* (Worcester, MA: Jonathan Grout, Jr., 1840); *Book of Bible Stories. A Present for a Good Scholar* (New Haven, CT: S. Babcock, 1842); *Pictures of Bible History* (Northhampton, MA: J. H. Butler, 1840); *Young Bible Reader* (Cincinnati, OH: William T. Truman [1843]); *Bible Stories and Pictures* (New Haven, CT: Sidney Babcock, 1850).

15. See Prothero, *Religious Literacy*, 82–3.

16. See Christopher De Hamel, *The Book: A History of the Bible* (New York: Phaidon Press, Inc., 2001), 259.

17. Ruth Elizabeth Adomeit catalogs over 150 such thumb Bibles published from 1750 through the 1800s in the United States, though many of these are second, third, or even twelfth editions of the same texts. See Ruth Elizabeth Adomeit, *Three Centuries of Thumb Bibles: A Checklist* (New York: Garland Publishing, Inc., 1980).

18. To list a few: *Scripture History* (New York: Wood, 1811), n.p.; *The History of the Holy Bible. Abridged* (New Haven, CT: Sidney's Press, 1817), 15–16; *The Attributes of God; An Account of the Creation and the Story of Joseph and His Brethren, Taken from Scripture* (New Haven, CT: Sidney's Press, 1818), 16–17; *History of the Holy Bible* (Hartford, CT: Cook & Hale, c. 1816–19), 6–8; *Scripture History, Abridged* (Boston, MA: Lincoln & Edmands, 1819), n.p.; *A History of the Bible* (no place of publication or publisher given, 1819); *Stories from Scripture for Small Children* (New Haven, CT: J. Babcock and Son, 1820), 24–30; *The Bible History* (Wendell, MA: J. Metcalf., 1828), 8–9; *A Short History of the Holy Bible: Embellished with numerous colored engravings* (Harrisburg, PA: G. S. Peters, 1838), 4; and *Little book of Bible stories for children.: With numerous engravings* (Worcester, MA: Dorr, Howland & Co. Spooner & Howland, printers, c. 1839 and 1841), 10–11.

Figure 1.2. Various thumb Bibles (on the top row) and chapbook Bible stories (on the bottom row) from the early nineteenth century. Note their size compared to the US quarter.

creature upon the face of the earth, except Noah and his family and those which were preserved with them in the ark. From these the earth was again peopled and replenished after the flood.[19]

Contemporary readers will note phrases such as "dreadful wickedness of man" and perhaps a greater emphasis on sin and destruction than found in most recent retellings of the story, but the retelling does not pause to add embellishments or lessons to the Genesis account of the story.

These brief summaries of Bible stories were quite common in the early nineteenth century. Along with other small books that covered the entire Bible,[20] popular individual Bible stories were often published in small eight-page

19. *History of the Holy Bible* (Hartford, CT: Cook & Hale, c. 1816–19), 6–8.

20. See also, for example, *Pictures of Bible history: With Suitable Descriptions* (Wendell, MA: J. Metcalf., 1826); *Child's book of Bible history.: With Engravings* (Worcester, MA: N. Hervey, c. 1855); and *Bible Stories, for the use of Sunday Schools and Children.; Illustrated with Twenty-four Engravings* (Boston, MA: Charles Gaylord, 1837).

chapbooks comprised of just two small folded pieces of paper, as with the chapbook *Noah and the Flood* from around 1835.[21] They stuck to the basic plots of Bible stories and included crude woodcut illustrations if any pictures at all. Reading them today, they do not seem very interesting or alluring compared to the colorful and entertaining children's Bibles of later years. These small books, however, may have been among the few possessions that young American children of the eighteenth and early nineteenth century owned. The narratives move along at a brisk pace and, though crude, the illustrations may have been the only pictures in any books that they owned. As such, parents may have found them to be helpful tools to introduce children to or remind them of the essential Bible stories that their authors felt children needed to know.

The most direct way that parents and educators have presented the Bible itself to children has been to offer the text of the entire Bible from a common translation. As religious historian Stephen Prothero notes, many early American children read the Bible from cover to cover multiple times before they entered adulthood.[22] For years, adults have created children's editions of the Authorized King James Version of the Bible, often printed in words with larger type in a single column. Many of these children's editions also omit chapter and verse numberings. They often include illustrations, at first rough woodcut illustrations and later colorful illustrations and paintings, to engage and maintain a child's interest. Many other children's editions of the King James Version of the Bible do not contain the entire text of the Bible, but only select stories that the editors deemed especially appropriate for children. These types of children's Bibles, while not the focus of this study, have been a mainstay of children's Bibles throughout the history of the United States.[23]

---

21. *Noah and the Flood* (Worcester, MA: H. J. Howland, c. 1835).

22. Prothero, *Religious Literacy*, 62.

23. To list just a few: *The Child's Bible* (Chicago: L. P. Miller & Company, 1884, 1889); Edward Tuckerman Potter, *Bible Stories in Bible Language* (New York: D. Appleton and Company, 1898); *Bible History for Schools and the Home. Authorized by the Evangelical Lutheran Augustana Synod* (Rock Island, IL: Augustana Book Concern, 1898); Joseph B. Gilder, *The Bible for Young People: Arranged from the King James Version with Twenty-Four Full Page Illustrations from the Masters* (New York: Century Company, 1902); Newton Marshall Hall, *The Bible Story: Volume One* (Springfield, MA: King-Richardson Company, 1906, 1917); Eva March Tappan, *An Old, Old Story-Book: Compiled from the Old Testament* (Boston, MA: Houghton Mifflin Company, 1910); Frances Jenkins Olcott, *Bible Stories to Read and Tell*, illus. by Willy Pogany (Boston, MA: Houghton Mifflin Company, 1915); Lorinda Munson Bryant, ed., *Bible Story in Bible Language* (King James Version) (New York: D. Appleton and Company, 1922); *The Book of Life, Volume One* (Chicago: John Rudin & Company Inc., 1923, 1925, 1927); *The Little Children's Bible* (New York: MacMillan Company, 1924); *The Older Children's Bible* (New York: MacMillan Company, 1924); *A First Bible* (New York and London: Oxford University Press, 1934); Newton Marshall Hall, *The Children's Bible* (New York: Western Publishing, 1981, 1965); *The Noah's Ark Bible* (Grand Rapids, MI: World Publishing, 1989); *Rainbow Bible* (Nashville, TN: Thomas

In the twentieth century some writers provided children with entirely new translations of the Bible to serve as an alternative to the archaic language of the King James Version or Revised Standard Version.[24] In the second half of the twentieth century, as English translations and paraphrases of the Bible such as *Today's English Version, The Living Bible,* and *The New International Version* were created that were accessible to younger readers, there was less of a need or a market for authors and publishers to create entirely new translations for children. Instead, many special children's editions of these new translations and paraphrase editions were soon published.[25] In the twenty-first century, especially, a growing trend in the US was to create separate brightly-colored editions of the Bible for children of each gender. Girls have been presented with Bible editions with titles such as the *Shiny Sequin Bible Holy Bible* (2011),[26] *The Precious Princess Bible* (2010),[27] and *The NIV FaiThGirLz! Bible* (2010),[28] while boys have been offered titles such as *The NIV Adventure Bible* (2011),[29] *The Super Heroes Bible: The Quest for Good Over Evil* (NIrV) (2002)[30] and the *Compact Kids Bible: Green Camo,* a 2007 International Children's Bible with a military-style camouflage cover from Thomas Nelson.[31]

Nelson, 1996); Lawrence O. Richards, ed., *The KJV Kids' Study Bible* (Grand Rapids, MI: Zonderkidz, 2001); *KJV Read to Me Bible for Kids* (Nashville, TN: Holman Bible Publishers, 2001); *The Princess Bible,* New King James Version (Nashville, TN: Thomas Nelson, 2008); *Holy Bible: King James Version, Kids Study Bible* (Grand Rapids, MI: Hendrickson, 2009); *The KJV Illustrated Study Bible for Kids* (Nashville, TN: Holman Bible Publishers, 2010).

24. See Henry A. Sherman and Charles Foster Kent, *The Children's Bible: Selections from the Old and New Testaments* (New York: Charles Scribner's Sons, 1922, 1947); John Stirling, ed., *The Child's Bible* (Indianapolis, IN: Bobbs-Merrill Company, ca. 1929); Harold Begbie, *The Children's Story Bible* (New York: Grolier Society, 1948); Edgar J. Goodspeed, ed., *The Junior Bible: An American Translation* (New York: MacMillan Company, 1948); and Allan Hart Jahsmann, *The Holy Bible for Children: A Simplified Version* (St. Louis, MO: Concordia Publishing House, 1977). See also J. F. Allen, et al., *Nelson's Picture Bible* (Nashville, TN: Thomas Nelson, 1973), a faithful paraphrase of select Bible stories.

25. See, for example, *The Children's Living Bible* (Wheaton, IL: Tyndale House, 1972); *Precious Moments Children's Bible: Easy-to-Read New Life Version* (Grand Rapids, MI: Baker Book House, 1999); *Family Bible: English Standard Version (ESV)* (Wheaton, IL: Crossway Bibles, 2004); *Holy Bible: International Children's Bible: New Century Version* (Dallas, TX: Word Publishing, 1983); *NIrV Discoverer's Bible for Early Readers* (Grand Rapids, MI: ZonderKidz, 2002); *The Beginning Reader's Bible,* compiled by Tama Fortner, illus. by Marijke ten Cate (Nashville, TN: Thomas Nelson, 2011).

26. *Shiny Sequin Bible. Holy Bible* (International Children's Bible) (New York: Tommy Nelson, 2011).

27. *The Precious Princess Bible* (NIrV) (Grand Rapids, MI: ZonderKidz, 2010).

28. *FaiThGirLz! Bible* (NIV) (Grand Rapids, MI: Zondervan, 2011).

29. *NIV Adventure Bible* (Grand Rapids, MI: Zondervan, 2011).

30. *The Super Heroes Bible: The Quest for Good Over Evil* (NIrV) (Grand Rapids, MI: Zondervan, 2002).

31. *Compact Kids Bible: Green Camo* (New York: Thomas Nelson, 2007). See also *NIV Boys Bible* (Grand Rapids, MI: Zondervan, 2011), 9.

The production designs and notes included in these Bibles frame the reading of the Bible for children as a gender-specific activity and tend to reinforce traditional gender roles. All translations of the Bible, including translations designed primarily for children, are interpretations of texts in and of themselves,[32] and the packaging of the Bibles and the notes they include certainly carry certain cultural values with them. Still, these children's editions of the Bible do not completely retell Bible stories in the same way as the children's Bibles described in the chapters that follow. As such, they illustrate the desire of many Americans to have their children read the Bible in language that is accessible and understandable to them.

Though this book focuses on the way Americans have retold Bible stories, these examples attest to the fact that the authors and publishers of many Bible-related books for children appear to have had no other agenda than to get children to learn the words and events found in the Bible itself for its own sake. Those who created these books may have had their own assumptions regarding what children would learn from the Bible, and careful analysis of the texts may reveal certain implicit lessons. These children's Bible resources, however, do not appropriate the stories of the Bible as freely as do the other children's Bibles examined in this book.

1.2. Changing the Story of Noah from the Genesis Account

Of all the Bible stories included in children's Bibles in America, none has been more popular than the story of Noah and the ark. The story of a devastating flood, a large boat full of animals, and a colorful rainbow seems to have made the story one that is appealing both to children and to the authors writing for them. The Genesis account of the story of Noah presents readers with a complex and nuanced depiction of the nature of God and provides children's Bible authors and illustrators with many opportunities to adapt and revise the story to serve their own various purposes. It is a story of epic events, with many gaps in the narrative, and it lends itself to many potential meanings.

While any summary of the story of Noah from Genesis is fraught with interpretive choices, some may find the following brief overview to be helpful.[33] According to Genesis 6–9, God sees the wickedness and violence of humankind and is sorry to have created people and animals on the earth. As a result, God decides to blot them out by means of a flood. God deems one human being, Noah, to be righteous and spares Noah, his family, and some of each of the animals of

---

32. Robert Alter, *The Five Books of Moses: A Translation with Commentary* (New York: W. W. Norton & Co., 2004), xix.

33. I am exceedingly aware of the presumptuousness of providing a summary of the story of Noah in a book that examines the ways in which other authors have retold and summarized the story of Noah. Still, I hope that this summary serves some as a helpful review of various episodes in the story of Noah as it is told in the Book of Genesis.

creation. God tells Noah that he is sending a flood and gives Noah somewhat detailed instructions for building an ark and gathering pairs of animals. Later, God tells Noah when to enter into the ark and then God shuts the door. Through the flood, all the living creatures outside of the ark perish. After the flood, Noah makes a burnt offering of animals to God on an altar. God gives Noah several commands and makes a covenant with humankind, setting a bow in the clouds as a sign of that covenant, and promises never again to destroy all flesh by water. Noah becomes the first man to plant a vineyard and at one point falls asleep drunk and naked. His son Ham sees him naked, but his other sons cover his nakedness. When Noah awakes, he proclaims a curse upon Ham's son Canaan. At age 950 years old, Noah dies. Children's Bibles include, omit, comment upon, or embellish these episodes in the story of Noah in a wide variety of ways and in the process create new stories that carry different meanings.

The authors of the Book of Genesis themselves likely drew upon previous sources and traditions as they composed the story. Some scholars have explored the ways in which the Genesis flood account may be partially dependent on other ancient Near Eastern flood myths.[34] Others have applied the Documentary Hypothesis outlined by Julius Welhausen to speculate on the possible earlier Hebrew sources lying behind the composition of the Genesis account of the story of Noah.[35] John Skinner, for example, breaks down his commentary on the flood narrative in terms of "The Flood according to J"[36] and "The Flood According to P."[37] The children's Bibles examined in this book, then, can simply be seen as following a long history of storytellers who draw upon source material to retell the story of the flood.

As an exercise in reception history, this book notes the changes children's Bibles make to the canonical text, such as adding and embellishing certain scenes, abridging or deleting others, and adding comments to the text, not out of a desire to chide the authors for being "unbiblical" or to privilege the canonical text's version of the story of Noah. Instead, this study examines the changes made from the Genesis account in order to see how those changes have functioned to present children with certain lessons and certain perspectives on life, God, morality, and the nature of the Bible itself. Many children's Bibles emphasize in their introductions that their versions of the Bible stories stay close to the biblical text and imply or state outright that this fidelity to the canonical text makes their children's Bibles more trustworthy than others, implying that their children's Bible retains more biblical authority. Given this high regard for the biblical text, it is instructive to note the changes they make from the canonical version of the story. Whether

---

34. See, for example, Lloyd R. Bailey, *Noah: The Person and Story in Historical Tradition* (Columbia, SC: University of South Carolina Press, 1989), 11–27.

35. See Julius Welhausen, *Prolegomena to the History of Ancient Israel* (New York: Meridian Books, 1957), 6–9.

36. John Skinner, *A Critical and Exegetical Commentary on Genesis* (New York: Charles Scribner's Sons, 1925), 150–8.

37. Ibid., 158–71.

these changes are made consciously or subconsciously, they function to present children with particular values and beliefs that may or may not be present in the original text. Some of the common changes made to the text include embellishments, abridgments, commentary such as explanations or moral and theological lessons to be learned, and illustrations.

1.2.a. Embellishing the story of Noah

As is the case with many Hebrew Bible narratives, the story of Noah as it is told in Genesis is quite laconic and has many "gaps." While many authors of children's Bible stories claim that they are merely trying to simplify the Bible's stories, they often expand them by filling in many of these gaps by drawing upon extra-biblical resources, passing on versions of the story that they have heard, or through the use of their own imaginations.

1.2.1.a(i). Common embellishments to the story of Noah

The story of Noah is one of the most familiar of all Bible stories. Many children and their parents would be surprised, however, to discover that many aspects of the story that are familiar to them are not actually included in the Genesis account.

Some embellishments to the story of Noah add detail and color to the narrative. The book of Genesis, for example, does not name any specific animals that are brought on the ark, but just provides broad categories of animals, stating that Noah's family entered the ark along with "every wild animal of every kind, and all domestic animals of every kind, and every creeping thing that creeps on the earth, and every bird of every kind—every bird, every winged creature. They went into the ark with Noah, two and two of all flesh in which there was the breath of life" (Gen. 7.14-15).[38] Many children's Bibles, however, lend nuance to their narratives by listing various animals and show them in illustrations that accompany the text. Some list farm animals such as cows, pigs, and goats; others describe an African menagerie of elephants, lions, tigers, and zebras entering the ark; while still others include a fanciful list of animals such as aardvarks, platypuses, and ladybugs. While such an extrapolation may seem reasonable, and such a list arguably may not have profound theological implications, the author's choice of animals and the way they are described entering into the ark often helps the author set the tone of her or his story as either a serious and profound account of an epic event, an exotic tale of another time and place, or a fun and amusing romp with silly animals on a boat.

The most common embellishments to the story of Noah are so ubiquitous that many people assume that they are part of the Genesis account when they actually cannot be found in Genesis or in any other part of the Bible. For example,

---

38. Unless otherwise noted, Scripture quotations are from the New Revised Standard Version Bible, © 1989 the Division of Christian Education of the National Council of the Churches of Christ in the USA.

Genesis makes no mention of anyone mocking Noah or his family while they built the ark or at any other time. Furthermore, there is no mention in Genesis of Noah or God warning people that a flood was coming or offering them a way to escape the judgment to come. As a matter of fact, Genesis makes no explicit mention of Noah having any interaction with any humans outside of his family. Genesis 7.18-23 notes that all living creatures outside of the ark died when the flood covered the earth, but the book makes no mention of whether those outside of the ark climbed to higher ground or cried out to get inside of the ark. If one concludes that any of these episodes must have occurred, they happen "off stage" in the Genesis account. Children's Bibles, however, have commonly added these and other episodes to the story of Noah in ways that serve a variety of agendas. Occasionally, children's Bible authors let their readers know when they are veering into the realm of speculation. Walter Russell Bowie, for example, suggests to readers of his book *The Story of the Bible*, "It does not take much imagination to know that the building of this ark must have caused comment" before proceeding to tell how Noah's neighbors must have thought that he was crazy.[39] More often, however, the embellishments are integrated into the story with no notice to the reader that the added episodes are not a part of the canonical version of the story.

1.2.a(ii). Sources of the embellishments to the story of Noah
These embellishments are not, of course, unique to children's Bibles and they certainly predate the existence of the United States of America as a nation. Jewish literature of the Second Temple period, for example, attests to Noah warning his neighbors and people reacting by mocking him or ignoring him.[40] According to the Sibylline Oracles, Noah, in response to God's command, preaches and tells people they should repent (1,150–70), but they respond by mocking him and calling him crazy (1,171–2). Noah in turn warns them of the coming flood (1,174–8). According to Flavius Josephus's *Antiquities of the Jews*, Noah tried to convince the people to repent (1,74). Philo of Alexandria, in his *Questions and Answers on Genesis* 2.13, does not have Noah preaching, but does suggest that God gave people a chance to repent. Rabbinic literature also elaborates upon the story of Noah. According to *Genesis Rabbah* 30.7, for example, Noah warned his neighbors that God would bring a flood but they responded with contempt for him.[41] Also in the Christian tradition, the Christian Church Father Ephrem the Syrian (c. 306–73) wrote, "When those of that generation gathered [to see] this novel sight, it was not to repent but rather to amuse themselves."[42]

39. Walter Russell Bowie, *The Story of the Bible* (New York: Abingdon Press, 1934), 35.

40. For a helpful overview, see Nadav Sharon and Moshe Tishel, "Distinctive Traditions about Noah and the Flood in Second Temple Jewish Literature," in Michael E. Stone et al., *Noah and His Book(s)* (Leiden and Boston, MA: Brill, 2010), 156–8.

41. See Aryeh Amihay, "Noah in Rabbinic Literature," in *Noah and His Book(s)* (Leiden and Boston, MA: Brill, 2010), 204.

42. Ephrem the Syrian, *Commentary on Genesis* 6.9.2, in *Fathers of the Church: A New Translation* 91.139 (Washington, DC: Catholic University of America Press, 1947).

For many Protestant Christian children's Bible authors, however, the New Testament serves as the sole scriptural authority that would permit them to augment the story as it appears in Genesis. Noah and the story of the flood are referenced in six passages of the New Testament, including Matthew 24.37-39, Luke 17.26-30; Hebrews 11.7, 1 Peter 3.18-22; 2 Peter 2.4-10, and 2 Peter 3.1-13. Strictly speaking, these passages, if accepted as authoritative sources, add little detail to the Genesis account of the flood narrative. According to 2 Peter 2.5, Noah was "a herald of righteousness" or, as sometimes translated, "a preacher of righteousness." This passage is often invoked to claim that Noah must have warned the wicked for years about the coming flood. However, 2 Peter makes no specific claims regarding at what point in his long life he did preach or if he specifically preached words of warning about the coming flood. As a matter of fact, if Matthew 24.39 is to be believed, the wicked "knew nothing until the flood came and swept them all away." In Matthew 24.38 and its parallel Luke 17.27, Jesus says that in the days of Noah, as will be the case at the time of the coming of the Son of Man, people "were eating, drinking, marrying, and giving in marriage." A few American children's Bibles' stories of Noah have made allusions to this passage and portrayed these seemingly benign activities as vices and as affronts to God that help justify the wicked people's destruction. Also, 2 Peter 3.1-13 speaks about both the waters of the flood and God's future judgment by fire, which some children's Bibles of the revivalist period draw upon and integrate into their stories as well.[43] Still, the New Testament alone seems to provide little in the way of clear support for many of the embellishments that often appear in Protestant Christian children's Bibles.

Some children's Bible authors draw upon other texts that hold authority in their particular traditions. Some children's Bibles written by members of the Church of Jesus Christ of Latter Day Saints (LDS), for example, include the common embellishment of Noah warning his neighbors of the coming flood and the people mocking him in return.[44] In their case, however, the episode is included in Joseph Smith's *Book of Moses* 8.19-21, which is part of the LDS standard work of scripture *The Pearl of Great Price*. In addition, *The Book of Moses* 8.18 explains that giants in the land were trying to kill Noah, but that God's protection was upon him, and several LDS children's Bibles integrate these events into their retellings of the story of Noah as well.[45]

---

43. References to God's judgment by fire can also be found in 1 Enoch and the writings of Flavius Josephus, Philo of Alexandria, and the Latin Vita Adam. For a helpful overview, see Sharon and Tishel, "Distinctive Traditions about Noah and the Flood in Second Temple Jewish Literature," 144–6.

44. See, for example, Emma Marr Petersen, *Bible Stories for Young Latter-Day Saints* (Salt Lake City, UT: Bookcraft, 1949), 24; *Scripture Stories* (Salt Lake City, UT: Church of Jesus Christ of Latter-day Saints, 1980), 9; and George D. Durrant, *Illustrated Stories from the Bible*, Vol. 1 (Provo, UT: Community Press, 1980), 39.

45. For example, Petersen, *Bible Stories for Young Latter-Day Saints*, 24; *Scripture Stories*, 9; and Durrant, *Illustrated Stories from the Bible*, Vol. 1, 39.

Some of the embellishments to the Genesis account of the story of Noah found in children's Bibles by Seventh Day Adventist authors can be traced to the writings of Ellen Gould White (1827–1915), whose visions and books hold authority for many Seventh Day Adventists. "Uncle" Arthur Maxwell's popular ten-volume *The Bible Story* was well known for having its first volume available in many doctors' and dentists' office waiting rooms in the later part of the twentieth century, complete with mail-in postcards inserted into the books to allow parents to subscribe to all ten volumes. The publicity for the set included endorsements by Methodist, Baptist, Catholic, and Lutheran clergy, and Maxwell makes no indication in his introduction that he is an Adventist or that he is writing specifically for Adventist children. The common embellishments of Noah warning his neighbors, his neighbors mocking Noah in return, and those neighbors crying out to enter the ark once the flood came, all play a significant role in Maxwell's extended retelling of the tale.[46] Maxwell's retelling contains little evidence, however, that he is drawing particularly from Adventist sources other than when he writes, "How Satan must have tried to sink the ark in the height of the tempest. Could he have done so, he would have succeeded in defeating God's purpose. But the ark did not sink. Miraculously it rode out the storm."[47] This episode is likely an allusion to Ellen G. White's emphasis on God's battle with Satan.[48]

Another popular children's Bible written by a Seventh Day Adventist author from the later half of the twentieth century is Arthur Whitefield Spalding's one-volume *Golden Treasury of Bible Stories* from 1954.[49] In his introduction, Spalding writes, "In some instances facts gained from non-Biblical sources have been included to make the setting clearer. The plain sense of the Bible text has been followed, without any attempt at indoctrination or sectarian interpretation."[50] Reading his account of the story of Noah, it seems clear that he is drawing from several of White's writings. Spalding writes, for example,

There were giants in the earth at that time, and they ruled over weaker people and made slaves of them, and killed and murdered as they pleased. There came to be great beasts, like giants among the animals, which the giants trained to fight and destroy weaker men and their homes and farms. Even in our day the bones of some of these giant animals are found buried in the earth, which show us how terrible were things in Noah's time.[51]

---

46. Arthur S. Maxwell, *The Bible Story*, Vol. 1 (Washington, DC: Review and Herald Publishing Association, 1953, 1973, 1975), 103–15.

47. Ibid., 117.

48. See Ellen G. White, *The Great Controversy; Between Christ and Satan* (Mountain View, CA: Pacific Press Publishing Association, 1888).

49. Arthur Whitefield Spalding, *Golden Treasury of Bible Stories* (Mountain View, CA: Pacific Press Publishing Association, 1954).

50. Ibid., 7.

51. Ibid., 41.

These scenes are likely drawn from White's visions described in *Spiritual Gifts* in which she writes, "There were a class of very large animals which perished at the flood. God knew that the strength of man would decrease, and these mammoth animals could not be controlled by feeble man."[52] Likewise, Spalding describes a scene in which he writes that when the flood came, "Some bound their children on great beasts, like oxen and elephants and even bears; for they knew these animals would climb for their lives."[53] Spalding likely drew this episode from White's *The Story of Patriarchs and Prophets* in which she wrote, "The beasts, exposed to the tempest, rushed toward man, as though expecting help from him. Some of the people bound their children and themselves upon powerful animals, knowing that these were tenacious of life, and would climb to the highest points to escape the rising waters."[54] Spalding's book was and still is found in many Protestant homes and church libraries, and many of its readers from other traditions may have assumed that these episodes were simply a part of the Genesis account that they had previously overlooked or forgotten.

Only on rare occasions do children's Bible authors cite any of these sources as authoritative sources for the embellishments they include in their stories. Some may not be aware of these sources and may simply be passing on versions of the story that they have heard from preachers or teachers or even from children's Bibles that they read as children. Often, children's Bible authors may not be aware of the sources of these embellishments or even aware that the embellishments that they include are not a part of the canonical version of the story.[55] Others may simply use their own imaginations to fill in gaps in the story. This book does not focus on determining the source the authors are drawing upon for their embellishments or whether or not they are aware of the ways in which they are adding to the story of Noah as it appears in the Genesis account. Instead, it focuses on the particular ways in which children's Bibles have used these embellishments in different ways to convey different lessons to children.

---

52. Ellen G. White, *Spiritual Gifts*, Vols III–IV (Washington, DC: Review and Herald Publishing, 1945), 121.

53. Spalding, *Golden Treasury of Bible Stories*, 42–3.

54. Ellen G. White, *The Story of Patriarchs and Prophets* (Mountain View, CA: Pacific Press Publishing Association, 1890, 1913), 100.

55. Anecdotally, while I was writing this book an author sent me a pre-publication copy of his children's Bible and asked me if I would read it and offer an endorsement. In his letter, the author indicated that he was particularly proud of the fact that his stories did not stray from the text of the Bible itself. I wrote back saying that I would not be endorsing any children's Bibles, but also pointed out that his story of Noah included scenes of Noah's neighbors mocking him and Noah warning them about the coming flood, which were not in the text of Genesis. He replied that he was unaware that those events were not in the book of Genesis, but was not troubled by it since one could logically conclude that these events must have happened. This is just one story, but it lends insight into the mindset of some authors.

1.2.b. Abridgments

Another common change that children's Bibles make to Bible stories is to abridge the text. The goal that many children's Bible authors state in their introductions is to simplify or clarify the Bible's stories for children. One way in which authors simplify the stories is by deleting what they see as extraneous and irrelevant details. For example, children's Bibles often abridge or delete certain aspects of God's instructions to Noah regarding the number of animals he is to gather. According to the Book of Genesis, God instructs Noah to gather seven pairs of all clean animals and one pair of all unclean animals (Gen. 7.2-3). In children's Bibles that retell the story, this is almost always simplified by saying that God commanded Noah to gather one pair of each animal. Children's Bibles also regularly abridge the Book of Genesis's account of God's detailed instructions to Noah on the size of various parts of the ark and the day upon which certain events occurred. While these aspects of the text have some significance, many readers would feel that they are not essential aspects of the story.

Many would argue, however, that the deaths of everything that had breath that was not on the ark is an essential part of the story. Children's Bible authors and illustrators, however, have either expanded descriptions of the death of the wicked or deleted any mention that anyone died in the flood in ways that are consistent with the views of childhood in the era in which they were writing and their own theological or moral agendas.

One part of the story of Noah that is excluded from the vast majority of children's Bibles is the episode about a drunken, naked Noah following the flood (Gen. 9.18-27). Some authors may delete this part of the life of Noah simply out of a desire to keep the story short or because they believe the subject matter is inappropriate for children. Others may see the tale as one that inconveniently offers a morally complex picture of Noah, so they may delete the story in order to preserve Noah as a positive role model for children.

In all of these cases, these abridgments can serve to promote or reinforce a variety of beliefs and values. Depending upon which episodes from the Genesis account that they exclude from their retellings, children's Bible authors are able to craft significantly different stories which serve to teach significantly different lessons to children.

1.2.c. Inserting moral and theology lessons, explanations and apologies

In addition to deleting details or embellishing the text, two other common ways that children's Bible storybook authors deviate from the biblical text is by adding or integrating moral or theological lessons to the story or by adding or integrating an explanation or apology for a problematic passage to the end of a story. This sort of direct commentary to the reader is the most explicit way in which the children's Bible authors reveal their own assumptions regarding the Bible and its stories and their own agendas for presenting Bible stories to children.

One of the more common changes twentieth- and twenty-first-century children's Bibles make is to insert a theological or moral lesson to be learned into the story.

As shall be examined in depth in chapters that follow, for example, the story of the death of sinners in the flood has often been used as a springboard for children's Bible authors to present children of their own time with a plan of salvation. In other children's Bibles, Noah has been held up to children as a role model who exhibits a wide variety of moral virtues ranging from obedience to patience.

Children's Bibles have also added explanation for confusing aspects of Bible stories and apologetics defending certain potentially troubling aspects of a story. Again, these comments are either integrated into the story or added as direct commentary to the reader at the end of the story. Some children's Bibles, especially those published in the late nineteenth century, added or inserted an explanation or apology to their retellings of potentially disturbing stories such as those of Abraham's binding of Isaac, Jephthah's sacrifice of his daughter, and the story of Elisha and the She-bears, with authors offering various explanations to children as to why God would ask Abraham to offer Isaac, or why the children of Bethel received such a harsh punishment for mocking Elisha. In the case of the story of Noah, children's Bibles have offered various arguments as to why God was entirely justified in destroying all people and animals except those who were on the ark or made the case that the destruction of the wicked was actually a gracious act. In a similar way, some of the relatively few American children's Bibles that include the episode in which Noah becomes drunk after the flood offer various excuses for Noah's behavior and explanations as to why he needed to curse Canaan. These statements seem to be born out of a desire to make sure children understand the story, to defend stories that may disturb children or make them think poorly of God or heroes of the faith, or to reinforce certain cultural norms and values.

Sometimes these lessons or explanations are set off in an alternate font or added to the end of the story in ways that make it somewhat clear to the reader that the lesson is the author's own commentary on the passage and not a part of the canonical text. More often, however, these lessons are integrated directly into the retelling of the story or added to the end with smooth transitions in ways that would make it difficult for many readers to tell where the retelling of the biblical story ends and where the children's Bible author's own commentary begins.

1.2.d. Illustrating the story

1.2.d(i). The role of illustrations in interpreting the story of Noah
A very important aspect of the way children's Bibles present the stories of the Bible to children is through the way the stories are illustrated. Artists and editors choose which episodes in each story to illustrate and thereby emphasize and underscore those aspects of the story. The style of the illustrations can also set a tone for the story. The illustrations can be realistic or impressionistic. They can convey a sense of historicity, evoke a sense of awe, or be drawn in a whimsical cartoon style. These choices of style convey to children a sense of what sort of book the Bible is as much or more than the words chosen to tell the story.

Throughout American history the authors of children's Bibles have often had little or no say in the illustrations included in the children's Bibles they produced.

In the nineteenth century, editors and publishers often chose to reprint classic or popular artist renderings of Bible stories, often with little regard for publication rights or for whether the tone of the illustrations was a good match for the way the author had retold the story. In more recent years, publishers often discourage the authors of children's literature from communicating with the artists of their books in order to allow the artists autonomy to convey their own artistic vision for the stories.

In the eighteenth and early nineteenth centuries, the printing technology of the time allowed only for very crude woodcut illustrations to appear in children's Bibles, but even these were too much of an appeal to children's amusement for some. The first prose children's Bible published in the United States, printed in Philadelphia by Andrew Steuart in 1763 and simply titled *The Children's Bible*, did not contain many illustrations. In the preface, the anonymous author noted that he or she had chosen to give the book a solid binding and to keep the cost down by forsaking illustrations. As the author put it, "I have chosen rather to give it a strong and handsome binding, than to increase the bulk of the volume by crowding it with ill-executed cuts, attended with a large expense and no manner of service; which may be necessary notwithstanding to promote the sale of nonsense, but the author apprehends that the BIBLE is no fit PLAY-THING FOR CHILDREN."[56]

Most children's Bible publishers, however, disagreed with this sentiment, at least when it came to including illustrations. Illustrations, whether they are the crude woodcuts of the nineteenth century or the colorful cartoon-style illustrations of the twenty-first century, soon became a mainstay of children's Bibles in America. Paul C. Gutjahr, in his book *An American Bible*, notes that only 16 percent of the Bibles published in America in the 1810s contained illustrations, while by 1870 59 percent of them did,[57] and the percentage of children's Bibles that contained illustrations was almost certainly higher. While some Americans may have initially had misgivings about including illustrations, most used them to make their books more appealing to young readers.

In the twenty-first century, a number of scholars have recognized the significant role that illustrations play in interpreting Bible stories for children. Bible scholar David Gunn explores the question of whether Bible illustrations may be more influential than biblical texts[58] and in the book *Text, Image, & Otherness in Children's Bibles: What Is in the Picture?* a variety of scholars explore the significance of the illustrations created for children's Bibles.[59] This book focuses on the interpretive power of the illustrations that accompany American children's Bible

56. *The Children's Bible* (Philadelphia, PA: Andrew Steuart, 1763), xii. Emphasis in original.

57. Paul C. Gutjahr, *An American Bible: A History of the Good Book in the United States, 1777–1880* (Stanford, CA: Stanford University Press, 1999), 37.

58. David Gunn, "Cultural Criticism," in Gale A. Yee, ed., *Judges & Method: New Approaches in Biblical Studies*, 2nd edn (Minneapolis, MN: Fortress Press, 2007), 205–7.

59. Caroline Vander Stichle and Hugh S. Pyper, eds, *Text, Image, & Otherness in Children's Bibles: What Is in the Picture?* (Atlanta, GA: Society of Biblical Literature, 2012).

retellings of the story of Noah. A number of the scenes not described in the Genesis account of Noah's ark, such as Noah being mocked while building the ark or while preaching to the people, the animals marching in line two abreast, or the attempts of people outside the ark to escape the flood, are among the most commonly illustrated scenes in children's Bibles and at times these scenes are illustrated even when they are not mentioned in the children's Bible's text. As Gunn suggests, these illustrations do not merely function as aids to understanding the written text of the story, but often make a greater impression upon children than the words of the story itself.[60]

1.2.d(ii). Illustrating children's Bibles from African and African-American perspectives
One aspect of the way American children's Bibles illustrate Bible stories that merits an extended discussion is the way in which the vast majority of them, past and present, depict the ancient Near Eastern people of the Bible as white people of Western European descent. Since the illustrators and publishers of the majority of these children's Bibles have been white people of Western European descent, this is one way that they have consciously and unconsciously passed on their assumptions that Christianity and Judaism are white religions and privileged themselves as being similar to the foundational figures of their faith.

For most of American history, there has been very little in the way of children's literature tailored for African-American children.[61] One benefit of recent developments in the book publishing industry and marketplace, however, is the recognition of "niche markets" and specialized marketplaces. According to Leonard Marcus, in his book *The Minders of Make-Believe*, the emergence of more children's books published by and for diverse groups of people, such as books tailored for African-American children, emerged especially during the 1990s.[62]

Ruth Bottigheimer, researching and writing on children's Bibles in the early 1990s, noted that at the time there had still been no children's Bibles composed specifically for African-American children in the United States.[63] Instead, in the majority of cases, children had to make do with Bible stories presented in a particularly Anglo-American way. As in American motion pictures, which often cast actors with light complexions and blue eyes in the role of Jesus or other Bible characters, the majority of children's Bibles and children's Sunday School curriculum materials depict Bible characters as white people of Western European descent.

60. Gunn, "Cultural Criticism," 205–6.

61. For a further exploration of this phenomenon, see Nancy Larrick's classic essay "The All-White World of Children's Books," in Osayimwense Osa, ed., *The All White World of Children's Books & African American Children's Literature* (Trenton, NJ: African World Press, Inc., 1995), 1–12.

62. See Leonard S. Marcus, *Minders of Make-Believe* (Boston, MA: Houghton Mifflin Company, 2008), 298–311.

63. Ruth B. Bottigheimer, *The Bible for Children: From the Age of Gutenberg to the Present* (New Haven, CT: Yale University Press, 1996), 47.

One exception to this rule was a collection of stories written by African-American missionary and author Lorenz Bell Graham. In 1947, Graham first published a series of Bible stories written in the idiom of the West African native storytellers he met there.[64] Graham titled the story of Noah "God Wash the World and Start Again," and tells the story of God instructing Noah to build the ark in the following manner:

> God go down and speak
> He say
> "Noah, O Noah!
> Hear My Word.
> I want you cut down plenty trees
> And make a ship.
> I want it be the biggest ship
> Man ever see.
> I want it be from here to there
> And plenty tight
> And when you finish so
> I come again."[65]

The book is illustrated by Ashley Bryan in the style of West African drawing. Though the story of Noah is illustrated only with an image of the ark upon the waters, the illustrations accompanying other Bible stories depict people such as Jonah, David, Isaac, Jacob, and Jesus as Africans, likely making it the very first collection of Bible stories published in the United States to do so.

For much of American history, the animals illustrated in children's Bible versions of Noah's ark have been a menagerie of animals native to the African continent such as elephants, lions, tigers, hippopotamuses, and more. Patricia Lee Gauch's 1994 children's book *Noah*, with vibrant paintings by Jonathan Green, however, is perhaps the first American storybook to depict Noah and his family as ancient Africans, including a spectacular image of Noah calling the animals to the ark (see Figure 1.3).[66] The illustrations open up new possibilities and new understandings of the ancient story.

One of the more creative examples of a children's Bible for African-American children is the book *Let My People Go*, by Patricia and Fredrick McKissack, published in 1998.[67] The authors put stories from the Bible into the narrative voice of Price Jefferies, a fictional free black abolitionist, who tells the stories

64. Lorenz Graham, *How God Fix Jonah*, illus. by Ashley Bryan (Honesdale, PA: Boyds Mills Press, 1946, 1974).

65. Ibid., 45–6.

66. Patricia Lee Gauch, *Noah*, illus. by Jonathan Green (New York: Philomel Books, 1994), 9–10.

67. Patricia and Fredrick McKissack, *Let My People Go: Bible Stories Told by a Freeman of Color*, illus. by James E. Ransome (New York: Atheneum Books for Young Readers, 1998).

Figure 1.3. Jonathan Green's painting of Noah calling the animals from Patricia Lee Gauch, *Noah* (New York: Philomel Books, 1994), 9–10.

in response to questions asked by his daughter Charlotte in Charleston, South Carolina in the years 1806–16. McKissack and McKissack creatively integrate the stories of Price and Charlotte Jefferies with stories from the Bible, and in the process draw connections between God's liberating work in the Bible, in the days of slavery, and in more recent times as well. In the story of "the Big Water," when Charlotte goes to visit one of her slave friends on a plantation, she discovers that the slaveholder has sent her away, and even the girl's own mother does not know where she has gone. In her bitterness and anger, Charlotte prays that God will just swallow up all the slaveholders. While Charlotte and her father ride back home in a row boat, they get caught in a storm and Charlotte is afraid that they are going to be caught in the Big Water God is sending to get all of the slaveholders. Price hugs his daughter and says, "God won't abide with slavery, and one day it will come to an end. But it won't be with Big Water again."[68] From there, Price tells the story of Noah and the ark. According to his version of the story, Noah's neighbors did not notice the coming storm, for, "They were too busy with riotous livin' and debauchery, don't you know?"[69] When the storm finally came, the sinners drowned and justice was served. When the flood subsides, God sends a rainbow and promises not to destroy the world by water again. Price assures his daughter, "All the hoping and angry wishes in the world can't make God break a promise. On that you can depend."[70] While the text offers insight to a particular time in African-American history and an interesting perspective on God and life, the

68. Ibid., 20.
69. Ibid., 23.
70. Ibid., 26.

illustrations included with the story were arguably just as significant or even more so. In his introductory "illustrator's note," the book's artist, James E. Ransome, explained that while previous Bible illustrations influenced his work, his illustrations had one major difference:

> The people would resemble those from the region of North Egypt and what we now know as Israel, Lebanon, Syria, Iraq, Jordan, Ethiopia, and north of Saudi Arabia—where most of the Old Testament stories took place. I would draw people with brown and olive complexions, Semites. I felt compelled to dispel the myth created by the European representations of Bible characters, so fixed in the minds of most of us.[71]

Ransome further explains, "I felt it was time to start educating our children about the true images of the people who gave the world the concept of one God and three religions: Judaism, Christianity, and Islam."[72]

In the same way, Thomas Nelson Publishers' *Children of Color Storybook Bible with Stories from the International Children's Bible* from 2001 depicts Bible characters that do not have the facial features and skin color of white Europeans or Americans. Instead, artist Victor Hogan illustrates characters such as Noah with a variety of facial features and variety of skin tones that are appropriate to the African and ancient Near Eastern settings of the stories (see Figure 1.4). The introduction to the book argues that its notes and illustrations will help build the self-esteem and confidence of children of color and connect them to their biblical heritage.[73]

It is significant that neither Hogan nor Ransome follow the pattern of so many white artists who preceded them in depicting Noah and other Bible characters just as members of their own race. Instead, they both chose to depict the people of the Bible as people of color with a variety of types of facial features and variety of skin tones. The goal of these and other similar children's Bibles created for African-American children[74] seems to be to show the diversity of races and ethnic heritages represented by the people of the Bible.

The examples cited here, however, are exceptions to the more common trend. The majority of American children's Bibles throughout history and that are still on the market today depict Bible characters with the coloration and facial features of white people of Western European descent.[75] In the last decades of the twentieth

---

71. Ibid., ii.

72. Ibid., vii.

73. *Children of Color Storybook Bible with Stories from the International Children's Bible*, illus. by Victor Hogan (Nashville, TN: Thomas Nelson, 2001), vii.

74. See, for example, *My Holy Bible for African-American Children* (Grand Rapids, MI: Zondervan, 2009).

75. See the helpful extended examinations of how children's Bible texts and illustrations treat "otherness" in Bible stories in the essays in Stichle and Pyper, *Text, Image, & Otherness in Children's Bibles: What Is in the Picture?*

Figure 1.4. Illustration by Victor Hogan of Noah and animals from *Children of Color Storybook Bible with Stories from the International Children's Bible*, illus. by Victor Hogan (Nashville, TN: Thomas Nelson Publishers, 2001), 14–15.

century and first decades of the twenty-first century, however, there seems to be a growing trend, even amongst children's Bibles that are not specifically aimed at children of color, to illustrate the Bible with people of color with a variety of skin tones.[76]

Through embellishing the story of Noah, abridging it, inserting moral or theological lessons into their retellings, offering explanations or defenses of aspects of the story, and through the way they illustrate the story, children's Bible authors and illustrators pass on their own embedded theologies and moral values in a variety of ways. Often, however, it is difficult to know whether the storytellers are aware of the changes they are making or not.

1.3. Children's Bibles' Claims and Caveats Concerning Staying Faithful to the Canonical Text

Most children's Bible authors offer their readers very little in the way of a philosophy of retelling Bible stories or a rationale for the way that they approach retelling Bible stories in their introductions. Of those that do, one of the most thoughtful and detailed descriptions of the task is offered by feminist Hebrew Bible scholars Alice Bach and J. Cheryl Exum. Bach and Exum note in the

---

76. See, for example, Alice Bach and J. Cheryl Exum, *Moses' Ark*, illus. by Leo and Diane Dillon (New York: Delacorte Press, 1989); *Holy Bible: Children's Illustrated Edition: Contemporary English Version* (New York: American Bible Society, 2000); and Desmond Tutu, *Children of God Storybook Bible* (Grand Rapids, MI: Zonderkids, 2010).

introduction to their 1989 collection of Bible stories, titled *Moses' Ark*, that their retellings are based on the original Hebrew language and contemporary biblical scholarship, but that they have also allowed themselves some freedom in their retellings. They explain:

> Retelling involves the filling of gaps. We all fill gaps by supplying our own selection of details when we read stories. For example, the biblical storyteller tells us nothing about life aboard Noah's ark during those drenching forty days and nights. Because today's readers may be curious about different things from ancient listeners, we have filled in the sort of details we think will help the stories come alive for our readers. Some details we can add without scholarly support. Surely all those animals made quite a racket as the rain fell endlessly![77]

This sort of thoughtful description of their process and rationale for filling gaps in the text, however, is rare among children's Bible authors.[78]

Some children's Bible authors who claim in their introductions that their goal is to remain as close to the words and events of the canonical text as possible are relatively successful in their efforts. Others explicitly tell readers that they are drawing on extra-biblical sources or their own imaginations to form new stories that differ from those found in the Bible itself. Still others, however, claim close fidelity to the biblical accounts but proceed to make significant changes to the story in their retellings. Any retelling or reframing of a story changes its meaning. As the examples described in the following section attest, however, children's Bible authors seem to have exceedingly diverse levels of awareness of how they are changing Bible stories.

1.3.a. Jewish children's Bibles: Passing on the original text and midrash

Most children's Bibles published for Jewish children in the United States have fallen into two broad categories. They have either stayed close to the words, events, and the tone of the Bible stories themselves or, conversely, the authors have openly acknowledged that they have drawn on extra-biblical sources and their own imaginations to compose creative new versions of the biblical tales.

Not every Jewish children's Bible that has been published in the United States falls into one of these two categories, however. While a small number of Jewish

---

77. Bach and Exum, *Moses' Ark*, 3.

78. Exum offers insightful reflections on the process of writing a children's Bible in her essay, "What Does a Child Want? Reflections on Children's Bible Stories," in Caroline Vander Stichele and Hugh S. Pyper, eds, *Text, Image, and Otherness in Children's Bibles: What is in the Picture?* Semeia Studies 56 (Atlanta, GA: Society of Biblical Literature, 2012), 333–45.

children's Bibles from the nineteenth,[79] twentieth,[80] and twenty-first centuries[81] have all freely adapted Bible stories, inserting moral teachings and embellishments, Penny Schine Gold has noted the ways in which Jewish children's Bibles published in the United States from 1915 to 1936 in particular tended to adapt and change Bible stories. In her book *Making the Bible Modern: Children's Bibles and Jewish Education in Twentieth Century America*, Gold examines children's Bibles from the era, such as Lenore Cohen's *Bible Tales for Very Young Children*[82] and Addie Richman Altman's *The Jewish Child's Bible Stories*,[83] and points out how the subtle changes of clarification, explanations of ancient customs, omissions of content that was deemed inappropriate for children (such as content dealing with issues of sexuality), some commentary on the nature of God, and some moral applications to the story crept into Jewish children's Bibles of the time. She notes that these changes, even if subtle, could significantly change the stories' meanings, and may have represented an attempt by the authors to help children integrate the Jewish faith with American culture.[84] Some of these and other children's Bibles for Jewish children will be examined in the chapters that follow.

Still, for the most part, Jewish children's Bible authors tend to be more self-aware of the changes they are or are not making to the canonical text than their Christian counterparts, or at least are more transparent and forthcoming about what they are doing. The goals of Jewish religious education seem to be such that most Jewish authors design their children's Bibles either to pass on knowledge of the Torah as part of their religious tradition, or they have consciously and transparently veered from the biblical accounts by drawing on midrash and other traditions to tell new stories for children.

1.3.a(i). Jewish children's Bibles that pass on knowledge of the Torah
Jewish children's Bibles that pass on much of the original words and phrases of the biblical text often explicitly state that this is one of their goals in their introductions, forewords, and prefaces. In the foreword of Mortimer J. Cohen's *Pathways through the Bible*, published by the Jewish Publication Society of America in 1946, the author explained his approach:

79. See, for example, Montefiore J. Moses, M. D., *Bible Stories for Jewish Children* (New York: Holt Brothers, 1879).

80. See, for example, Sholem Asch, *In the Beginning: Stories from the Bible*, trans. by Caroline Cunningham (New York: Schocken Books, 1966).

81. See, for example, Julie Downing, *A First Book of Jewish Bible Stories* (London and New York: DK Children, 2002).

82. Lenore Cohen, *Bible Tales for Very Young Children* (Cincinnati, OH: Union of American Hebrew Congregations, 1934).

83. Addie Richman Altman, *The Jewish Child's Bible Stories* (New York: Bloch Publishing Company, Inc., 1949).

84. Penny Schine Gold, *Making the Bible Modern: Children's Bibles and Jewish Education in Twentieth Century America* (Ithaca, NY: Cornell University Press, 2004), 117–78.

While the Jewish Publication Society translation of the Bible has been used as the basic text, liberty has been taken occasionally to modernize that text by eliminating difficult words, obscure phrases and archaic expressions, or by substituting modern equivalents for old English words. Sometimes, too, verses have been transposed or rearranged in order to make the reading smooth and unobstructed, and the thought clear.[85]

Cohen indeed takes this approach in his retelling of Noah's ark. He offers a condensed version of the text, without any of the common embellishments or abridgments.[86] Where the book does offer some interpretation, however, is the titles and brief introductions that open each story. The chapter on the story of Noah, for example, is titled "The Cleansing Flood" and it is introduced as follows:

Men multiplied and spread over the earth, and evil increased with them. So heartless did they become that, according to our sages, they put clothes on their marble statues to protect them against the winter's storms, but neglected the poor who died of the bitter cold. It was such wrongdoing that brought on the the [sic] destruction of mankind by the flood. Only one family escaped—that of the righteous Noah. Many ancient peoples believed that a flood had once destroyed almost all mankind, but only the Bible explained it to be the result of man's evil deeds.[87]

Through this title and introduction, the author frames the reading of the text, but the words and phrases of his version of the story stay close to the words in Genesis.

Similarly, Rabbi Hyman E. Goldin's *A Treasury of Bible Stories* argues for the value of the original wording as it is found in the Bible in his foreword. He explains that he has followed the pattern of the original text, while updating the language: "The unforgettable, fascinating Bible stories are here told in simple, beautiful and edifying style of prose and poetry as they are told in the original; but they are told in the language of today, following the best sources available."[88] He adds that, "The moving, dramatic and inspiring manner of the biblical narratives, as they are told in the original, is likewise retained."[89] Goldin's representation of the story of Noah is indeed a paraphrase that stays close to the biblical text. Since he is focused on simply updating the language of the text, he adds in none of the common embellishments such as Noah preaching to his neighbors or the people mocking Noah, and includes the references to seven pairs of clean animals and to all living things dying in the flood. This is not to say that Goldin makes no changes to the story of

85. Mortimer J. Cohen, *Pathways through the Bible* (Philadelphia, PA: Jewish Publication Society of America, 1946), x.

86. Ibid., 12–16.

87. Ibid., 12.

88. Hyman E. Goldin, *A Treasury of Bible Stories* (New York: Twayne, 1958), n.p.

89. Ibid., n.p.

Noah. He does, for example, choose to end the story before the post-flood episode of a drunken, naked Noah and his sons.[90]

The acclaimed novelist, essayist, and translator Lore Segal provides a thoughtful preface to her 1987 children's Bible *The Book of Adam to Moses*. In it she acknowledges that, in the opinion of many, there were already more than enough children's Bibles in print. Her approach, she explains, is one of a translator, privileging the words of the text itself over attempts at clarity, referencing the work of Bible scholar Robert Alter in the process:

> And finally, I have retained the "and ... and" construction though it may irritate the modern ear, which expects to hear "when ... then." A footnote in Robert Alter's *The Art of Biblical Narrative* explains to me my own instinct in this matter: statements connected by "and" have equal value, whereas clauses beginning with "whereas," "when," "because," "although" not only subordinate one to another but specify their logical relationship in a way the Bible generally does not. Why should we be wiser?[91]

Segal's retranslation of the story of Noah from Genesis 7.11-14 reads, "And Noah was six hundred years old when the flood came upon the earth, and the fountains of the great abyss burst open, the floodgates of heaven opened up, and Noah went into the ark with his sons, Shem, Ham, and Japheth, and his wife, and his son's wives, and every kind of animal, and every kind of creeping thing, and every kind of chirping, flying bird."[92] This desire to pass on the tone and feel of the passage extends to Leonard Baskin's black and white illustrations in the book. His illustration of a gathering of animals that accompanies the story is realistic and serious in tone, not a fun illustration of cartoon-style smiling animals.[93]

The desire to stay close to the language of the biblical text itself can also be seen in the 2004 storybook *Noah's Ark*, adapted by Alison Greengard and illustrated by Carol Racklin-Siegel. The story is presented in Hebrew and English, and the book is printed to be opened on the left side, as is the Torah. The introduction explains that the book is actually closer to a translation than a retelling:

> The account of Noah and the great flood is told in Genesis 6–9, and although we have omitted words and sentences to keep the language simple and tighten the narrative, we have not changed or added any text. Each page offers a meaningful—but not always literal—translation.[94]

90. Ibid., 19–22.

91. Lore Segal, *The Book of Adam to Moses*, illus. by Leonard Baskin (New York: Alfred A. Knopf, 1987), x.

92. Ibid., 10.

93. See ibid., 9.

94. Alison Greengard, *Noah's Ark*, illus. by Carol Racklin-Siegel (Albany, CA: EKS Publishing Co., 2004), n.p.

The introduction concludes by passing on the goal of the book, explaining, "We hope that readers of all ages will enjoy this telling of *Noah's Ark* and come to appreciate the language and beauty of the Hebrew Bible."[95] That said, the Hebrew and English texts are both abridgments of the Genesis account. So, for example, there is no mention of God's command for Noah to gather seven pairs of clean animals, only to "take two of every living animal to live with you in the ark."[96] The book ends with what it calls a "literal translation" of its abridged Hebrew text of the story of Noah's ark.

Ellen Frankel perhaps best explains the contrast between Jewish children's Bibles and Christian children's Bibles. In the introduction to her 2009 *JPS Illustrated Children's Bible*, she observes that in Christian children's Bibles, "the biblical stories were expurgated, abridged, rewritten, and more often than not, Christianized. The Bible was thus turned into a morality play for children."[97] She then offers reflections on the contrast between Jewish Bibles for children and many Christian children's Bibles:

> The Jewish community has also long used the Bible for moral instruction of its children, but it has done so not by rewriting the original text as in Christian children's Bibles but by filtering it through the interpretations and fables of the rabbinic sages. Jewish tradition has always regarded the Hebrew Bible as the foundation of its "core curriculum" of lifelong learning.[98]

Frankel writes that she sought to anchor her retellings closely to the wording of the New Jewish Publications Society translation (NJPS),[99] and indeed she makes only subtle changes in her slight paraphrasing of the NJPS version of the story of Noah's ark and other stories. She maintains God's command to gather seven of each clean animal, for example. As with all paraphrases, Frankel does use some interpretive license in her adaptation of the text. Where the NJPS has "The earth became corrupt before God; the earth was filled with lawlessness" (Genesis 6.11),[100] she writes, "By now the earth had become violent and wild."[101] Frankel, however, does not insert any of the common embellishments to the story and does not add any lessons to be learned into the middle or to the end of the story.

These and other Jewish children's Bibles have passed on to children knowledge of the words, events, and tone of Bible stories and do not add morals or

95. Ibid., n.p.

96. Ibid., 4.

97. Ellen Frankel, *JPS Illustrated Children's Bible* (Philadelphia, PA: Jewish Publication Society, 2009), xi.

98. Ibid., xi.

99. Ibid., xii.

100. *Tanakh: The Holy Scriptures: The New JPS Translation According to the Traditional Hebrew Text* (Philadelphia: The Jewish Publication Society, 1988), 11.

101. Frankel, *JPS Illustrated Children's Bible*, 15.

explanations to the end of their stories.[102] By doing so, they help children remain aware of their biblical heritage and tradition.

1.3.a(ii). Jewish children's Bibles as midrash

While many Jewish children's Bible authors stay quite close to the wording and events described in the Bible, others take a decidedly different approach. Instead, they draw upon extra-biblical sources, create dialogue and scenes of their own, and explicitly tell their readers that they are doing so.

The title of Rabbi Hyman E. Goldin's book from 1931, *Bible and Talmud Stories: Volume 1 from the Beginning to the Death of Moses*, for example, cues the reader that Goldin is not drawing upon the text of the Torah alone for his stories. Goldin draws upon the tradition found in Midrash Devorim, the Kabbalistic Zohar, and elsewhere that criticizes Noah for not caring for the people of his generation. After Noah and his family survive the flood, Noah cries out, "O Lord of the World! You are called the Merciful, and you should have had mercy upon your creatures."[103] According to Goldin, "'O you foolish shepherd'; replied God, 'is it only now you bethink yourself to speak to me?'"[104] God chides Noah for at first caring just for his own safety and only asking for mercy for others after the rest of the world was destroyed. Noah realizes his error. Goldin, then, creatively integrates elements of the Talmud into his retelling of the stories of the Bible to teach children a lesson about compassion for others.

In 1989, Rabbi Marc Gellman, perhaps best known for co-hosting the television show *The God Squad* with Monsignor Thomas Hartman, offered a collection of his Bible stories for *Moment Magazine* in a book titled *Does God Have a Big Toe? Stories about Stories in the Bible*. In Gellman's "Author's Note" at the beginning of the book, he writes, "The best way to understand a story in the Bible is to make up another story about it. And that is what I have done in this book."[105] He continued, "I am a Jew and I am a rabbi. In my tradition the people who write stories about stories in the Bible are called *darshanim*, and the stories they write about the stories in the Bible are called *midrashim*. A *midrash* is the Jewish name for a story about a story in the Bible."[106] Gellman explains that while he has read the old *midrashim* and learned from them, the stories in the book are new. He claims that "They are modern *midrashim*" and offers them in "a way that the love of the Bible shines forth."[107]

---

102. See, for example, Laaren Brown and Lenny Hart, *The Children's Illustrated Jewish Bible* (New York: DK Publishing, 2007), and Alfred J. Kolatch, *Classic Bible Stories for Jewish Children* (Middle Village, NY: Jonathan David, 1994).

103. Hyman E. Goldin, *Bible and Talmud Stories: Volume 1 from the Beginning to the Death of Moses* (New York: Star Hebrew Book Company, 1931), 26.

104. Ibid., 26.

105. Marc Gellman, *Does God Have a Big Toe? Stories about Stories in the Bible* (New York: Harper & Row, 1989), vi.

106. Ibid., vii.

107. Ibid., vii.

Gellman's approach can be seen in two stories he tells about Noah and the ark. In the first story, each animal assumes that God must be like him or her. The elephant, being the biggest, thought God must be big like him, and so went to the mountain to ask it not to end the world. The eagle, who flew the highest of any animal, asked the cloud, while the lion, who roared the loudest, asked the thunder not to end the world.[108] Finally, the fish spoke up and said, "In the oceans and seas and rivers and lakes where we live, water is everywhere. There is water above and water below. There is water all around. If the water is everywhere, God must be everywhere too."[109] God then appears and says to the animals, "When I end the world, I will save two of each kind of animal so that when the world starts over, you can start over too. But as for the fish ... I will save *all* of them, because only they knew where to find God."[110]

In the next chapter, Gellman explains that Noah's friends Jehaz and Jabal did not understand his reasons for building the ark. As he puts it, "Noah's friends thought he was nuts."[111] When the rains came, however, Jehaz and Jabal bang on the door of the ark and say, "Hey Noah, you rat, let us in! We're your *friends*! You can't float off and leave us here to drown. Save us, Noah! Save us!"[112] According to Gellman, "Noah looked down with tears in his eyes and said, 'I didn't pick me. God picked me. What can I do?'"[113] The following scene is remarkable for being both humorous and quite sad:

> Noah's friends Jehaz and Jabal came to the ark dressed in a zebra suit. They demanded to be let in. Noah knew it was them. They were too lumpy to be a zebra. "Let us—I mean, let me in," they said. "You forgot me when you gathered in all the animals. I am a Jehaz—I mean—a zebra." Noah looked down on his friends and spoke through his tears.[114]

Noah tells his friends, "I love you. I am sorry for you, sorry for the animals, sorry for me, and sorry for God."[115] Gellman ends the tale by writing:

> Then the great rains came and flooded all the earth.
> Some say it was just rain, but others say that it was God's tears.[116]

Though approached with an element of humor, Gellman does not avoid the melancholy and tragic nature of the story of the flood.

108. Ibid., 27–8.
109. Ibid., 28.
110. Ibid., 29.
111. Ibid., 32.
112. Ibid.
113. Ibid.
114. Ibid., 33.
115. Ibid.
116. Ibid.

Mordicai Gerstein, in the introduction to his 1999 storybook *Noah and the Great Flood*, informs the reader that "In the Jewish tradition, many legends have arisen around the stories of the Bible."[117] He adds that "Here, then, is the story of Noah, enriched by these legends."[118] So, for example, Gerstein's story begins with Noah being born and with light of every color streaming from his eyes, which his wise great-grandfather recognizes is a sign "that one day, because of Noah, there will be a bridge of light between heaven and earth, and the world will end and begin again."[119] The story goes on to depict Noah preaching to the cruel giants who roam the land and sneer and jeer at him.[120] Gerstein draws upon several legends to tell a more interesting tale for children.

As these examples attest, Jewish children's Bibles tend either to reflect a primary goal of passing on the words, phrases, and events of the Torah itself as a part of Jewish religious tradition, or participate in the tradition of midrash by producing new versions of the stories based upon Jewish legends, midrashim, and their own imaginations. While some of the latter of these, such as Gellman's stories, clearly attempt to pass on certain values and perspectives to children, they differ from many Christian children's Bibles in that they do not describe their revised stories to readers as merely simplified versions of the Bible stories themselves.

1.3.b. Christian children's Bibles' approaches to retelling the story

As Ellen Frankel noted in the introduction to her *JPS Illustrated Children's Bible*, Christian children's Bibles have as a rule appropriated the biblical text more freely than their Jewish counterparts.[121] Many authors and publishers of Christian children's Bibles state in their introductions that their only goal is to simplify the Bible for children and to make its message clear, but then proceed to make changes to Bible stories and insert commentary without informing their readers that they are doing so.

Most Christian children's Bibles either offer no preface or introduction that describes their approach to retelling Bible stories or, if they do include one they use it to extol the grandness and value of Scripture and seek to assure parents that they are staying very faithful to the biblical text. Over the years some authors and editors, however, have written explicitly about their task, offering a philosophy of retelling of sorts. Very often, the authors suggest that they only make minor changes to the biblical text that do not change its meaning in any significant way. A close reading of these retellings, however, often reveals that this is not the case.

---

117. Mordicai Gerstein, *Noah and the Great Flood* (New York: Simon & Schuster Books, 1999), n.p.

118. Ibid., n.p.

119. Ibid., n.p.

120. Ibid., n.p.

121. Frankel, *JPS Illustrated Children's Bible*, xi.

1.3.b(i). Christian authors who acknowledge they are changing the stories
While many Christian children's Bible authors seem to be unaware or are unforthcoming about the changes they are making to Bible stories, a few appear to be very well aware of these changes and offer their readers a rationale for making those changes. The following, then, represent exceptions to the general rule, and serve as contrasts to the more prevalent trend.

One example of this approach can be found in Walter De La Mare's popular 1929 offering *Stories from the Bible*, published for decades in both Britain and the United States. De La Mare, an English poet and novelist who was also known for his ghost stories for children, had a somewhat ambivalent relationship with his Christian faith. In the introduction to *Stories from the Bible*, De La Mare suggests that "the very simplicity and austerity of the Old Testament stories, their conciseness" can lead to misunderstandings.[122] To help him communicate the meaning of the text to children, he says that he strove to remember "what the matchless originals in the Bible itself meant to me when I was a child."[123] In retelling the story of Noah, then, De La Mare allows himself the freedom to create scenes that add emotional texture to the story. For example, according to De La Mare, at night when Noah and his sons rested from their labors, "Only the nightingale poured on into the starry dark a song of delight, that yet seemed to echo with grief and exile."[124] One wonders if this melancholy scene of the night was a memory of some retelling of the story De La Mare heard as a child. He adds another dramatic interlude in his story:

> Strangers sometimes came that way, men with their hunting-dogs—men of great stature and faced like the hawk; keen and ferocious. Noah greeted them with civility and offered them food and drink. But when he solemnly warned them of the horror and destruction that were soon to come upon the earth, they merely mocked at him. They surveyed with their hard bright eyes the great clumsy wooden ship that lay casting its vast shadow on the grass beside it in the light of the sun, then turned their heads and stared insolently into his face as if into that of a man without wits, or with a mind ridden by the haggard deceits of insanity.[125]

From his introduction it is clear that De La Mare is aware that he is at times veering from the Genesis account and, at least in his introduction, makes his readers aware of this as well.

Ralph Milton is more blunt about it. He titles the introduction to his 1996 *The Family Story Bible* "Have Fun! A Word to Adults." In it, he acknowledges that he adds his own details and integrated some moral applications for the stories, and

---

122. Walter De La Mare, *Stories from the Bible* (New York: Alfred A. Knopf, 1961), 10.
123. Ibid.
124. Ibid., 46.
125. Ibid., 47.

suggests that "if that bothers you, maybe you need to find another book."[126] In his retelling of the story of Noah, for example, along with adding some of the more common embellishments to the story, Milton inserts a brief scene in which Noah's grandchildren complain about the odor, supported by an illustration by Margaret Kyle of a boy holding his nose. Milton writes, "Inside the ark it was pretty smelly. The animals would sometimes fight with each other. 'This place stinks!' said the grandchildren."[127] According to Milton, Noah concurred. "He wanted to get off that smelly ark as much as anyone."[128] This smelly subplot does not seem to support any significant theological or moral agenda, but it does add texture to the story and illustrates the sort of artistic license that some writers allow themselves in adapting Bible stories.

Changes such as these do not necessarily foist a clear moral or theological lesson onto readers, but they do change the tone and nature of the story. De La Mere and Milton are well aware of the sorts of changes they are making and let their readers know that they are making them. As shall be seen, however, these authors are exceptions to the more common trend.

1.3.b(ii). Christian authors who claim fidelity to the text but make significant changes to the story
Some Christian children's Bible authors have been fairly successful at following through on the creative restraint they promise in their introductions and a few have cued their readers to the fact that they are making significant changes from the canonical accounts. Many more Christian children's Bible authors, however, have claimed that they remain faithful to the words and events of the Scripture but have actually proceeded to change the stories of the Bible in significant ways.

James "Uncle Jim" E. Chessor's *Short Bible Stories: Retold in Simple Language*, published by the Gospel Advocate Company in 1924, is one example of a children's Bible that claims to make only minor changes to the biblical text. Chessor's book is subtitled *Eighty-Five Select Bible Stories, Each Complete in Itself, and Faithful to the Sacred Text*. In his "Prefatory," Chessor writes that he has used many exact quotations from the American Revised Version of the Bible, and insists that he has made only a few changes for the sake of clarity:

> These changes were made after much hesitancy, for fear that, in human frailty, the sacred text would not be represented accurately. Nor have I allowed myself to record imaginary scenes or incidents, or conversations. With prayer and purpose of heart, I have endeavored to be true to the inspired word of God.[129]

---

126. Ralph Milton *The Family Story Bible*, illus. by Margaret Kyle (Louisville, KY: Westminster John Knox Press, 1996), 7.

127. Ibid., 21.

128. Ibid.

129. James E. Chessor, *Short Bible Stories: Retold in Simple Language* (Nashville, TN: Gospel Advocate Company, 1924), 4.

Chessor's retelling of the story of Noah, however, reveals that he actually allowed himself a measure of freedom in imagining the scenes described in the Bible. Regarding Noah's neighbors, he writes:

> No doubt the faithless people laughed and jeered at him, but he was not persuaded away from duty by ridicule. He worked at the task many years—a hundred, perhaps. He made every part exactly as God said it should be.
>
> But Noah was also a preacher of righteousness. While the long-suffering of God waited, Noah warned the people that destruction would surely overtake them unless they would repent. But they gave no heed.[130]

He continues:

> No doubt the people laughed in glee when they beheld this curiously built structure standing solitary and dark against the horizon, a water craft where there was no water. To the wicked world the idea of a flood seemed absurd.[131]

Here, by writing "No doubt," Chessor offers a caveat of sorts to his embellishment of the mocking neighbors and, by referencing the New Testament claim that Noah was a preacher, covers his inclusion of Noah's warnings to his neighbors. He adds, without any caveat or support, the natural conclusion that, "The doomed people began to forsake their homes, rushing to higher places for safety. Animals ran pell-mell everywhere, seeking refuge and finding none."[132] He extends this scene as follows:

> What became of the wicked people of the world? They were all drowned—not one escaped! There was no place to flee. If they sought the hills for refuge, the flood reached them there; if they climbed into tall trees, the waters swept them away; if they reached mountain peaks, the floods carried them to watery graves. Death met them everywhere. It was an appalling destruction.[133]

Chessor then ends his retelling by integrating the following commentary upon the story:

> Nevertheless, another and still more dreadful destruction awaits the world at the last day. Then the "elements [heavenly bodies] shall be dissolved with fervent heat, and the earth and the works that are therein shall be burned up." In that awful day the wicked shall be destroyed, but the righteous shall be saved.[134]

130. Ibid., 17.
131. Ibid., 18.
132. Ibid., 20.
133. Ibid.
134. Ibid., 21.

Despite Chessor's stated intent to represent the sacred text accurately, avoid imaginary scenes, and remain true to the word of God, he allows himself freedom to embellish and abridge the Genesis account of the story of Noah and to add his own message of warning and call to salvation to the story. As shall be seen throughout the rest of this book, Chessor is far from alone in claiming to stay true to the canonical version of the story yet significantly revising it in ways that pass on certain beliefs or values, and is more reserved in his revisions than many others.

Perhaps no American children's Bible has been as popular or enduring over the years as the one by the American Methodist Episcopal clergyman Jesse Lyman Hurlbut. *Hurlbut's Story of the Bible Told for Young and Old* was first published in 1904 and has remained in print through numerous editions to the present day. So trusted was Hurlbut's children's Bible that some printings were published with black false leather textured covers and red paint on the edge of each page, just like regular Bibles published at the time, perhaps suggesting to consumers that it might serve as a faithful edition of the Bible itself. In his introduction, Hurlbut argues against those who would rewrite the Bible in ways that serve purposes beyond faithfully relating "the Sacred Narrative."[135] He seems to say that he will not embellish his stories when he writes, "I have refrained from adding to the Bible record any imaginary scenes or incidents or conversations."[136] Furthermore, he claims that in his book, "The Bible stories are made plain, but they are not rewritten or changed."[137] Hurlbut also emphasizes his opposition to children's Bibles that added morals or theological teachings to the end of their stories:

> In my opinion many books for children containing stories from the Bible are greatly marred by the evident attempt to interject a body of divinity into them, to make them teach doctrines which may be right or may be wrong, but are not stated in the Scripture stories ... [Some seek] to connect with Bible stories the deepest and most mysterious doctrines ... others contain moral reflections and applications which may be useful, but are not contained in the text of the story. I have sought to explain what needs explanation, but to avoid all doctrinal bias, and not to be wise above what is written.[138]

Reading these statements, one might assume that Hurlbut's retellings would be almost entirely free from embellishments or moralizations. This, however, is not the case.

Hurlbut passes on to children more of the details of the biblical text than most books that retell Bible stories and he adds fewer embellishments and comments than many others. Still, even Hurlbut makes several subtle changes to the story

---

135. Jesse Lyman Hurlbut, *Hurlbut's Story of the Bible told for Young and Old* (Chicago: John C. Winston, Co., 1904), 12.

136. Ibid., 11.

137. Ibid.

138. Ibid.

of Noah as it is presented in Genesis. He suggests, for example, that "it must have seemed very strange to all the people around, to build this great ark where there was no water for it to sail upon" and speculates that Noah's wicked neighbors "no doubt laughed at Noah for building a great ship where there was no sea."[139] He also adds a brief description of the scene of the people outside the ark, which Genesis does not do, writing that "the people had left their houses and ran up to the hills" and that "Some had climbed up to the tops of higher mountains, but the water rose higher and higher, until even the mountains were covered and all the people, wicked as they had been, were drowned in the great sea that now rolled over all the earth where men had lived."[140] At the end of the story, Hurlbut makes another subtle change. Instead of simply relaying, as Genesis does, that God told Noah that the rainbow was a sign of his promise never to destroy the earth with a flood, Hurlbut addresses his readers directly and reframes God's promise as a lesson to be applied by the readers themselves: "So, as often as we see the beautiful rainbow, we are to remember that it is the sign of God's promise to the world."[141] When compared to the great liberties many Christian children's Bible authors take with the Genesis account, these changes seem minor and Hurlbut likely felt that these revisions to the text were only making the story of Noah and its meaning more plain and clear to his readers. As later chapters will detail, however, even these seemingly subtle changes and additions serve to significantly reframe the stories for children.

These changes to the canonical versions of the stories and the lessons offered may not be considered radical interpretations of the text by people of their time and may be the common form of the story told in many sermons and religious education lessons of their day. In the case of children's Bibles, however, these adaptations and lessons are integrated into versions of the stories that are presented to their readers as a faithful version of the contents of the Bible itself.

1.4. Conclusion

What accounts for the ways in which authors and illustrators change the stories of the Bible, even while they often insist that they are remaining faithful to the biblical accounts? While it is difficult if not impossible to surmise the intentions of authors, these children's Bibles themselves offer no evidence that their authors are anything but sincere in their efforts to make the content and meaning of the Bible clear to children, and there is no evidence that they are consciously distorting the Bible stories in order to serve their own particular agendas for children. In most cases the authors of children's Bibles appear to understand the Bible as the holy scripture of their faith communities, and as such assume that its stories pass on the values and beliefs of those faith communities. From their perspectives

139. Ibid., 44.
140. Ibid.
141. Ibid., 46.

and their contexts, they read the stories of the Bible in ways that lead them to recognize particular beliefs and values in it.[142] When they take on the task of retelling the stories to children, they want these values and lessons to become clear for the younger generation. In this sense, their retellings do remain "faithful" to the Bible as they understand it.

Again, the purpose of this study is not to criticize or mock those authors and illustrators who change the story of Noah from how it appears in the Book of Genesis, even if those authors claim fidelity to the text. Instead, the chapters that follow will note how these authors use embellishments, abridgments, direct commentary, and illustrations to craft new versions of the story of Noah that speak to their time and place. The chapters that follow demonstrate how the story of Noah has been used throughout American history to present children with diverse images of God, different perspectives on salvation in Jesus Christ, a wide variety of moral and spiritual virtues, and perspectives on Bible stories as profound historical events or engaging and entertaining tales.

142. This phenomenon is not limited to the retelling of Bible stories. For more on how myths, Bible stories, and fairy tales have been retold to reinforce cultural values, see John Stephens and Robyn McCallum, *Retelling Stories, Framing Culture: Traditional Story and Metanarratives in Children's Literature* (New York: Garland Publishing, Inc., 1998).

Chapter 2

THE BIBLE AS THE REVELATION OF GOD: THE STORY OF NOAH AND THE CHARACTER OF GOD

2.1. Introduction

Oh! How dreadful it is to disobey such a powerful God, who can destroy us in a moment, if he please![1]

> Samuel G. Goodrich, *Peter Parley's Book of Bible Stories*, 1834

The wicked people would not go into the ark, nor believe Noah when he told them that the water was soon coming to drown them all. God waited in mercy many years, for He did not wish them to perish. But they would not repent nor believe, nor turn to God; and, at last, He sent rain from heaven and water out of the sea, and washed away the wicked people.[2]

> John Williamson Tyler, *The Bible Story Newly Told for Young People*, 1901

"I'll keep you safe!" God promised His friend.[3]

> Sally Lloyd-Jones, *Tiny Bear's Bible*, 2007

The desire to teach children about the nature of God lies at the heart of Jewish and Christian religious education. Many parents, teachers, and clergy see it as a religious duty to pass on their faith tradition's view of God to the next generation. But who is God, and how should children understand their relationship to God? Should the thought of God observing their every word and action fill children with a sense of abject fear, minor discomfort, or a warm feeling of comfort and assurance?

The Genesis account of the story of Noah presents readers with a complex and nuanced depiction of the nature of God and provides children's Bible authors

---

1. Samuel G. Goodrich, *Peter Parley's Book of Bible Stories* (Boston, MA: Lilly, Wait, and Co., 1834), 19, and Lucy Barton, *Bible Letters for Children* (London: John Souter, 1831), 11.

2. John Williamson Tyler, *The Bible Story Newly Told for Young People* (n.p.p.: William S. Whiteford, 1901), 21–2.

3. Sally Lloyd-Jones, *Tiny Bear's Bible*, illus. by Igor Oleynikov (Grand Rapids, MI: Zondervan, 2007), n.p.

and illustrators with many opportunities to adapt and revise the story to serve their own purposes. Throughout American history, children's Bible authors and illustrators have adapted this story of God, the flood, Noah, and the ark to teach children a variety of lessons about the character of God. As the three short quotes that open this chapter suggest, the character of God as revealed in American children's Bibles has gone through a number of changes. Of course not every American children's Bible fits neatly into predefined categories matching certain themes with their dates of publication. As a matter of fact, there is often a lag between when certain beliefs become widespread and when they find their expression in children's Bibles. In other cases, evidence of the popular beliefs of previous years seems to linger in children's Bibles much longer than one might expect. At the same time, different faith communities have different beliefs that they have expressed in children's Bibles through the years. In general, however, the character of God in American children's Bibles seems to have evolved in three general phases. In the early decades of the republic, God was presented to children as an unapologetically wrathful judge who destroys the wicked in His (in American children's Bibles, God is almost always referred to exclusively as a male) righteous anger. Later in the nineteenth century, a kinder, gentler God emerged, one who only reluctantly corrects or punishes people. Finally, in the later half of the twentieth century and early twenty-first century, God is presented as someone who is a friend who always keeps people safe.

2.2. Stories of a God of Wrath and Judgment

2.2.a. Puritan theology, mortality rates, and childhood development studies

Many of the earliest children's Bibles published in the United States unapologetically present children with stories of a wrathful God who metes out judgment and death upon those who are disobedient. Twenty-first-century readers of these children's Bibles are often surprised to find no attempts to sanitize or minimize the judgment and death present in the Bible stories, including that of Noah and the ark, and instead find stories that actually emphasize and expand upon these themes. Several aspects of the times, however, help explain why the presence of these motifs in children's Bibles from early in America's history are not only understandable, but to be expected.

The Puritan theology that was birthed in England and crossed the ocean to New England emphasized the sinfulness of humankind and the providence and judgment of God. As Stephen Prothero has put it, "The Puritans, in short, were a God-fearing rather than a Jesus-loving people, obsessed not with God's mercy but with His glory, not with the Son but with the Father."[4] The themes of God's righteous judgment upon sinners and the imminence of death were prominent in both Puritan thought and Puritan literature for children. Children were

4. Stephen Prothero, *American Jesus* (New York: Farrar, Straus and Giroux, 2003), 45.

often taught about the sinfulness of humankind and just wrath of God in their theological education. Still, the stories of the Bible were only occasionally used to convey this message. While children were immersed in spiritual matters through stories, hymns, and theological catechisms, and lessons on God's judgment, children's Bibles and Bible catechisms were usually not retold to teach these lessons but rather seemed designed simply to help children learn the stories and the words of the Bible for their own sake. Still, much of the other religious education material of the time emphasized the themes of the judgment of God and the ever-present specter of death for humankind.

In order to gain perspective on the religious education of children and children's Bibles in particular in the early days of the American republic, it will be helpful to take a step back and establish a baseline or point of departure in order to understand the Puritan heritage and approach to children's education that the nation inherited from England and its colonial period.

Nathaniel Crouch's *Youth's Divine Pastime*, published in London in 1691, is just one children's Bible from the Puritan era that emphasizes themes of judgment and death, but it provides a striking example of a children's Bible that is full of stories of sex, violence, and death. Not only did Crouch fail to omit the Bible's more scandalous stories, but he appears to have intentionally selected stories precisely because of their more sordid content. The stories in the first volume included "David and Bathsheba," "Jezebel eaten by dogs," "Two bears destroy forty children," and "The Death of Ananias and Saphira." The first volume ends with a story titled "Upon Death" accompanied by a gruesome illustration of a skeleton and the poem "Upon Heaven, and Upon Hell":

Where nothing's heard but Yells,
    And Groans, and woful [*sic*] Cries,
And where the Fire ne're [*sic*] abates,
    The Worm there never dies.

That worm which ever gnaws,
    And tears their Bowels out:
The Pit upon them shuts its Jaws:
    It's terrible no doubt.[5]

The second volume continues in the same vein, including the stories "Joseph and Potifer's wife," complete with a small woodcut illustration of Potiphar's wife reclining on her bed with naked breasts while pulling off Joseph's robe,[6] "The Levite and his Concubine," "Phinehas Killeth Zimri and Cozbi," "Achan Stoned to Death," "The Prophet Slain by a Lyon," "Dinah Rafish'd," "Deborah and Barak," as well as the stories of Lot's drunken incest with his daughters, Jephthah killing his daughter, Herod killing the children of Bethlehem, and the beheading of John

5. Nathaniel Crouch, *Youth's Divine Pastime*, Vol. 1 (London: n.p., 1691), 85.
6. Nathaniel Crouch, *Youth's Divine Pastime*, Vol. 2 (London: n.p., 1691), 48.

the Baptist. The text and the illustrations included in these retellings do not leave nudity (naked breasts are often depicted) or gruesome violence to the imagination of the children.

When Crouch takes up the story of Noah's ark, then, it is not surprising that his words emphasize horror, death, and violence even more than the words of Genesis would to his readers:

> When Men by Sin and Violence
>   Did stain the Earth with Blood,
> God doth resolve to wash them thence
>   By Waters of a Flood.

> Yet did he warn them before he struck,
>   *Noah* was sent to tell,
> They by their Sins would God provoke
>   To cast them down to hell![7]

The poem concludes:

> Then some unto the Mountains flee,
>   And others climb the Trees,
> Here one cries out, *Ah! Woe is me*,
>   He Death and Judgment sees.[8]

The title of Crouch's book suggests that it provides youth with a divine pastime, but its stories of sex, violence, death, and God's judgment are not the sort of stories most parents would offer their children in the twenty-first century. While the stories and descriptions of sexual activities soon faded from prominence in children's Bibles, tales that focused on judgment, violence, and death persisted for many years that followed.

How could parents and religious educators expose children to such sordid stories of violence, judgment, and death? Why did they feel that it was important to emphasize these themes? Why did they believe it would it be helpful for children to understand these things? To better understand why this approach to religious education came naturally, it is helpful to understand the Puritan theology of England and early America, the pervasive presence of death in the life of children in the American colonies and early republic, and the prevailing perspective (or lack thereof) on childhood development at the time.

The theology of the Church went through significant changes from the Puritan era to the days of the Christian revivals that swept through the American colonies during the First Great Awakening, beginning in the 1730s. Partly in response to the intellectualism of the Enlightenment, revivalists such as Jonathan Edwards

---

7. Crouch, *Youth's Divine*, Vol. 1, 10.
8. Ibid., 11.

and George Whitefield preached in ways to elicit an emotional as well as intellectual response to the Gospel. Though many of these revivalist preachers held that believers were elect, or predestined for salvation, even they looked for a quick, spontaneous, and often emotional conversion experience to confirm one's election.

One of the most famous sermons of the Great Awakening was Edwards' sermon "Sinners in the Hands of an Angry God," which he preached at the Bath Road Baptist Church in Kingston, Ontario, Canada, in July 1741. Edwards' sermons were about more than just the judgments of an angry God, but it is instructive to note that his message of God's judgment was delivered to children as well as to adults. Near the end of the sermon, Edwards says,

> And you, children, who are unconverted, do not you know that you are going down to hell, to bear the dreadful wrath of that God, who is now angry with you every day and every night? Will you be content to be the children of the devil, when so many other children in the land are converted, and are become the holy and happy children of the King of kings? And let every one that is yet of Christ, and hanging over the pit of hell, whether they be old men and women, or middle aged, or young people, or little children, now hearken to the loud calls of God's word and providence.[9]

A great appreciation of God's power, wrath, and judgment, as well as an appreciation of God's saving grace and mercy, was central to the theology of both the Great Awakening and what is often referred to as the Second Awakening that followed in the early nineteenth century. Adults believed that children needed to be warned that God's judgment might come at any time. As Steven Mintz writes in his book *Huck's Raft: A History of American Childhood*, "Children's early consciousness of their mortality and the severity of divine judgment was considered a particularly useful tool for shaping behavior."[10]

Another factor that helps explain the ubiquitous presence of death in early American religious education materials is the morality rate of the times. Children were not shielded from the subject of death because, for one reason, they could not be. Even at the end of the nineteenth century, one child out of six died before the age of five,[11] and children often saw siblings and adult family members die at home rather than in the hospital.

Also, it is helpful to recognize that this approach to the religious education of children in early American history came well before the days of modern childhood development studies and even before the Romantic view of children as innocents who needed to be protected from the harsh realities of the world

9. Jonathan Edwards, Henry Rogers, Sereno Edwards Dwight, and Edward Hickman, *The Works of Jonathan Edwards, Vol. II* (London: W. Ball, 1839), 11.

10. Steven Mintz, *Huck's Raft: A History of American Childhood* (Cambridge, MA: Harvard University Press, 2004), 19.

11. Ibid., 134.

became popular in the United States. In this era, children were often perceived as little adults, smaller in size and with less knowledge and vocabulary than their elders, but still able to perceive abstract concepts and to be exposed to subject matter such as death and violence that would in later years be perceived as not age appropriate.

The first prose children's Bible published in the United States offers a striking illustration of this perspective on children. The book, by an anonymous author, was simply titled *The Children's Bible*. It was first published in London but then republished in Philadelphia by Andrew Steuart in 1763.[12] Actually, the majority of children's Bibles and other children's religious education materials published in America in the colonial period and the early days of the republic were first published in England. American publishers selected certain popular English books to reprint that they felt would be appropriate to American readers, and in other cases, American authors simply chose to borrow liberally from the texts of English children's Bibles, often without giving any credit to their sources. In any case, the frontispiece of *The Children's Bible* depicts a man reading to young children, but the children are drawn in the same dress and same bodily proportions as adults, only smaller in size (see Figure 2.1).

These factors also help explain the way adults spoke to children about death in the eighteenth and early nineteenth centuries. As parents and teachers were reminding children of their sinfulness, they were also warning them about the potential nearness of their deaths. English theologian John Norris's 1694 book, *Spiritual Counsel, or, The Father's Advice to his Children*, is a striking example of this sort of religious education of children. Norris gives his children the following advice: "Be as much also in the contemplation of the four last things, Heaven, Hell, Death and Judgment. Place yourselves frequently upon your Deathbeds, in your Coffins, and in your Graves."[13] In David E. Stannard's book, *The Puritan Way of Death*, he notes that "The child of the Puritan was told to 'think how it will be on a deathbed'; to consider the terror of certain separation from, and even betrayal by, parents and loved ones; and to imagine what his well-deserved torments in Hell would be like."[14] Steven Mintz observes that "As early as possible, children were taught to prepare for death. Ministers admonished children to reflect on death, and their sermons contained graphic descriptions of hell and the horrors of eternal damnation."[15]

This practice of teaching children to prepare for death continued into the eighteenth century, as can be seen in the 1777 edition of *The New England Primer*. The popular primer taught children about the imminence of death through the well-known prayer, "Now I lay me down to take my sleep, I pray the Lord my

12. *The Children's Bible* (Philadelphia, PA: Andrew Steuart, 1763), frontispiece.

13. John Norris, *Spiritual Counsel, or, The Father's Advice to His Children* (London: S. Manship, 1694), 76.

14. David E. Stannard, *The Puritan Way of Death* (New York: Oxford University Press, 1977), 171.

15. Mintz, *Huck's Raft*, 20.

Figure 2.1. Frontispiece of *The Children's Bible* (Philadelphia, PA: Andrew Steuart, 1763).

soul to keep, If I should die before I wake, I pray the Lord my soul to take."[16] Likewise, even while learning the letters of the alphabet in the primer, children were reminded about death through lessons such as, "T: Time cuts down all, Both

16. *The New England Primer* (Boston, MA: Edward Draper, 1777), n.p.

great and small," "X: XERXES did die, and so must I," and "Y: While youth do chear [sic], death may be near."[17]

Such teachings on death continued throughout much of the nineteenth century. The American Sunday School Union published a monthly journal of Bible stories and morality tales from everyday life titled *The Youth's Friend* that often told tales of children who died when breaking God's law. To cite just one example, the October 1830 issue contains a story titled "The Sabbath Breaker Punished; Or, The Effects of Sabbath-Breaking." The titular Sabbath Breaker is a boy by the name of Henry Mees who played hooky from Sunday School one day. He took a walk by a river, slipped on a plank, fell into the river, and drowned. According to the story, "He had not been a great while in Sunday School, and his conduct was generally pretty good; but it is a very awful thing to die suddenly; still more so to die in the act of breaking the commandments of God."[18] The story concludes that children should live with a healthy fear of God's judgment: "Let Sabbath-breakers beware! The Lord is a holy God; he hates sin, and he often punishes those who break his laws; if not in this world, he will in the next."[19] As Sunday School historians Robert W. Lynn and Elliott Wright put it, "If sex is the common preoccupation of Americans in the mid-twentieth century, then death was the obsession of evangelical Protestants in the first half of the nineteenth."[20]

A strong strain of religious education of children in the United States in the late eighteenth and early nineteenth centuries, then, focused on convincing children of their own sinfulness and reminding them of the potential nearness of death and judgment of God.[21] Adults appear to have had a number of motivations for making sure that children were aware that they might die suddenly. This chapter examines the ways in which the threat of impending death impacts the way God is portrayed in children's Bible retellings of the story of Noah and the ark, while the chapters that follow will demonstrate how the threat of death in the story is used to instruct children regarding salvation and moral virtues.

When twenty-first-century readers who are unaware of these factors look at eighteenth- and nineteenth-century children's Bibles, they are often struck by the seeming emphasis on death and God's wrath and judgment on sinners. By the time of the American Revolution in the late eighteenth century and during the revivals of the nineteenth century, there was actually less of an emphasis on frightening children about death and God's judgment than there had been

---

17. Ibid., n.p.

18. "The Sabbath Breaker Punished; Or, The Effects of Sabbath-Breaking," *The Youth's Friend* (October 1830): 157.

19. Ibid.

20. Robert W. Lynn and Elliott Wright, *The Big Little School*, rev. edn (Birmingham, AL: Religious Education Press, 1980), 70–1.

21. See Anne M. Boylan, *Sunday School: The Formation of an American Institution 1790–1880* (New Haven, CT: Yale University Press, 1988), 147, and Lynn and Wright, *The Big Little School*, 121–2.

during the Puritan era.[22] Most children's Bibles of the time were actually quick to mention the mercy of God as well as God's judgment. Still, the aftereffects of the Puritan approach to religious education did not all immediately disappear with the Second Great Awakening or the dawn of the nineteenth century.

Rather than edit out stories of judgment and death from children's Bibles, these stories were often included. For example, the story from 2 Kings 2.23-24 of Elisha cursing the children of Bethel and the she-bears killing 42 of them is rarely included in children's Bibles of the twentieth and twenty-first centuries. In the late eighteenth and early nineteenth centuries, however, if a children's Bible were to include just ten to fifteen stories from the Bible, the chances are that this story would be chosen and that one of the book's few illustrations would be devoted to a scene of bears eating children (see Figure 2.2).[23] In other cases, most children's Bibles in the late eighteenth and early nineteenth centuries make no attempt to soften or apologize for the presence of so much death and judgment but instead elaborate on the biblical stories in ways that highlight those very aspects. The story of Noah's ark in children's Bibles of the time provides a helpful example of how this was done.

2.2.b. Noah's ark as the story of God's wrathful judgment on the world

In contrast to other ancient flood stories, the Book of Genesis provides a moralistic reason for the flood. The Gilgamesh Epic's story of the flood does not comment on the reason for the flood and the ancient Atrahasis Epic suggests that the reason for the flood was simply that God was disturbed because humankind was becoming too noisy. The Genesis account of the story of the flood, however, makes it clear that God sends the flood to destroy humankind because of its moral wickedness.

How has the story of Noah's ark been appropriated to teach children about a God of wrath and righteous judgment? It was done in several ways. While Genesis notes that all living things outside of the ark were destroyed when the flood came, it does not provide any details or description of their plight as the waters rose. In the late eighteenth and early nineteenth centuries, however, these aspects of the story were often highlighted in various ways in children's Bibles. More often than not, the story was titled "The Deluge." The aspects of these children's Bible retellings of the story of Noah that stand out the most to contemporary readers are (i) the extended descriptions of people drowning that go well beyond the brief reporting that all outside the ark had died found in the book of Genesis; (ii) the explicit warning to children of the dangers of provoking God's wrath and judgment that are integrated into the story or tacked onto the end of it; and (iii) the disturbing illustrations of the people outside of the ark in distress as they are

22. Gary Laderman, *The Sacred Remains: American Attitudes Toward Death, 1799–1883* (New Haven, CT: Yale University Press, 1996), 53.

23. See, for example, *Scripture History* (New York: Wood, 1811), n.p.; *Little Book of Bible Stories for Children.: With Numerous Engravings* (Worcester, MA: Dorr, Howland & Co., 1839), 19–20, and *Stories from the Bible* (Northampton, MA: E. Turner, 1843), n.p.

BEARS TEARING CHILDREN.

Figure 2.2. Woodcut illustration of "Bears Tearing Children" from *Stories from the Bible* (Northampton, MA: E. Turner, 1843), n.p.

being overwhelmed by the flood waters. Some of these children's Bibles also note God's mercy and protection for people like Noah and his family. Unlike many children's Bibles from later eras, however, this mercy and protection is not unconditional. It is clearly contingent upon the people loving and obeying God.

2.2.b(i). Extended descriptions of drowning and warnings of God's judgment
Some of the earliest published retellings of the Bible for children in America were in verse. The necessary task of rhyming words and keeping the story brief meant that creativity was needed, which often led authors to include their interpretive flourishes to the Bible stories and their poems. Benjamin Harris's *The Holy Bible in Verse*, which was published in 1717 in Boston, serves as a very early example of this phenomenon. Harris briefly tells the story of Noah in verse, framing it as a story of judgment and mercy. As the story begins, God is distraught with humankind's sinfulness:

At which he cries out in despair,
My Grief is more than I can bear.
Man's Wickedness grows very great

For which a Deluge God does threat,
It comes and in it all are drown'd,
Save only *Eight*, who mercy found.[24]

The God of the verse is an emotional God and the one who possesses agency in the story. Due to God's grief and despair over humankind's wickedness, God "threats" the deluge, which drowns everyone save eight. Mercy is found in this story, but it is made clear that God's mercy was reserved only for the eight members of Noah's family

John Taylor's *Verbum Sempiternum*, first published in 1614 in England, was available in the colonies as early as 1750. A third edition was published in Providence in 1774 as a miniature thumb Bible. In his note "To the Reader" Taylor writes, "With care and pains out of the Sacred book, / This little Abstract for thee have took: / And with great reverence have I cull'd from thence, / All things that are of Greatest consequence."[25] The beginning of Taylor's brief poetic retelling of the Book of Genesis takes up four of the 280 small pages of the book and briefly tells the tale of creation, humankind's sinfulness, and God's mercy and judgment:

GENESIS
JEHOVAH here of Nothing all things makes,
And Man, the chief of all, his God forsakes,
Yet by th' Almighties Mercy 'twas decreed,
Heaven's Heir should satisfy for Man's misdeed.
Men now live long, but do not act aright.
For which the flood destroys them all but eight.
Noah, his Wife, their Sons, with those they wedd:
The rest all perished in that watery bed.[26]

This verse, too, speaks of God's mercy, but also makes it clear that only eight are saved from being destroyed by the flood. Taylor's readers are left with the provocative, frightening, and memorable image of all others perishing in a "watery bed."

In the opening dedication of *The Children's Bible* from 1763 the author prepares children for stories that reveal a God of anger, justice, and mercy, and tells them, "For when you hear of GOD's being angry with and punishing people, for their disobedience of his Holy Word, may you not immediately reason with yourself, and think with great justice, that he will punish you likewise, if you disobey him."[27]

In retelling the story of Noah, *The Children's Bible* does not shy away from describing the harsh judgment of God. In transitioning from the story of Cain and Abel to the story of Noah, the text reads,

24. Benjamin Harris, *The Holy Bible in Verse* (Boston, MA: John Allen, 1717), n.p.

25. John Taylor, *Verbum Sempiternum*, 3rd edn (Providence, RI: n.p., 1774), n.p.

26. Ibid., n.p.s. Note that I have retained the original spellings of many words here and in other direct quotations from eighteenth- and nineteenth-century texts.

27. *The Children's Bible*, vi–vii.

Thus, my dear child, you have seen the dreadful consequences of vice in particular persons; but the world soon grew so intolerably wicked, that GOD ALMIGHTY could endure it no longer, and he resolved to destroy it all at once. However, as he never punishes the innocent with the guilty, there was one *Noah*, who was a pious and virtuous man, and him GOD ALMIGHTY determined to save, together with his whole family.[28]

When the flood covered the earth, however, the text makes it clear that "all the wicked inhabitants of it were utterly destroyed."[29] The author manages to keep the retelling quite brief but still expands the Genesis account in order to underscore the omnipotence of GOD ALMIGHTY and to make it clear to the reader that the wicked deserved to be punished and received their due punishment accordingly.

Reverend Thomas Smith's collection of Bible stories, *The Sacred Mirror; or Compendious View of Scripture History*, was first published in the United States in 1806. In his preface, he writes to "my young readers,"[30] although, as is the case with many male clergy authors of children's Bibles, the vocabulary he uses seems quite advanced. Smith presents the flood to children as "the awful decree of Omnipotence":[31]

In this posture of affairs, while vice and profligacy were daily gaining ground, and every religious duty was rapidly sinking into neglect, the Almighty determined to chastise mankind for their unrighteousness; but he graciously allotted them one hundred and twenty years for repentance, mercifully observing, that they were but flesh. As, however, they still continued incorrigible, and the friendly admonitions of Noah were totally disregarded, God is emphatically said to have decreed their destruction, together with that of the beasts of the field, and fowls of the air. The Divine Justice, however, was sweetly tempered with mercy, and a reservation was made, by which the earth might be replenished when the threatened deluge should subside.[32]

Smith ends his tale with words about the love of God and the wickedness of humankind: "Thus was desolation brought upon the earth by the wickedness and impenitence of mankind; and thus was the love of God manifested in the preservation of the only family, consisting of eight persons, which retained the profession and practice of religion in the midst of universal licentiousness."[33]

28. *The Children's Bible*, 19. Emphasis in the original.

29. Ibid., 19–20.

30. Thomas Smith, *The Sacred Mirror; or Compendious View of Scripture History* (Boston, MA: Samuel H. Parker, 1806), iii.

31. Ibid., 12.

32. Ibid., 11.

33. Ibid., 12.

According to Smith, God is the omnipotent agent of divine justice who must carry out an awful decree. Smith's God is also presented as a God of mercy, though only merciful to the one family that was not wicked, impenitent, and licentious.

The story of Noah and the ark is also retold in *The Child's Library of Useful Knowledge* from 1806, a volume that also contains non-biblical stories and poems. According to the story,

> God sent rain forty days and forty nights; and all men lost their lives, except for Noah and his family: they were kept alive in the ark, which was a sort of ship, the first that was made, which God told Noah how to build. All animals died too, but those which God caused to go in the ark. The waters stood so as to cover all the high hills; the whole globe was one deep sea. But the ark was lifted up, and in it God saved Noah and his family; but cut off all the wicked people.[34]

These sentences clearly juxtapose the safety of Noah and the animals on the ark with the fate of the wicked. The unnamed author appears not to have trusted that readers would grasp the implicit message, however, because the very next sentence offers direct commentary to the reader: "We must fear God, and love him, and keep his laws."[35] Children, then, are left with the lesson that God is a God whom they must both fear and love.

The small, 190-page book *A Short History of the Bible and Testament* from 1817 stays relatively close to the wording and tone of the Genesis account of the story of Noah. The full story of Noah and the ark is told as follows:

> Adam disobeyed God, and all his children disobeyed him too, so that in time the whole world was full of wickedness, and God determined to punish it by a flood of water, which should drown them all. Only Noah and his family remembered to love and to worship him; and they alone were saved. They built an ark by God's directions, and went into it, with animals of every kind, two and two: while the rain poured down in torrents, the floods burst over the rivers, and rushed in from the foaming seas! For many months the ark rode about upon the waters; and not a leaf, not a mountaintop was seen, till at length the waters began to dry away, the ark rested upon a high hill; and Noah and his family went out praising God who had saved them from the mighty deluge.[36]

Though this is only a brief, abridged summary of the story, it certainly does not shy away from revealing a God who punishes and kills the wicked. The story suggests that Noah and his family were spared because they remembered to love and worship God, a fact that seems to serve as a warning to children that they would be wise to do the same.

34. *The Child's Library of Useful Knowledge* (Pittsburgh, PA: Zadok Cramer, 1806), 9.

35. Ibid., 9.

36. *A Short History of the Bible and Testament* (Hartford, CT: Cooke & Hale, 1817), 15–17.

The theme of God's judgment upon the wicked can also be seen in the 1834 small thumb Bible, *The Child's Bible*, written by "a Lady of Cincinnati," who was rumored to be Harriet Beecher Stowe.[37] The book's retelling of the story of Noah recounts how the wicked people were drowned and Noah was saved. The story concludes, "The Lord will always preserve those that love and obey him. So when the flood of his wrath shall come upon the wicked, the righteous need fear no harm."[38] The book, then, raises the prospect of the flood of God's wrath being meted out in the present day, but also adds the theme of God's protection. That protection, however, is contingent upon whether or not one loves and obeys God.

Bible Stories with Suitable Pictures, a 16-page "Mini Book" published some time between 1821 and 1831, also includes the themes of punishment and salvation in its brief summary of the story of Noah. As the story begins, "the whole world was full of wickedness, and God, determined to punish it by a flood of water, which should drown them all."[39] The story concludes "and Noah and his family went on praising God, who had saved them from the mighty deluge."[40] According to the book's short account, then, God's initial inclination is to drown everyone by means of a flood but then demonstrates mercy by saving Noah and his family.

The short book *Scripture History, or Short Sketches of Characters from the Old Testament* from 1829 includes an illustration at the top of each page, a poem retelling the Bible story in the middle of the page, and a lesson to be gleaned from the Bible story at the bottom of the page. For the story of Noah, the small woodcut illustration shows Noah kneeling before the ark with arms outstretched in praise. In a somewhat dubious effort at rhyming, the poem declares, "The mighty waters of the Flood, Proclaim a sin-avenging God."[41] The lesson included at the bottom of the page explains, "Sin makes God angry. All the people delighted in doing evil, except Noah."[42] The text suggests to readers that they would not want to make this sin-avenging God angry and would want to avoid doing evil, especially if they are deriving any delight in their sinful escapades.

As was the case with Nathaniel Crouch's *Youth's Divine Pastime* of 1691, a high percentage of the Bible stories chosen for inclusion in *Pictures of Bible History with Suitable Descriptions* include a level of violence and death that was not uncommon in educational materials of its time. The short, 24-page chapbook from 1826 is very brief in its retelling of the story of Noah and seems to have adapted many of

37. See Charlotte M. Smith, "The Joys of Miniature Books," *Books at Iowa* 41 (November 1984). http://www.lib.uiowa.edu/spec-coll/bai/smith2.htm (accessed April 28, 2015).

38. *The Child's Bible* (Philadelphia, PA: Fisher and Brother, 1834), 30. The book measures 2¼" x 1⅞" and is 192 pages long.

39. *Bible Stories with Suitable Pictures* (Worcester, MA: Dorr & Howland, c. 1821–31), 13–14.

40. Ibid., 16.

41. *Scripture History, or Short Sketches of Characters from the Old Testament* (New York: Mahlon Day, 1829), 5. Similarly, P. C. Headley would write of "Jehovah's avenging waters" in *Bible Chats with Children* (Philadelphia, PA: John E. Potter and Company, 1895), 56.

42. Ibid.

its retellings from 1817's *A Short History of the Bible and Testament,* but abridges the stories even further. According to the story, "Adam disobeyed God, and all his children disobeyed him too, so that in time the whole world was full of wickedness, and God determined to punish it by a flood of water, which should drown them all. Only Noah and his family remembered to love and worship him; and they alone were saved."[43] The author makes the blunt point that God is punishing the wicked, and explicitly tells the reader that they all drowned, and that Noah and his family were saved, again because they remembered to love and worship God.

As has been noted, many early American children's Bibles were simply republications of English children's Bibles that publishers and their customers deemed appropriate for American children. Other early American children's Bibles, however, were created by American authors who crafted and redacted their text by freely borrowing from children's Bibles previously published in England. Some of these American authors gave some indication in their introductions that they were drawing on other sources, but the majority did not.

For example, Lucy Barton was an English author whose retelling of the story of Noah seemed to have especially resonated with American authors. Barton's *Bible Letters for Children* (1831) tells her readers that "God declared that as a punishment for the sin of the world, He would bring a flood of waters upon the earth that should destroy every other living thing."[44] After explaining how the flood covered the tops of the highest mountains, Barton then inserted the following direct commentary to her readers: "Oh! how dreadful it is to disobey such a powerful God, who can destroy us in a moment, if he please! But this mighty God is also called, in the Bible, the God of love; and the same Being who commanded the waters to destroy the earth, condescends to love little children, if they do but wish and try to please *Him.*"[45] According to Barton's narrative, God is powerful, and it is dreadful to disobey God. Children are explicitly told that God could destroy them at any moment. The first line appears to be designed to frighten children at the prospect of making God angry. The second line tells children that God is merciful, but it is a condescending mercy that is only given when children try to please God.

A number of American children's Bible authors found the image of God in Barton's direct commentary quoted above so helpful that they included those words verbatim in their own texts. Samuel G. Goodrich, author of the extremely popular Peter Parley series of children's books, inserted Barton's words into his 1834 book, *Peter Parley's Book of Bible Stories,*[46] as did *A Child's Book of Sunday Reading,* which was republished by various publishers in the early 1940s,[47] and

---

43. *Pictures of Bible History with Suitable Descriptions* (Wendell, MA: J. Metault, 1826). Later republished with the identical pages and contents as *Pictures of Bible History* (Northampton, MA: John Metcalf, 1836), 7.

44. Barton, *Bible Letters,* 11.

45. Ibid., 12.

46. Goodrich, *Peter Parley's Book,* 19, and Barton, *Bible Letters,* 12.

47. *Child's Book of Sunday Reading* (Worcester, MA: N. Hervey, 1840), n.p., and *Child's Book of Sunday Reading* (Worcester, MA: G.B. Matthews, c. 1840), n.p.

Bible Stories for the Young with Colored Engravings from 1842.[48] All of these American authors seemed to find Barton's words useful as they sought to appropriate the story of Noah's ark to warn children about a God of judgment who is at the same time a God of love—albeit conditional love—and mercy.

The Rev. I. B. Watkins wrote and published a children's Bible in the 1820s that became quite popular in both Britain and the United States when published in a thick, two-volume set in 1851 titled *Tallis's Illustrated Scripture History for the Improvement of Youth*. The author uses vocabulary appropriate for quite advanced readers and places a clear emphasis on God's wrathful judgment as well as God's merciful salvation. The text begins, "The rebellious spirit of Adam, which caused his ignominious expulsion from Paradise, brought 'sin into the world,' and left it a wretched legacy to his posterity. In time the growing depravity of mankind, became more than Divine patience could longer endure."[49] The story continues with the observations, "Terrible indeed was the scene then witnessed: tremendous the effects of God's wrath"[50] and "as no sin can escape the eye of the Omniscient, so no defence can save the transgressor from his mighty arm."[51] The author suggests to the reader that to sin against God today is foolish, stating, "The mind recoils shuddering at the thought, yet men who would tremble to receive the sentence of a human judge, carelessly trample on the laws of God."[52] After arguing that no one can truthfully say the location of the mountain on which the ark rested, the author concludes the story by sharing the following lesson from the story of Noah:

> The history of the Deluge will lead the serious reader to reflect how dreadfully comprehensive Divine wrath can be; but while we shudder at the thought, it will be remarked that God is as potent to save as to punish, and often since the days of Noah it has been found, that while dreadful judgments were spreading far and wide universal ruin and despair, the good man in [sic] his family has been saved from peril, and remained, not only uninjured, but serene till the storm had passed away.[53]

The text explicitly talks about God's power, God's wrath, and how dreadful God's judgment can be. As a matter of fact, the words "dreadfully" and "dreadful" are both used in the complex sentence, underscoring the point that children should have a respectful dread of God's wrath and power.

That these children's Bibles mention that God causes the flood or that the world and its inhabitants are all drowned is not remarkable. These are, after all, aspects

---

48. *Bible Stories for the Young with Colored Engravings* (Worcester, MA: S. A. Howland, 1842), n.p.

49. *Tallis's Illustrated Scripture History for the Improvement of Youth*, Vol. I (London and New York: J. & P. Tallis, 1851), 9.

50. Ibid.

51. Ibid.

52. Ibid., 9–10.

53. Ibid., 10.

of the story of Noah as it is presented in Genesis. Later children's Bibles, however, would often go to some lengths to avoid explicitly describing these aspects of the story or presenting children with an image of God as a wrathful judge whom they should fear. The majority of these earliest American children's Bibles, however, do not hesitate both to name God as the one who brings the flood and to describe the flood as God's righteous and wrathful judgment on a wicked world. As much as these texts may have invoked the fear of God in children of the time, the illustrations that accompanied these stories may have had an even greater impact on the children who saw them.

2.2.b(ii). Illustrating the deluge
One feature of many nineteenth-century American children's Bibles that immediately strikes many contemporary readers is the presence of illustrations that depict the death of children and the frightening nature of God's judgment. In the case of the story of Noah, the Book of Genesis briefly reports that all people and animals that were not in the ark died in the flood, but it does not describe a scene outside of the ark. There is no description of how those outside of the ark reacted when the flood came, how they tried to save themselves, or how they might have called out to Noah to be allowed to enter the ark. This scene outside the ark, however, is one of the most common scenes illustrated in American children's Bible stories of the nineteenth century. Even when the story of Noah had just one or two pictures accompanying the text, the scene of people being overwhelmed by floodwaters was one that publishers commonly chose.

The lone illustration accompanying the story of Noah in *Pictures of Bible History with Suitable Descriptions* from 1826 is a small woodcut of the ark afloat in the background while a distraught man, woman, and child are struggling to hang onto a tree on a small island in the midst of the waters, underscoring the theme of judgment upon the wicked.[54]

Bible Stories for the Young with Colored Engravings from 1842 includes another illustration of the deluge with people holding onto branches or riding swimming horses.[55] The images and description of drowning animals may have been especially poignant to children, who may have identified with their sorrowful, innocent faces.

Two thick two-volume sets, John Howard's *The Illustrated Scripture History for the Youth* from 1863 and Tallis's *Illustrated Scripture History for the Improvement of Young* from 1851, both illustrated their retellings of the story of the flood with the same woodcut illustration of a man and a woman holding a baby in despair on what is left above water of a mountaintop while the waters of the flood overwhelm them (see Figure 2.3). A snake mockingly rides the waves next to the man's head. The caption in Tallis's version reads:

---

54. *Pictures of Bible History with Suitable Descriptions*, 7.
55. *Bible Stories for the Young with Colored Engravings* (Worcester, MA: S. A. Howland, 1842), n.p.

THE DELUGE
The windows open'd of the sky,
    O'erwhelmed the globe in one vast sea.
And sinners feel, condemn'd to die
    How terrible our God can be.[56]

The most common illustrations reproduced in nineteenth-century children's Bibles to accompany the story of Noah are three illustrations by French artist Gustave Doré. Doré's well-known Victorian drawings were done in a highly romanticized, neoclassical style. His pencil drawings were turned into fine woodcuts and were included in many nineteenth-century and even some twentieth-century children's Bibles in America. The single illustration that has been used to accompany the story of Noah in more American children's Bibles than any other is Doré's *The Deluge*, an image that focuses on children in distress (see Figure 2.4).[57] The illustration depicts naked adults, with strips of cloth and branches strategically placed for modesty's sake, being overcome by the flood. These adults attempt to lift naked children above the waves and onto a small rock, presumably all that is left above water of the tip of a mountaintop, which is already home to a wild tiger that is trying to save her cubs. Another Doré illustration, titled *The World Destroyed by Water*, depicts a mass of naked people in distress climbing to higher ground along with a variety of wild beasts including elephants and bears while the ark appears far in the background. Another of his illustrations used in several children's Bibles is *The Dove Sent forth from the Ark*, which depicts the majestic image of the ark run aground on dry land as the waters have receded to reveal bare land littered with the naked, dead bodies of humans and animals (see Figure 2.5). Any one of these images could have frightened children into contemplating the awful judgment of God for days to come, which indeed may have been the desired effect.

By the final years of the nineteenth century, graphic descriptions of the fate of the wicked outside of the ark were becoming increasingly less common in American children's Bibles, and the number of children's Bibles that presented God to children as an unapologetically wrathful judge became increasingly rare as well. Still, Doré's illustrations continued to be used. At times the illustrations

---

56. *Tallis's Illustrated Scripture History*, 8.

57. See, for example, Charles Foster, *The Story of the Bible from Genesis to Revelation Told in Simple Language* (Philadelphia, PA: Charles Foster Publishing, 1873), 19–21; John Howard, *The Illustrated Scripture History for the Young* (New York: Virtue and Yorston, 1876), 11; J. L. Sooy, *Bible Talks with Children: The Scriptures Simplified for the Little Folk* (New York: Union Publishing House, 1889), 16; Carolyn Hadley, *From Eden to Babylon: Stories of the Prophets, Priests and Kings of the Old Testament* (New York: McLoughlin Brothers, ca. 1890), 14–15; J. W. Buel and T. DeWitt Talmage, *The New Beautiful Story* (Philadelphia, PA: Historical Publishing Company, 1892), 45; Russell H. Conwell, *Bible Stories for Children* (Philadelphia, PA: W. W. Houston & Co., 1892), 16; Mary A. Lathbury, *Bible Heroes: Stories from the Bible* (Boston, MA: DeWolfe, Fiske & Co., 1898), 5, and many more.

THE DELUGE.

(GEN. CH. VII. V. 11, 12.)

THE DELUGE CAME, SO DREAD AND DARK.
OF WATERS FALLN FROM HEAVENS FOUNT ;
BUT GOD PRESERVED GOOD NOAHS ARK
UNTIL IT RESTED ON THE MOUNT.

Figure 2.3. Illustration from John Howard's *The Illustrated Scripture History for the Young* (1863), 11.

chosen for children's Bibles appear to be selected simply because of their availability or familiarity rather than because they fit the tone of the text. In some instances a significant dissonance exists between more gentle texts and the harsh illustrations that accompany them.

Russell H. Conwell's version of the story of Noah in his *Bible Stories for Children* from 1892 is a case in point. Conwell, the Northern Baptist minister known for his famous "Acres of Diamonds" sermon and for being the founder and first president of Temple University, tended to present a kinder and gentler version of events than many of his predecessors. Conwell's text does, however, include a scene in which people are begging to get inside the ark: "Men and women and children were calling on God to save them, but they had all led bad lives, and God would not listen to their prayers, for He intended to punish them with death for their sins."[58] Doré's popular *The Deluge*[59] and his less common illustration *The*

58. Conwell, *Bible Stories for Children*, 17.
59. Ibid., 16.

Figure 2.4. Gustave Doré's *The Deluge*, c. 1866, found in many nineteenth-century children's Bibles.

Dove Sent Forth from the Ark,[60] both of which show people dying or already dead from the flood, accompany Conwell's retelling. Conwell may or may not have had much of a hand in choosing the illustrations accompanying his text. In any case, the book's two graphic illustrations of death by the flood would likely have had a more lasting impact on its young readers than Conwell's kinder and gentler text.

60. Ibid., 18.

THE DOVE SENT FORTH FROM THE ARK

Figure 2.5. Gustave Doré's *The Dove Sent Forth from the Ark*, c. 1866.

In similar fashion, Mary A. Lathbury's *Bible Heroes: Stories from the Bible* from 1898 presents a more child-friendly text, but frightening illustrations. Lathbury, a Methodist Episcopal perhaps best known as the librettist of the hymn "Break Thou the Bread of Life," designed her children's Bible to be a book of Bible stories written by a mother for other mothers. Lathbury's account of Noah sets a friendly tone. She writes about Noah's family entering the ark: "Into their great black house, and through the window in the top came flying the little families of birds and insects, from the tiny bees and humming birds, to the great eagles, and through the door on the side came the families of animals, two by two, from the little mice to the tall giraffes, and the elephants, and when all had come the Lord shut them in."[61] She muses, "Think how glad the sheep and cows were to find fresh grass, and the birds to fly to the green trees."[62] Lathbury ends the story with the reassuring message that, "He still sends the rainbow to show us that He is taking care of this world, and will always do so."[63] Still, one suspects that Doré's illustration *The Deluge*[64] that accompanies the story would have had at least as much of a lasting impact on many of its young readers as Lathbury's more comforting text.

Alternative versions of the scene depicted in Doré's *The Deluge* continued to be used in children's Bibles at the end of the nineteenth century. The sole illustration accompanying the story of Noah in Rev. Alvan Bond's *Young People's Illustrated Bible History*, from 1871, is a full-page engraving titled *The Deluge* by American artist E. Sears. Sears's illustration depicts a very dramatic tableau in which waters are flowing and lightning is striking, while a despairing group of people looks very small and powerless in the foreground. In his text, Bond describes God's plan to "destroy the wicked people and wash them all away."[65] Likewise, the illustration by an unnamed artist of *The Deluge* used in F. J. Knecht's *The Child's Bible History*, from 1898, depicts a cluster of men, women, and a child on the small portion of a mountaintop remaining above the sea while another person is seen drowning in the sea (see Figure 2.6).[66] It is a disturbing image, with people clearly in distress, as the small image of the ark is seen in the distant background.

After the first couple of decades of the twentieth century, illustrations and descriptions of people drowning in the flood became less and less common in children's Bibles, though some do exist.[67] Some of the most horrific images and descriptions of the flood from the twentieth century came from writer and artist

61. Mary A. Lathbury, *Bible Heroes: Stories from the Bible* (Boston, MA: DeWolfe, Fiske & Co., 1898), 6.

62. Ibid.

63. Ibid.

64. Ibid., 5.

65. Alvan Bond, *Young People's Illustrated Bible History* (Norwich, CT: Henry Bill Publishing Company, 1878), 28.

66. F. J. Knecht, *The Child's Bible History* (St. Louis, MO: B. Herder, 1898), 15. For a similar image, see *Favourite Bible Stories for the Young* (London, Edinburgh and New York: T. Nelson & Sons, 1896), 11.

67. See, for example, *The Children's Bible* (New York: Golden Press, 1962); Turner Hodges and Elizabeth MacLean, *The Bible Story Library*, Vol. One (New York: American Handbook and Textbook Co., 1963), 20–1; Kenneth N. Taylor, *Family-Time Bible* (Wheaton, IL: Tyndale House Publishers, 1992), n.p.; and Jennifer Rees Larcombe, *Through-the-Bible Storybook*, illus. by Alan Parry (Grand Rapids, MI: Zondervan, 1992), 13.

Basil Wolverton, who is best known for his grotesque and humorous illustrations for *Mad Magazine*. Wolverton had been an atheist before he came to the Christian faith through listening to Herbert W. Armstrong's Radio Church of God radio program. Wolverton was baptized by Armstrong, made an elder in the church, and became a member of its Board of Directors.[68] Rather than have him preach, Armstrong set Wolverton the task of producing *The Bible Story Book*, which was first published in 1958 and continued publication into the 1970s.

Wolverton's retelling of Noah's ark included a large, horrific image of terrified men and women screaming and crying as their heads bob just above the waters outside the bow of the ark.[69] The text provides a graphic and dramatic description of the people who screamed for Noah to let them into the ark.

> But with the rain falling in torrents on the ark, probably Noah and his family couldn't even hear the frantic yells of those about to drown just outside. As the water grew higher and higher and the ship came up off its resting place, desperate hands clawed feebly at the pitch-smeared plank. Then the hands disappeared in the muddy water, and there were no more screams.[70]

Wolverton also depicted horrific apocalyptic images set in the contemporary world based on the Church's interpretation of the Book of Revelation.[71] Illustrations such as these would evoke fear in the children and adults who saw them, and were clearly designed to do just that.

As the examples in this section attest, many of the illustrations of the deluge that accompanied the earliest American children's Bibles seem to be designed to evoke the horrors of being drowned outside of the ark. At the same time, these children's Bible texts often spoke of a God of wrath and veered from the Genesis account in order to offer extended descriptions of the horrible plight of those outside the ark. These texts and illustrations would have served well the purposes of passing on to children what children's Bible authors likely saw as a healthy fear of God and God's judgment, tempered with some grateful acknowledgment for God's mercy to those who are obedient.

2.3. Stories of a Less Frightening and More Long-suffering God

While children's Bibles of the late 1700s and early 1800s presented children with a God who was a wrathful judge, by the 1830s and beyond more authors began to underscore the point that God was patient and long-suffering. In his book *The*

---

68. Herbert W. Armstrong, "At Last! Here is the Bible Story Book," *The Plain Truth* 23:11 (November 1958): 5.

69. Basil Wolverton, *The Bible Story*, Vol. I (Pasadena, CA: Ambassador College Press, 1961), 43.

70. Ibid., 44.

71. Basil Wolverton, *The Wolverton Bible* (Seattle, WA: Fantagraphics Books, 2009), 264ff.

Figure 2.6. Illustration by unnamed artist from F. J. Knecht, *The Child's Bible History* (St. Louis, MO: B. Herder, 1898), 15.

Sacred Remains: American Attitudes Toward Death, 1799–1883, Gary Laderman notes, "Instead of the evangelism of fear—the harsh rhetoric and emphasis on human depravity that characterized the Puritan worldview—a softer, sentimentalized imagination and religious sensibility developed near the beginning of the nineteenth century."[72] Still, this was the era in which Julia Ward Howe wrote of the Lord's "terrible swift sword" in "The Battle Hymn of the Republic" (1861), and a number of children's Bible authors still wrote about the terrible and swift judgment that awaited those who tested God's patience. Many, then, tried to balance the message that God would judge sin with the image of a somewhat more approachable, nicer, and more merciful God.

The American revivals affected the way in which preachers and teachers used the Bible and, at the same time, American views of childhood were beginning to change. In the 1830s and beyond, evangelical, revivalist preachers embraced the power of a well-told story. Rather than preaching a rational message about adherence to strict doctrine, they used artful, often emotional, storytelling. Sermon audiences of the revivalist era were not content to have their preachers proclaim the harsh truth of God's judgment. Instead, congregations looked for their preachers

72. Laderman, *Sacred Remains*, 53.

and leaders to exhibit more populist tendencies and to retell the biblical stories in ways that seemed more interesting, appealing, and relevant to their lives.[73] The preachers often obliged, reshaping and elaborating upon biblical stories in dramatic ways and drawing on theatrical methods to deliver their sermons with a flair that made their messages both exciting and appealing.[74] The so-called Second Great Awakening of the late 1700s and early 1800s was an ecumenical turn towards Arminian theology, placing a greater emphasis on human choice, and preachers attempted to tell stories that made the human choice to turn towards God or away from God very clear to their listeners. These characteristics endured and became central characteristics of the revivalism of the nineteenth century in America.

At the same time, views of childhood were changing as well. While still well before the influence of modern-day childhood development studies, literature in America—especially literature produced for the upper classes—began to reflect increasingly Romantic views of childhood as a time of innocence during which children should be sheltered from the concerns of adulthood. Similarly, in 1847, theologian and Congregational pastor Horace Bushnell published his *Views on Christian Nurture*, arguing for a more sentimental view of children. Rather than sinners born into depravity whose only hope was to be converted, Bushnell argued that children were to be seen as Christian from birth, able to be nurtured in faith and morality from infancy.[75] Likewise, instead of trying to get children to be little adults and to act as grown up as possible as soon as possible, Bushnell encouraged parents to let their children play and enjoy their childhood, even if it meant that they might miss a devotional or two.

These disparate factors all found expression in American children's Bibles from about the 1830s and into the early decades of the twentieth century. If Christians of the time wanted their religious leaders to seem friendlier and more down to earth, then perhaps they wanted a God who demonstrated those characteristics as well. They began to grow concerned with how children were being exposed to violence. At the same time, reflecting an increased emphasis on human agency and self-industry, biblical storytellers tended to frame their stories in ways that emphasized the choices that humans made. Given these factors, it is not surprising that children's Bible authors in the nineteenth and early twentieth centuries found ways to adapt the story of Noah that presented children with a somewhat less harsh and more merciful image of God. These adaptations involved tempering the images of death and devastation in the story of Noah and placing greater emphasis on the choices made by humans in the story.

To do this, children's Bibles used a number of techniques. These included the strategic use of common embellishments to the story of Noah, presenting Bible stories as a dialogue between children and a loving parent or grandparent who can

---

73. Cf. Prothero, *American Jesus*, 50–2.

74. See, for example, Harry S. Stout, *The Divine Dramatist: George Whitefield and the Rise of Modern Evangelicalism* (Grand Rapids, MI: Eerdmans Publishing Company, 1991).

75. Horace Bushnell, *Christian Nurture* (New York: Charles Scribner's Sons, 1888, 1916), 4.

answer any concerns children might have with the stories, and the use of euphemisms for the death and destruction of animals and humankind.

2.3.a. Warning the wicked mockers: Using embellishments to soften the story of the flood

Children's Bibles commonly add two episodes to the story of Noah in children's Bibles that are not included in the book of Genesis, namely Noah warning people that the flood is coming and the presence of Noah's mocking neighbors who are often very mean and continually jeering at Noah while he preaches to them or faithfully works to build the ark. While these two embellishments have been around in various forms for centuries,[76] it is still striking to see how they are present in nearly every American children's Bible that retells the story of Noah.

These embellishments allow authors to build a satisfying narrative arc. By having Noah warn people that a flood is coming, the story is given some drama that is not present in the Book of Genesis. Will the people listen to Noah's warnings? Will they be saved from the flood? The fact that Noah warns the people, and in many versions of the story God tells Noah to warn people, also establishes Noah and God as the nice heroes of the narrative. Noah is not callously and secretly planning to be saved from the flood while he knows his neighbors are going to drown, and God is not planning to drown the people without fair warning. Also, by adding scenes in which Noah's neighbors mock Noah and scoff at his warnings, the neighbors are established as the villains of the piece. The Book of Genesis describes the flood as being worldwide, which one would assume means that many people who had never seen Noah building the ark nor heard his warnings would have drowned when the floodwaters came. By establishing scenes in which people are mocking Noah, however, the narrative can present the villains, those who were being mean to the nice man Noah and defiantly ignoring God's warnings, as the ones who die in the flood. The flood, then, provides children with a satisfying conclusion to the narrative. The flood is presented not as the capricious act of a vengeful God but as the reasonable consequence for mean people who mocked Noah and refused to listen to his gracious warning from a just and merciful God.

Children's Bibles use these embellishments in a number of creative ways. The chapters that follow demonstrate how these embellishments are used to help call children to salvation and virtuous living. This chapter will focus on how these embellishments are used to demonstrate God's kindness and patience, redeeming

---

76. See, in particular, *Sanhedrin* 108b in the Talmud on Noah sternly warning his neighbors and his neighbors jeering at him. For more on early writings from the Talmud, Josephus, and other sources, see Louis H. Feldman, "Questions about the Great Flood, as Viewed by Philo, Pseudo-Philo, Josephus, and the Rabbis," *Zeitschrift für die Alttestamentliche Wissenschaft* (*ZATW*) 115:3 (September 2003): 408–11. See also Stephen R. Haynes's helpful review of midrashic treatments of the story of Noah in *Noah's Curse: The Biblical Justification of American Slavery* (Oxford: Oxford University Press, 2002), 26ff.

God from being the quick to anger, terrible judge presented in many earlier children's Bibles.

A good example of the use of these embellishments for this purpose can be seen in the very popular children's book, first published in Britain in 1837, titled *Line Upon Line*. Favell Lee Mortimer, the widow of the Reverend Thomas Mortimer, the popular minister of the Episcopal Chapel in London, wrote the book, and US publishers released several editions of it.[77]

Mortimer's retelling of the story of Noah informs the readers that "God was very angry with the wicked people and he determined to punish them."[78] According to Mortimer, Noah gave the wicked people plenty of warning that the flood was coming: "Noah told the people to leave off their wickedness. But they would not mind. Still they went on eating and drinking, and not thinking of God, nor trying to please him."[79] Mortimer's retelling does not shy away from the part of the story in which people drowned and even mentions that children drowned, but her wording seems to suggest that the only ones who drown were those who heard Noah's warnings but ignored them. Thus, the responsibility for the consequences that follow is placed firmly upon those who mocked Noah and ignored his message, and not upon God:

> Then it began to rain. It rained all day and all night. What did the wicked people think now? How they must have wished that they had minded Noah! If they climbed trees, the water soon reached to the tops; if they went up high mountains, as high as the clouds, the water rose as high as they; for it rained forty days and forty nights. All beasts, and birds, and men, and children died, except those on the ark.[80]

After the flood is over, Mortimer notes that the wicked are no longer there: "Noah saw all the green hills and fields again; but where were all the wicked people? he would never see their wicked faces again."[81] In this approach, then, the narrative makes no apology for the flood or that God is the one who brings the flood. By introducing Noah's warnings and focusing on the deaths of those wicked people who ignored Noah's warnings, however, the story is made less objectionable to children's sensibilities and perhaps puts God in a better light. Like a loving parent, God needed to punish the wicked, and the people had a responsibility to listen to God.

Mortimer's approach seemed to strike a chord with a number of American children's Bible authors, as a number of children's Bibles, such as D. P. Kidder's

---

77. See, for example, Favell Lee Mortimer, *Line Upon Line* (Greenfield, MA: L. Merriam, 1860), and Favell Lee Mortimer, *Line Upon Line* (Philadelphia, PA: Henry Altmus, 1897).

78. Ibid., 20.

79. Ibid.

80. Ibid., 21.

81. Ibid., 22.

Bible Stories for Children (1851),[82] C. R. Graham's *My Mother's Bible Stories* (1896),[83] and Annie R. White's, *Bible Story Land: for Home, School and Sunday-School* (1891),[84] all borrowed from Mortimer practically word for word in their versions of the story of Noah's ark. Kidder's text reads, "How did these poor people, when they were drowning, wish they had listened to the warnings of Noah!! All beasts and birds, and men, and children died, except those that were in the ark."[85] The story, then, does not shy away from the deaths of those outside of the ark, and specifically notes that children were among those who died. If the children reading the text were to empathize with those drowning children, they might have been struck by the fact that the doomed children in the story regretted that they did not listen to Noah's warnings and wonder what kind warnings adults might be giving them that they may be ignoring. Those children had been given a choice and had chosen poorly.

Other children's Bibles excuse the flood by suggesting that justice demanded that God send the flood, even if God did not necessarily relish the task. In the 1840s, the author of *The Child's Instructor: or Stories from the Bible* introduces his or her tale by writing,

> At the time Noah lived, the world was very wicked, and God was justly angry with people on account of their sins. God, however, bade Noah admonish and warn them; and he did so. He told them, that their sins, if they did not repent of them, would prove their ruin. Still they would not leave off their wickedness; so God determined to punish them; and he sent his servant to tell them, that he would bring a flood of water over the earth, and drown them all.[86]

The author introduces God's judgment with the editorial comment that God was "justly" angry and embellishes the story to say that Noah warned the sinners, that God commanded Noah to warn them and gave them time to repent, and that only when they would not stop being wicked did God finally need to "punish" them. Only after the author gives children those implicit and explicit explanations for God's judgment does the text state that God sent the flood to "drown them all."[87]

In a similar manner, in the early 1850s, a children's Bible titled *Bible Stories* explains:

> Noah was told to preach to people, and for more than a hundred years did he

82. D. P. Kidder, *Bible Stories for Children*, Vol. I. (New York: Lane & Scott, 1851), 36–40.

83. C. R. Graham, *My Mother's Bible Stories* (Philadelphia, PA: Globe Bible Publishing Co., 1896), 50–3.

84. Annie R. White, *Bible Story Land: for Home, School and Sunday-School* (Chicago, IL: National Publishing Co., 1891), 24–8.

85. Kidder, *Bible Stories for Children*, 39–40.

86. *The Child's Instructor: or Stories from the Bible* (Boston, MA: William Henshaw, 1842), 11.

87. Ibid.

say, that if they did not repent, God would surely destroy them. In the mean time, he was building an ark, or large vessel, which would contain his family and some of every kind of beast and bird. They did not believe in Noah's warning, and he was obliged to enter the ark with his family, and close its doors. God caused terrible rain to pour down on the earth, and it was totally covered with water. Noah, in his ark, rode safely over the waters, but all the rest of mankind were drowned. They learnt, when it was too late to repent, that God will surely punish sin, although he is longsuffering, and delights in showing mercy.[88]

According to this story, Noah warned the people for over 100 years. God is presented as merciful and long-suffering, even delighting in showing mercy. The story suggests that God will punish sin, but that God does so only reluctantly, not as a triumphant demonstration of power.

Still other children's Bibles reduce God's culpability for the flood by emphasizing the choices made and the eventual regret of those who drowned. Unlike the children's Bibles discussed in the following chapter, these children's Bibles do not explicitly connect the story of Noah to a call for salvation in Jesus Christ, but one can almost hear the altar call as the authors warn their readers against waiting too long to repent of their sins as did those in Noah's day.

In Isabella Child's 1853 miniature thumb Bible, *The Child's Picture Bible*, the author emphasizes that the wicked would not listen to Noah's warnings: "Noah was told to preach to the people, and for more than a hundred years did he tell them, that if they did not repent, God would sure destroy them ... The people did not believe in Noah's warning, and continued as wicked as ever."[89] When the flood came, these wicked people received their judgment, with the implicit warning that readers should not wait too long to repent: "[A]ll the rest of mankind were drowned. They learnt, when it was too late to repent, that God will surely punish sin, although he is long suffering, and delights in showing mercy. This awful judgment of God is known by the names of the Deluge or the Flood, both words expressive of the immense quantity of water by which it was accomplished."[90] God is long-suffering and merciful, then, but it is still possible to wait too long to repent and to receive God's awful judgment.

In a similar way, Sophia G. Ashton integrates into her story of Noah the message that God will forgive those who repent, but will judge those who do not. In her 1861 book, *Frankie's Book about Bible Men*, she writes, "He is a long-suffering and a forgiving God, and, perhaps if those wicked men had all said, 'We have done very wrong; we have not believed God, nor minded him; we are afraid he is really going to drown us ...' But they did no such thing. O, it is a dreadful thing not to be sorry when we have done wrong."[91] God, then, is long-suffering

---

88. *Bible Stories* (New York: John Levison, 1851), 22–5.

89. Isabella Child, *The Child's Picture Bible* (Boston, MA: G. W. Cottrell, 1853), 15.

90. Ibid.

91. Sophia G. Ashton, *Frankie's Book about Bible Men* (Boston, MA: J. E. Tilton and Company, 1861), 25.

and ready to forgive, but also a God who will punish those who are not sorry for their wrongdoings.

In Charles Foster's *The Story of the Bible*, first published in 1873, the author writes of Noah, "The Bible says he was a preacher; he used to speak to the people about God, and about the punishment that was coming upon them for their sins. But they would not repent."[92] Later in the story Foster writes of the people who had not listened to Noah: "How glad they would have been to go with him into the ark, but it was too late."[93] Foster places emphasis on the tragedy of their failure to repent by speculating, "No doubt they climbed up to the highest places on the hills and mountains; but the hills and mountains were covered at last."[94] Foster's version of the story, then, places the blame on those who drown and shows that, by their regret, they acknowledge their own responsibility for their fate.

Bible History; to which is added A Short History of the Church was released in 1879 with no listed author but with the approbation of Cardinal John McCloskey, the Archbishop of New York, who would later become the first American cardinal. The book uses the popular Roman Catholic spelling of "Noe" from the time and highlights Noe's repeated warnings to the wicked and their persistent mocking of him:

> During this time Noe did not cease to exhort men to repentance, warning them of the dreadful judgment which was about to fall upon them. They mocked at his words; for they gloried in their riches and strength, and did not believe that God could destroy them. Even when the time was come, and they saw Noe entering the ark with all his family, they continued dancing and feasting, marrying and giving in marriage. Scripture tells us that in the last days of the world, the wicked will act in a similar manner.[95]

Along with the common embellishments of Noah's persistent warnings and the neighbors' harsh mocking, an allusion is made to Jesus' description in Matthew 24.37-39 of how people acted in the days of Noah, and how they would act in the final days, along with the notion that the neighbors did not think that God could destroy them. This last element raises the issue of blasphemy and direct challenge to God's power and authority that are implicitly answered when the flood finally comes.

In 1889 the American Tract Society published *The Bible in Picture and Story*, a large hardcover book by Mrs. L. S. Houghton that included many illustrations. According to Houghton,

92. Charles Foster, *The Story of the Bible from Genesis to Revelation* (Philadelphia, PA: Charles Foster, 1873), 20.

93. Ibid., 21.

94. Ibid.

95. *Bible History; to which is added A Short History of the Church* (New York: P. O'Shea, 1879), 15.

While Noah was building the ark he continually preached to the people around, warning them what was going to happen and urging them to turn away from their sins and serve God. But no one paid any attention to him. And as Noah was a long time building the ark, they became quite used to his preachings, and went on their own wicked way just as much as if they had never been warned.[96]

Having been so warned, the wicked people still do not repent. They are even dismissive of the rain when it begins, but soon "the terror of the people became greater and greater. Oh, how they must have gazed after the ark, riding safely on the top of the water, and wished that they had gone in there before it was too late!"[97] These words again seem to imply that the ones who are caught in the flood are those who ignored Noah's warnings. The text also implies that all those who would have wanted to enter the ark would have been welcomed there and would be safe from the flood. Further, in the spirit of many American Tract Society publications, the text contains an implicit warning of the dangers of waiting too long to repent and turn to God. God, then, is not presented as a God who arbitrarily destroys all the people of the world save one family. Instead, God gave a group of people plenty of warnings and a chance to escape the flood in the ark, but those people dismissed the warnings and chose to be wicked until it was too late.

In 1890, Henry Frederic Reddall compiled a group of Bible stories and songs by other authors into a very large volume titled *Golden Memories of the Book of Books in Picture, Song, and Story*, with Bishop John P. Newman of the Methodist Episcopal Church providing an introduction. The first page of the story of "Noah and the Deluge" is accompanied by a picture of despairing people clinging to small islands while others are drowning in the midst of the waters of the flood.[98] Noah worked on building the ark, but according to the story, that was not his only job.

And Noah not only worked at building the ark. The Bible says he was a preacher; he used to speak to the people about God and about the punishment that was coming upon them for their sins. But they would not repent nor believe what he told them; so that he had to hear their wicked words and see their wicked acts all the time he was building the ark. Yet he worked on patiently, until at last he finished it as God had commanded him.[99]

The culpability of the wicked, then, is made clear. God sent them a preacher to warn them. Noah preached on an ongoing basis, but they would not repent and responded with hostile words towards Noah, who in contrast to their wicked behavior remained patient, hard-working, and obedient to God. At the point

96. L. S. Houghton, *The Bible in Picture and Story* (New York: American Tract Society, 1889), 15.

97. Ibid., 15–16.

98. Henry Frederic Reddall, ed., *Golden Memories* (New York: Hunt & Eaton, 1890), 127.

99. Ibid., 128.

when the floodwaters cover the earth, the text provides an extended reflection on the fate of the wicked and their regret at not repenting in time:

> What were those men to do who would not obey God nor listen to the preaching of Noah? Before the rain came they thought there would be no flood, and that Noah wanted only to make them afraid. Now the flood had come, and they saw that all he had told them was true. How glad they would have been to go with him into the ark! But it was too late. No doubt they climbed up to the highest places, on the hills and mountains, but the hills and mountains were covered at last; there was no other place for them to go, and all the people in the world, except those few in the ark, were drowned. And every beast and bird and little insect, except those in the ark, was drowned also. Then all the earth was covered with water. There was no land to be seen anywhere; only the ark could be seen floating alone, with the water all around it and the sky above.[100]

The reader senses that the people were just so wicked that they needed to be killed and, after all, God had given them plenty of chances to repent and obey. Children once more are left not so much with an image of a God whom they should fear, but the image of a kind and reluctant judge who provides for those who will obey. Still, children are shown that those who do not obey God will be judged.

Isabel C. Byrum was the author of several children's Bibles. In *Beautiful Stories from the Good Old Book* (1904), she opens her story by establishing a loving God who loves the good man Noah: "When God saw how much Noah loved him and how he tried to teach the people to love him, he loved Noah and said that he would save him, his wife, his three sons, and their wives, but that he was going to send rain upon the earth until everything else that was alive would be drowned."[101] Byrum then describes Noah warning people about the flood and telling them that they could be saved from it. She explains: "All the time when he was not working on it he was preaching to the people, trying to get them sorry for their sinful ways, that they might be saved also; but they would not hear."[102] Byrum establishes, then, that the people had fair notice and the opportunity to be saved, but simply chose to ignore Noah's warnings. Their death in the flood is not ignored, but Noah's efforts and their unwillingness to repent make the results more palatable. Byrum writes, "Oh, how sorry the people must have been that they had not listened to what Noah had said and had been forgiven their sins, so that they too could go into the ark! But it was too late. God would not listen to their cries, and the waters soon covered them up and they died."[103] By suggesting that the people were sorry, Byrum implies that they acknowledged that they were responsible for their fate. They understand that God had offered forgiveness and they had neglected it.

---

100. Ibid., 129.

101. Isabel C. Byrum, *Beautiful Stories from the Good Old Book* (Moundsville, WV: Gospel Trumpet Company, 1904), 24.

102. Ibid., 26.

103. Ibid.

Byrum adds to the poignancy of the scene by suggesting the image of the people crying out to God and God ignoring their cries.

Byrum's *Our Darlings' ABC Book* devotes a page to an illustration and a short rhyme featuring each letter of the alphabet and then tells a fuller narrative of the story on the facing page. Byrum writes of Noah, "N is for Noah; with beasts large and small, He entered an ark, thus saving them all."[104] In her narrative of the story she relates that,

> Noah lived in a time when the people were very wicked. Never had so much sin been known among the people. Noah was sorry to see the people so wicked, and he told them so. He said that God was going to send much rain upon the earth and that everybody would die. There was only one way to escape. That way was to get inside the ark, or large house-boat, which Noah meant to build.
> The people just turned away and would not listen.[105]

In a departure from the biblical text, Byrum suggest that everyone was invited to enter the ark. The choice and the fault, therefore, again lay with the people who were more sinful than at any other time in history. They simply would not heed God's warning. The wicked in Byrum's brief tale do not mock Noah. They simply turn away. The tale of the flood, then, is presented as a very regrettable and avoidable state of affairs. If only the people had accepted Noah's invitation to enter the ark, the narrative seems to say, all would have been spared.

Reverend A. J. Kynett was the Corresponding Secretary of the Methodist Episcopal Board of Church Extension in the late nineteenth century. According to his version of the story of Noah, in his book *Sacred Pictures and Their Teachings: Grand Old Stories from the Good Old Book for Young and Old* from 1892, the very carpenters and workers Noah hired to build the ark were wicked and mocked him, and though he constantly warned them, they would not change their ways: "The carpenters and other workmen Noah had employed were wicked men; and they made sport of Noah. The rain had never before fallen in such a great way and they did not think there was any danger of a flood."[106] Kynett continues, "Noah was a preacher and all the time he was working on the ark, he spoke to the people about God, and how He was going to punish them for their sins. But they would not believe what Noah said, and kept on in their wicked ways."[107] In Kynett's description of the scene, he explicitly notes that children drown: "The water rose higher than the mountains, and every man, woman and child on the earth was drowned, except those who were in the ark."[108] The drowning was not God's fault,

---

104. Isabel C. Byrum, *Our Darlings' ABC Book* (Anderson, IN: Gospel Trumpet Co., 1908), 30.

105. Ibid., 31.

106. A. J. Kynett, *Sacred Pictures and Their Teachings: Grand Old Stories from the Good Old Book for Young and Old* (Philadelphia, PA: Keystone Publishing Co., 1892), 23.

107. Ibid., 24.

108. Ibid.

however, but the people's fault. According to Kynett, "Noah and his family were no doubt sorry that so many people were drowned in the deep water. But they had to suffer for their own evil ways."[109] This description again sympathetically frames the flood not as the triumphant death of the wicked at the hands of a mighty righteous God but as a regrettable occurrence that only needed to happen because the people would not repent.

Henry Davenport Northrop was a doctor of divinity and the author of a number of non-fiction books for children. In his very large volume *Charming Bible Stories: Written in Simple Language* (1894), Northrop also emphasized the fact that the people who drowned were given plenty of warning, but that they were very wicked and had openly laughed at Noah's warnings:

> [Noah] told them God was going to drown the world for their wickedness but they did not believe what he said. They went on eating and drinking and pleasing themselves, and doing everything just as usual. Noah told them that they were in danger, but they only laughed at him. And so year after year passed away. Noah still worked hard at the ark, which was to save him and his family from the great flood of waters, and he still went on preaching and warning his neighbors.[110]

As Northrop continues the story, he gives much attention to the plight of those outside of the ark, far more than is present in the Book of Genesis.[111] Northrop then adds a brief scene in which Noah ponders a world without his neighbors after the flood: "All his acquaintances and his neighbors were dead. As Noah thought of all this he felt thankful for his great deliverance. He built an altar—that is, he made a heap of stones—and upon this heap, or altar, he offered a sacrifice to the Lord."[112] Unlike some other children's Bibles of the time, in this story the death of his neighbors does not make Noah sad but instead makes him grateful for the mercy that was given only to him and to his family.[113]

"Grandpa" Reuben Prescott wrote another thick children's Bible, published in 1887 and titled *Grand Father's Bible Stories*. Prescott tells his readers that none of Noah's neighbors had ever seen the sea or a large boat:

---

109. Ibid., 25.

110. Henry Davenport Northrop, *Charming Bible Stories: Written in Simple Language* (Philadelphia, PA: Monarch Books, 1894), 25–6.

111. Ibid., 27.

112. Ibid., 29.

113. Northrop would later release a large, 250-page children's Bible, with only very slightly revised wording, under the title *From Eden to Calvary; or through the Bible in a Year with our Boys and Girls* with brightly colored pictures and a title page that proclaimed it "The Greatest Bible Book for Young People Ever Published." The wording of the story of Noah is almost identical to that of his previous book. See Henry Davenport Northrop, *From Eden to Calvary; or through the Bible in a Year with our Boys and Girls* (Philadelphia, PA: National Publishing Company, 1900), 23–5.

They must have wondered what Noah and his sons were making, and perhaps, laughed at him; for if he told them that a great flood was coming which should cover the earth and destroy all living things except such as God had chosen to save, they were so unbelieving and wicked, and had so forgotten what they might have been told of the power of God, that they would not think Noah was speaking the truth."[114]

Having established that Noah warned his neighbors and that they responded by laughing at him, the rest of Prescott's retelling of the story of the flood recalls those of the earlier decades of the nineteenth century, with an extensive description of the people trying to escape the flood and a dramatic illustration to accompany it. The illustration, titled "THE FLOOD DESTROYING THE EARTH," shows adults attempting to pass small children up high into trees and trying to rescue an old man who is struggling in the water. As with other illustrations, the floodwaters apparently make people's clothes fall off them, with one woman's breast bared.[115] The text reads,

> At first the little streams and great rivers rose and covered the fields. Then the waters rose higher and higher, drowning the cattle and the wild animals which fled into caves. Men and women, trembling with fright, and knowing now how great was the power of the Lord whom they had forgotten, and how truly Noah had spoken when he told them why the ark was built, climbed the hills to safety.[116]

Prescott makes it clear that those outside of the ark struggled in vain:

> But still the waters rose higher and higher. The valleys became one great sea; the smaller hills were covered. People who were too weak to climb were swept away by the great rush of waters, and others sought safety on the lofty mountains. But the rain poured down the sides of the highest hills, and men and women were carried away to death by the force of the waters.[117]

Prescott, then, does not at all gloss over the deaths of the wicked or that God was the one who sent the flood as judgment upon them. The flood in the story proves the might of God even to those who may have forgotten about it or who may doubt it.

Later, however, after recounting the story of the rainbow, he provides some direct commentary to the reader that seems intended to leave them with a positive impression of who God is:

114. Grandpa Reuben Prescott, *Grand Father's Bible Stories* (Chicago: C. W. Stanton Company, 1897), 28.
115. Ibid., 29.
116. Ibid.
117. Ibid.

God never fails, but what he promises that he performs. Whenever we see the rainbow in the clouds—and we may very often see it after a heavy storm of rain—we should remember how once God destroyed the wicked people of the world, all but a few righteous men and their families, and how he preserved them because Noah believed in him, and did as he was commanded. Let us remember, too, that God promised Noah, and, through him, promised us, that he would not again destroy the world with a flood of water.[118]

While God destroys the wicked, God preserves those like Noah who believe and obey. Prescott concludes by telling readers that the story that had just been told was intended "to remind us of God's power and goodness."[119] After giving an extended description of the horrible flood that God sent, Prescott then seems to take special care to leave his young readers with assurances of God's goodness.

The Child's Bible History of 1898 by the Rev. F. J. Knecht, D.D., a Roman Catholic priest, was actually translated and adapted from a German children's Bible by J. Schuster and G. Mey. The book appeared in multiple editions during the 1890s. Knecht's book is interesting in that it presents its Bible stories in numbered paragraphs. Some of these are taken directly from the words of the Bible; others are embellishments to the biblical text. Given that these embellishments are written in a biblical style of language, contain numbered paragraphs similar to numbered Bible verses, and that they are inserted in the middle of actual verbatim verses from the Bible, readers could easily get the impression that the whole story, including Knecht's embellishments, is taken directly from the words of the Bible. The following is a sample of his retelling of the story of Noah, which includes Noah's warning to those around him:

3. Noe did all things as God had commanded. He spent a hundred years in building the ark, and never ceased to preach penance to the people.

4. But they heeded not the warning; they ate, and drank, and held great feasts.[120]

Knecht, then, integrates a reference to penance and the reference to people eating and drinking in Noah's day from the Gospel of Matthew 24.37-39. Knecht follows his retellings with Bible catechism-style questions for the reader, which includes questions regarding his embellishments as well as questions on the parts of his text taken directly from the Bible. For the Noah story, Knecht's questions include "How many years did Noe spend in building the ark?" and "Did the people heed his warning?"[121] Knecht is more subtle than most in making his point, but his embellishments to the text and subsequent questions help underscore the point

118. Ibid., 31.
119. Ibid.
120. F. J. Knecht, *The Child's Bible History: Adapted from the Works of J. Schuster and G. Mey* (St. Louis, MO: B. Herder, 1898), 14.
121. Ibid.

that those who were drowned were given fair warning of the destruction to come and were given a choice of whether to face God's judgment or not.

In 1900, author Jean S. Remy wrote a book entitled *The Lives of the Presidents Told in Words of One Syllable*,[122] and in 1909 she followed it up with *Bible Stories for Little Children: In Words of One Syllable*. Remy's retelling of the story of Noah's ark includes the common embellishments of people mocking Noah and later begging to get into the ark. She writes that when the waters rose to the tops of the hills, "a great fear came in their hearts; they fled to the Ark, to beg No-ah to let them in; but this, God would not let him do, for these peo-ple, as you know, had made fun of God's word; and so, he would not give them His love and care."[123] Remy's retelling suggests that Noah might have let the wicked people into the ark but that it was God who would not allow it. The story suggests that the reason God lets them drown and withholds love from them is that they had mocked Noah and God's word.

Sarah Elizabeth Dawes, author of *Bible Stories for Young People*, which was first published at least as early as 1903, wrote that she offered her stories "without note or comment. There has been no attempt at criticism and no explanation of events narrated other than the Bible gives. This has seemed the wisest course to pursue in writing for children these oldest of stories."[124] Her version of the story of Noah, however, does offer its own take on the story, increasing the role of Noah's wicked neighbors: "When Noah told them why he was building it, and of the great rain that was coming, none of them believed it. No doubt they thought he was a silly old man to make himself all that trouble for nothing."[125] The reader witnesses the flood from their point of view: "This terrible storm of rain came pouring from the sky for forty days and forty nights, and we may be quite sure that the poor drowning people laughed no more at the great boat. They climbed first the little hills, and then the mountains, to escape the flood, and as they did so, they must have wished that they, too, might have a safe home in the ark."[126] Again, the drowning people regret that they had not listened to Noah.

In George Hodges' *The Garden of Eden: Stories from the First Nine Books of the Old Testament* from 1909, the wicked laugh not only at Noah's warnings but even after it rained!

> Then Noah told them of the coming flood, and tried to get them to stop their bad ways, that they might live and not be drowned. But the neighbors only laughed at Noah, and said he must be crazy to build a boat on dry land, and so

---

122. Jean S. Remy, *The Lives of the Presidents Told in Words of One Syllable* (New York: A. L. Burt Company Publishers, 1900).

123. Jean S. Remy, *Bible Stories for Little Children: In Words of One Syllable* (Philadelphia, PA: Henry Altemus Company, 1909), 22.

124. Sarah Elizabeth Dawes, *Bible Stories for Young People* (New York: Thomas Y. Crowell, 1923), n.p.

125. Ibid., 7.

126. Ibid., 8.

they went back to their wicked lives. Sometimes, when it rained, they thought of Noah, but the rain cleared away, and they laughed again, and were worse than ever.[127]

Such brazen mocking may seem worthy of punishment, but as the story continues, Hodges does not return to the mocking neighbors. There is no mention that they or anybody else drown in the flood, only that God preserved Noah and his family.

Upon her death in 1916, Charlotte F. Wilder was hailed as "one of the most noted women of the Middle West and American Methodism."[128] According to one obituary, "In every civic reform she was a leader. She was a Great Heart to whom no need appealed in vain."[129] Wilder's ministry seemed to be focused on giving those who found themselves in difficult circumstances a second chance in life. She wrote an account of the story of the flood in her 1911 book, *The Child's Own Book*, Volume 1. Note how the story goes to some length to explain just how many chances Noah and God gave the mockers to change their mind and be safe from the flood: "Noah did as God told him. He talked to the peo-ple and tried to have them love God. He told them they would be de-stroyed if they were not good but they laughed at No-ah. He built his great boat and asked the peo-ple if they did not want to go in, but they laughed more than ever."[130] In Wilder's version, God and God's agent, Noah, really want the people to be good and are offered the chance to go enter the ark and be saved. The only reason the people drowned is because they did not want to go into the ark. It was their choice. Wilder's story does not mention anyone other than Noah's family after these laughing people rejected Noah's invitation, so there is no speculation about whether or not they had a change of heart once the floodwaters rose. Instead, they are conveniently omitted from the rest of the story.

While many children's Bibles were primarily an attempt to help children read the Bible by putting it into language other than the archaic language of the Authorized or King James Version of the Bible, when it came to writing his 1930 children's Bible, *The Bible Story: A Connected Narrative Retold from Holy Scripture*, Rev. James Baikie intentionally emulated that language. He writes in the preface:

> One of the enduring charms of the Bible story in its English dress is the matchless dignity and grace of the language in which it is told in our Authorised Version. To anything like this no other narrative can pretend; but an effort has been made to maintain a form of language which, while avoiding what is archaic and unintelligible, shall yet avoid also what is unduly familiar and modern,

127. George Hodges, *The Garden of Eden: Stories from the First Nine Books of the Old Testament* (Boston, MA: Houghton Mifflin Company, 1909), 8.

128. G. W. Isham, "Mrs. C. F. Wilder," *Woman's Missionary Friend* 49:2 (February 1917): 65.

129. Ibid.

130. Charlotte F. Wilder, *The Child's Own Book*, Vol. 1 (Chicago: Howard-Severance Company, 1911), 44–5.

and preserve something of the savour of more ancient times and more stately manners.[131]

Baikie proceeds to use this stylized language even when he veers significantly from the text of the Bible and composes new scenes in this pseudo-biblical language. In telling the story of Noah, Baikie writes:

> Year after year the mighty vessel was a-building. The men of the plain, who dwelt beside Noah, came and marveled at it, as the gaunt ribs rose and were clothed with the planks; and they would mock and jeer at the madman who wasted his own and his sons' time and strength on such a folly. When they jeered and questioned, Noah spoke to them of righteousness, and of God's coming judgment upon iniquity, but none would listen.[132]

After establishing that the wicked people repeatedly refused the warnings they had been given, Baikie provides the readers with an extended, dramatic narrative of how they received their just rewards:

> First the muddy waters swept over the great plains, and houses dissolved in the furious waves, and all folk fled in terror to the hills, and the ark rocked and shivered where it lay, till at last it lifted and went drifting over what had been fertile fields and happy homes. Foot by foot the floods crept up the hillsides, and men drew their loved ones and their treasures higher and higher up the slopes, till at length they were forced to seek the great mountains behind. And still the rain lashed upon them from above, and the cold waters swelled from beneath to their very feet. Then they fought for standing room on the mountain summits, and the weaker fell one by one into the tide of death. At last there came a day when the horror-stricken people in the drifting ark saw neither man nor beast nor speck of land remaining; but from grey horizon to grey horizon naught but an infinite and weary waste of desolate waters. The judgment of God was accomplished, and of all the race of man there was left that handful within the ship of deliverance.[133]

In Baikie's story the wicked had been given plenty of warning and plenty of chances to change their ways. Still, the flood is clearly an instrument of God's judgment and Baikie gives an extended description of the horror of the deluge.

As the early decades of the twentieth century passed, however, the approach taken by Edna B. Rowe in *Bible Studies for Little Folk* became more common. In Rowe's version of the story, God is sorry, and Noah feels sorry for the wicked people. There is talk of fun animals, and unless one is paying careful attention,

---

131. James Baikie, *The Bible Story: A Connected Narrative Retold from Holy Scripture* (New York: MacMillan Company, 1930), viii.

132. Ibid., 11.

133. Ibid., 12.

one might miss the fact that in this version of the tale there is no direct mention of anything as unpleasant as people or animals drowning. According to Rowe's story, "God looked down upon the world He made and saw how wicked the people were. He was sad. He was sorry He had made the world. He saw that the only way to make the earth a happy, good place in which to live was to punish the wicked people."[134] The fact that God was sad and could find no other way to resolve the issue serves to create sympathy for God, but runs the risk of creating a less omnipotent image of God in the minds of children. Still, Rowe provides a rationale for why God had to do what he did in order to make the world better in the long run. According to her version of the story, Noah is also sorry for the people and that they have to die: "Noah felt sorry for the wicked people. He tried to make them good, so that God would not have to punish them, but they would not listen."[135] Once the story proceeds from that point, however, there is no mention that any person or animal is drowned in the flood. As a matter of fact, the narrative takes on a more playful tone as Rowe describes giraffes, squirrels, toads, mice, butterflies, and last of all, two little snails entering the ark.[136] Through the narrative, it is established that neither God nor Noah wanted the flood, and the death of those outside of the ark is de-emphasized.

Reverend P. Henry Matimore was a professor of education at Loyola University who dedicated his 1929 book, *A Child's Garden of Religious Stories*, to "His Eminence George Cardinal Mundelein." Matimore's account of the story of Noah begins, "God was very angry with these sinful people, for He had been kind to them, and had given them many blessings."[137] In so doing, he immediately rationalizes God's anger and seeks to establish God's kindness. Matimore explains that God "planned to punish evil people by destroying them in a terrible flood."[138] In so doing, Matimore does not shy away from telling children that God was the one who brings the flood or that God is going to punish people and destroy them through the flood. Matimore puts the embellishment of Noah's neighbors to good use:

> For years and years, Noe's family worked on the ark. The wicked people often gathered to watch them. They made fun of Noe for building such a boat on dry land. But nothing could weaken Noe's faith nor his desire to obey God. Sometimes Noe tried to talk to the people about God and His punishment of sin, but they only laughed at him. He and his sons worked on, cheerfully and patiently.[139]

134. Edna B. Rowe, *Bible Stories for Little Folk*, illus. by Otto Stemler with copies from the Old Masters (Cincinnati, OH: Standard Publishing Company, 1926), 20.

135. Ibid., 21.

136. Ibid.

137. P. Henry Matimore, *A Child's Garden of Religious Stories*, illus. by Carl Michel Boog (New York: Macmillan Company, 1929), 21.

138. Ibid.

139. Ibid., 22–3.

Through this, not only does Matimore establish that the wicked people were mean to Noah, but also that Noah warned them about God's punishment and that they responded with scorn.

By the time the flood comes, Matimore has prepared his readers for the harsh fate of these wicked people, describing the scene as follows:

> The frightened people fled from their homes in the beautiful valleys, and ran to the hills and mountains to escape drowning. Many of them must have gone to the ark and begged Noe to let them enter. But they were doomed to disappointment.
>
> The rain kept falling … People climbed higher and higher on the hills, but the water continued to come closer and closer to them. Soon it covered the hills. Even those who had run to the top were drowned.[140]

The description is accompanied by an illustration by Carl Michel Boog of people huddled on islands as the floodwaters rise. Matimore does not avoid or play down the fate of the wicked. They are doomed and they drowned.

Reading the narrative, though, one can easily get the impression that it is only the wicked people who laughed at Noah and ignored his warnings who are killed, not every person in the world. They are also the ones who make God sad after God had been so kind to them. So God is not just a cruel, arbitrary judge who kills everyone for their wickedness: God is patient and kind but must punish evil people.

David R. Piper's *Youth Explore the Bible: A New Story of the World's Most Popular Book*, from 1941, describes humankind as "submerged in a riotous flood of wickedness."[141] As Piper put it, "So the Deluge came, though not without warning."[142] As a matter of fact, as the wicked people mocked Noah, "the thud of his ax became a daily sermon of warning," but rather than heeding the warning, the people "regarded the ark as a huge joke."[143] The narrative seems to create the impression that everyone who would drown was in earshot of Noah's preaching and hammering, thus making it more palatable to Piper's young readers that they would drown in the flood.

Marian M. Schoolland's introduction to her 1947 book, *Marian's Big Book of Bible Stories*, explains to the reader her understanding of the primary purpose of the stories of the Bible: "They are a revelation of God. They reveal His thoughts and plans; they reveal His manner of dealing with mankind; they reveal His very self—His love and anger, His mercy and care. In fact, the prime purpose of each Bible story is just that—to show us God."[144]

---

140. Ibid., 25–6.

141. David R. Piper, *Youth Explore the Bible: A New Story of the World's Most Popular Book*, illus. by Beatrice Stevens (Boston, MA: W. A. Wilde Company, 1941), 9.

142. Ibid.

143. Ibid.

144. Marian M. Schoolland, *Marian's Big Book of Bible Stories*, illus. by Dirk Gringhuis (Grand Rapids, MI: Wm. B. Eerdmans Publishing Company, 1950), n.p.

Schoolland's account is rare because she attends to a concern that some children may have had, namely that so many presumably innocent plants and animals died in the flood. Schoolland helps explain their deaths by writing, "He saw that His beautiful earth was no longer the same as it was in the beginning. There were many thorns and weeds where beautiful flowers used to be. Many of the animals were wild; they fought each other and even ate each other."[145] Humans do not fare any better. According to Schoolland, "They did not pray. They played and danced and did only what they wanted to do. They did not take care of God's plants and animals. They did not even think about God."[146]

Instead of presenting God as the transcendent holy being, Schoolland invites children to witness the scene from God's point of view. As the story proceeds, she writes, "God was very sorry to see all the other people living in sin. He loved the people and wanted them to love Him. But they would not."[147] Schoolland's account draws the reader to empathize with and even have sympathy for God, a character who is about to destroy the vast majority of life on the planet. In the process, however, the narrative presents what may be seen as a vulnerable God who is not able to get people to be good and not the almighty protagonist who drives the action, as was the case in many earlier retellings of the story of Noah.

Schoolland continues her narrative by adding embellishments of Noah warning the people and the people mocking Noah, using them to highlight just how fair, loving, and patient God is and how wicked and foolish the others were:

> Sometimes people came to see what Noah was doing. He told them about the flood that was coming. He told them to stop living in sin. He told them to live for God. They only laughed at him. They would not listen. They did not think the flood would ever come.
>
> From heaven God watched. He gave people a long, long time. He gave them one hundred and twenty years' time. He was kind to them. But they would not listen. They still lived in their sinful way. And Noah went on building the ark.[148]

Having established that God is a kind God and that the deaths in the flood were not really God's fault, the story concludes, "All the wicked people had drowned. Noah and his family and the animals inside the ark were safe."[149] Schoolland's choice of words suggests that it is those very people who mocked Noah and did not heed his warnings that died. Also, the story immediately moves on to assure the reader that Noah and all those inside the ark were kept safe.

Marianne Radius had quite a family legacy behind her when she wrote her 1968 children's Bible, *The Tent of God: A Journey through the Old Testament*. Her father was Princeton Seminary Professor of the Bible, Geerhardus Vos; her

---

145. Ibid., 25.
146. Ibid., 26.
147. Ibid., 27.
148. Ibid.
149. Ibid., 29.

mother Catherine Vos wrote the bestselling *Child's Story Bible* in 1934;[150] and her husband was William T. Radius, who taught in the Classics Department of Calvin College. Radius's children's Bible seems to be a bit of a throwback to children's Bibles of earlier times. It is one of the few children's Bibles from the later half of the twentieth century to refer to God as a terrifying judge in her story of Noah's ark, though she also goes to some length to balance God's character in the story. Radius has Noah working on the ark for 120 years and suggests that one of the reasons for this is that 120 years gave Noah plenty of time to warn his neighbors about the coming flood. In response, Radius reports, they just laughed at him and mocked him.[151] According to Radius, Noah gives them a stern warning about a God who punishes the wicked: "You can laugh at us, but no man can laugh at God. Put away your wicked, violent deeds, and pray to Him for forgiveness. For the day is surely coming when He will punish those who do not trust in Him."[152] The mockers just scoff. Radius then writes, "Every man on earth except Noah's family drowned. Each one had now to appear before the very God he had mocked—to appear, and to answer for his wicked life. It is a fearful thing for a sinful man to fall into the hands of the living God!"[153] Radius summarizes the story and her lesson by describing to children a God who is both a terrifying judge and a tender father:

> If God is a terrifying Judge to those who have defied Him, you will not find there could be a more tender Father than He is to those who trust in Him. Not for a moment, night or day, did God take His eyes off Noah and the ark. Every second His almighty arm was stretched out to protect and to reassure His child. We know this for certain because God Himself wrote it down in the Bible.[154]

Radius's version, then, hearkens back to the earlier children's Bibles described above that refer to God as a frightening judge who brought the flood to punish the wicked. Despite Radius's high view that "God Himself" wrote the Bible, she does not refrain from embellishing the story of Noah or inserting direct commentary into it in order to make her point.

Radius and these other children's Bible authors sought to moderate God's image by explaining to children that God was also a merciful God who gave the wicked plenty of chances to repent and escape judgment. As mentioned above, these embellishments and their use in children's Bibles do not stay neatly in one era or another. Though the use of Noah's mocking neighbors as the ones who drown would become less popular in the later half of the twentieth century, there

150. Catherine F. Vos, *Child's Story Bible* (Grand Rapids, MI: William B. Eerdmans Publishing Company, 1934).

151. Marianne Radius, *The Tent of God: A Journey through the Old Testament*, illus. by Chris Soffel Overvoorde (Grand Rapids, MI: William B. Eerdmans Publishing Company, 1968), 34.

152. Ibid., 35.

153. Ibid., 36.

154. Ibid.

have certainly been some later children's Bibles that do so.[155] Many later children's Bibles would also soften God's image by including episodes in which an emotional God is quite distraught over the necessary deaths of the wicked people outside of the ark.[156]

These children's Bibles creatively appropriated the embellishments of Noah warning his neighbors and his neighbors' mocking responses in ways that move the focus away from God's act of judgment and toward God's patience and saving acts. In the process, they soften the harshness of God and God's judgment for their young readers.

2.3.b. A dialogue between children and a wise and loving parent

Another strategy used in some children's Bibles to present children with the story of God's judgment upon the world and yet still defend God's actions was to tell their Bible stories as part of a conversation between an adult and a child or group of children. These children's Bibles used the embellishments of Noah warning people and the people mocking and ignoring him in return, but also used the framing device of a conversation to help explain away the more troubling aspects of the story. As seen in the section above, there were several children's Bibles in the later half of the nineteenth century with titles such as *My Mother's Bible Stories* and *Grand Father's Bible Stories*. These titles in and of themselves seem to suggest a kinder, less harsh approach to telling the Bible's stories to children. Instead of presenting the stories as objective, ancient, holy writ, they are presented as stories told by a kindly parent or grandparent. In addition to those children's Bibles, however, there emerged a small subgenre of children's Bibles that employed the strategy of including the storyteller and their children as characters in the story. Through this device, the children in the framing narrative are able to serve as stand-ins for the reader, asking questions and raising concerns that the author might anticipate young readers would have about stories such as that of Noah in which God destroys most of the living things on the earth. The parent or grandparent is then able to present a harsh view of God's judgment but also provide an answer or apologetic to the children who may be troubled by it. Following the parent's explanations, the children characters are able to give the readers a role model who demonstrates how they should readily accept the explanation that has been given to them

In 1832, for example, *Scripture Prints, with explanations in the form of familiar dialogues,* by the prolific British children's literature author Mary Sherwood, was published in the United States.[157] Through the framework of conversa-

---

155. See, for example, Julie Downing, *A First Book of Jewish Bible Stories* (London: DK Children, 2002), 13, 17.

156. See Ralph Kirby, *The Bible Story with Living Pictures* (New York: Harper and Brothers, 1960), 17, and David Daniel, *The Complete Book of Bible Stories for Jewish Children* (Jersey City, NJ: KTAV Publishing House, Inc., 1971), 19.

157. Mary Sherwood, *Scripture Prints, with explanations in the form of familiar dialogues* (New York: Pendleton and Hill, 1832).

tions between a wise grandmother and her grandchildren about Bible stories, Sherwood is able to insert concerns that children may have with the stories and commentary on those stories from a reliable and trustworthy character. To her granddaughter, Sophia, the grandmother reasons that Noah must have warned people about the coming flood:

> *Sophia* … But those people must have wondered that he was making this great building for; and I dare say they thought him very foolish or quite mad.
> *Grandmother.* There is no doubt but that he warned them of the evil that was coming; for Noah is called in the New Testament "a preacher of righteousness"; and we may imagine how many opportunities this holy man would have of preaching during that time, or whilst the long suffering of God waited whilst the ark was preparing.[158]

Later, the grandmother is able to offer a rationale for God inflicting such horror upon the world: "The destruction of the earth by water, is given to us who live in the latter ages of the world, as an awful warning, and one which should ever be present with us."[159] Still later in the story, a grandson named George is troubled when looking at an illustration of the deluge: "*George.* I am sorry for it, for I do not like it; it is a dark, dismal, horrid picture: it makes me uncomfortable to look at it."[160] As Grandmother continues to tell the story, George is again troubled and raises the question of whether Noah might not have let some of those who were drowning into the ark.

> *George.* Don't you think, grandmamma, that the people, when they found the waters rising, gathered round the ark, and made a great noise, and tried to persuade Noah to take them in?
> *Grandmother.* That might have happened, George, although the Bible does not mention it; but whatever noise and clamor those poor perishing creatures might have made, they could not be let in.[161]

Whenever the children offer a rationale for why the people acted the way they acted or express concern for the way God acted or that all the people drown, Sherwood employs the character of the grandmother who calmly and wisely defends God's actions and explains why they were reasonable and justified.

In addition to her book *Bible Stories for Young People*, noted above, Sarah Elizabeth Dawes also wrote several books for the New York American Tract Society. Her *Hours with Mamma*, published in the 1860s, merits an extended examination. Dawes manages to employ a number of techniques that would be utilized by various children's Bible authors of the time in order to soften the

---

158. Ibid., 95–6.
159. Ibid., 106–7.
160. Ibid., 109.
161. Ibid., 111.

potentially harsh and uninviting content of the story of Noah. First of all, she frames all her stories as a conversation between curious children and a loving "mamma."[162] Second, she introduces the entire story of Noah by noting that God was grieved and that God is long-suffering, but still must destroy the wicked: "The Bible says that God grieved to see so much wickedness on the earth. He bore it for a great while, for he is long-suffering and slow to anger; but at last he determined to destroy all who had so wickedly disobeyed him."[163] Readers are not given a rationale as to why God's patience finally ran out, but God is given credit for holding back for so long. Third, as with many children's Bibles before and after her own, Dawes establishes the idea that the wicked were warned and that the wicked mocked Noah:

> Of course Noah could not build such a strange floating house without attracting a great deal of attention; and he tried by his example and by preaching to convince the wicked people around him that God was surely going to destroy mankind by the flood. But no one believed his words; and no doubt a great many of them laughed at him, and called him a foolish old man. Nevertheless he believed that what God had said he would surely bring to pass.[164]

The fact that Noah tried to warn the wicked people, but that those wicked people laughed at him and called him a foolish man, are presented as a given part of the story. Dawes underscores the folly of the wicked by describing their persistence in being wicked and ignoring Noah's warnings, again making an allusion to the description of Noah's day and the end days in Matthew 24.37-39: "The wicked people that Noah had so often warned in vain, still kept on in their folly and sin, and were eating and drinking, and making themselves merry at the very time that Noah and his family were going into the ark for safety."[165] Here, the integration of the Matthew passage serves to depict the wicked people as particularly unrepentant. Still, as a mother herself, Dawes was aware that the death of all living things would be troubling to children and puts these concerns into the mouth of one of the story's children, allowing the mother to answer him:

> "But, mamma," said Charlie, "did not a great many, when they saw that the rain had really come, try to get into the ark?"
> "Yes, Charlie, perhaps they did; but you must recollect that after Noah and his family had entered, God shut them in, and it was too late then for any more to enter. Perhaps you think that these people who lived before the flood were very foolish; but there are a great many in these days who are more foolish and wicked than they, for although God tells them so often in his word, and by his

---

162. Sarah Elizabeth Dawes, *Hours with Mamma* (New York: American Tract Society, 1866), 27.
163. Ibid., 24.
164. Ibid., 25.
165. Ibid., 26.

ministers, that unless they repent and forsake their sins they can never dwell with him, yet they keep on in their wickedness until they are called to die, and then it is too late.[166]

Dawes' use of the embellishments of Noah's warnings and the mocking neighbors accomplishes two purposes. First of all, in reading the narrative as it is laid out, the reader is led to think only of those wicked, foolish people who heard Noah's warnings and cruelly mocked him as the ones who were killed in the flood. There is no mention of those who lived beyond the sound of Noah's voice or were not present to laugh at Noah or call him foolish. Second, it allows Dawes to teach her young readers some lessons for today, namely that they should listen to God's ministers and not to wait too long to repent and forsake their wicked ways. Also, by emphasizing how persistently foolish and wicked the people were, and how often they were warned, children are perhaps more likely to understand God's actions and not blame God for killing so many people.

Laurie Loring frames the Bible stories in her book *Little Truths for Little Folks; Bible Stories* (1877) as a dialogue between a mother and her sweet daughter named Goldlocks (not to be confused with Goldilocks). When Mamma tells the story of the return of the dove, Loring uses the character of Goldlocks to articulate concerns that sensitive children might have with the story of a flood that kills countless people:

"Did the dove find any live folks?"
"No; all the people were drowned except Noah's family. They were in the ark."
"What did God do it for, mamma?"
"Because the people were so wicked."
"Be all the wicked folks drownded [sic.] now, mamma?" Goldlock's blue eyes
  opened wide as she asked this.
"No, darling. God promised never to destroy the people by flood again."[167]

Mamma is able to offer commentary in the middle of the story of Noah that God had to drown the people because they were wicked and immediately afterwards assure Goldlocks and the reader that God will not destroy people by flood in the present and proceeds to tell Goldlocks the story of the rainbow and God's promise of no more great floods.

Through the framing device of a parent or grandparent in dialogue with children, along with the use of the embellishments of Noah warning the people and the people rejecting those warnings, these children's Bibles could retain some of the harsher elements of the story of Noah and still defend God's character by having caring adults explain to children why the flood needed to take place.

---

166. Ibid., 26–7.
167. Laurie Loring, *Little Truths for Little Folks; Bible Stories* (Boston, MA: D. Lothrop & Co., 1877), 11–12.

2.3.c. Euphemisms and allegories

As shall be discussed in more detail below, twentieth-century versions of the story of Noah tend to downplay or skip over the judgment of God and the death of the people altogether. Children's Bibles that did tell about God's judgment sometimes employed the use of various euphemisms or allegories for the flood and the death of the people. This is yet another strategy that children's Bible authors used to interpret the flood, defend God's actions, and make the prospect of a worldwide flood more palatable to their young readers.

One subtle change in wording that many nineteenth-century children's Bible authors make, perhaps in an effort to relate the flood to children's own experiences, is to describe the deluge as God's way of "punishing" wicked people. The Book of Genesis itself does not use the word "punish" or the concept of punishment to describe God's rationale for wiping out all living things with a flood. For children, however, the word "punish" would probably evoke the sense of correction or discipline. It is not surprising, then, that many nineteenth-century children's Bibles use the word "punish" to describe what God was doing by destroying people with the flood.[168] In *Bible Stories for Little Children*, published in 1955 by the Union of American Hebrew Congregations, author Betty R. Hollender took an approach that her young readers would understand when she wrote, "Once upon a time all the people on the earth were bad. So God decided he would have to punish them. They were all bad except one man. His name was Noah. Noah was a good man. So God decided not to punish him."[169] The use of the word "punish" or "punishment" and the descriptions of being bad or good were certainly concepts that children would understand and were ways in which they could relate the flood to their own experiences.

Again, religious education and the discipline children received at the hands of adults emphasized that if one is good and obedient one is rewarded; if one is bad one is punished. A description of the flood as God's way of punishing wicked people would evoke in children the sense of correction or discipline. It is worth noting, though, that those who drowned outside of the ark did not benefit from any discipline or correction; they were blotted out and destroyed, not disciplined so that they might have the opportunity to learn to live better lives in the future. By framing the flood as a punishment, however, God is placed in a role similar to that of children's parents and teachers who punish those who are bad.

Perhaps the most common use of a euphemism regarding the flood is the word "wash" or "washing." As was the case with several of the examples cited above, the

---

168. See, for example, *The Children's Bible* (1763), 19–21; *A Short History of the Bible and Testament*, 15–17; *Bible Stories with Suitable Pictures*, 13–14; Goodrich, *Peter Parley's Book*, 19; *Pictures of Bible History with Suitable Descriptions*, 7; *Tallis's Illustrated Scripture History*, 10; Conwell, *Bible Stories for Children*, 17; and Montefiore J. Moses, *Bible Stories for Jewish Children* (New York: Holt Brothers, 1879), 26.

169. Betty R. Hollender, *Bible Stories for Little Children* (New York: Union of American Hebrew Congregations, 1955), 2.

children's Bible examples that follow avoid saying that God brought a flood that killed flesh and blood people but instead describe the flood as washing away evil.

The prolific English author Charlotte Yonge provides a prime example of this approach. Many of Yonge's books were published in the United States, including *Young Folks' Bible History*, which was published in Boston in 1880. According to Yonge's account of the story of Noah, "[God] said that he would destroy these wicked people, and wash away the evil from the earth by a great flood."[170] She comes back to the image at the end of the tale, writing, "Then Noah knew the sad time of the flood—a whole year—was over, and the earth had been washed from all her stains."[171] Yonge acknowledges to children that the flood was a sad event, but the metaphor offers a rationale for why it was ultimately a good thing. Yonge's books gave great attention to class distinctions and often reflected prejudices that did not transfer smoothly to the American context.[172] In Yonge's account of the flood, readers may infer that she was not very troubled that the world had been rid of the riff raff and unpleasantness.

Mrs. Helen W. Pierson, author of books for children such as *History of the United States in Words of One Syllable* and *History of England in Words of One Syllable*, described the flood as though God was cleaning house in her 1900 book *The Bible Story: In Easy Words for Children*. According to Pierson,

> In time the men in the world grew so full of sin that God said He would sweep them from the face of the earth.
> But there was a good man named No-ah that God loved. So He told him of the great flood He meant to send to wash the world clean once more.[173]

If Pierson's story gives the sense that wicked people were a nuisance to be swept away, John Williamson Tyler's 1901 children's Bible, *The Bible Story Newly Told for Young People*, portrays God as having a considerable amount of angst over whether or not to send the flood.

> The wicked people would not go into the ark, nor believe Noah when he told them that the water was soon coming to drown them all. God waited in mercy many years, for He did not wish them to perish. But they would not repent nor believe, nor turn to God; and, at last, He sent rain from heaven and water out of the sea, and washed away the wicked people."[174]

---

170. Charlotte M. Yonge, *Young Folks' Bible History* (Boston, MA: D. Lothrop Company, 1880), 20.

171. Ibid., 24.

172. Gillian Avery, *Behold the Child: American Children and Their Books 1621–1922* (London: Bodley Head, 1994), 8.

173. Helen W. Pierson, *The Bible Story: In Easy Words for Children* (New York: McLoughlin Brothers, 1900), 12.

174. John Williamson Tyler, *The Bible Story Newly Told for Young People* (n.p.p.: William S. Whiteford, 1901), 21–2.

God is presented in a sympathetic light as someone who was merciful but who needed to do what had to be done. The use of the euphemism of washing away the wicked people further softens God's act.

Addie Richman Altman uses the same euphemism in *The Jewish Child's Bible Stories* from 1915. In Altman's story of Noah, God speaks to Noah in plain, conversational language. God tells Noah, "It will rain so much that all the wicked people will be washed away, and the world will be clean again."[175] Once the flood comes, there is no explicit description of people drowning or in despair. Instead, Altman recalls the euphemism of washing, stating, "There never was so much rain, either before or since then; and it was called 'The Flood,' because it washed away the cities, and the houses, and everything in them."[176] According to Altman's tale, God is a friend to Noah, helping him along the way, and washing the world so that it will be clean again.

In the foreword to her 1925 book *Fireside Bible Stories*, A. Gertrude Krottjer explains that she would not be drawing moral lessons from her stories explicitly but instead would use Bible stories that would make her points implicitly: "No direct moralizing has been done, but rather an attempt made to select such stories whose moral lesson will leap forward without seeking. The characters are such as have always and will always live and they speak and are actuated through the influence of the same general emotions and principles by which man has been and is ever aroused."[177] While those who died in the flood may disagree, Krottjer begins her retelling of the story of the flood by writing, "The story of Noah who built the ark and of what happened to him is a very nice one."[178] From the beginning of her narrative it is clear that Krottjer is not going to tell it as a tale of a wrathful God in order to frighten children. She continues her narrative by establishing that God's plan was for people to be happy, but the people were just so wicked it could not be so: "[God] had made so many plans to make His people happy if only they would not disobey his laws, but it seemed in vain. Always they grew more wicked. There seemed nothing left to do but destroy them and start a whole new world."[179] Krottjer's story includes the embellishments of Noah warning the people and the wicked people mocking him in return. She begins the story by introducing the metaphor of God washing the earth: "'With a great flood I shall wash the earth clean,' God said. 'Only you and your family shall be saved.'"[180] As she continues to embellish the story, Krottjer extends the narrative of the fate of the mocking neighbors and names some exotic animals. According to

---

175. Addie Richman Altman, *The Jewish Child's Bible Stories* (New York: Bloch Publishing Company, Inc., 1949), 22.

176. Ibid., 23.

177. A. Gertrude Krottjer, *Fireside Bible Stories: Old Testament. Retold for Children*, illus. by Joseph Eugene Dash (Chicago: Just Right Books, 1925), 7.

178. Ibid., 25.

179. Ibid., 26.

180. Ibid.

Krottjer's tale, while these animals seem to understand that the flood was coming, the foolish, mocking people do not have a clue.[181]

Krottjer adds a lighter tone to the deluge with the words, "Pitter, patter came the rain."[182] She then concludes her tale by returning to the metaphor she introduced earlier: "All the wickedness had been washed away."[183] In the end, then, Krottjer still does not clearly state that the wicked people actually drown, but instead writes that the abstract concept wickedness had been "washed away."

Tailer Andrews' *Bible Stories for Children* from 1927 offers a variation on this theme. It uses the image of a cleansing but does not in any way gloss over the horror of the flood for those who died. In the story, the mocking neighbors are used as a foil to Noah and his faith in God. According to Andrews, "We can be sure that many people mocked at Noah building this large boat so far from the sea. But Noah believed God and obeyed Him."[184] Andrews provides readers with a scene that is absent from Genesis: "It was a dreadful, even a horrible sight. The terrified men and women, carrying their helpless children, and the savage animals fleeing from death, fled to the heights to escape the rising flood of waters, and they fought for their lives."[185] This dreadful, horrible event, in which helpless children were drowned, is presented as a cleansing incident: "The earth was cleansed and the evildoers, with their wicked haunts, were swept away. But the ark floated safely upon the waters, and Noah and his household and all the beasts he had taken with him were saved alive."[186] When Noah leaves the ark, he finds a cleansed and beautiful world:

> It was cleansed, and full of beauty and charm. The green grass was sprouting, and flowers were in bloom.
>
> All those who had vexed God and done evil, who had been thieves and brawlers had been drowned. But it was a silent world, and Noah understood how great was God's goodness to him and to his household in sparing them alive.[187]

Andrews' conclusion suggests that those who drowned were all thieves and brawlers and the fact that they are dead is one that would make Noah and the reader happy and one that would make people appreciate the goodness and might of God and the nice clean world God has provided for them.

Dom Hubert Van Zeller's 1949 book, *Old Testament Stories: Scripture Textbooks for Catholic Schools*, delivers a broader view of salvation than the tale of individual

---

181. Ibid., 27–8.

182. Ibid., 29.

183. Ibid.

184. Tailer Andrews, *Bible Stories for Children*, illus. by C. W. Kelsey (New York: J. H. Sears & Company, 1927), 10.

185. Ibid., 10–11.

186. Ibid., 11.

187. Ibid., 12.

sinners and the salvation of a few individuals often highlighted in Protestant children's Bibles. To begin his story, Van Zeller offers an interesting perspective on the sinfulness of humankind and uses the image of God washing the earth:

> You would have thought that in the days when people lived to a very great age indeed, mankind would gradually become wiser and milder and more inclined to peace. Not at all. As the population grew, so the sins of man grew too; and the family of Seth was as bad as any. In order to cleanse the world God decided, quite simply, to wash it. He sent a flood.[188]

The solution to the world's sin problem is simple, at least for God. God must wash it. According to Van Zeller's tale, however, Noah is not happy about the destruction of the wicked. When he looks outside of his window and sees the devastation, Van Zeller suggests that it "must have been saddening indeed."[189] After telling readers how the flood waters receded and God made a covenant with Noah, Van Zeller uses the flood as an image of baptism for the world: "The world which had sinned had been baptized; and the grey sky which for forty days had loosed its burden upon the earth had now put on its choicest colours to celebrate the ceremony. Man has been given another chance."[190] For Van Zeller, if the flood was a symbol of baptism, the rainbow serves as a metaphor for an archway to heaven:

> High above the altar and against the cloudless blue, the great sweep of God's rainbow proclaims that through a new archway must man find his way to heaven. There is perhaps a moment's silence … a sense of awe … downcast looks and the effort to concentrate. Blinking and fluttering and stretching our legs we all go off together in the joy of our new-found freedom and resolve."[191]

For Van Zeller, then, the flood serves as a metaphor for both washing and baptism, while the rainbow offers the image of a bridge between earth and heaven.

This motif endures in more recent children's Bible retellings of the story of Noah. In 1984, for example, Alice Joyce Davidson's *Alice in Bibleland Storybooks* tells the story of a young girl from the present named Alice. Alice reads a magic, giant Bible that allows her to walk into the past and enter into Bible stories. In *The Story of Noah*, Davidson emphasizes the fact that Noah was good while the other people were very bad. The sweet, innocent-looking young Alice watches the people:

> She saw wicked, wicked people
>   Who did a lot of wrong,

---

188. Dom Hubert Van Zeller, *Old Testament Stories: Scripture Textbooks for Catholic Schools* (Westminster, MD: Newman Press, 1949), 8.

189. Ibid., 9.

190. Ibid., 10.

191. Ibid., 10–11.

And instead of singing praise to God,
    They sang this awful song:
"Ha, ha, ha, he, he, he!
    We're as wicked as can be!
Up with evil, down with good.
    Down with love and brotherhood!"[192]

According to the text, however, "Noah and his family were very, very good."[193] Davidson uses the language of washing to describe the flood:

The water covered houses,
Tall trees and mountains, too,
As God washed all things bad away
Just as He said He'd do.[194]

In Davidson's story there is no mention that any people, even those people who gloried in their wickedness, died or were covered with water. It was just the houses, trees, and mountains. Instead of specifying that bad people were washed away, the text only says that "all things bad" had washed away. According to this brief stanza, the fact that people and things were washed away is not a reason to question God's character. Instead it is evidence of God's good character as it demonstrates that he followed through on what "He said He'd do."

This euphemistic approach to the story of the flood has made its way into twenty-first-century children's Bibles as well. In *The Lion Read & Know Bible*, a 2008 Bible storybook published in Britain but also available in the United States, author Sophie Piper does not specifically mention that anyone drowned in the flood; instead she writes, "When it is ready, I am going to send a flood to wash the bad old world away."[195] When the flood ends and Noah and his family can leave the ark, the happy tale has a happy ending. According to Piper, "Noah and his family laughed for joy. 'Thank you, God,' they cried. 'Thank you for keeping us safe.'"[196]

Sarah Young wrote a 2004 devotional for adults, titled *Jesus Calling: Enjoying Peace in His Presence*, in which she puts daily words of comfort into the mouth of Jesus. The Jesus of the devotional does not challenge readers to work for justice or better serve others but instead offers words of personal peace, assurance, and affirmation to the reader, along with calls to trust and obey him. The book proved to be very popular and has led to a whole series of devotional books for a variety of

192. Alice Joyce Davidson, *The Story of Noah*, illus. by Victoria Marshall (Norwalk, CT: C. R. Gibson Company, 1984), n.p.

193. Ibid.

194. Ibid.

195. Sophie Piper, *The Lion Read & Know Bible*, illus. by Anthony Lewis (Oxford: Lion Childrens, 2008), 27.

196. Ibid., 35.

age groups, including the *Jesus Calling Bible Storybook* from 2012. Young also uses the euphemism of washing: "Before long, the whole earth was covered with water. God's flood destroyed the bad things and washed them all away. Yet everyone and everything in the ark were safe and sound because Noah did what God said."[197] Again, as is the case in many of these versions, it is not the wicked people and animals who drown, but bad things that are washed away.

Bessie Edmond Andruss took a unique allegorical approach in her version of the story of Noah. In *Bible Stories as Told to Very Little Children*, from 1932, she offers a fascinating approach to retelling Bible stories using the metaphors of "Love" and "error." In the preface to her book, Andruss argues for an intentional spiritualization of Bible stories: "I found ... that the more spiritual the stories were, the better they understood them. It was very clear to these children that evil or error was really nothing in the presence of divine Love. Thus, to tell them that divine Love destroyed evil, not men, was to present a consistent God to them, whom they could love and obey."[198] Andruss carries out this approach in her retelling of Noah and the ark in which *God* does not destroy wicked *people*, but rather *Love* wipes out *error*. She begins the story:

> Now, God loved Noah very much, because Noah was always good and kind and loved everybody, and would do everything that God told him to do. Noah taught his three sons to love God too.
>
> Now, all the other people at the time would not do what God told them to do, but instead they listened to error who told them to be naughty children, and not to listen to Love as Noah always did.
>
> So Noah told them not to listen to error, but listen to God, for God was Love. But these people only laughed at good kind Noah, and poked fun at him.[199]

The story continues by explaining that "there was going to be a great big rain, which would rain and rain and rain, until it would be a big flood of rain over everything."[200] This growing flood becomes a metaphor for the way error grows: "That is the way error works. If you listen to error, it gets bigger and bigger, until it gets so big it just bursts!"[201] It is worth noting that for Andruss it is not God, but error that causes the flood waters to fall: "So when God shut the door of the Ark, with Noah and his family inside with the animals, then error began at once to pour down the rain."[202] According to Andruss, Noah and his family were not concerned, "for they knew that Love was with them all the time, and had given

197. Sarah Young, *Jesus Calling Bible Storybook*, illus. by Carolin Farias (Nashville, TN: Thomas Nelson, 2012), 32.

198. Bessie Edmond Andruss, *Bible Stories as Told to Very Little Children*, illus. by Olivette (New York: Coward-McCann, Inc., 1932), 11.

199. Ibid., 13.

200. Ibid., 14.

201. Ibid.

202. Ibid.

them this beautiful Ark to keep them safe, and it could not rain on them. So the Ark just went sailing along on the water and they were all so happy because they were all good children."[203] Andruss begins to end her tale on a positive note, telling readers of the rainbow "which Love puts in the sky to tell His children not to fear."[204] She tells children that they have nothing to fear from the God of Love and that it was error that had destroyed itself. "Now, while Noah and his family were safe in God's Ark, error, which had made it rain so hard that it had become a flood, was destroyed."[205] Andruss ultimately concludes her story with the observation, "So you see, error just punished itself as it always does, while God's perfect children were all happy and thanked Love for taking care of them as He always does."[206]

Through the use of these interpretive allegories, Andruss distances God from the judgment of the flood. God is Love. God does not kill wicked people. God's children are perfect and happy. The flood is not an act of God, but error destroying itself.

2.3.d. Conclusion

It is evident that many children's Bibles of the nineteenth and early twentieth centuries anticipated the concerns children might have with the image of a God who would send a flood to kill countless people. They addressed this concern in a number of ways. Many creatively used the embellishments of Noah's warning people and the wicked mocking him in return to suggest to the reader that God gave those who died every chance to repent and be saved but that they were so wicked that God eventually had to let them drown. Other children's Bibles used these embellishments and also framed their narratives as conversations between children and loving parents who could gently answer children's concerns. Later, some children's Bibles used euphemisms and allegories to avoid saying directly that God killed people. As shall be seen, in the second half of the twentieth century children's Bibles more often dealt with the difficulties raised by the image of people drowning in the flood by quickly glossing over the event or by avoiding it altogether. The image of God in children's Bibles was not that of a God of wrath but that of a friendly God who keeps children safe.

2.4. Stories of a Friendly God Who Keeps Children Safe

The late nineteenth and early decades of the twentieth century saw a growing awareness of child development and increased concern for what was appropriate

---

203. Ibid., 14–15.
204. Ibid., 16.
205. Ibid.
206. Ibid.

for children to see and hear.[207] In the first half of the twentieth century, several psychologists, such as Sigmund Freud,[208] Jean Piaget,[209] and Erik Erikson,[210] began to formalize theories of child development. In truth, however, the work of educators such as G. Stanley Hall and progressive educators such as John Dewey, along with the enforcement of mandatory school laws in the United States, had already been raising America's awareness of what children could comprehend and raising issues of what was appropriate and inappropriate to present to children. As a matter of fact, Dewey spoke on the topic of child development at the very first meeting of the Religious Education Association in 1903 and stressed the need to understand the full implications of the fact that "the mind of a child is not identical to the mind of an adult."[211] While the Religious Education Association itself did not publish a curriculum, its engagement with progressive educational theories influenced groups such as the Graded Lesson Conference, organized by J. W. Barnes in 1906, and other groups that led to an increasingly graded curriculum that accounted for the understanding and sensitivities of children at different age levels.[212]

At the same time, in the early decades of the twentieth century, child mortality rates began to drop significantly and an increasing number of people died in hospitals as opposed to dying at home.[213] As a result, death was no longer a common occurrence in the life of children, and they were no longer being taught that death was always near. Death became increasingly hidden from children, and the topic of death gradually came to be avoided with children altogether.[214] As Lynn and Wright put it,

> By the turn of the century the death music of the old-time Sunday school had acquired a dismal reputation. Such songs as "The Grave" and "Death of a Pious Child" were dismissed by the disdainful epithet, "mortuary hymns." The strongest critic of these songs was the "religious education" movement of the

207. See Mintz, *Huck's Raft*, 186–91, for a more detailed description of the scientific study of children and its influence during these years.

208. Sigmund Freud, *Three Contributions to the Sexual Theory*, trans. A. A. Brill (New York: Journal of Nervous and Mental Disease Publishing Company, 1910).

209. Jean Piaget, *Origins of Intelligence in Children*, trans. by Margaret Cook (New York: International University Press, 1952).

210. Erik H. Erikson, *Childhood and Society* (New York: W. W. Norton, 1950).

211. John Dewey, "Religious Education as Conditioned by Modern Psychology and Pedagogy," *The Religious Education Association: Proceedings of the First Annual Convention, Chicago, February 10–12* (Chicago: Religious Education Association, 1903), 60.

212. Frank Glenn Lankard, *A History of the American Sunday School Curriculum* (New York: Abingdon Press, 1927), 280–1.

213. Mintz, *Huck's Raft*, 134, and Samuel H. Preston and Michael Hains, *Fatal Years: Child Mortality in Late Nineteenth-century America* (Princeton, NJ: Princeton University Press, 1991).

214. Stannard, *Puritan Way of Death*, 189; Laderman, *Sacred Remains*, 7.

early twentieth century, a group of reformers sensitive to the promptings of progressive theories of John Dewey and other Liberals.[215]

Following World War Two, Americans sought to present themselves and their children with idyllic images of domestic peace and prosperity. Dr. Benjamin Spock, in his book *The Common Sense Book of Baby and Child Care* (1946), assured parents that their children were not depraved creatures born into sin but children who should be showered with love and warm affection.[216] As adults, many members of the Baby Boomer generation would look back at their child-hoods as a happy time of innocence when their parents and other adults protected them from many of the fears and concerns of adulthood, including topics such as death and the potential judgment of God upon the world.[217] They were assured that adults would take care of them and that they were safe.

By the twenty-first century, an extensive study of adolescent religious beliefs in the United States would reveal that these perspectives had permeated the religious lives of American teenagers from nearly every faith and denomination. In the book *Soul Searching: The Religious and Spiritual Lives of American Teenagers*, Christian Smith and Melinda Lundquist Denton reported on the findings of the National Study of Youth and Religion conducted from July 2002 to March 2003. Through extensive interviews with teenagers from a wide variety of faith tradi-tions, they identified the prevailing view of God held by American teenagers (ages 13–17) practicing and non-practicing and across religious and non-denom-inational boundaries. Smith and Denton labeled this prevailing view as "Moral Therapeutic Deism."[218] According to this view, God exists and wants people to be nice to one another. The central goal of life is to be happy and feel good about oneself. A key characteristic of this view is "God does not need to be particularly involved in one's life except when God is needed to resolve a problem."[219] God has very little in the way of expectations for humankind. God wants people to be nice to one another, but makes very few demands upon them. Still, God is always there to protect them and to save them if they are in a bind. Smith and Denton summarize the view, writing, "This God is not demanding. He actually can't be, because his job is to solve our problems and make people feel good."[220] Although there is no similar study of American teenagers from the nineteenth century with which to contrast this study, one suspects that the teenagers of that day would have viewed God as much more demanding and less likely to be standing at the

---

215. Lynn and Wright, *Big Little School*, 82.

216. Benjamin Spock, *The Common Sense Book of Baby and Child Care* (New York: Duell, Sloane and Pearce, 1946).

217. Mintz, *Huck's Raft*, 275.

218. Christian Smith with Melinda Lundquist Denton, *Soul Searching: The Religious and Spiritual Lives of American Teenagers* (Oxford: Oxford University Press, 2005), 162–70.

219. Ibid., 163.

220. Ibid., 165.

ready to help when one was in trouble. Teenagers of a century ago certainly did not grow up reading children's Bibles that presented them with this view of God.

Given these conditions, it is not surprising to find that throughout the twentieth century children's Bibles increasingly began to avoid frightening stories of violence and death. Stories such as that of Elisha, the children of Bethel, and the she-bears soon disappeared from all but the most inclusive children's Bibles. In retelling the story of Noah, many children's Bibles dealt with the troubling image of people drowning in the flood not by offering explanations for God's behavior but by simply avoiding the fact that God caused the flood or that people died in the flood altogether. Illustrations and descriptions of the plight of those outside of the ark became increasingly rare. Given the cultural factors at work, one might anticipate that, by the end of the twentieth century, the image of God presented in children's Bibles is not a God who was demanding and judgmental but rather a loving heavenly friend who keeps them safe in times of trouble.

2.4.a. Children's Bibles for the very young: God our friend who keeps us safe

While there were some nineteenth- and early twentieth-century children's Bibles aimed at younger readers,[221] and some publishers such as Golden Books and Arch Books who published various versions of the story of Noah for younger readers in the mid-twentieth century,[222] it was especially in the late twentieth and early twenty-first centuries that an increasing number of children's Bibles were produced for preschoolers, toddlers, and even babies.[223] If baby boomers

221. See, for example, Gertrude Smith, *Baby Bible Stories* (Philadelphia, PA: Henry Altemus Company, 1904); Elisabeth Robinson Scovil, *Wee Folks Stories from the Old Testament: In Words of One Syllable* (Philadelphia, PA: Henry Altemus Company, 1920); Louise M. Pleasanton, *A Nursery Story of the Bible* (New York: Frederick A. Stokes Company, 1920); Rosamund D. Ginther, *Bible Stories for the Cradle Roll*, 5 vols (Nashville, TN: Southern Publishing Association, 1933); and Lenore Cohen, *Bible Tales for Very Young Children* (Cincinnati, OH: Union of American Hebrew Congregations, 1934). Despite their titles, these children's Bibles tended to be written for an elementary age reading level and not for preschool children.

222. See Annie North Bedford, *Walt Disney's Noah's Ark* (New York: Simon and Schuster, 1952); Barbara Shook Hazen, *Noah's Ark*, illus. by Tibor Gergely (Racine, WI: Golden Press, 1969); and Jane Latourette, *The Story of Noah's Ark*, illus. by Sally Matthews (St. Louis, MO: Arch Books, 1965).

223. See V. Gilbert Beers, *The Toddler's Bible*, illus. by Carole Boerke (Colorado Springs, CO: Cook Communications Ministry, 1992); Betty L. Aldridge, *The Toddler's Activity Bible* (Nashville, TN: Thomas Nelson, 1992); Carolyn Nabors Baker and Cindy Helms, *The Beginners Bible for Toddlers*, illus. by Danny Brooks Dalby (Dallas, TX: Word Publishing, 1995); *Baby's First Bible*, illus. by Colin and Moira Maclean (Pleasantville, NY: Reader's Digest Books, 1996); Robin Currie, *The Baby Bible Storybook*, illus. by Cindy Adams (Eastbourne: Chariot Books, 1994); *Baby's Bible*, illus. by Mandy Stanley (Cincinnati,

were raised to have a sense of safety and comfort, they seem to have wanted their children and grandchildren to know these feelings of love and safety from a very young age. While children's Bibles created for children grade school age and older often teach lessons related to virtues and salvation, the vast majority of those designed for preschool children teach them the lessons that God is their friend and that God will keep them safe no matter what. God's grace and Noah's safety no longer appear to be dependent on being good or doing what God commands. Given the cultural trends and understanding of young children, these trends are perhaps not surprising, but the cumulative effect of the many, many examples that follow gives one the impression that parents and teachers are obsessed with assuring children that God is their friend and that God keeps them safe. These children's Bibles reinforce the point with friendly cartoon images of Bible characters. As a matter of fact, the image of a smiling Noah with a host of smiling modern-day zoo animals graces the cover of many children's Bibles, such as the *Spark Story Bible* from 2009 (see Figure 2.7).[224] In these versions of the story of Noah, there is no need to use euphemisms or allegory to describe people drowning in the flood since there is often no mention that God caused the flood or that anyone died in the flood. The story is simply about how God keeps Noah and the animals safe.

One of the most popular children's Bibles of the late twentieth and early twenty-first century is *The Beginner's Bible*, first released in 1989. The original version, written by Karyn Henly, was in print from 1989 to 2004 and sold over 5 million copies. Henly is a graduate of Abilene Christian University and received a Masters of Fine Arts degree from Vermont College. Dennas Davis provides fun, child-friendly illustrations of Bible characters who almost always wear smiles on their faces. Noah smiles as he starts his carpentry work,[225] and Noah, his family, and the animals are all wearing smiles as they face the reader as if posing for a photograph.[226] The story of Noah is titled "The First Rainbow," and Henly's text explains, "People began to forget about God. They began to do bad things. There was only one good man. His name was Noah."[227] The fact that others are drowned in the flood is vaguely hinted at when God says, "I am sorry that I made people. I will start all over again,"[228] but there is no explicit mention that anyone drowned in the flood. Instead, the focus is on the fact that "Noah and his family and all the

OH: Standard Publishing, 2003); *Baby Blessings Baby's Bible* (Norwalk, Connecticut, CT: Standard Publishing, 2004); and Sally Ann Wright and Honor Ayers, *Baby's First Bible* (Lutherville, MD: Anno Domini Publishing, 2012).

224. Patti Thisted Arthur et al.'s *Spark Story Bible* (Minneapolis, MN: Augsburg Fortress, 2009).

225. Karyn Henly, *The Beginner's Bible: Timeless Children's Stories*, illus. by Dennas Davis (Sisters, OR: Questar Publishers, Inc., 1989), 29.

226. Ibid., 33.

227. Ibid., 29.

228. Ibid., 30.

Figure 2.7. Artist Peter Grosshauser's wraparound cover image from Patti Thisted Arthur et al.'s *Spark Story Bible* (Minneapolis, MN: Augsburg Fortress, 2009).

animals were safe and dry inside the ark."[229] After leaving the ark, the theme of safety is underscored when "Noah thanked God for keeping them safe."[230]

The revised version of *The Beginner's Bible*, released in 2005, takes a similar approach. If anything, it draws the reader into further sympathy for God by telling them, "God was sad that everyone but Noah forgot about him. He told Noah about his plan to start over."[231] It also makes more of an effort to frame the story as a happy one in which God keeps us safe. Even in the midst of the flood, "Everyone inside the ark was safe. Noah and his family were very happy."[232]

Kenneth N. Taylor, author of the popular *Living Bible* paraphrase of the Bible, also wrote a number of children's Bibles. Each page that is devoted to the story of Noah in Taylor's *My First Bible in Pictures*, from 1989, underscores the theme of safety. In the three pages of text and three illustrations devoted to the story of Noah, no one outside of Noah's family is mentioned or seen. The first page recounts that God told Noah to build a huge boat and ends, "Noah and all his family will be safe in the boat."[233] The second page describes Noah building the ark and gathering the animals and ends, "There are two giraffes and two tigers and two ducks. They will all be safe in the ark when the flood comes."[234] On the

229. Ibid., 33.

230. Ibid., 35.

231. Catherine DeVries, ed., *The Beginner's Bible: Timeless Bible Stories* (Grand Rapids, MI: Zondervan, 2005), 28.

232. Ibid., 31.

233. Kenneth N. Taylor, *My First Bible in Pictures* (Wheaton, IL: Tyndale House Publishers, 1989), n.p.

234. Ibid.

third page, Taylor writes, "It rained and rained and rained. Soon everything was covered with water. But Noah's boat is floating on the water. Yes, God took care of Noah and his family and the animals in the boat. God takes care of you, too."[235] The emphasis is upon assuring children of God's care for Noah and for them. There is no need for Taylor to explain or excuse the fact that people drowned in the flood since that is not mentioned in the narrative.

My Bible Pals Storybook, developed by Diane Storz with Greg Holder for children ages 2–5 years, begins the tale "Ark Full of Animals" by establishing that God is indeed the one who is sending the flood, but assures the reader that Noah and the animals will be safe. According to the story, "God told Noah to build a BIG boat. 'I'm going to send a lot of rain,' said God. 'You and your family will be safe inside the ark. You will keep animals safe there, too.'"[236] The story ends by explaining that Noah left the ark, "And the first thing that Noah did was thank God for keeping everyone safe!"[237] In this version of the story, God is the one who sends the rain, but there is no mention that anyone dies, and so the story seems to imply that God kept everyone safe.

Pilgrim Press's 2003 offering, *The Pilgrim Book of Bible Stories*, usually does not add or delete many details from the canonical accounts. Still, Mark Water's text avoids dealing with the devastation of the flood by moving the narrative along quickly to place Noah and his family already on the ark. The story begins, "God told Noah to build an ark. When the rains came, Noah and all his family went into the ark. With them, they took two of every creature on earth."[238] The story moves along briskly to the scene in which God places the rainbow in the sky, and ends with, "All of Noah's family looked at the dazzling colors in the rainbow and knew that God loved them."[239] Here, God is not only the one who keeps people safe, but the one who loves them as well.

Catherine DeVries takes a similar approach in her *Adventure Bible Storybook* from 2009. She avoids the unpleasantness of people drowning entirely by beginning the story with Noah already on the ark, relaxing in a hammock and listening to the rain.[240] The story ends with Noah praying, "Thank you for promising to save me, my family, and the animals."[241]

In one of many children's Bibles of the twenty-first century created just for young girls, *The Sweetest Story Bible*, author Diane Stortz titles her story of Noah's

235. Ibid.

236. Diane Stortz and Greg Holder, *My Bible Pals Storybook*, illus. by Jodie McCallum (Cincinnati, OH: Standard Publishing Company, 1996), 10.

237. Ibid.

238. Mark Waters, *The Pilgrim Book of Bible Stories*, illus. by Diana Shimon (Cleveland, OH: Pilgrim Press, 2003), 23.

239. Ibid., 25.

240. Catherine DeVries, *Adventure Bible Storybook*, illus. by Jim Madsen (Grand Rapids, MI: ZonderKids, 2009), 18.

241. Ibid., 23.

ark "Safe in a Big Boat."[242] Stortz's version contains no mention of mean mockers, and there is no mention or illustration of anyone in the story other than Noah and his family who are all kept safe. The story concludes with a nice, friendly conversation between Noah and God:

> "Thank you for taking care of us!" Noah told God.
> "I will always take care of you," God said. He promised never to flood the earth again. He made the rainbow to remind everyone of his promise.[243]

Each story in *The Sweetest Story Bible* concludes with a young girl in a pink dress presenting readers with a "Sweet Thought" placed inside a pink heart and some "Sweet Words." For the story of Noah, the Sweet Thought is "God keeps us safe," and the Sweet Words are "We trust in the Lord our God—Psalm 20:7."[244] Like many other children's Bibles created for young girls, Stortz presents God's world as a nice, sweet and safe place to live with a nice, caring God looking over the people in it.

In some children's Bibles, God is introduced to children not as an intimidating, transcendent, holy, and majestic figure, but as a folksy-sounding friend to Noah who engages him in clever repartee. In the 1997 Arch Book *Noah's 2-by-2 Adventure*, for example, after God tells Noah to get his hammer and build an ark, Noah's response shows the two have a good rapport:

> "Yes, Sir, God," said Noah.
> And he built a boxy boat.
> "Now," said God, "My critters
> And your family can stay afloat."[245]

Miriam Sagasti's illustrations show Noah surrounded by smiling, friendly, and cuddly animal friends. As the story ends, God speaks again, and Noah and the animals respond:

> God then said, "I promise
> Not to drown the world again."
> Noah and his family
> With the critters said, "Amen!"[246]

242. Diane Stortz, *The Sweetest Story Bible: Sweet Thoughts and Sweet Words for Little Girls*, illus. by Sheila Bailey (Grand Rapids, MI: Zondervan, 2010), 20. For a very similar version of this story in a board book for younger girls, see Diane Stortz, *The Sweetest Story Bible for Toddlers*, illus. by Sheila Bailey (Grand Rapids, MI: Zondervan, 2010), n.p.

243. Stortz, *Sweetest Story*, 25.

244. Ibid.

245. Carol Wedeven, *Noah's 2-by-2 Adventure*, illus. by Miriam Sagasti (St. Louis, MO: Concordia Publishing House, 1997), 4.

246. Ibid., 14.

In this story, Noah models a comfortable friendship with God.

In Pat Alexander's *My First Bible* from 2002, God often speaks using informal or colloquial language. In the story of Noah, God explains the reason for the flood by saying, "I have to get rid of all this nastiness."[247] The story, however, provides readers with no explicit description of what exactly happens to the nastiness. At the end of the story, after the flood, she notes that Noah's family is thankful: "'Thank you, oh thank you, God,' they said, 'for keeping us all safe.'"[248]

The Bible characters in Lois Rock's 2004 storybook *Five-Minute Bible Stories*, including God, are spunky, confident, and sometimes even flippant. Rock writes, "One day, God came to have a closer look at the world, and God saw all the wicked people. 'I'm sorry I ever made the place,' said God. 'It's become a disaster zone.'"[249] In her brief retelling of the story, Rock moves the focus away from either judgment or safety in order to emphasize the fun celebration that follows the flood:

> Noah and his crew clapped as the long line of creatures hurried away, crawling and jumping, walking and running, leaping and flying. They were eager to build homes and raise families.
> "And now for our own party," said Noah.
> As they celebrated, God gave them a promise.
> "I will never send a flood like that again."[250]

God speaks in colloquial terms and almost seems to reveal a twinge of regret over bringing the flood to earth.

In these stories, God is not the frightening judge who is punishing sin that is presented in children's Bibles of a century earlier or even a benevolent deity to look upon with awe and wonder. Instead, God is accessible and folksy, using witty and amusing language in casual conversation with Noah. Throughout all these versions of the story, it is also made very clear that God keeps Noah and the animals happy and safe.

Many American evangelicals of the late twentieth and early twenty-first centuries take the approach that every Bible story is directly applicable to every reader's life today and believe that people can and should have a very personal relationship with God. Many children's Bibles produced during this time reflect these perspectives by giving the story of Noah a very personal application. The fact that God kept Noah and his family safe is assumed to mean that God keeps each individual child who is reading the book or being read the book in the present safe as well. While this is the implicit message of most of these late

247. Pat Alexander, *My First Bible*, illus. by Leon Baxter (Intercourse, PA: Good Books, 2002), 29.

248. Ibid., 37.

249. Lois Rock, *Five-Minute Bible Stories*, illus. by Richard Johnson (Minneapolis, MN: Augsburg Books, 2004), 16.

250. Ibid., 19–20.

twentieth-century and early twenty-first century versions of the story of Noah, in many cases the point is made explicitly as well by telling the reader not only that God cares for Noah, but that God cares for "you" or "us" or "me."

For example, Christian author Thomas Womack, writing under his occasional pen name Mack Thomas, makes this sort of direct application in *The First Step Bible* from 1994. As Womack describes the scene, "Inside the boat God keeps us safe … until the day the water is gone. Then God says, 'Come out, everyone, come out!' And we are so glad God keeps us safe!"[251]

Each story in the *My Bible Pals Storybook* concludes with a suggested prayer under the heading "Pray With Me." The prayer that follows the story of Noah is "God, you took care of Noah and the animals, and you take care of me. Thank you. I love you, God. Amen."[252] The story of Noah and the accompanying prayer speak to children of a close, warm, and loving relationship with God and teach children not only that God kept Noah safe, but that God takes care of them and keeps them safe as well.

Standard Publishing's 2004 *Touch-and-See Bible* does not list an author and states that it is based on the New Living Translation but is a typical Bible storybook that freely retells Bible stories for young children. The short, one-page story of Noah is titled "God Cares for Noah" and concludes, "Water soon covered the earth. But God kept Noah and his family safe!"[253] The book includes a Bible verse after each story at the bottom of the page. In this case, the direct link between God keeping Noah safe and God keeping children safe is made through quoting Psalm 55.22 in the New Living Translation: "God will take care of you."[254]

The revised edition of Susan Elizabeth Beck's *God Loves Me Bible* from 2004, created for children ages 2–4, features a built-in frame in the middle of the front cover of the book so that parents can place a photograph of their child in the middle of the cover, under the title, and surrounded by illustrations of a smiling monkey, giraffe, zebra, lion, and birds. This feature seems to be designed to personalize the Bible and help each child see the Bible as his or her book that relates directly to his or her life. Gloria Oostema's illustrations show everyone smiling, animals included, and each story ends with a reminder that God loves the people in the Bible story just completed, "and God loves me!" So, for example, the story of Noah begins by establishing a friendly relationship between God and humankind, stating, "Noah was God's friend."[255] The story concludes with the words "God loved Noah and his family and the animals. And God loves me!"[256] God not only keeps the child reading the book safe, but loves the child as well.

---

251. Mack Thomas, *The First Step Bible* (Sisters, OR: Gold 'n Honey Books, 1994), 37.

252. Storz, *My Bible Pals*, 10.

253. *Touch-and-See Bible*, illus. by Eileen Hine (Cincinnati, OH: Standard Publishing, 2004), n.p.

254. Ibid.

255. Susan Elizabeth Beck, *God Loves Me Bible*, rev. edn (Grand Rapids, MI: Zondervan, 2004), 10.

256. Ibid., 11.

In 2008, David C. Cook republished Robin Currie's text from *The Baby Bible Storybook* in two editions: *The Baby Bible Storybook for Boys* and *The Baby Bible Storybook for Girls*. Other than the different titles, the books are identical except that the storybook for boys has a blue cover and the storybook for girls has a pink cover. Currie's story of Noah concludes, "God took care of Noah. God takes care of you too."[257] Immediately following the story, a prayer is added, saying, "Dear God, I'm glad You take care of all the animals and me! Amen."[258] God's care for Noah is related directly to God's care for the child.

The Beginning Reader's Bible (2011) includes abridged Bible stories taken from the International Children's Bible translation. Each story concludes with a "Pray God's Word" feature in a box, which, in effect, offers readers a lesson to take away from the story. The story of selections from Genesis 6–9 concludes with the prayer, "Lord, keep us safe. Always protect us. Protect me, God, because I trust you.—Psalm 12:7; 16:1."[259] The multivalent story offered in the passages excerpted from Genesis 6–9 is summarized, in effect, with a message of God keeping the reader safe. In this case, the text of the story is initially allowed to speak for itself, without extended revision, but the prayer at the end serves to drive home to children the primary lesson that God will keep them safe.

Every other page in Connie Morgan Wade and Diane Storz's 2012 *Rhyme Time Bible Stories: Noah's Ark* repeats the refrain,

> With a zzz, smack, pound, and whack built a floating zoo.
> God saved Noah, he'll save you."[260]

Again, a direct connection is made between God saving Noah and God saving the child who is reading the story or having the story read to him or her.

Roma Downey, the star of the long-running CBS television show *Touched by an Angel*, wrote *Roma Downey's Little Angels Bible Storybook* (2012). The story "God Sends a Big Flood" begins, "God told Noah that a big flood was coming. He wanted Noah to be safe so he told Noah to build a big boat."[261] Each story ends with an "I learned that …" feature. For the story of Noah, the lesson is "God makes promises to his people. If I will trust his promises, I can be at peace. I

257. Robin Currie, *The Baby Bible Storybook for Boys*, illus. by Gonstaza Basaluzzo (Colorado Springs, CO: David C. Cook, 2008), n.p., and Robin Currie, *The Baby Bible Storybook for Girls*, illus. by Gonstaza Basaluzzo (Colorado Springs, CO: David C. Cook, 2008), n.p.

258. Currie, *Baby Bible Storybook for Boys*, n.p.

259. *The Beginning Reader's Bible*, illus. by Marijke ten Café (Nashville, TN: Thomas Nelson, 2011), 12.

260. Connie Morgan Wade and Diane Stortz, *Rhyme Time Bible Stories: Noah's Ark*, illus. by Laura Ovresat (Cincinnati, OH: Standard Publishing, 2012), n.p.

261. Roma Downey with Carolyn Larsen, *Roma Downey's Little Angels Bible Storybook* (Carol Streams, IL: Tyndale House, 2012), 36.

can know that he is taking care of things."[262] The lesson provided at the end of the story actually echoes the message of most episodes of *Touched by an Angel*. Namely, God loves people, has a specific plan for each of their lives, and will take care of them. People can find peace, but only if they will trust in God's plan for their lives.

In these examples, children are not only assured that God will keep all people safe, in a general sense, but that God keeps them safe in a very personal way.

A number of children's Bibles use the story of Noah's ark to provide children and their parents with an image of God as a loving parent who keeps children safe. They do this by comparing how God rocks the ark by the waves of the flood with a parent rocking a child to sleep or comparing how God keeps Noah and his family safe in the ark with a parent who keeps his or her children safe and sound in a warm and cozy bed during a stormy night.

Tracy L. Harrast's 1995 *My Baby and Me Story Bible*, for example, tells of how Noah builds the boat and gets the sheep, lions, and elephants inside. Harrast then explains the story and gives parents an activity to conduct with their children: "God keeps them all safe in the big boat. I'll rock you like you're riding in the big boat. Back and forth. Back and forth. God keeps you safe too."[263] Although the allegory may be lost on the babies, God rocking the ark is compared to a parent rocking a cradle.

Leslie Eckard's *Beginning Bible Stories: Blessings for Baby* from 2001 makes a similar analogy: "Pitter-pat! Rain covered the whole earth, but Noah, his family, and the animals were safe and dry."[264] Eckard ends the story by writing, "Like a father who cradles his baby in his arms, God protects all his creatures. Bless all living things and those who care for them."[265]

Lori C. Froeb's *Fisher-Price Little People: Noah and the Animals* from 2012 features illustrations of a smiling Noah and his wife, and smiling animals based on the Fisher-Price toy of Noah and Ark. Froeb begins the story by highlighting the theme of safety: "God told Noah, 'Build an ark, and make it long and wide. Soon I'm sending lots of rain, but you'll be safe inside.'"[266] In the midst of the flood, "the rain came down for forty days and lightning lit the sky. Inside the ark, the animals stayed cozy, warm and dry."[267] Even during the worst of the rains, the animals are smiling, happy and content, warm, cozy, and dry.

In these stories the ark, which earlier children's Bibles often imagined as a frightening or at least very uncomfortable place, is used to conjure up the image

---

262. Ibid., 37.

263. Tracy L. Harrast, *My Baby and Me Story Bible*, illus. by Gloria Oostema (Grand Rapids, MI: Zondervan Publishing House, 1995), 12.

264. Leslie Eckard, *Beginning Bible Stories: Blessings for Baby* (Nashville, TN: Broadman & Holman, 2001), n.p.

265. Ibid.

266. Lori C. Froeb, *Fisher Price Little People: Noah and the Animals* (White Plains, NY: Reader's Digest Children's Books, 2012), n.p.

267. Ibid.

of a rocking cradle or warm and cozy bed and children are led to imagine God as a kind parent who keeps them safe and warm.

God as the one who keeps little ones safe is also a theme that is central in Sally Lloyd-Jones's *Tiny Bear's Bible* from 2007. The cover features an illustration by Igor Oleynikov of a small huggable bear in pink overalls grinning ear to ear and jumping up in pure joy. The Bible stories are given titles such as "God Keeps Moses Safe," "God Protects Daniel," and "Jesus Stops a Scary Storm." The story of Noah, titled "God Promises to Rescue Noah," immediately begins with the theme of safety and by establishing God as a friend:

"I'll keep you safe!" God promised His friend.
"My world has gone wrong and I'm starting again."
So God sent a flood, and they all sailed away,
And floated and floated, for day after day![268]

According to the story, God is the one who causes the flood, but the text does not mention that anyone drowns and seems to suggest that "they all" sailed safely on the ark. The story ends, "When their boat landed safely, they all said, 'PHEW!' And when God makes a promise, you know that it's true!"[269]

The production design of three offerings by Zondervan Publishers' children's division, ZonderKids, perhaps best illustrates adults' desire to have children relate the Bible and God to warm and friendly feelings. In 2007, ZonderKids offered another edition of Lloyd-Jones's *Tiny Bear's Bible*. This one has a plush cover shaped and designed to look like a cute smiling teddy bear with blue overalls, and the packaging includes the words, "A bear to hug, a Bible to love."[270] Here, the message of comfort is delivered not only through words and pictures, but through a tactile element as well. The text of this children's Bible, as noted above, repeatedly assures children that God will keep them safe. This edition of the book, however, doubles as a teddy bear that they can cuddle. The *Baby's Hug-a-Bible*, from 2010, also written by Lloyd-Jones, is designed with a soft, faux lamb's wool cover. The official product description reads as follows: "A Bible you can hug! In this soft and cuddly book, little ones will find a collection of ten favorite Bible stories in rhyme, filled with comforting truths and promises. Keep God's word close to baby's heart in this perfect introduction for the very young to the stories of the Bible and to God's great love for them."[271] The story of Noah's ark is accompanied by Claudine Gévry's colorful illustration of a smiling panda, two giraffes, and a crocodile on the boat with Noah and the dove. Lloyd-Jones's text again presents readers with a friendly and helpful God. She begins the story of Noah by asking children, "Who kept Noah safe from harm? Who brought him safely through the storm?"[272] She soon provides

268. Lloyd-Jones, *Tiny Bear's Bible*, n.p.

269. Ibid.

270. Ibid.

271. Ibid.

272. Sally Lloyd-Jones, *Baby's Hug-a-Bible*, illus. by Claudine Gévry (New York: HarperFestival, 2010), n.p.

the answer, "Yes, God's the one. And guess what too? Yes, little one, God cares for you."[273] P. J. Lyons's *Little Lion's Bible*, from 2011, has a cover made of soft artificial fur in the shape of a small lion. The packaging invites children to "Cuddle Up with Little Lion and Know God's Love."[274] The one-page story of Noah, titled "God's Friend Noah," begins "in a time when folks were bad, Only Noah made God glad. God said 'Noah, build a ship, Pack a zoo, and take a trip.'"[275] The accompanying illustration by Melanie Mitchell shows a happy Noah with a smiling panda, puppy, giraffe, and a shy Little Lion, all on a small, overstuffed ark. Still, even though there is mention that folks were bad, the fact that all living things that had breath perished in the flood is naturally erased from this retelling, as it is in all of these fuzzy children's Bibles. More significant than the details of the text of the stories themselves, however, is the fact that the Bible itself, and by extension the God who is described within it, has literally become a warm and fuzzy feeling for children.

2.4.b. The case of the Brick Bible: Against the tide

The extent to which the story of Noah has become a story of God's care rather than God's judgment, and a story of how God keeps children safe rather than that God might destroy them, is best illustrated by a book that at first glance may seem like an exception to the rule. Brendan Powell Smith, who according to an article in *Rolling Stone* magazine is an avowed atheist,[276] started posting his irreverent adaptations of Bible stories online in 2001. Smith's stories are illustrated with photographs of Bible scenes he has created with Lego blocks and Lego Minifigures. These have been published in a variety of formats for adult readers, including *The Brick Bible: A New Spin on the Old Testament*. Seeing the scenes Smith has created, one suspects that he and his readers take some pleasure in using children's toys to depict the sex and violence in Bible stories that is often glossed over in religious education materials and sermons. Smith, however, claims to have a serious religious education goal. In his introduction to the book, he claims "I have been inspired to do this for one reason: people should really know what's in the Bible. For a book that so many of us consider our ultimate moral guide and the very word of God, it can be shocking to consider how few people ever actually read it."[277] The results may be considered irreverent but are surprisingly faithful to the words and events of the Bible. The story of Noah and the flood includes some disturbing scenes of the flood waters overcoming those outside the ark and even has Noah's family and the animals walking through skeletons and corpses as they leave the ark.[278]

---

273. Ibid.

274. P. J. Lyons, *Little Lion's Bible*, illus. by Melanie Mitchell (Grand Rapids, MI: Zondervan, 2011).

275. Ibid.

276. C. Spencer Beggs, "Brick Testament," *Rolling Stone*, October 6, 2005, 98.

277. Brendan Powell Smith, *The Brick Bible: A New Spin on the Old Testament* (New York: Skyhorse, 2011), 7.

278. Ibid., 27–9.

Given the disturbing nature of Smith's scenes, it is quite remarkable to find that some of his adaptations have been turned into an actual children's Bible intended for children. Smith's 2012 *Noah's Ark: The Brick Bible for Kids* uses images that are toned down a bit from those he created for his adult readers, but they are still quite harsh compared to most twenty-first-century children's Bibles. God is a character who appears throughout the story and Smith's Lego Minifigure version of God is male, has long white hair, a beard, wears a white robe, and is colored in the standard yellow color of most Minifigures, as is Noah and his family. Instead of wearing a friendly face and a smile like Noah, God wears a scowling frown and angry eyebrows throughout the story.

The story begins, "God decided He would wash away all the people and animals of the world with a great flood."[279] While Smith's retelling does use the image of washing, he also does not shy away from the fact that it is not just a principle, such as evil or error, that is being washed away, but people and animals who are actually drowning. As the story continues, it includes some scenes that could be disturbing to young children. In one scene, people who are clearly in distress, with panicked expressions on their faces, are shown running from the rising waters.[280] The following page has the somewhat benign text, "The water rose so high that the ark Noah built was lifted off the ground."[281] The photograph on the page, however, shows Lego Minifigures now naked and with distressed, pained, and panicked expressions on their faces as they are overwhelmed by the floodwaters. There are also various portions of Minifigures bodies, such as a stray arm, leg, and head, broken apart from the rest of their bodies and floating in the water. One suspects that Smith had fun creating the scene, but in any case it presents an image that could be quite distressing to young children. Smith's text on the following page leaves no doubt that "all the people drowned."[282]

As Smith continues the story, he also includes the scene of Noah offering a goat on an altar, a scene that is often mentioned but rarely illustrated in children's Bibles of the twentieth and twenty-first centuries. The text reads, "Noah was thankful to God, so he built an altar and made an offering."[283] The accompanying image shows an altar made with Lego bricks, wood, and on top of it a gentle-looking goat. Noah stands by the altar holding a lit torch in one hand and a shiny knife in the other. Smith does end his story on a positive note, with the rainbow in the sky and God's promise to never again drown the world.[284]

While Smith's version of the story could be seen as more faithful to the Genesis account of Noah's ark than many other children's Bibles of its day, it is interesting to note that the publishers include a fairly lengthy letter to parents at the beginning

---

279. Brendan Powell Smith, *Noah's Ark: The Brick Bible for Kids* (New York: Sky Pony Press, 2012), 6.

280. Ibid.

281. Ibid., 20.

282. Ibid., 21.

283. Ibid., 28.

284. Ibid., 29–31.

of the book. Reverend Wanda M. Lundy, who the book informs readers is the Director of the Doctor of Ministry Program at New York Theological Seminary, is the author of the letter. Lundy tells parents that the book provides "child-friendly illustrations of the biblical story by utilizing a familiar toy, LEGO® building blocks, to introduce difficult subjects, such as the drowning of all the world's people by God (which is illustrated in this book)."[285] As Lundy continues, she warns parents that the story could be distressing to their children and encourages them to use the story as the beginning of a conversation:

> Your child might ask hard questions like "Why did God make the people drown?" or "Why would God kill people?" Depending on your child's age, your child may really be asking you if he is going to be drown [sic] or if God is going to kill her. Try turning the question into a conversation about the child's safety. Reaffirm that you will be there to help your child through any difficult times in life. Explain to the child that every time he sees a rainbow in the sky, it is a reminder of God's love for all creation.[286]

Lundy concludes, "A great value of the Bible is that it challenges us to think about who we are in the world and how we are to be in relationship with each other. The story of Noah and the ark is a story that can bring us closer to each other and closer to God."[287]

In terms of its content, then, Smith's Brick Bible version of the story of Noah is the exception that proves the rule. Unlike most children's Bibles of the twenty-first century, it does include images of a God who is angry rather than happy and who kills those outside of the ark. However, precisely because it does so, it is evident that the publishers felt it necessary to switch the narrative by instructing parents to assure their children that they are safe and that God loves them. Whereas children's Bibles of the eighteenth and nineteenth centuries would have used this tale precisely in order to warn children of God's righteous anger and that God could and would destroy them at any time if they were not obedient, the gospel of the twenty-first century is that children, especially young children, are to be made to feel that they are loved and that they are safe.

2.4.c. Concluding remarks on stories of a friendly God who keeps children safe

Children who get their perspective on the character of God from these late twentieth- and early twenty-first century children's Bibles will likely continue to grow into the teenagers who hold to the Moral Therapeutic Deism described by Smith and Denton. God is there to keep children safe from the storms of life. The one difference, however, is that many of these children's Bibles of the twenty-first century seem to model a more personal and intimate friendship with God than

---

285. Ibid., 1.
286. Ibid.
287. Ibid.

the studies showed. God not only takes care of Noah in a time of storm but in many cases is considered a friend with whom one can chat.

Though each of these children's Bibles nuances their message in subtle ways, the remarkably persistent message in all of these many examples of late twentieth- and early twenty-first-century children's Bible retellings of the story of Noah is that God is a friendly God who keeps people safe. Since so many children's Bibles use the story of Noah to convey this message, it would be easy to forget that the exact same story was commonly used in the 1830s and the decades that followed to teach children the lesson, "Oh! How dreadful it is to disobey such a powerful God, who can destroy us in a moment, if he please!"[288]

2.5. The Character of Allah in Children's Qur'ans

The later years of the twentieth century and early years of the twenty-first century have also seen the publication in the United States of a few storybooks with stories from the Qur'an. Unlike Christian and Jewish children's Bibles, the prophets are either not pictured or their faces are obscured. References to Noah, or "Nuh," are scattered throughout the Qur'an, so it is interesting to note which parts of the story are selected and highlighted by these books to present different perspectives on the character of Allah.

In 1998, Iman Publishing offered a box-set collection of six board books by Siddiqu Juma titled *Stories of the Prophets from the Qur'an*. The set included books devoted to Adam, Nuh (Noah), Ibrahim (Abraham), Musa (Moses), Isa (Jesus), and Muhammad. The story of Nuh begins, following the account in the Qur'an, with Nuh rather than God first complaining about the wicked people. According to the story, "Nuh (*pbuh*) complained to Allah: 'These people do not believe in you, they laugh at me when I tell them about you and your creations.'"[289] Later in the story, Juma follows the Qur'an's account that some outside of Nuh's family believed and were saved: "Only a few people believed in Nuh (*pbuh*) and got into the ark with him."[290] Unlike many Christian storybooks for young readers written during this time, Juma does not avoid the fact that, "Everybody drowned except for those on the sea."[291] The rest of the story, however, plays out in much the same way as many Protestant Christian children's Bibles do. The people mock Noah: "Allah told Nuh (*pbuh*) to build a huge ark. People laughed at him because there was no sea for him to sail in the ark."[292] Noah tries to warn them: "Nuh (*pbuh*) warned the people that heavy rains would fall and drown all the unbelievers."[293]

---

288. Goodrich, *Peter Parley's Book*, 19, and Barton, *Bible Letters*, 11.

289. Siddiqa Juma, *Nuh (Noah) (Peace be upon him)* (Elmhurst, NY: Tahrike Tarsile Qur'an, Inc., 1998), n.p.

290. Ibid.

291. Ibid.

292. Ibid.

293. Ibid.

While these story elements do not appear in the Book of Genesis, they do appear in the Qur'an (cf. Qur'anic verses 11.38). According to the last two pages of the book, "Nuh (*pbuh*) led all the creatures safely unto dry land. Nuh (*pbuh*) and his companions were filled with joy to breathe the cool fresh air and see the wonderful creations of Allah."[294] The story, then, ends by noting the blessings of Allah's creation.

Saniyasnain Khan's *My First Quran Storybook* from 2007 is similar to many Christian children's Bibles in the way that it emphasizes the message that Allah kept Nuh and his family safe and puts less emphasis on the destruction of the wicked. The book is filled with colorful illustrations of smiling animals, landscapes, and various scenes, but the prophets themselves are not illustrated. According to the book's story of "The Ark of Nuh," Nuh "would go house to house and talk to people about Allah" and that "the people laughed at Nuh."[295] Khan's text does not avoid the fact that the people drowned in the flood. As Khan puts it, "They said, 'We are not scared of the rain!' They were not scared of Allah. They all drowned in the flood."[296] Khan's retelling emphasizes, however, that "Everybody was safe in the boat"[297] and that, while everyone was afraid during the storm, "Allah was watching over them."[298] After the flood, "they thanked Allah for keeping them safe."[299] Khan closes the tale by noting, "Allah made the flood and the Ark of Nuh (*pbuh*) a Sign and warning to future generations."[300] Like many twenty-first-century Christian children's Bible authors, Khan emphasizes Allah's care for people and how Allah keeps them safe.

Ruth Woodhall and Shahada Sharelle Abdul Haqq's *Stories of the Prophets in the Holy Qur'an* from 2008 places less emphasis on the fact that Allah kept Noah safe than on the importance of believing in God and God's prophets. The illustrations do show people, but the faces of the prophets are always turned away from the reader and obscured by hoods. This version points out that, as Noah preached, "Only the weak, the poor, and the common people believed his words. His message came as mercy to their hearts."[301] Meanwhile, "the rulers, the rich, the strong, and the powerful" rejected his message.[302] Abdul Haqq relates the story from the Qur'an, passed over by Khan, that Noah's wife and son were disbelievers and would not join him on the ark. They, therefore, were not spared from the flood. When Noah asks God why his son had to die, "God replied that

294. Ibid.

295. Saniyasnain Khan, *My First Quran Storybook* (Nizamuddin West, New Delhi: Goodword, 2007), 74.

296. Ibid., 78.

297. Ibid., 77.

298. Ibid., 78.

299. Ibid., 80.

300. Ibid.

301. Ruth Woodhall and Shahada Sharelle Abdul Haqq, *Stories of the Prophets in the Holy Qur'an* (Somerset, NJ: Tughra Books, 2008), 14.

302. Ibid.

the Prophet Noah's son was not of the righteous people."[303] Noah then apologizes for questioning God, "for God knows what we do not know."[304] According to the story, when "the earth had been washed clean of wrong doers," God stopped the rain and the waters.[305] Later, as Noah lay dying, he gathered his surviving sons and passed on some of the key teachings of Islam. Specifically, "he warned his sons never to forget that there is no god but God. He also warned them that they should never worship any other thing, and that they should avoid being full of pride."[306] The emphasis, then, is on remembering to worship God and God alone. Those who are disbelievers are excluded from the safety that God provides.

Like children's Bibles, then, this small sample of children's Qur'ans suggest that these authors draw from their holy Scripture in diverse ways in order to highlight different aspects of the character of Allah.

2.6. Conclusions

One can glean many lessons from this survey of children's Bibles. For one thing, it demonstrates just how multivalent and malleable these biblical narratives can be. Throughout history, parents, religious educators, and clergy have struggled with the story of Noah and how to use it to teach children what they believe about who God is and how God relates to humankind. This survey illustrates the myriad of ways in which this has been done.

In terms of theology proper—that is, the understandings of who God is and how God acts—the God of children's Bibles has gone through a remarkable transformation in terms of both behaviors and personality over the course of American history. If the primary message of children's Bibles' adaptations of the story of Noah in the late eighteenth and early nineteenth century was that children should not consider themselves safe from God's wrath or from death, by the later half of the twentieth century, most children's Bibles retold the same Bible story in ways that taught children the exact opposite lesson: that God is their friend and that God will keep them safe no matter what. God, then, has been transformed from a God who is a righteous judge whom sinners should fear to a kinder and gentler God who is patient and ready to forgive but eventually obliged to judge for justice's sake and finally to a friendly God whose only agenda is to keep people safe.

These stories also illustrate the changing goals of religious education in America. In this chapter alone the story of Noah's ark has been used to convey very different lessons to children about the character of God and the natural world in which they live. Do our children need to understand the world as a dangerous place where death is near and the divine force at work in the world as one that is potentially threatening if one does not pay it proper homage? Or should children

303. Ibid., 16.
304. Ibid.
305. Ibid., 18.
306. Ibid.

be persuaded that the story of Noah is not as harsh and frightening as it may seem at first glance and that God is not cruel, hasty, or unreasonable in doling out divine judgment? Or should the story of Noah be used to assure children that they live in a safe world with a friendly Deity who loves them, cares for them, and will always keep them safe?

The chapters that follow expand the scope of the study to explore even further uses of the story of Noah in children's Bibles, including how the story has been adapted and appropriated to teach children various lessons regarding salvation and the life of virtue.

Chapter 3

THE BIBLE AS A SOURCEBOOK OF SALVATION: THE STORY OF NOAH AS A STORY ABOUT SALVATION IN JESUS CHRIST

My dear reader, if you have not entered into this ark of safety; if you have not trusted in Christ,—delay it no longer. A deluge is coming,—the deluge of God's terrible displeasure against sin in the future world—fear lest it may overwhelm you in endless and hopeless ruin![1]

T. H. Gallaudet, *Scripture Biography for the Young* (1838)

Did you know that when God saved Noah in the ark, it was part of his plan to save us? That is true because one day Jesus, our Savior, would be born as a far-off grandchild in Noah's family. There was only one way to be saved from the waters of the flood: you had to go through the door of the ark. And there is only one way to be saved from our sin. Jesus said, "I am the way" (John 14:6). The next time you see a rainbow in the sky, don't just remember the way God saved Noah. Remember Jesus and the way his death brought salvation to us.[2]

Marty Machowski, *The Gospel Story Bible: Discovering Jesus in the Old and New Testaments* (2011)

3.1. American Christianity's Focus on Jesus

Throughout American history, a significant number of children's Bibles have transformed the story of Noah's ark into a story about salvation in Jesus Christ. The previous chapter examined a number of children's Bibles that used the story of Noah and the flood to warn children about the wrath of God and assure them of God's mercy. Many of the examples in this chapter follow the same pattern but go a step further by making explicit connections between the story of Noah's ark and

1. T. H. Gallaudet, *Scripture Biography for the Young, with Critical Illustrations and Practical Remarks*, Vol. 1, *Adam to Jacob* (New York: American Tract Society, 1838), 67–8.

2. Marty Machowski, *The Gospel Story Bible: Discovering Jesus in the Old and New Testaments* (Greensboro, NC: New Growth Press, 2011), 14.

salvation in Jesus Christ. Taking a story that even by conservative estimates takes place over 2,000 years before Jesus' birth and turning it into a story about him may be troubling to some, but it represents a significant strain in the way Christians have used the Hebrew Bible. These examples attest to the desire of many children's Bible authors and publishers to pass on to children their belief that Jesus Christ is central to their faith and the central focus of their Scriptures, including the stories of the Hebrew Bible.

For nearly 200 years, American Christians have had a special relationship with Jesus Christ. This statement may seem obvious and somewhat redundant. In his book, *American Jesus: How the Son of God Became a National Icon*, however, Stephen Prothero details the particular ways in which American Christianity transitioned from the Puritans' focus on God the Father to a faith that has increasingly focused on the person of Jesus Christ. As Prothero notes, "In Puritan theology, Christ had a limited role to play; Jesus had almost none."[3] From the 1830s to the 1850s, however, preachers increasingly shifted focus from God to Jesus.[4] This focus on Jesus Christ continues. Prothero notes that, in contrast to the fading belief in Christianity in Europe, two-thirds of Americans claim to have made a personal commitment to Jesus Christ.[5] As Prothero puts it, "In the United States today, virtually all Christians are Jesus people."[6]

Furthermore, throughout America's history, American ministers and authors from a variety of theological perspectives have encouraged Christians to see Christ throughout their Old Testament. The early eighteenth-century minister Edward Taylor's collection of sermons titled *Upon the Types of the Old Testament* encouraged readers to see Christ both in the person of Noah and the ark.[7] The prominent nineteenth-century American physician William Hanna Thomson wrote *The Great Argument, or Jesus Christ in the Old Testament*.[8] In the twentieth century, Kenneth E. Trent offered *Types of Christ in the Old Testament: A Conservative Approach to Old Testament Typology*.[9] In the twenty-first century, David Murray wrote *Jesus on Every Page: 10 Simple Ways to Seek and Find Christ in the Old Testament*.[10] These authors represent just a few of the many American

---

3. Stephen Prothero, *American Jesus: How the Son of God Became a National Icon* (New York: Farrar, Straus and Giroux, 2003), 11.

4. See Prothero, *American Jesus*, 52–5.

5. Ibid., 11.

6. Ibid., 43.

7. Edward Taylor, *Upon the Types of the Old Testament*, ed. Charles W. Mignon (Lincoln, NE: University of Nebraska Press, 1989).

8. William Hanna Thomson, *The Great Argument, or Jesus Christ in the Old Testament* (New York: Harper, 1884).

9. Kenneth E. Trent, *Types of Christ in the Old Testament: A Conservative Approach to Old Testament Typology* (New York: Exposition Press, 1960).

10. David Murray, *Jesus on Every Page: 10 Simple Ways to Seek and Find Christ in the Old Testament* (Nashville, TN: Thomas Nelson, 2013).

Bible scholars and pastors who have encouraged their readers to see Jesus Christ in the stories of the Old Testament in a wide variety of ways.

How, then, do American children's Bibles reflect the country's focus on Jesus Christ? For a significant number of children's Bible authors, illustrators, and publishers, devotion to Jesus Christ means that the story of Noah should be transformed into a story that is ultimately about salvation in Jesus Christ or Christ's Church. While the examples examined in this chapter do not represent all or even the majority of children's Bibles that have been published in the United States, they are a significant sampling and reflect a significant strain of American Christianity. Furthermore, these examples help illustrate how important it has been to some American Christian parents and other Christian leaders that their children come to understand and accept salvation in Christ and that they recognize the Bible, including the Hebrew Bible, as a thoroughly Christian book.

3.2. Noah as a Type of Christ

3.2.a. Typological interpretation

Christian authors have been using the story of Noah, the flood, and the ark to reflect upon their faith since the writing of the New Testament.[11] Early Christian literature saw the ark as an Old Testament "type" of Christ fulfilled in Jesus' life and work and made allegorical interpretations of Noah's life and Noah's ark that related them to Christ, Christ's Church, and salvation.[12] Throughout the Middle Ages, allegorical and typological interpretations of Scripture were the norm. Protestant reformers, however, attacked the use of allegorical and typological interpretations and instead argued that readers should seek the literal sense of Bible passages. With the emergence of the historical-critical method in biblical studies, many nineteenth- and twentieth-century Bible scholars viewed allegorical or typological interpretations as suspect or rejected them entirely. Others, however, defended the use of types under certain conditions by making a clear distinction between typological readings and allegorical readings of Scripture.[13]

Those who argued that typological interpretations of the Scriptures were legitimate argued that the New Testament, in places, models this approach. Adam,

---

11. See, for example, Mt. 24.37-39, Lk. 17.26-30, Heb. 11.7, 2 Pet. 2.4-10, and 2 Pet. 3.1-13.

12. See, for example, Justin Martyr's "Dialogue with Trypho," in Justin Martyr, *Writings of Saint Justin Martyr* (New York: Christian Heritage, Inc., 1948), 360, and Origen's "Genesis Homily II," in Origen, *Homilies on Genesis and Exodus*, trans. Ronald E. Heine (Washington, DC: Catholic University of America Press, 1981), 86.

13. For a helpful brief survey of this history, see Brevard S. Childs, *Biblical Theology of the Old and New Testaments: Theological Reflection on the Christian Bible* (Minneapolis, MN: Fortress Press, 1992), 13–14.

they argued, could be seen as an Old Testament type that is realized in the New Testament antitype of Jesus Christ (Rom. 5.12-17). In his influential book *The Typology of Scripture*, first published in Britain in 1847 and then published in the United States in a second edition soon afterward, Scottish theologian Patrick Fairbairn drew a clear distinction between allegories and types. According to Fairbairn, allegories could be based upon fictitious stories or actual events, while types "indispensably require the reality of the facts or circumstances stated in the original narrative."[14] Furthermore, Fairbairn argued that while allegorical inter-pretations often veer significantly from the point of the original story, typological interpretations require that "the same truth or principle be embodied alike in the type and the antitype."[15] In almost all cases, this truth related to redemption history. In the case of the story of Noah and the flood, Fairbairn does not argue that the ark is a type of Christ. Instead, he explores the statement that Noah and his family "were saved through water. And baptism, which this prefigured, now saves you" (1 Pet. 3.20a-21b). For Fairbairn, this serves as a type because, in his view, the flood actually took place and it contains the same spiritual truth as baptism does. In order to find the same truth in Noah's flood as is found in Peter's words about baptism and salvation, Fairbairn makes the point that Noah and his family were not saved *from* the flood, but *by* the flood. To do this, Fairbairn argues that Noah was saved not from drowning in the flood, but from "the real danger—the corruption, enmity, and violence of ungodly men."[16] This influence of ungodly men was, according to Fairbairn, the very thing "which wasted the church of God, and brought it to the verge of destruction."[17] Therefore, Fairbairn argues that the deluge was Noah's baptism or "the means of his salvation from an outward form of spiritual danger."[18] He concludes, "So that the deluge, considered as Noah's baptism, or the means of his salvation from an outward form of spiritual danger, was not less essentially connected with a work of judgment than with an act of mercy."[19] The flood, then, was a type of baptism because it was a historical event and represented the same spiritual truth as baptism, and because both were means by which people were saved from spiritual destruction by the influence of ungodly men.

Given the popularity of typological interpretations by nineteenth-century preachers and the renewed defense of typology in the twentieth century,[20] it is surprising to discover that while there are a few early nineteenth-century children's Bibles that use the term "type" before Fairbairn's work or the renewed defense of the approach in the 1930s, the term "type" is rarely if ever used in children's Bibles in the years that follow. Still, most Protestant children's Bibles adhere to the principal

14. Patrick Fairbairn, *The Typology of Scripture* (Philadelphia, PA: Smith and English, 1854), 18.

15. Ibid., 19.

16. Ibid., 282.

17. Ibid.

18. Ibid., 283.

19. Ibid.

20. Childs, *Biblical Theology*, 13.

distinction between a type and allegory by drawing a connection between Noah's ark and Jesus Christ. They refrain, however, from engaging in extended allegorical interpretations. Instead, they attempt to find the same spiritual truth in Noah's salvation through the ark and believers' salvation in Jesus Christ.

3.2.b. Noah's ark described as a "type" of Christ in early nineteenth-century American children's Bibles

An early American example of a book that calls the ark a "type" of Christ is the 1830 edition of the American Sunday School Union's *Union Questions on Selected Portions of Scripture*. The *Union Questions*, which were used with all ages, including children, had both "primary questions" and "interpretive questions." The primary questions were printed in large type and, like Bible catechisms, focused on matters of biblical content. So, for example, the primary questions on the story of Noah in Genesis chapter six were questions that asked readers to recall words from the verses, such as,

> 9. How does the ninth verse begin? ...
> What kind of man was Noah?
> With whom did Noah walk?[21]

and

> 10. How many sons had Noah, and what were their names?[22]

The *Union Questions* interpretive questions, however, which were printed in smaller type, often in these early years led readers to reflect on the state of human-kind's sinfulness and need for salvation in Christ. Regarding the story of Noah in Genesis chapter six, for example, these interpretive questions asked:

> What will become of those who *now* will not flee for refuge to the hope laid
>   before them in the gospel?
> Whose fault will it be if they are for ever shut out from Christ and heaven?
> What does Jesus say in Luke xiii. 24, to those who sin away the time until it is
>   too late?[23]

and,

> What do you learn from Noah's conduct in patiently waiting for the command
>   of God? Prov. i. I, 5, 6.

21. *Union Questions on Selected Portions of Scripture*, Vol. III (Philadelphia, PA: American Sunday School Union, 1830), 25.
22. Ibid.
23. Ibid., 29.

What do you learn of the dealings of God with the wicked, from this account
  of the flood?
Why is the ark considered a type of Christ?
… In whom alone can you find safety on that awful day?[24]

The *Union Questions*, then, did not limit itself to being a pure Bible catechism, asking questions only about the words of the Bible itself. Here, one of the few questions calling readers to make theological interpretations of the story asks readers to consider the ark as a type of Christ.

Scripture History, or Short Sketches of Characters from the Old Testament, published in 1829, is an early example of a children's Bible that uses the word "type" to describe Noah's ark. Each page from the short book includes an illustration, a poem retelling the Bible story, and a lesson at the bottom of the page. For the story of Noah, the small woodcut illustration shows Noah kneeling before the ark with arms outstretched in praise. The poem on the page reads,

THE FLOOD
The mighty waters of the Flood,
Proclaim a sin-avenging God,
But those who in the ark were found,
Were saved when all besides were drown'd.
That ark a type of Christ we deem:
O may our souls be found in Him.[25]

In a dubious effort at rhyming, the poem declares, "The mighty waters of the Flood, Proclaim a sin-avenging God."[26] The poem, then, does little to minimize the harsh judgment of God. God is a sin-avenging God and all the people drowned. The lesson at the bottom of the page explains, "That ark was a type of our Lord Jesus Christ. None will be saved at last, but those who are found in Him."[27] This example, then, highlights the potential judgment of God and draws a connection between the ark and Jesus Christ. It does not, however, explicitly call children to repent and turn to Christ as do many children's Bibles from later in the century. Instead, it concludes with the relatively passive sentiment, "may our souls be found in Him."

In 1832's *Scripture Prints, with explanations in the form of familiar dialogues*, Mary Sherwood, a prolific Calvinistic writer of her time, takes a similar approach.[28]

24. Ibid., 32.
25. *Scripture History, or Short Sketches of Characters from the Old Testament* (New York: Mahlon Day, 1829), 5.
26. Ibid.
27. Ibid.
28. For an interesting analysis of Mary Sherwood's writing, see Neil Cocks, "'Scripture Its Own Interpreter': Mary Martha Sherwood, *The Bible* and Female Autobiography," *Nineteenth-Century Gender Studies* 7:3 (Winter 2011). http://www.ncgsjournal.com/issue73/cocks.htm (accessed May 25, 2014).

Sherwood has a wise grandmother teach her granddaughter Sophia the "emblem" of the ark:

Grandmother … What is the ark like, Sophia? Of what is it the emblem?
Sophia. Indeed, grandmamma, I am not able to say.

Grandmother. It is a type of the church of Christ, wherein all who are spiritually admitted, will be carried safely through the storms of life, and landed on a new earth, where seed-time and harvest, day and night, summer and winter, shall never cease.[29]

Later, Grandmother concludes, "The door, then, of the ark, was a type of Christ our Lord. Whilst this door was open, it was a type of mercy to the people before the flood."[30] Sherwood, then, distinguishes two separate types of Christ in the story. The ark is a type of the Church. Meanwhile, the door to the ark serves as a type of Christ. Readers may infer that they should enter this door, but Sherwood does not urge readers to turn to Christ in the manner in which many children's Bibles of the revivalist era would.

The authors of these three books name the ark (or the door of the ark) a "type of Christ" and apparently felt that it was worthwhile to introduce or remind youth of the term "type." In so doing, they provide anecdotal evidence that the term and concept was present in the American Christian mindset in the earlier years of the nineteenth century before the writings of Fairbairn and others popularized it in more formal biblical studies. In the years that followed, children's Bibles would assume even more human agency on the part of their readers and explicitly call children to repent and turn to Christ to escape the judgment of God. Given the popularity of books for adults on biblical "types" of Christ in the nineteenth and twentieth century, however, it is interesting to note that children's Bibles from the years that followed these examples rarely if ever use the term "type" to describe the relationship between Noah's ark and Jesus Christ to children.

3.3. The Story of the Deluge as an Altar Call to Christ in the Nineteenth Century

3.3.a. Revivalism in nineteenth-century America

Throughout the later nineteenth century, a significant number of American children's Bibles retold the story of Noah's ark and other Bible stories in a manner similar to how revivalist preachers used the texts, emphasizing God's judgment on the wicked and salvation through Jesus Christ. Before examining examples of

29. Mary Sherwood, *Scripture Prints, with explanations in the form of familiar dialogues* (New York: Pendleton and Hill, 1832), 102.
   30. Ibid., 111.

how the story of Noah and the ark was adapted to highlight these themes, it will be helpful to establish some of the contexts in which these children's Bibles were produced.

It is difficult to understand Christianity in the United States without understanding the influence of the Christian revivals that swept the American colonies during the First Great Awakening beginning in the 1730s and continued through the so-called Second Great Awakening of the nineteenth century. From the 1830s to 1850s, sermons in America began to focus increasingly on the person of Jesus and Jesus Christ's role as savior to lost sinners.[31] As the revivalist movement in the United States progressed further into the nineteenth century, Christian educators focused increasingly on human agency by calling children to make the decision to repent and turn to God for salvation.

Many Protestant Christians' theological beliefs led them to assume that young children were born in depravity and could do nothing on their own to please God until the time of their conversion. Only after they made a personal decision to repent and turn to Jesus Christ as their savior could God's work of sanctification begin and could children do good. These beliefs led to an emphasis on the need for personal salvation and had a profound effect on the Christian education of children. Those who held to this view did not attempt to teach children to act morally, for they believed that their children were incapable of being good before their moment of conversion. As detailed in the previous chapter, much religious education for children in the eighteenth and early nineteenth centuries focused instead on putting the fear of God into children and making them totally aware of their sinfulness and mortality and need of salvation.[32] As Kenneth O. Gangel and Warren S. Benson put it,

> The practical outcome of the foregoing beliefs was that parents were to teach their children that they were not Christians and that when they reached such an age as appropriate for deep conversion, they should respond to Christ in faith. Prior to that time it was the parents' duty continually to point out the sinfulness of the child to him and to prepare him for conversion at a later date.[33]

The nineteenth-century Congregational minister and theologian Horace Bushnell characterized the prevailing view of his time as one that assumed "that the child is to grow up in sin, to be converted after he comes to a mature age."[34] Bushnell

---

31. See Prothero, *American Jesus*, 52–5.

32. Cf. Steven Mintz, *Huck's Raft: A History of American Childhood* (Cambridge, MA: Harvard University Press, 2004), 17.

33. Kenneth O. Gangel and Warren S. Benson, *Christian Education: Its History & Philosophy* (Chicago: Moody Press, 1983), 279.

34. Horace Bushnell, *Christian Nurture* (New York: Charles Scriber's Sons, 1888, 1916), 4.

argued against this approach, but his view was not accepted by the majority of the people of his time.

A strong strain of religious education of children in the United States, then, beginning in the mid-1800s and continuing into the twentieth century, focused on convincing children of their own sinfulness, reminding them of the potential nearness of death and judgment of God, and encouraging them to turn to Christ for salvation.[35]

3.3.b. Revivalists' use of the story of Noah as a call to salvation

Revivalist preachers had a long tradition of using the story of Noah as a sermon text to call sinners to repentance and salvation. In the 1740s, during the Great Awakening, Jonathan Edwards used the story of Noah as the primary text for his sermon "The Manner in Which Salvation of the Soul is to be Sought."[36] Over a century later, in 1885, revivalist preacher Dwight L. Moody used the story of Noah as the text for his sermon "Day of Rest: Come Thou Into the Ark"[37] in a very similar manner. These sermons, preached over a century apart, illustrate the persistent use of the story of Noah as a story that calls people to repent and turn to Christ for salvation. The sermons both use the embellishments, not in the Genesis account, of Noah preaching words of warning to his neighbors, Noah's neighbors mocking him and ignoring the warnings, and the wicked crying out for help when the flood comes and regretting that they had not heeded Noah's warnings of God's coming judgment. The preachers use these embellishments to transform the story of Noah into a compelling call to salvation. Edwards' and Moody's sermons provide a template of sorts for how to use the story of Noah as a compelling call to salvation. Both preachers proclaimed to their audiences that 1) Noah preached and provided fair warning to the people of his day and preachers in the present day give sinners the same warning of God's coming judgment. 2) The wicked mockers of Noah's day ignored the warnings of God's coming judgment and people today should not ignore the warnings of God's coming judgment. 3) When the flood comes, the mockers wish they had repented in time and so it shall be with those in the present day who put off repenting and do not immediately turn to Christ for salvation. 4) In Noah's day the unrepentant were judged by the water of the flood, but in the present day God will judge the world by fire. 5) There are implicit and explicit connections between God's mercy in providing Noah's safety

35. See Anne M. Boylan, *Sunday School: The Formation of an American Institution 1790–1880* (New Haven, CT: Yale University Press, 1988), 147, and Robert W. Lynn and Elliott Wright, *The Big Little School*, rev. edn (Birmingham, AL: Religious Education Press, 1980), 121–2.

36. Jonathan Edwards, "The Manner in Which Salvation is to be Sought," in *Sermons of Jonathan Edwards* (Peabody, MA: Hendrickson Publishing, Inc., 2005), 357–75.

37. Dwight L. Moody, "Day of Rest: Come Thou Into the Ark," *The Aroha News* 4:175 (October 23, 1886): 8. A scan of the newspaper page can be found at http://paperspast. natlib.govt.nz/cgi-bin/paperspast?a=d&d=TAN18861023.2.48 (accessed May 9, 2014).

and salvation in the ark and God's mercy to people in the present day shown by providing them with safety and salvation in Jesus Christ. 6) Finally, the sermons emphasize the agency of humankind in salvation by focusing on the need for humans to choose to repent and turn to Jesus Christ for salvation and safety from judgment. Many children's Bibles of the nineteenth century follow this same pattern when they retell the story of Noah's ark.

One compelling feature of these sermons that stands out to current readers is their references to God's judgment of the earth by fire in the present day. The connection between the flood and future judgment by fire has New Testament precedence. In 2 Peter 3.6 there is an allusion to the flood, and 2 Peter 3.7 then warns that "the present heavens and earth have been reserved for fire, being kept until the day of judgment and destruction of the godless." References to a second, future judgment of God by fire can also be found in 1 Enoch and the writings of Flavius Josephus, Philo of Alexandria, and the Latin Vita Adam.[38] Matthew Henry's Commentary helped make the connection between the flood and a future judgment by fire well known to Americans. Henry's Commentary on 2 Peter was written in 1706 but was more widely available and influential in the eighteenth century.[39] In his comments on 2 Peter 3.7, Henry wrote "but the ruin that awaits this world, whenever it comes, will be absolutely a universal one; there will not be any part but what the devouring flames will seize upon, not a sanctuary left any where for the inhabitants to flee to, not a single spot in all this world where any one of them can be safe."[40] He continues by observing that "the old world was destroyed by water, but this is reserved unto fire, which shall burn up the wicked at the last day."[41] Many American clergy had access to Henry's reading of this passage.

Several of the children's Bibles examined below make the same reference to judgment by fire. The authors of these books tell how God provided a rainbow as a promise to never flood the world again but are not content to leave the story there. Instead, they apparently feel uneasy about leaving children with the comfort and reassurance that God would not flood the world again. Instead, to underscore the urgent need to seek salvation, they immediately follow the story of the rainbow with the warning that God will destroy the world by fire in the present day.

3.3.c. The reason the wicked needed to be punished and people need salvation

Another intriguing issue that the story of Noah and children's Bible adaptations of the story raise is the reason that God felt the need to punish the wicked, or,

38. See Sharon and Tishel, 144–6.

39. Allan M. Harman makes the point that Philip Henry, Charles Wesley, and George Whitfield were all reading Matthew Henry's in the eighteenth century. See Allan M. Harman, "The impact of Matthew Henry's *Exposition* on eighteenth-century Christianity," *Evangelical Quarterly* 82:1 (2010): 14.

40. Matthew Henry and Thomas Scott, *Commentary on the Holy Bible: Matthew–Revelation* (Nashville, TN: Royal Publishers, 1979), 415.

41. Ibid.

put another way, how does Christ's sacrifice save sinners from judgment? St. Anselm and John Calvin offered two slightly different theories of atonement. For Anselm, humankind's disobedience and sinful life dishonors God. To restore God's honor, God must seek satisfaction for this offense. Jesus Christ's sacrifice serves as satisfaction that restores God's honor. For John Calvin, the issue is the law. Humankind's sin violates the law and, because of God's righteous nature, God must punish that sin. Jesus Christ, then, stands as a substitute for humankind and receives the punishment for humankind's violation of the law.[42] Most children's Bibles do not provide a clear rationale one way or another as to why the wicked need to be judged. Other children's Bibles considered below, however, seem to reflect one approach or the other.

3.3.d. Nineteenth-century children's Bibles using the story of Noah as a call to repentance and salvation from God's judgment through Jesus Christ

As described in the previous chapter, many children's Bibles of the revivalist era used various strategies to adapt the story of Noah in ways that urge children to repent and accept God's mercy. The examples in this chapter take the additional steps of making an explicit connection between Noah's ark and Jesus Christ or between the ark and the Church of Jesus Christ and calling children to make a personal decision to turn toward salvation in Christ. At times, one can almost hear the strains of Charlotte Elliot's 1835 hymn "Just as I Am Without One Plea" as the authors make their own none-too-subtle plea for children to turn to Jesus Christ for salvation.

Sunday Evenings; or, An easy introduction to the reading of the Bible from 1832, written by an author identified only as female and the author of "The infant Christian's first catechism," serves as an early example of a children's Bible that uses the story of Noah to call children to salvation in Christ.

The author presents Bible stories through dialogues between a mother and her son Edward. The mother in the story suggests that there are two reasons that God had Noah work so hard to build the ark. She tells Edward, "There is no doubt, my child, that God could have made the ark for Noah; but God wished to try Noah's faith and obedience."[43] Mother also tells Edward, "And perhaps there was another reason for desiring Noah to build an ark, and such an ark as would take a long time to make, which was, that God wished to give the people plenty of time to repent."[44] The author alludes to 2 Peter 2.5 as evidence that Noah gave them plenty of warning:

42. For a helpful brief survey of classical models of atonement, see Tyron Inbody, *The Faith of the Christian Church* (Grand Rapids, MI: William B. Eerdmans Publishing Company, 2005), 218–23.

43. *Sunday evenings; or, An easy introduction to the reading of the Bible* (New York: J. & J. Harper, 1832), 29.

44. Ibid.

All the while Noah was building the ark these wicked people had time to repent, that is, to be sorry for their sins, and to begin to serve God. They saw Noah building his ark, and he had told them, you may be sure, what he was doing, and why he was doing it; and begged them over and over to leave off their wickedness, and to serve the Lord. There is no doubt of this, because Noah is called in the Bible a "preacher of righteousness"; which means, that he preached to the people, and tried to teach them what was right. But all would not do.[45]

After underscoring that the wicked people had plenty of time to repent in this way, the mother describes the flood:

Then was the whole of that pleasant earth covered with water. Think how dreadful it must have been! All the trees, and flowers, and fruits, all the houses also were swept away; the waters were exceedingly great; so great, that all the tall mountains and high hills under the whole heaven were covered, and all flesh died that moved upon the earth, both of fowl, and cattle, and beast, and of creeping thing; and every man, woman, and child, all who had the breath of life in them, *died.*[46]

The author, then, makes a special point of detailing that every "child" died, and for good measure italicizes the word "died" in the text.

After the mother tells Edward of these dreadful effects of disobeying God, she quickly shifts to telling him about the happy results of obeying God: "See here, my dear boy, how able God is to take care of those who serve him. Think of that little family, riding safely on those mighty waters, fearing no evil, for God was with them! See the happiness of serving God."[47] Mother does not stay focused exclusively on the positive, however, but also gives Edward a lesson about sin: "Learn, again, my child, to hate sin. Think how God must hate it, when it caused him to destroy that beautiful world which he had such pleasure in making, and all those people whom he had made to be good and happy here, and to live with him for ever afterward in heaven."[48] Here, then, the narrative introduces that image of heaven and the hope of living with God in heaven.

After describing Noah and his family's time on the ark, Mother describes Noah's sacrifice to God and God's promise, marked by a rainbow, to never destroy the world by flood again. Like many authors of her time, however, this author seems uncomfortable with leaving children with this assurance of safety from a gracious God. Instead, she moves directly from God's promise to never flood the earth again to a word of warning:

Though this pretty world is never to be drowned again, the Bible tells us that it is, one day, to be burned up with fire. Yes, this earth, and those beautiful bright

---

45. Ibid., 30.
46. Ibid., 31.
47. Ibid., 32.
48. Ibid.

heavens which are above it, shall one day melt away in the great heat of that fire, which God shall send to destroy the world, and all the wicked people that shall then be found in it. That day will be as dreadful to the wicked as the flood was to the people of the old world.[49]

The author then offers assurance by writing, "God will be able to take as much care of the righteous when he burns this world as he did of Noah when he drowned the old world."[50] She concludes, "In that great day, when this earth shall be burned up with fire, our blessed Saviour will be there to take care of all those who belong to him; they will be as safe with our Lord Jesus Christ as Noah was in the ark."[51] Thus, the entire narrative leads up to making an analogy between Noah's safety from the waters of the flood in the ark and the safety from the fire of judgment that people in the present day can find in Jesus Christ.

Reverend Thomas Hopkins Gallaudet's *Scripture Biography for the Young*, published by the American Tract Society in 1838, follows a similar pattern. Gallaudet attended Yale University and Andover Theological Seminary, and became one of the pioneering figures for education for the deaf in North America. The book was quite popular, being republished in several editions with several bindings. Gallaudet devotes twelve pages of his book to the story of "The Deluge," which allows him plenty of space to expand on the story and use it to make several points to his readers.

According to Gallaudet, Noah's neighbors mocked him, but "Noah, not withstanding, told them what God had threatened, and warned them of their danger. He exhorted them to repent of their great wickedness, and in mocking Noah, and despising God; while he kept on, obeying and trusting God and building the ark."[52] By adding this episode, Gallaudet establishes that God through Noah urged the wicked to repent and characterizes the wicked people as people who mock Noah and despise God.

Later in the narrative, Gallaudet suddenly transitions into allegory and direct commentary to the reader, urging them to turn to Jesus Christ for their salvation. He asks the reader, "Have you gone into *that ark of safety* which he has provided, to secure you against a vastly greater evil than *the deluge* was?"[53] In case the message is lost on the reader, Gallaudet then makes the point explicit, underscoring it from the rest of the text with italics, writing, "*Jesus Christ is our only ark of safety.*"[54] He elaborates with a direct plea to the reader that is similar to those given at the end of tent meeting sermons of the time: "My dear reader, if you have not entered into this ark of safety; if you have not trusted in Christ,—delay

49. Ibid., 38.

50. Ibid.

51. Ibid., 39.

52. T. H. Gallaudet, *Scripture Biography for the Young, with Critical Illustrations and Practical Remarks*, Vol. 1, *Adam to Jacob* (New York: American Tract Society, 1838), 64.

53. Ibid., 67. Emphasis in the original.

54. Ibid. Emphasis in the original.

it no longer. A deluge is coming,—the deluge of God's terrible displeasure against sin in the future world—fear lest it may overwhelm you in endless and hopeless ruin!"[55] Gallaudet, then, uses both the message of the threat of God's judgment and promise of safety from judgment for the faithful that he finds present in the story of Noah to call his readers to turn to Jesus Christ.

Gallaudet brings home his call to repentance by describing how the wicked had been warned yet they were surprised and terrified when the flood came and they received God's punishment.[56] He subtly reminds his readers that children, as well as men and women, drowned in the flood by painting a terrifying picture: "Men, women and children,—all, all were buried in the waters! How terribly did this show the displeasure of God against sin. For remember, it was to punish the inhabitants of the world for their very great wickedness, that this dreadful calamity befell them."[57] As if to counterbalance this God of judgment, Gallaudet writes about this "longsuffering"[58] God: "How kind and merciful he is in not destroying you as he did the wicked persons in Noah's time! He is giving you time for repentance. He is inviting you to come to Christ, and trust in him, and have all your sins forgiven, and be safe under his protection and blessing, both in this world and in that which is to come."[59] Gallaudet, then, calls children to recognize that this powerful and terrifying God is being kind and merciful to them by virtue of the fact that God is not destroying them. He invites them to turn to Christ to be "under his protection" from the terrible judgment of God.

Favell Lee Mortimer's book, *Scripture Facts in Simple Language*, published by the American Tract Society in the late 1840s, included the story of "The Great Rain." The American Tract Society also published this story separately as a short pamphlet-style chapbook along with many other such chapbooks used to promote biblical knowledge, moral living, and its evangelistic efforts. As discussed in the previous chapter, Mortimer's books *Peep of the Day* and *Line Upon Line* were very popular and emphasized, at least compared to later children's Bibles, a very harsh and judgmental God. The version of the story of Noah that Mortimer tells in *Scripture Facts in Simple Language* certainly does not gloss over the deaths of those outside of the ark, but it also leads more explicitly into a message of salvation in Jesus Christ.

Mortimer begins her tale of Noah and the flood by telling her readers stories of children who drowned in the 1824 flooding in St. Petersburgh in Russia in 1824, in which approximately 10,000 people died. Once having established the horror of that scene, she writes, "But a more dreadful event happened once. The whole world was drowned. Yes, all the people in the world were drowned, and all

---

55. Ibid., 67–8.
56. Ibid., 68–9. Also note that, like several of his contemporaries, Gallaudet seems interested in theories that tried to pinpoint the exact date of the flood.
57. Ibid., 69–70.
58. Ibid., 73.
59. Ibid., 73–4.

the beasts and birds, except one family, and a few beasts and birds with them."[60] Mortimer, therefore, prepares children for the horrors to come.

According to Mortimer, Noah did his best to warn the people: "None of the wicked people went in. Noah had often begged them to repent and to turn to God, but they had not minded. They would not believe that they should at last be drowned."[61] The wicked, then, had plenty of opportunity to repent. In an apparent allusion to Matthew 24.37-39, which Mortimer seems to present as proof of their wickedness, Noah's neighbors go on with their lives:

> They thought that one day would be like another, and that no sad day would ever come; so they built houses, and planted gardens, and married wives, and ate and drank, and never thought of God, or thanked him for giving them food and all their pleasures. They did not wish to go into the ark with Noah; they liked much better staying in their fine gardens and houses.[62]

This blasé disregard for God, the narrative seems to suggest, justifies their fate. The narrative highlights the neighbors' disregard for and dishonor for God, and therefore seems to follow Anselm in suggesting that the people are being punished for their disregard for God rather than because the law was violated. Mortimer underscores the judgment of God by embellishing the Genesis account by speculating on the actions of those outside of the ark: "Every body was drowned, and every beast and bird. If people climbed to the tops of trees, the water soon reached them, and if they mounted the high hills, the waters at last covered them; there was no way of escaping from the anger of God."[63] Mortimer's narrative suggests that one cannot escape the anger and judgment of God, especially if they wait too long to repent: "Once God would have heard the prayers of these sinners, but now it was too late—they were all drowned."[64] The scene, then, is all the more dreadful because it could have been avoided if only the sinners had repented in time.

After describing how Noah and the animals survived the flood, and how God placed a rainbow in the sky, Mortimer writes, "That rainbow puts us in mind of God's kindness to Noah."[65] She then makes a somewhat abrupt segue into a message of salvation:

> But I have not told you of all his kindness. Did you ever hear how he sent his only Son, the Lord Jesus Christ, to die for wicked men? Yes, he did send him, and Jesus was nailed to a great piece of wood called a cross. He died instead of

---

60. Favell Lee Mortimer, *Scripture Facts in Simple Language* ([United States]: American Tract Society, [1848]), 2.

61. Ibid., 4.

62. Ibid.

63. Ibid., 5.

64. Ibid.

65. Ibid., 7.

you; he is willing to save you from going to hell. Do you wish to turn from all wicked ways? Do you wish to be saved as Noah was?"[66]

Mortimer, then, transitions from the story of Noah in the past directly into an altar call encouraging children in the present to accept Jesus as their savior. The reference to "a great piece of wood called a cross" is presumably an effort to draw an analogy between the cross and the ark. The call to salvation is a call to turn away from wickedness and towards Jesus, with an allusion to substitutionary atonement found in the idea that Jesus was sent to "die for wicked men."

Like others of her time, Mortimer seems uneasy about leaving children with the comfort of knowing God's promise that the earth will never again be destroyed by a flood: "A dreadful day is coming, when the world shall be burned up ..."[67] God, however, provides salvation from this judgment. Mortimer concludes her story by explaining that "those who love God as Noah did, shall be caught up and saved from the fire. What I am telling you is quite true. Do believe me. The people would not believe Noah, and they were drowned. All I have told you is written in the Bible, which is the book of God."[68] Mortimer, then, leaves children with the message that they will be saved from this judgment of fire if they will love God as Noah did.

The following examples of children's Bibles from the second half of the nineteenth century all follow a similar pattern. While many of them claim in their introductions that they are only making minor changes to the biblical text for the sake of clarity, they all add the embellishments of Noah repeatedly warning the wicked people of the coming flood and the people mocking him in return. These embellishments are creatively used to highlight the human agency of the wicked in rejecting God's call to salvation, and the children's Bibles then all highlight the horror of God's righteous judgment through extended descriptions of the plight of the wicked and illustrations such as the drawings of Gustave Doré discussed in the previous chapter or other, similar illustrations of men, women, and children being overcome by the floodwaters. They also all explicitly connect the story of Noah's ark to salvation in Jesus Christ and often integrate these connections right into the middle of their flood narratives.

For example, according to *Half Hours with the Bible; or, The Children's Scripture Story-Book*, a book written in the 1860s by an author identified only as "Mrs. Grive," Noah's ark relates to Jesus in several ways:

Such was the refuge God provided for His servant Noah and his family; and He has shown similar mercy to the whole of mankind. For God has provided another ark, or place of safety, for lost and ruined sinner; and when God looks down now from His holy dwelling-place in heaven, He can see that even the very thoughts of men's hearts are desperately wicked; and, therefore, He has

---

66. Ibid.
67. Ibid.
68. Ibid., 7–8.

provided an ark for these perishing souls to flee to. Do you know what that ark is called? It is the Holy Saviour Jesus Christ; the only offering which the world could produce to appease the just anger of an offended God. He provided the ark; and the same love provided the Saviour, the ark of our strength—the refuge from the storm of trouble and the flood of sin. He has in Himself all things necessary for our support and salvation, just as the ark contained all that was necessary for Noah and his family.[69]

Grive seems to follow Anselm's view of humankind's need for salvation. Their sin has offended God and God's just anger deserves satisfaction. Only Jesus could provide that satisfaction. At the same time, Grive compares God's observation of the wicked in Noah's day to God's view of the wicked in her readers' day. She draws an analogy between the refuge for perishing souls that the ark could provide in the day of the flood with the refuge for sinners that Jesus Christ can provide. Finally, just as the ark contained everything its passengers needed, so does Jesus provide all that Grive's readers would need in their day.

Having established these analogies, Grive makes an appeal worthy of a revival sermon's altar call: "Many years was the ark building. Long it stood open, while Noah vainly tried to persuade the hardened sinners to enter the door. So Christ is always ready, always at hand to save; he stands waiting, he is willing and able to save all who would go unto him."[70]

Despite the stated intentions to stick close to the words of the Bible and to allow the words of the Bible itself to make its own impression on the minds of children, Grive seems to have been unable to resist adapting the story and commenting on it. Her desire that children might know of and find salvation in Jesus Christ appears to have compelled her to adapt the story and use it to serve this purpose.

In a similar way, in *Young People's Illustrated Bible History* from 1871, Rev. Alvan Bond writes, "And the ark may remind us of the Lord Jesus Christ. If we are in Him, by faith, then we shall be safe for ever from God's anger, as Noah was safe in the ark from the waters of the flood."[71] Bond makes no explicit claim that the ark is a type of Christ, but suggests that it may remind the reader of salvation in Jesus Christ. For Bond, the issue is that God is offended and God is angry. For him, like Anselm, God's anger at being ignored must be appeased and, just as the ark saved Noah, Jesus Christ saves believers from God's anger.

In 1887, Rev. George A. Peltz, who served as an associate pastor to Russell H. Conwell at Philadephia's Baptist Temple, released *Grandpa's Stores: or Home Talks about the Wonderful Book*. Peltz seems to draw upon Jonathan Edwards' 1740 sermon "The Manner in Which the Salvation of the Soul is to be Sought," in which Edwards proclaims, "All the blows of the hammer and axe, during the progress

---

69. Mrs. Grive, *Half hours with the Bible: or, The Children's Scripture Story-Book* (New York: McLoughlin Brothers, [1867]), 21–2.

70. Ibid., 22.

71. Alvan Bond, *Young People's Illustrated Bible History* (Norwich, CT: Henry Bill Publishing Company, 1878), 28–9.

of that building, were so many calls and warnings to the old world, to take care for their preservation from the approaching destruction. Every knock of the workmen was a knock of Jesus Christ at the door of their hearts: but they would not hearken."[72] In a similar fashion, Peltz has the character of Grandpa Goodwin explain to the gathered children that as Noah built the ark he also spread the message of salvation:

> He did preach. At his work and in his rest, he told the story over and over, and warned the people of the coming flood. Every blow of his axes and hammers was a call to men to turn from their sins and be saved, and yet nobody came. That is why only Noah and his family were saved. Nobody else was willing to enter the ark.[73]

Whether Peltz is drawing directly upon Edwards or upon others who copied Edwards, or making his own creative connection, he offers readers an imaginative interpretation of Noah's work that creates a synergy between Noah's work ethic and evangelism.

In 1889's *Bible Talks with Children: The Scriptures Simplified for the Little Folk*, Rev. J. L. Sooy presented a generally kinder and more loving God than many of his contemporaries. Even this book, however, includes full-page reproductions of Doré's *The Deluge* and *The Dove Sent forth from the Ark*. After describing how the flood covered the earth, Sooy interjects a direct appeal to children to come to the Ark of salvation.

> Now, dear children, why did God show Noah such grace? I will tell you. It was because God saw that Noah was righteous—that means that he tried to be good; and next, because he believed what God said to him. O, it does always pay to obey our Heavenly Father! Can you tell me, who is our Ark of Salvation? "JESUS." Yes, that is right. Outside of Him all is ruin and death. And to you who are yet outside is the loving message given, "Come thou into the Ark." O, come to-day.[74]

Sooy's quotation of Genesis 7.1, to "Come thou into the Ark," may also have been an allusion to D. L. Moody's famous sermon of that title that he preached in December 1885.[75] Like that sermon, Sooy appropriates the story of Noah's ark to tell children a compelling story about their need for salvation in Christ.

72. Jonathan Edwards, "The Manner in Which the Salvation of the Soul is to be Sought." http://www.jonathan-edwards.org/Seeking.html (accessed May 6, 2014).

73. George A. Peltz, *Grandpa's Stories: or Home Talks out of the Wonderful Book* (Toronto: Best Brothers, 1887), 72.

74. J. L. Sooy, *Bible Talks with Children: The Scriptures Simplified for the Little Folk* (New York: Union Publishing House, 1889), 16–18 (page 17 is devoted to Gustave Doré's illustration of *The Deluge*).

75. D. L. Moody, "The Day of Rest. Come Thou Into the Ark. An Address by D. L. Moody," *The Aroha News* 4:175 (October 23, 1886): 8.

Carolyn Hadley's book from around 1890, *From Eden to Babylon: Stories of the Prophets Priests and Kings of the Old Testament,* also uses Doré's *The Deluge* as an illustration and her text describes the scene outside of the ark: "The people who were outside the ark was [*sic*] very frightened now, but Noah could not let any come in. It was too late,—God had shut the door."[76] She then expresses distress over the fact that people then and now do not turn to God for salvation: "Oh, why did they not seek for safety before it was too late? Why do people now go on sinning till they die, heeding not the warnings of those who beg them to seek safety in Jesus, the True Ark, ere it is too late?"[77] Hadley, then, ends her story of Noah with an urgent call to salvation in Jesus.

While most American children's Bibles of the nineteenth century that use the story of Noah as a call to salvation in Christ do not explicitly use the language of "type," they still draw a direct connection between Noah and his family's salvation from the flood in the ark and the salvation available through Jesus Christ to sinners in their own day. The way they use the image of the ark and connect it to the work of Jesus Christ is more like a type than an extended allegory.

3.4. Twentieth-Century Connections to Christ in the Story of Noah

In twentieth-century America, some children's Bibles continued the practice of using the story of Noah to tell children about salvation in Jesus Christ. These retellings shared many characteristics with the previous century, but they tended to be more focused on informing children about various analogies that could be drawn between the ark and Jesus Christ than on urging them to escape God's wrath and find salvation in Jesus Christ.

Ethel Hudson's *Bible Heroes,* published in 1926, serves both as a throwback to the children's Bibles of the revivalist era and as a precursor to twenty-first-century children's Bibles that frame the entire Bible as the story of Jesus. In her foreword Hudson writes, "In sending out this little volume of BIBLE HEROES, it is my purpose, not only to make real each hero, but also to help the young people to see that God used each one to hold up to the world a picture of Jesus. Each chapter tells a story of God's love for a lost world. All center around one Hero, Jesus Christ."[78] She follows this pattern throughout her book. Hudson does not add Noah's preaching or his mocking neighbors to her version of the story of Noah and the flood, but she still highlights humankind's sin. In a section titled "God foretells the coming judgment" she writes:

76. Carolyn Hadley, *From Eden to Babylon: Stories of the Prophets Priests and Kings of the Old Testament* (New York: McLoughlin Brothers, c. 1890), 15.

77. Ibid. For a similar narrative, see Catherine Burnham, *From the Creation to Moses* (New York: Geo. A. Leavitt [1870]), 30–1.

78. Ethel Hudson, *Bible Heroes: For Use in the Junior B.Y.P.U.* (Nashville, TN: Sunday School Board of the Southern Baptist Convention, 1926), 6.

God looked down from heaven upon the pretty world that he had made and saw it again in blackness. This time it was the blackness of sin. How it grieved God to know that the man he had made in his image and likeness had so soon turned away from him and was worshiping Satan. God saw that man's thoughts were evil continually, and he said: "I will destroy man, whom I have created, from the face of the earth; both man, and beast and the creeping things, and the fowls of the air."[79]

Hudson then concludes her story with a section titled "The Last Judgment" in which she makes a direct connection between Noah's ark and Jesus:

Noah gave to the world a beautiful picture of Christ. There is to be another judgment and it is to be a judgment of fire. God, through Noah, provided an ark of safety for the first judgment, and he has already provided an ark of safety for the second judgment. This is the ark of Jesus. All have sinned and must be punished. Jesus came and took our punishment. He was beaten with many stripes until the blood streamed from his body; then when the cruels [sic] nails pierced his hands and feet, blood streamed from them. He went through the judgment for us. When we accept him, we go into the Ark of Safety; and God closes the door to make us secure. As the ark was pitched within and without with pitch, our ark is covered with blood, and no fire of judgment can reach us. Satan can no longer claim us as his own, for, though we sin, as did Noah, we cannot go back through the judgment, for it has already passed.[80]

Like children's Bible authors of the previous century, Hudson draws a graphic connection between Noah's safety from judgment through the ark and the message of substitutionary atonement through Christ's death on the cross. Christ's death, she suggests, grants people a chance to escape final judgment and she even makes reference to a coming judgment by fire.

The foreword of Ruth Hogue Bobb's *A Bible Highway: Charted for Boys and Girls*, published in 1941 by the International Child Evangelism Fellowship, explicitly tells teachers that they should look for opportunities to use the Bible stories as tools for evangelism. Bobb instructs teachers that, while using the stories in her book, "Wherever it fits in naturally, without being strained or forced, the Gospel message should be presented and an opportunity for decisions prayerfully offered."[81] Bobb proceeds to suggest, "Because a child is in Sunday School or regularly attends one of our classes, it should never be taken for granted that he is born again."[82]

In her story of Noah, Bobb explains, "For more than a hundred years Noah worked on the building of the ark and told people that God would destroy with a

---

79. Ibid., 24.

80. Ibid., 30.

81. Ruth Hogue Bobb, *A Bible Highway: Charted for Boys and Girls* (Chicago: International Child Evangelism Fellowship, 1941), n.p.

82. Ibid.

flood all the wicked people on the earth. They must have laughed at Noah; for they did not believe him."[83] Near the midpoint of Bobb's retelling of the story of Noah, just after she describes the animals and Noah's family entering the ark, Bobb interjects, "The ark was the only safe place for all of them in the flood of God's judgment. Today you and I are in the only safe place from God's judgment, if we are in Christ—trusting in Him. Are you safe in Him?"[84] The ark, then, becomes an allegory for salvation in Christ. Bobb ends her chapter on Noah by explaining, "God loves us; and He wants us to love and obey Him by accepting His way to reach Heaven. That way is the Lord Jesus Christ. 'I am the way ... no man cometh unto the Father but by me.' *John 14:6*. Is He *your* Way?"[85] Bobb is not content to retell the story of Noah as it appears in Genesis, and then to allow the teachers to look for opportunities to share the Gospel, as advised in the foreword. Instead, she integrates the message of salvation in Christ into the story of Noah and ends the chapter with direct commentary to readers in which she makes it clear that the salvation message is the primary lesson they should learn from the story.

These twentieth-century children's Bibles provide evidence that Protestant American children's Bible authors continued the previous century's pattern of using the story of Noah's ark to teach children their beliefs about salvation in Jesus Christ. They tend to do so, however, in subtly different ways. The tone of these twentieth-century examples is different to those of the previous century. For example, while nineteenth-century children's Bibles often highlighted the threat of God's judgment and urged children to turn to Christ, their twentieth-century counterparts tend to have less of a sense of urgency to create a conversion moment for the reader. The twentieth-century authors tend instead to use the story to inform children about the connection to Noah and Jesus Christ and inform them about salvation in Jesus Christ.

The children's Bibles in this section also reflect the twentieth-century American's tendency to avoid the subject of death with children. As noted in the previous chapter, this tendency becomes evident in the United States around the 1920s. Compared to children's Bibles from the nineteenth century, then, these twentieth century children's Bibles tend de-emphasize the deaths of the wicked. The authors instead choose to focus on God's need to punish sin, and the salvation that God provided through the ark and through Jesus Christ.

Finally, in a manner similar to examples from the nineteenth century, these twentieth-century Protestant children's Bibles do not engage in elaborate allegorical interpretations. Although they do not use the term "type," they tend to use the ark in a manner consistent with a typological interpretation, and not an allegorical interpretation, of Noah's ark and how it relates Jesus' saving work.

83. Ibid., 9.
84. Ibid.
85. Ibid., 10.

3.5. Noah's Ark as a Type of the Church in Roman Catholic Children's Bibles

While Protestant authors emphasized the need for personal salvation through Jesus Christ, a number of nineteenth- and twentieth-century Roman Catholic children's Bible authors highlighted the role of baptism and the Church in human-kind's salvation. While many Protestant authors suggest that the ark is a type of Jesus Christ, their Roman Catholic counterparts tend to look to the ark as a type of the Church of Jesus Christ.

Precedence for the connection between the ark and the church can be found in Jerome's *Dialogue against the Luciferians*, dating to approximately 376 CE. Jerome alludes to 1 Peter 3.20-21 when he writes, "Noah's ark was a type of the Church, as the apostle Peter says."[86] Jerome proceeds to suggest many parallels between the ark and the Church. Among these, the ark housed many kinds of animals, while the Church houses the righteous and sinners alike. The ark had many rooms, while the Church has many mansions. Eight souls were saved in the ark, while the number eight can be found in several places in Scripture. The raven did not return to the ark, but the dove announced peace on earth. Meanwhile, through baptism "that most unclean bird the devil is expelled and the dove of the Holy Spirit announces peace to our earth."[87] Jerome engages in these allegorical inter-pretations to find theological significance in the story of Noah and the Church of his day. Some Roman Catholic children's Bibles allude to Jerome's interpretation in their retellings of the story of Noah.

In 1862, the D. & J. Sadler & Company in New York published an edition of *The History of the Holy Bible, Comprising the Most Remarkable Events in the Old and New Testaments, Interspersed with Moral and Instructive Reflections, Chiefly out of the Holy Fathers*, a book first published in Britain in 1780, that also compared the ark to the Church. The book proved to be quite popular, remained in print, and the publisher revised the text into smaller and larger editions as well.

The book has an interesting history. The Rev. Joseph Reeve, a former Jesuit, set out to translate an edition of the book written in France around 1683 by Nicolas Fontaine, who wrote under the pseudonym Royamount. The reason Fontaine wrote under the pseudonym is that he was a Port-Royal Monsieur and was accused of Jansenism, a movement condemned as a heresy. As a result, Fontaine was imprisoned in the Bastille. Like many Puritans and revivalists, Jansenism placed great emphasis on human depravity and the necessity of divine grace. In his preface, Reeve notes Fontaine's Port Royal connections and his "enthusiastic system of theology" and therefore confesses to correcting and altering the text as

---

86. Jerome, *Dialogue Against the Luciferians* 22, in Phillip Schaff and Henry Wace, eds, *The Principal Works of St. Jerome*, trans. by W. H. Fremantle (Edinburgh: T&T Clark, 1892), 331. Volume 6 of Select library of Nicene and post-Nicene Fathers of the Christian Church. Series 2 . Available as part of the *Christian Classics Ethereal Library*. http://www.ccel.org/ccel/schaff/npnf206.vi.iv.html (accessed May 23, 2014).

87. Jerome, *Dialogue Against the Luciferians*, 331.

he goes, resulting in quite a free adaptation of Fontaine's original text.[88] The result is a book that is in many places similar to those written by revivalists, but is in other places more particularly Roman Catholic in its perspective.

As the story of Noah begins, the retelling seems to match some of the characteristics of American Puritan and revivalist authors. The text does not add the common embellishment that Noah preached to and warned his neighbors of the impending flood, but rather seems to assume that the implicit warning that God was about to judge the world with a flood unless they repented of their sins should have been obvious to anyone who saw Noah building the ark,[89] and makes an explicit connection between the judgment of the flood and the last judgment.[90] The text continues, revealing a God who makes threats and who will not be ignored:

> He cannot with indifference see his threats disregarded, his admonitions slighted, and his mercy abused. Men must not fancy that their numbers, or their wealth, or worldly power will be able to screen them from the vengeance that their crimes deserve. When summoned to appear before the tribunal of an omnipotent judge, they will find, that the whole world will be as little able to stand against the fires of the last day, as against the waters of the deluge.[91]

A small woodcut illustration depicts naked people, including an unobstructed view of a woman's naked breasts that may be surprising to today's readers, trying to climb trees as the floodwaters overwhelm them. Although Reeve initially does not include a scene in which Noah's neighbors laugh at him before the rains begin, later, as he tells his readers of the neighbors' deaths, he writes that they had laughed:

> Then did those unhappy mortals who had laughed at Noah's prudent forecast, most bitterly bewail their folly; with deep despair did they then see themselves swallowed up by the resistless waves, and the more sensibly did they feel the stroke of their destruction, as they had received the power and timely notice to prevent it.[92]

Neither Fontaine nor Reeve minimize the horror of the deluge and neither of them do much to make their text easily accessible to younger readers. The retelling of the Noah story itself seems quite consistent with Protestant retellings.

The conclusion to the story, however, follows a common pattern of Roman Catholic children's Bibles as it offers an interpretation from the early Church:

---

88. Joseph Reeve, *The history of the Holy bible, comprising the most remarkable events in the Old and New Testaments, interspersed with moral and instructive reflections, chiefly taken from the Holy fathers* (New York: D. & J. Sadler & Company, 1862), iii.

89. Ibid., 23.

90. Ibid.

91. Ibid.

92. Ibid., 24.

"The holy fathers have considered the ark of Noah as a figure of the church of Christ."[93] The text proceeds to extend the analogy: "The church, like the ark, has triumphantly risen above the storms that have been raised to depress her,"[94] finally adding, "This [the Church] is the refuge which all must flock to, who desire to be saved; this is the sanctuary, out of which no salvation can be found."[95] Like Jerome, then, the interpretation of the story of Noah moves beyond the limits of a type to engage in some allegorical use of the story.

In 1881, the Right Rev. Richard Gilmour, the Bishop of Cleveland, offered *The Bible History* as part of the Catholic National Series that was created for use in Catholic schools in the United States. Gilmour offers a relatively unembellished retelling of the story of Noah. After he retells the tale, he adds a brief allegorical commentary, similar to Jerome's commentary, in a smaller font, that reads, "The impenitent sinner is like the raven that returned not to the Ark, while the dove is like the faithful son that finds its rest only in Jesus Christ and His church."[96] Like a number of Catholic writers of the time, Gilmour uses the Latin spelling of "Noe" rather than the "Noah" of Protestant versions of the Bible. After recounting the story, he asks questions in the style of a Bible catechism. These include, "How long did the deluge continue? Where did the Ark rest? How did Noe know the waters were gone? How long was Noe in the Ark? What did Noe offer? What covenant did God make?"[97] Gilmour, however, then calls children's attention not to the Bible passage but to his commentary by asking, again in a smaller font, "What is said of the raven and the dove?"[98] Gilmour, then, does not dwell on the ark as an allegory or type of Christ and the Church. Instead, in the tradition of Jerome, he focuses on an allegorical reading of the raven and the dove as two types of people and their response to Jesus.

Hazel Gillmore Alden's *The Kingdom of Heaven. An Instruction in The Catholic Faith for Children*, from 1907, engages in a complex allegory comparing the ark and the Church:

> Did you ever think how much this Ark is like the Church? It may not seem so at first, but remember that the Holy Catholic Church is the Ark of Salvation, and those who are in the Church are being saved from death just as those in Noah's Ark were being saved—only we are being saved from the death of our souls instead of our bodies as they were. Christ built the Church, our Ark of Salvation, as Noah built his ark, and each built just as God the Father told him. We enter the Church through Holy Baptism, and that is why we put the Baptismal Font near the Church door. You will find that the part of the Church where the Font stands is called the "nave," which means "ship." We know that our Ship will

93. Ibid.
94. Ibid.
95. Ibid.
96. Richard Gilmour, *Bible History* (New York: Benzinger Brothers, 1881), 16.
97. Ibid.
98. Ibid.

not sink in the flood of wickedness that covers the world, because it is built according to God's plan, and our Ark will hold us safely, because Christ built it for our Salvation.[99]

Alden, then, not only sees the Holy Catholic Church as the "Ark of Salvation" but also finds connections between holy baptism and the entrance to the church and the nave of the church as part of the church. It is a bit of a mixed metaphor, but it allows Alden to impress upon children the belief that salvation is found in the Church.

Rather than presenting the story of Noah as the tale of a handful of mocking sinners and the salvation of one family, Dom Hubert Van Zeller's 1949 *Old Testament Stories: Scripture Textbooks for Catholic Schools* emphasizes a more universal perspective on salvation. After telling readers how the flood waters receded and God made a covenant with Noe, Van Zeller follows the teaching of 1 Peter 3 by using the flood as an image of a baptism for the world:

> The world which had sinned had been baptized; and the grey sky which for forty days had loosed its burden upon the earth had now put on its choicest colours to celebrate the ceremony. Man has been given another chance.[100]

If the flood was a baptism, for Van Zeller the rainbow serves as an archway to heaven:

> High above the altar and against the cloudless blue, the great sweep of God's rainbow proclaims that through a new archway must man find his way to heaven. There is perhaps a moment's silence … a sense of awe … downcast looks and the effort to concentrate. Blinking and fluttering and stretching our legs we all go off together in the joy of our new-found freedom and resolve.[101]

One could make the case that Van Zeller's comparison of the flood and baptism was a typological interpretation, consistent in some ways with the original meaning of the story of the flood. His interpretation of the rainbow as an archway to heaven may be more difficult to place in the category of typological interpretation, however, and fall instead into the category of an allegorical interpretation.

In 1955, the Catholic Book Publishing Company offered readers Rev. Lawrence G. Lovasik's *New Catholic Picture Bible*, which continued to be republished for decades to follow. Lovasik uses the story of Noah as an opportunity to pass on the story of Shem and the Messiah to come:

---

99. Hazel Gillmore Alden, *The Kingdom of Heaven. An Instruction in The Catholic Faith for Children* (New York: Church Publishing Company, 1907), 29.

100. Dom Hubert Van Zeller, *Old Testament Stories: Scripture Textbooks for Catholic Schools* (Westminister, MD: Newman Press, 1949), 10.

101. Ibid., 10–11.

God made a new promise to Noah. He promised that He would bring mankind again into His favor, if men would worship Him alone and be faithful to His service. God also gave him the hope of the Redeemer. To his son Shem, and to those who came after him, fell the great task of protecting the worship of the true God and the promise of the Messiah.[102]

For Lovasik, then, the story of Noah connects to Christ not through a typological or allegorical interpretation, but through the lineage of Noah and his son Shem.

Sister Jane Marie Murray and Eugene S. Geissler give readers a quick tour of the entire Bible with an eye towards salvation in 1961's *The Story of Salvation*. They use the stories of Noah's ark and the Tower of Babel to quickly establish humankind's sinfulness and need of a savior. According to the book, "The story of the deluge teaches the truth of the terrible misfortunes sin brings upon men. Noe escapes the flood because he has been living a God-fearing life."[103] Murray and Geissler, however, do not attempt to draw a direct analogy between Noah or the ark and Jesus Christ and they do not end their story of Noah with an immediate plea for readers to find salvation in Christ or the Church. Instead, they take a longer approach to their retelling of the Bible's stories by ultimately emphasizing the role of the Church. After completing the retelling of the New Testament, Murray and Geissler describe aspects of the life of the Church, explaining, "In the Church, Christ continues to the end of time."[104] The book concludes, "The Church will triumph eternally, and Christ will reign forever."[105] This interpretation, then, has more in common with some twenty-first-century evangelical interpretations of the Bible as one long story of the history redemption in Christ than with other Roman Catholic children's Bibles.

Sister Mary Theola's story of "Noe," first published in 1960[106] but republished in 1983's *The Catholic Children's Bible*, integrated reflections on sin, the nature of God, and salvation through the Church. She writes, "Wickedness had reached its fullness. In their lawlessness the wicked jeered at God."[107] Theola cautions children that "God sees all things, both good and evil. And now, the day of reckoning was at hand."[108] As she continues to tell the story, she suggests, "The building of the ark should have served as a warning of the tribulation that was to follow, but it

102. Lawrence G. Lovasik, *New Catholic Picture Bible* (New York: Catholic Book Publishing Company, 1955, 1981), 15.

103. Sister Jane Marie Murray and Eugene S. Geissler, *The Story of Salvation* (Notre Dame, IN: Fides Publishers Association, 1961), 6.

104. Ibid., 152.

105. Ibid., 166.

106. Mary Theola, *Catholic Bible Stories* (New York: Regina Press, 1960).

107. Mary Theola, *The Catholic Children's Bible*, illus. by J. Verleye (New York: Regina Press, 1983, 2008), 37.

108. Ibid.

provoked ridicule instead of repentance."[109] Theola does not spare children from warnings of tribulation or from relatively advanced vocabulary.

Theola integrates into her retelling comments on the themes of God's mercy and justice as she sees them in the story. As the rains fall, she comments, "The measure of God's mercy reached an end. God's justice would be satisfied."[110] At the end of the story, she concludes, "Looking at God's part in the story of the Flood, we see His justice, His impatience with sin, and His holiness that cannot tolerate corruption. On man's part, the story shows the ugliness of sin, its rapid growth and the depth that human malice can reach in man."[111] Interestingly, Theola seems to follow John Calvin's soteriology more than St. Anselm's soteriology. It is sin and corruption that God cannot tolerate, not a personal affront to God's honor. Earlier, however, as she notes that "the wicked jeered at God," she seems to support Anselm's view.

Rather than choosing between the ark as a type of the Church or the flood as a type of baptism, Theola makes the case that the ark is a figure of both baptism and the Catholic Church: "The ark is a figure of Baptism and also of the Catholic Church. The salvation granted to Noe as he was lifted upon the flood-waters, stands for the saving waters of Baptism."[112] She continues, alluding to the Church Fathers' use of the ark as an allegory or type of the Church: "And the ark, even in the early days of the Church, was looked upon as foreshadowing it. The Church like the ark, is a means of salvation."[113] Theola's retelling, then, serves to impress upon her young readers the importance of the Catholic Church and the sacrament of baptism.

In many of the chapters of this book, one can find only subtle differences between Catholic and Protestant authors' use of the story of Noah in children's Bibles. The examples in this section are an admittedly small sample, but they suggest that Protestant and Catholic children's Bibles that connect the flood to issues related to salvation tend to differ in precisely the sort of ways one might expect. Protestant children's Bible authors use the ark to call readers to a personal commitment to Jesus Christ, whereas Roman Catholic writers emphasize the role of the Church in salvation. Roman Catholic children's Bibles also appear to draw more on the analogy between the flood and baptism found in 1 Pet. 3.20-21, a connection that Protestant children's Bibles largely ignore in favor of claiming that Jesus Christ is the ark—a claim not made in the New Testament. In so doing, Catholic children's Bibles emphasize the role of the sacrament of baptism in the life of the faithful. Finally, based upon these examples, Roman Catholic authors tend to be more open to allegorical interpretations than their Protestant counterparts.

109. Ibid., 38.
110. Ibid.
111. Ibid., 39.
112. Ibid., 40.
113. Ibid.

3.6. Noah Talks to Jesus in Seventh-Day Adventist Children's Bibles

At least two Seventh-day Adventist authors have affirmed the divinity of Jesus Christ by having Jesus appear as a leading character in the story of Noah. As is the case with many Christian communities, the Seventh-day Adventists have engaged in a long debate over the exact nature of the trinity and the nature of the incarnation in particular. Was Christ begotten, therefore created in time by God the Father? Or is Christ eternal and pre-existent with an underived divine nature?[114] The following authors affirm Jesus Christ's pre-existing nature by depicting Jesus speaking to Noah before, during, and after the flood.

Rosamond D. Ginther makes Jesus the hero or main character of every story of her *Bible Stories for the Cradle Roll*. The book, published in 1933 by the Southern Publishing Association, is written for boys and girls "from birth to four years of age."[115] In Ginther's version of the story of Noah, which she titles "The First Big Boat and the Man Who Built It," it is Jesus, and not God, who is the primary divine character in the story. Ginther begins her tale, "Noah was a good man; he loved Jesus and tried to do the things that pleased Him. He had some little boys, and he taught them to love Jesus. I think Noah must have taken his boys on his knee, just as your daddy takes you on his knee, and he told them stories about Jesus and His Father, and how much They loved little children."[116] Ginther does, then, acknowledge the first person of the trinity, Jesus' Father. The focus of the narrative, however, is clearly on Jesus. Jesus is the one who Noah loves, and Noah tells his children stories of Jesus. Ginther continues, "But there were many, many fathers living near Noah who did not love Jesus, and they did not teach their little boys and girls to love Him. The boys and girls were very naughty. They did not mind their fathers and mothers. It made Jesus sad to see all these people doing wrong. He was glad that Noah and his boys would not do wrong, as their neighbors did."[117] According to the story, "Jesus was so sad, and He thought about what He could do to make the earth good again. It had been a pretty place; but the people were so naughty, it was being spoiled."[118] Ginther, then, encourages children to empathize with Jesus, who grieves for the world because it is so wicked.

Ginther includes the embellishments of Noah preaching to his neighbors and the neighbors mocking Noah, but in language young children might understand: "Jesus is going to send rain out of the sky until everything is covered, and He wants you to be in the ark so you will not be hurt. But do you know what the

---

114. For a helpful historical survey of these debates, see Merlin D. Burt, "History of Seventh-day Adventist Views on the Trinity," *Journal of the Adventist Theological Society* 17:1 (Spring 2006): 125–39.

115. Rosamond D. Ginther, *Bible Stories for the Cradle Roll* (Nashville, TN: Southern Publishing Association, 1933), 7.

116. Ibid., 36.

117. Ibid.

118. Ibid.

people did? Some of them laughed."[119] Noah still tries to convince them, telling them, "Yes, it will rain, because Jesus said it would."[120] Still, however, the neighbors would not believe him.

When describing the coming of the flood, Ginther spares her young audience an explicit statement that these wicked people drowned or died, simply noting that the flood covered up everything. Instead, she writes that when the flood came, "the people in the ark were all safe. Jesus and the angels were caring for them. Jesus loved Noah and his family, and He loves us. Jesus loves everyone and will take care of those who love Him."[121] When the storms come and the waves rock the ark, "Noah was not afraid. He said to his family, 'Jesus said He would take care of us, and we need not be afraid. I know Jesus will keep his promise.' And Jesus did."[122] Jesus, then, is the one who keeps Noah and his family safe.

The book does not make it clear whether Ginther felt that it was not helpful to distinguish between the persons of the trinity for her young audience or if she did not make much of the distinction in her own theology of the trinity. Perhaps Ginther simply felt that Jesus would be a friendlier and more personable character for her young readers than God the Creator. Also, though Jesus is the protagonist of the story and though Ginther says "Jesus loves everyone and will take care of those who love Him," her book does not include as explicit an appeal for repentance and salvation for her young readers as some other children's Bibles do.

Years later, *The Wonderful World of the Bible for Children*, first published in Portugal in 1999 but republished in the United States in English in 2003, took a similar approach to Ginther's book. Jesus appears in Charlotte F. Lessa's text and João Luiz Cardozo's illustrations of every story from the Old and New Testaments that is in the book. Lessa begins the story of Noah, "Of all the people living on the earth, only one family remained who loved Jesus. It was Noah's family. Noah enjoyed obeying Jesus. Noah and his family prayed to Jesus every day."[123] The next page contains a traditional image of Jesus with a beard and white robe standing next to Noah looking over building plans (see Figure 3.1), accompanied by the text, "One day Jesus said, 'Noah, the people on earth are very bad. I am going to destroy the world with rain.'"[124] After telling the tale of the flood, Lessa concludes her story, "Noah and his family gathered to thank Jesus for His care. 'Noah,' Jesus said, 'do you see this rainbow? It's a sign that I will never again send a flood to destroy the whole earth. And look how beautiful the rainbow is!'"[125] As with Ginther's tale, Jesus is the one who cares for Noah and his family.

119. Ibid., 37.

120. Ibid., 38.

121. Ibid.

122. Ibid., 40.

123. Charlotte F. Lessa, *The Wonderful World of the Bible*, illus. by João Luiz Cardozo (Hagerstown, MD: Review and Herald Publishing Association, 2003), 26.

124. Ibid., 27.

125. Ibid., 33.

One day Jesus said, "Noah, the people on earth are very bad. I am going to destroy the world with rain—so much rain that it will cover everything with water. I want you to build a very big boat. I want you, your family, and everyone who believes what I'm telling you to go into the boat when it's finished."

Figure 3.1. Illustration of Jesus and Noah looking at blueprints for the ark by João Luiz Cardozo from Charlotte F. Lessa, *The Wonderful World of the Bible* (Hagerstown, MD: Review and Herald Publishing Association, 2003), 27.

These two children's Bibles, then, emphasize Jesus and his divine pre-existence by taking the extraordinary step of making Jesus present with Noah and other Hebrew Bible characters.

3.7. Twenty-first-Century Stories of Noah's Ark as Part of the Entire Bible's Story of Redemption History

In the twenty-first century, a trend in children's Bibles emerged that took a subtly different approach to the story of Noah and indeed all of the stories of the Bible. Not only could an analogy be drawn between salvation for Noah in the ark and salvation for people in the present day in Christ and not only was Noah's ark one of a handful of "types" of Christ, but these children's Bibles suggest that the entire Bible is actually one cohesive story about salvation in Jesus Christ. Furthermore, for a number of evangelical authors, it is important to impress upon their readers not only that the stories of the Bible point to Jesus Christ, but that all thirty-nine books of the Old Testament and all twenty-seven books of the New Testament are part of one unified book with one unified story of redemption history. Often the covers or introductions to these children's Bibles explicitly proclaim this message.

David Helm's 2004 *The Big Picture Story Bible* is a case in point. Helm presents God's plan of salvation through Jesus Christ as the "big picture" of the Bible. Helm, a graduate of Wheaton College and Gordon-Conwell Theological Seminary, and pastor of Holy Trinity Church in Chicago, tells readers, "This book takes you through the stories of the Bible with colorful illustrations so you will see the big picture of God's love for you."[126] The storybook forms a seamless narrative that uses the stories of the Bible to tell young readers the story of salvation history from an evangelical perspective. Throughout the book, Helm repeats the promise that God would send a "forever king" who finally arrives with the birth of Jesus.[127] Gail Schoonmaker's illustrations of the stories are often drawn as if the reader was looking straight down upon the characters, presumably from a God's-eye perspective. Helm's text keeps the story moving, quickly making transitions across books of the Bible and even across the testaments, to present the stories of the Bible as one unified story of salvation. Helm's account, like several other twenty-first century children's Bibles, also clearly assigns human emotions to God but, unlike those from centuries before, the emotions God feels are not wrath or anger but sadness and compassion.

In retelling the story of Noah, Helm writes that people were evil, which "made God very sad."[128] According to Helm, "All the peoples of the earth had rejected him as king"[129] and so "God decided to judge all the peoples of the earth."[130] At the end of the account of the story of Noah, accompanying an illustration looking down on Noah and his family as they sacrifice at the altar, Helm writes, "Do you know what the flood teaches us? God will judge every single person who rejects him as king. And do you know what God's judgment teaches us? Every

---

126. David Helm, *The Big Picture Story Bible*, illus. by Gail Schoonmaker (Wheaton, IL: Crossway Books, 2004), back cover.

127. Ibid., 268.

128. Ibid., 59.

129. Ibid.

130. Ibid., 60.

single person needs God's blessing."[131] Helm is more reserved than others who take a similar approach to telling children the story of the Bible as the story of redemption history. He does not engage in typological or allegorical interpretations to connect the stories directly to Jesus Christ. Instead, he focuses on broad themes of humankind's sin, God's judgment, God's saving grace, and the promise of a forever king.

Sally Lloyd-Jones's very popular 2007 offering, *The Jesus Storybook Bible: Every Story Whispers His Name*, is explicitly designed to lead children to see salvation through Jesus Christ as the end of every story in the Hebrew Bible as well as the stories of the New Testament. ZonderKids offers the following description of the book, on its back cover:

> *The Jesus Storybook Bible: Every Story Whispers His Name* tells the story beneath all the stories in the Bible. At the center of the story is a baby, the child upon whom everything will depend. Every story whispers his name. From Noah to Moses to the great King David—every story points to him. He is like the missing piece in a puzzle—the piece that makes all the other pieces fit together.[132]

After recounting the story of Noah, his mocking neighbors, and the flood, Lloyd-Jones adds,

> It was a new beginning in God's world.
> It wasn't long before everything went wrong again but God wasn't surprised, he knew this would happen. That's why, before the beginning of time, he had another plan—a better plan. A plan to one day send his own Son, the Rescuer.[133]

The story of the flood, then, is not a story in which God regrets making humankind, but instead a story that fits into the plan God had all along. Lloyd-Jones relates the story of how God placed a rainbow in the sky, and draws on the interpretation of the rainbow as symbolic of the bow as a weapon of war and destruction:

> God's strong anger against hate and sadness and death would come down once more—but not on his people, or his world. No, God's war bow was not pointing down at his people.
> It was pointing up, into the heart of heaven.[134]

Lloyd-Jones's warm words speak of the heart of heaven, but they allude to God's anger and potential judgment as well. God's anger, however, is not directed at

131. Ibid., 65.
132. Sally Lloyd-Jones, *The Jesus Storybook Bible: Every Story Whispers His Name* (Grand Rapids, MI: ZonderKids, 2007), back cover.
133. Ibid., 47.
134. Ibid.

sinful people, but at hate, sadness, and death. God will mete out God's anger, apparently, upon Jesus on the cross.

Sin and salvation are the predominant themes throughout Starr Meade's *Mighty Acts of God: A Family Bible Story Book* from 2010. She titles the story of Noah, "Noah and the Flood: God Judges Sin and Saves from Judgment. Genesis 6–9."[135] Meade's story in many ways recalls the retellings of the story from the era of the revivalists.

Meade opens her retelling by asking children if they ever had to weed a garden, and then transitions into a metaphor of God needing to weed the earth of evil people. To make clear her message of salvation, Meade integrates into her retelling a running commentary on the motivations of the characters and the theological significance of the events: "God hates sin and always punishes it."[136] She explains, "So God said he would destroy what he had made because it had become so evil."[137] Still, Meade further explains, "But God is also full of mercy and grace, and he provides a way for people to be saved from the punishment they deserve."[138] She also suggests that Noah "must have urged them to find safety with him in the ark—but no one listened."[139] Even after the animals entered the ark, the people did not believe. According to Meade, this is because "they did not want to give up the sinful ways they loved. They did not believe God would punish them and they chose not to obey him. They rejected the only way of safety: Noah's ark."[140] Meade notes that God had waited patiently for many years for people to repent, but in the end the rain came and kept on coming: "Everything died in this judgment God sent, except those who trusted in the salvation God provided."[141] In case the children have not recognized the point, she concludes her story by explaining, "He is merciful and patient with sinners. We should also remember the flood, though, and remember that God always punishes sin. His judgment will fall on all who fail to make use of the salvation he provides."[142] Meade, then, assures her readers that God is a God of mercy, but warns them that God is a God of judgment as well and will judge those who do not make use of God's salvation.

According to Mary Machowski's *The Gospel Story Bible: Discovering Jesus in the Old and New Testaments*, published in 2011, each story of the Bible points to Jesus. Machowski is a Family Life Pastor at Covenant Fellowship Church, a Sovereign

---

135. Starr Meade, *Mighty Acts of God: A Family Bible Story Book* (Wheaton, IL: Crossway, 2010), 26.

136. Ibid., 27.

137. Ibid.

138. Ibid.

139. Ibid. It is interesting to note that Meade's description of events follows the pattern of many other children's Bibles. What starts off as a qualified speculation, "he must have urged them …," soon becomes an unqualified part of the description of events, as the story assumes that Noah's neighbors rejected his warnings.

140. Ibid.

141. Ibid.

142. Ibid., 28.

Grace Ministries church in Glen Mills, Pennsylvania. According to the publisher's description of *The Gospel Story Bible*, it helps people realize that every Bible story points to Jesus:

> It is easy to forget Jesus in the midst of frantic schedules, family squabbles, and conflicting priorities. But the truth is that he is the hero of every story, including these ordinary ones. This is why Marty Machowski puts God's plan of salvation in Christ on continuous display in *The Gospel Story Bible*. The easy-to-read storybook introduces your family to many captivating people, places, and events from the Bible's Old and New Testaments, showing how each one ultimately points to Jesus.[143]

Every single Hebrew Bible story, then, concludes with a connection to a message of salvation through Jesus Christ. For the story of God's promise to Abraham, the message is "Through Abram we have all been blessed, just as God promised, because it is by the death and resurrection of his great-far-off grandson Jesus that all those who believe inherit the promise of Abram forever!"[144] Regarding God's covenant with Abraham, "Like Abram, we are saved when we trust in what Jesus did for us."[145] For baby Moses, "Jesus, like Moses, grew up to rescue God's people from slavery. But it was a different kind of slavery—a slavery to sin."[146] Regarding the Ten Commandments, he makes the point that "None of us can obey God perfectly. None of us except Jesus! When we put our faith in him, Jesus takes away our sin and gives us his perfect record of obedience."[147] The point of the story of David and Goliath is that "Before David delivered the men of Israel from Goliath, they stood helpless against him just as we are helpless to save ourselves and need Jesus to deliver us from our sin. David's life points to Jesus, and this story helps us see that we are not saved by our own strength, but by God's power."[148] Reflecting on Hezekiah, Machowski observes that "The sacrifices Hezekiah offered in the temple held back God's judgment for a while, but only the blood of King Jesus shed as a sacrifice for our sins can save his people forever."[149]

Machowski summarizes the story of Noah by making several points:

> Did you know that when God saved Noah in the ark, it was part of his plan to save us? That is true because one day Jesus, our Savior, would be born as a far-off grandchild in Noah's family. There was only one way to be saved from the waters

143. http://gospelstoryforkids.com/portfolio/gospel-story-Bible-2/ (accessed June 26, 2013).

144. Marty Machowski, *The Gospel Story Bible: Discovering Jesus in the Old and New Testaments* (Greensboro, NC: New Growth Press, 2011), 17.

145. Ibid., 18.

146. Ibid., 55.

147. Ibid., 68.

148. Ibid., 114.

149. Ibid., 137.

of the flood: you had to go through the door of the ark. And there is only one way to be saved from our sin. Jesus said, 'I am the way' (John 14:6). The next time you see a rainbow in the sky, don't just remember the way God saved Noah. Remember Jesus and the way his death brought salvation to us.[150]

Machowski's summary alludes to several connections between the story of Noah and Jesus and salvation. He indicates that the ark saved a person who was an ancient ancestor of Jesus. He uses the door to the ark as an analogy for the way people can turn to Jesus as the door to salvation. He even calls children to remember Jesus and Jesus' death as their source of salvation whenever they see a rainbow. All of these lessons and all of these insights are evidence of Machowski's strong desire to link every story—and even several aspects within one story—to Jesus and salvation.

Rondi DeBoer and Christine Tangvald's 2011 offering, *My Favorite Bible*, created for children ages 4–8, frames the entire Bible around the motif of Jesus as "the Promised One." According to the book's introduction, "This promise of God is the focus of the whole Bible. Every story reflects the Promised One. Every event prepares the way for His coming. Every page proclaims the truth that Jesus is our one and only Savior."[151]

According to DeBoer and Tangvald, then, Noah sees the ark and is "Amazed as he gazed upon God's plan of salvation. God knew exactly how He would save His creation. He provided the one and only way … The Ark."[152] Later, after the flood, as Noah offers a sacrifice, DeBoer rhapsodizes about God's plan of salvation: "Oh! The wonderful plan of God! Noah built an altar to the Lord and thanked God for His one way of salvation, the ark."[153] The analogy between Noah's one way of salvation and Jesus as the one way of salvation may not be apparent to young readers or even their parents. Deboer and Tangvald, however, end each Bible story with a "Family Talk" that somewhat interprets the analogy. Still, they do not directly state that Jesus is the Promised One until they reach the New Testament. Only then do they reveal that Jesus is "the Promised One." In the case of the story of Noah, the authors explain, "The Promised One is like that ark. He is the only way to be saved from the blood of our sin. Like the one door of the ark that Noah and the animals went through to be saved, the Promised One is our one door, the only way we can enter into a joyful life with God forever."[154] Even given this explanation, the analogies may not be clear to 4-to-8-year-old children for whom the book is designed, but the authors convey their theological perspective, namely that the entire Bible is the story of Jesus, to the adults who read the book.

Sarah Young, author of the popular "Jesus Calling" series of devotionals, writes in the preface of her 2012 *Jesus Calling Bible Storybook*, "This book tells

---

150. Ibid., 14.

151. Rondi DeBoer and Christine Tangvald, *My Favorite Bible* (Grand Rapids, MI: Baker Publishing House, 2011), 63. Bold type in the original.

152. Ibid.

153. Ibid., 70. Bold type in the original.

154. Ibid., 72.

the wonderful story of God's great love for His people. It shows that the center, the beginning, and the end of this story all focus on Jesus."[155] She concludes her story of Noah by explaining to children, "God knew that bad things would happen again. But He already had another plan. One day, He would send His Son, Jesus, to save children from evil."[156] Young's take on Noah is different from many others in that she does not attempt to draw a direct correlation between Noah's salvation and salvation in Jesus Christ. Instead, she simply concludes that evil would continue in the world and so God already had plans for Jesus to come to save children from it.

A couple of children's Bibles offer abridged text from modern translations of Bible stories followed immediately by explanatory text that makes an explicit connection between each story and Jesus Christ. *My First Hands-On Bible*, published by Tyndale House Publishers in 2011, presents illustrated and abridged versions of Bible stories from the New Living Translation. Immediately following each story the book offers a "Jesus Connection" in big letters that span the bottom section of two pages followed by some craft and activity ideas loosely related to each story. For the story of Noah on the ark, the book offers "The Jesus Connection—Noah saved the animals by putting them on the ark. And God sent someone to save us—Jesus!"[157] For the story of God's covenant with Noah and the rainbow, the book offers, "The Jesus Connection: Here's another promise God made: He forgives us because Jesus died for our sins."[158] Many children love animals, and it is interesting to note that the editors choose to remind their readers that Noah saved the animals, rather than that God saved Noah and his family. The authors, then, connect Noah's saving act to God's saving act of sending Jesus to save people. While the editors do not change or adapt the biblical text, then, the explanatory notes connect the story of Noah directly to salvation through Jesus.

In a very similar manner, the cover of *The Big Picture Interactive Bible Storybook* describes itself as "Connecting Christ throughout God's Story." The book, published by B & H Publishing in 2013 and not to be confused with *The Big Picture Story Bible* discussed above, presents illustrated and abridged versions of Bible stories from the Holman Christian Standard Bible translation. Every story is followed immediately with a "Christ Connection." For the story of Noah, the Christ connection is as follows:

> Christ Connection: The story of the flood shows us how serious God is about sin. He will not leave sin unpunished. But the story of Noah also shows us how loving God is. He provided a rescue plan for one righteous man—Noah. The rescue was extended to Noah's family. This story points ahead to a greater rescue! Jesus, the only perfectly righteous person, came to take the punishment

---

155. Sarah Young, *Jesus Calling Bible Storybook*, illus. by Carolin Farias (Nashville, TN: Thomas Nelson, 2012), n.p.

156. Ibid., 35.

157. *My First Hands-on Bible* (Carol Stream, IL: Tyndale House, 2011), 28–9.

158. Ibid., 32–3.

for sin. We trust His act of obedience and are saved from the punishment our sin deserves.[159]

Here, the editors immediately follow the story by telling readers that the rescue of Noah points to the rescue of humankind through salvation in Christ. While the publishers of these two children's Bibles do not change the wording of the Genesis account of the story of Noah or add any episodes to help make their theological point, their introduction and cover text, along with immediately following each and every story of the Hebrew Bible and New Testament by drawing explicit connection to Jesus Christ, teach parents and children a Christocentric approach to the Bible.

B & H introduced this approach to the Bible to even younger readers in 2014 with *The Big Picture Interactive Bible Stories for Toddlers from the Old Testament.* The cover again announces that the book is "Connecting Christ throughout God's Story." While the text of the story of Noah does not explicitly mention Jesus Christ, it seeks to prepare toddlers for the plan of salvation. The story of Noah is retold as follows: "The people of the earth had become evil, and God was sorry He had made them. Only Noah obeyed God. In His grace, God saved Noah and his family. God is holy and will punish sin. He is also gracious and will save those who believe in Him."[160] Each story in the book ends with a Big Picture Question and a Big Picture Answer. Here, the question is "Why does sin separate people from God?" and the answer is "God is holy and separate from sin."[161] These theological concepts may be beyond the understanding of most toddlers, but the book's existence serves as concrete evidence of how important these theological concepts are to some twenty-first-century Christians and how important they feel it is to pass that understanding on to their children as soon as possible.

Finally, a couple of twenty-first-century children's Bibles draw analogies between Noah's ark and salvation in Jesus in ways that recall the approach of earlier centuries. The 2007 Arch Book, *A Man Named Noah: The Story of the Great Flood and God's Promise*, by Karen N. Sanders, has only the story of Noah in it, but it also connects the story of Noah with faith in Jesus Christ. Arch Books are popular small books published by the Lutheran-Church Missouri Synod's Concordia Publishing House that tell one Bible story each. Sanders retells the story of Noah in rhyme. She notes that neighbors mock Noah, or as she rhymes it, "'You're sick in the head!' the neighbors said."[162] When the flood comes, however, there is no explicit mention that these neighbors or anyone else died in the deluge. Furthermore, the text does not strike a triumphant chord, but is rather mournful:

159. *The Big Picture Interactive Bible Storybook* (Nashville, TN: B & H Publishing, 2013), 6.

160. *The Big Picture Interactive Bible Stories for Toddlers from the Old Testament* (Nashville, TN: B & H Publishing, 2014), n.p.

161. Ibid.

162. Karen N. Sanders, *A Man Named Noah: The Story of the Great Flood and God's Promise*, illus. by Marcy Ramsey (St. Louis, MO: Concordia Publishing House, 2007), n.p.

"Noah," with dread, God sadly said,
"I've decided to make it rain.
A flood will swirl over the entrance to the world
And get rid of sin and pain."[163]

Put this way, the rain does not kill people or animals, but rather gets rid of the abstractions of sin and pain. While this makes for a good rhyme, it may seem like a remarkable claim for children who have continued to experience sin and pain since the time of the flood.

While the story does not focus on the judgment of the wicked, it does eventually turn the story of Noah's ark into a message of faith in Jesus Christ. On the last page of the story, Sanders explains,

God promised then that never again
Would He flood the entire earth.
Now our faith we base on baptismal grace
And the gift of Jesus' birth.[164]

In case the analogy is lost on children, Sanders ends her tale with the rhyme,

Our water comes down from a Christ-based crown.
God's love makes us remark,
"Since You say so, Lord, we'll trust you, Lord,
Like Noah, who built the ark."[165]

Sanders' connection for her readers, then, is that they should trust the Lord in the way Noah trusted God when he built the ark.

Angie Smith draws connections to the cross of Jesus in the story of Noah's wife in her 2014 book *For Such a Time as This: Stories of Women from the Bible, Retold for Girls*. Smith retells her story of Noah's wife in a way designed to prepare the reader for the analogy to Christ that follows. She opens her story, "*Thud. Thud. Thud.* Noah's wife watched as he hammered, her eyes shining with love for him."[166] Noah's wife has to watch her husband endure the "mocking crowds."[167] When the rain begins to fall, she hears it go "*Drop, drop, drop.*"[168] This all prepares readers for the end of the story, when, according to Smith, "Many, many years later, the sound of a hammer pounding would pierce the silence again, driving nails into

163. Ibid.
164. Ibid.
165. Ibid.
166. Angie Smith, *For Such a Time as This: Stories of Women from the Bible, Retold for Girls*, illus. by Breezy Brookshire (Nashville, TN: B & H Publishing Group, 2014), 10.
167. Ibid.
168. Ibid., 13.

the wood of a cross. *Thud. Thud. Thud.*[169] Having drawn the analogy between the hammer thuds of Noah building the ark and the hammer thuds of nailing Jesus to the cross, Smith extends the analogy to women who observe people mocking someone they love: "While the crowds mocked Him, there would be women who knew what He was doing for God—what He was doing for them. Standing high above the ground, the cross would bring life instead of death."[170] Finally, Smith makes a graphic analogy between the drops of water as the rain began in Noah's day with the drops of blood Jesus shed: "The window of heaven would open again, and scarlet-colored droplets would rain from high above. Jesus Himself would be hung to cleanse us, and the flood of mercy would make us right with Him forever. *Drop, drop, drop.*"[171] Thus ends Smith's extended analogy between the story of Noah's ark and the story of Jesus on the cross.

While reading examples from earlier centuries that draw connections between Noah's ark and other Hebrew Bible stories to Jesus Christ, readers today may get the sense that the authors were aware that they were actively appropriating Bible stories to speak to their own faith and finding meanings that may never have been intended by the original authors. After reading some of the introductions and back cover blurbs from these twenty-first-century children's Bible authors, however, one gets the sense that the authors sincerely believe that the stories of the entire Bible are and always were primarily part of a cohesive message about salvation that would come through Jesus Christ.

In the twenty-first century, many Christians have, out of a sense of ecumenicity and respect for the Jewish faith, refrained from using the name Old Testament, referring to it instead as the Hebrew Bible or First Testament. The children's Bibles noted above, however, offer evidence that the practice of approaching the Old Testament as a thoroughly Christian and Christ-centered book is not fading, but growing in influence and popularity among some American Christians.

3.8. Conclusions

New Testament scholar Warren Carter notes that early Christians read the Septuagint, a Greek translation of the Hebrew Bible, "with Jesus-glasses on,"[172] seeing in it numerous references and prophecies of Jesus Christ. The children's Bibles examined in this chapter illustrate that Christians have continued this practice centuries later throughout US history.

American Christianity has had a particular focus on the person of Jesus Christ and the need for people to make a personal decision for salvation by making a personal commitment to Jesus Christ. The fact that children's Bibles in the US

169. Ibid., 14.
170. Ibid.
171. Ibid.
172. Warren Carter, *Seven Events that Shaped the New Testament World* (Grand Rapids, MI: Baker Academic, 2013) 35–7.

would appropriate the story of Noah's ark to teach children about salvation in Jesus Christ and Christ's Church is, therefore, not surprising. The children's Bible authors discussed in this chapter appear to have felt compelled to use the Bible stories as a plea for repentance and salvation. These authors only occasionally delve into particular theologies of soteriology or Christology. It was enough, it seems, to point children towards repentance, salvation, and toward Jesus.

The children's Bibles described in this chapter reveal certain trends in the ways that children's Bible authors retell the story of Noah during certain eras of American history. They also serve as a reminder, however, that on the basic grass-roots level reflected by children's Bibles, American Christians have not marched lockstep according to certain formally established timelines set for America's religious history. The presumed end of the Puritan era, for example, did not mean that children would no longer be reminded of their sinfulness or warned about God's judgment on sinners. Likewise, the end of the revivalist or evangelical century did not mean that Hebrew Bible stories would no longer be appropriated for evangelistic purposes. The term "type" was often used in children's Bibles before it found a wider use in formal biblical studies. Many later Protestant children's Bible authors followed the principles of typological interpretation, but rarely used the term "type" or "typology."

As seen in the previous chapter and the chapter that follows, it is also worth noting the remarkable multivalency of biblical narratives such as the story of Noah. The previous chapter detailed ways in which the story of Noah has been used to teach lessons about the character of God. The following chapter reveals how the same story has been used to teach particular moral virtues to children. The examples in this chapter all use the story of Noah in yet another way: to point children to Jesus Christ and salvation. Furthermore, not only do these children's Bibles use the story of Noah to point to Christ and salvation, they do so in a wide variety of ways that convey a wide variety of theological, biblical, and practical perspectives on the life and saving work of Jesus Christ and the Church.

It is worth noting that the majority of children's Bibles by Christian authors published in the United States do not transform the story of Noah's ark into a story about salvation in Jesus or the Christian Church. Still, the examples in this chapter attest to a noteworthy strain of American Christianity that has read and appropriated the stories of the Hebrew Bible through the lens of Christianity and Christian salvation.

Concern for children's salvation was one of the first goals of religious education in the United States, and it continues to be the primary goal of many religious educators today. While many children's Bibles have retold their stories in ways that highlight a salvation message, by the end of the nineteenth century another goal had emerged that would become the most common in the way that children's Bibles used Bible stories with children: namely to teach children particular moral virtues.

Chapter 4

THE BIBLE AS A BOOK OF VIRTUES: NOAH AS A MODEL OF VIRTUES AND VICES

Almost all the people in the world were naughty; so naughty, that they never thought of God, or recollected to do what he desired them to do; but they did just what they liked themselves, without caring whether God was pleased or displeased. There was one man who was good: his name was Noah. He was sorry to see so much wickedness, and he tried to make his children good, like himself and always did what he thought would please God.[1]

Scriptural Stories for Very Young Children, 1814

Noah worked every day on the ark. He worked for many years. His sons helped him. Sometimes it was easy. Sometimes it was hard. Sometimes it was fun. Sometimes it was boring. But they knew they were doing God's special work. Noah did everything God told him to do. He was happy because his work made his family strong.[2]

Carolyn Nabors Baker, *The Beginners Bible Tales of Virtue: A Book of Right and Wrong*, 1995

Mrs. Noah kept busy cleaning up after the animals and keeping her family fed and the clothes cleaned.[3]

Carolyn Larsen, *Little Girls Bible Storybook for Mothers and Daughters*, 1998

Children's Bibles retell Bible stories more as a means of passing on cultural moral values and virtues than for any other purpose. To put it another way, the majority of American children's Bible authors have not used Bible stories to promote their own sectarian doctrinal views but rather to instill in children values shared by the wider culture that would be accepted across sectarian bounds. In the Puritan era in America, most children's Bibles were designed simply to transfer knowledge of the

---

1. *Scriptural Stories for Very Young Children* (Philadelphia, PA: Kimber & Conrad, 1814), 23.

2. Carolyn Nabors Baker, *The Beginners Bible Tales of Virtue: A Book of Right and Wrong*, illus. by Kelly Pulley and Lisa Reed (New York: Little Moorings, 1995), 81.

3. Carolyn Larsen, *Little Girls Bible Storybook for Mothers and Daughters*, illus. by Caron Turk (Grand Rapids, MI: Baker Book House, 1998), 32.

words and stories of Scripture to children. During the time of the revivals, many children's Bibles presented the stories of the Bible in ways that called children to salvation. Since the second half of the nineteenth century, however, while Americans have used children's Bibles to serve a wide variety of purposes, the most common way that children's Bibles have used Bible stories has been to pass on specific moral virtues that the dominant culture of America (read "middle-class and upper-class white Protestants") agreed was necessary to make children good citizens. These virtues included spiritual values such as praying regularly and showing devotion to God, but more often the virtues they have taught relate to broader, secular public values such as obedience, hard work, and loyalty.

Children's Bibles that taught culturally accepted virtues became increasingly common in the 1900s. By the end of the twentieth century, children's Bibles had commonly become collections of stories that each taught a moral for living a virtuous life comparable to a collection of Aesop's fables. Through adapting the language of the text and adding a "moral" to the end of the stories, these children's Bibles appear to be designed to insure that children would glean a certain moral or a particular set of morals from each Bible story. Individual children's Bibles, however, use the same Bible stories in very different ways to teach children a wide variety of moral virtues depending on the authors' assumptions or agendas.

4.1. Philosophical, Theological, and Educational Shifts in America's Understanding of Children and Childhood

Moral education has been a part of the general education and religious education of children from the beginning of American history.[4] Between 1850 and 1920, however, a number of gradually overlapping factors seem to have coalesced to create an environment that was conducive to Bible stories being used as fables with each story used to teach a particular moral lesson. The factors that contributed to this shift are complex, gradual, and coincide with the transition to a modern approach of reading the Bible that seeks to analyze and extract concepts or virtues from it rather than to know the content of the Bible itself. These factors, which I detail in the pages that follow, include 1) philosophical and theological shifts in the understanding of children and morality; 2) a growing sense of urgency for the moral education of American children; 3) an increasing openness among American Christians to using narrative literature to pass on moral lessons to children; 4) the role of the Bible in the public school; and finally 5) a desire for religious education materials that would be acceptable to a wide range of Christian denominations.

Throughout the nation's history, Americans have made several significant philosophical and theological shifts in their understanding of childhood. In the

---

4. B. Edward McClellan, *Moral Education in America: Schools and the Shaping of Character from Colonial Times to the Present* (New York: Teachers College Press, 1999), 22–3.

late eighteenth and early nineteenth centuries, many Christians' Calvinistic views led them to believe that children were not capable of learning to act morally prior to conversion. As a result, adults believed there was little value in trying to teach children moral values before they reached the age of accountability and came to a saving faith in God. The moral and spiritual education of children, then, focused not on teaching children particular morals but rather on the knowledge of God and spiritual things. By the end of the nineteenth century, however, many came to abandon this view and embrace John Locke's belief that childhood was a "blank slate" and that children were malleable in their moral formation. This understanding of children as blank slates led to the belief that parents and educators could and should write upon that slate with good values and good character. Romantic ideals of children as pure, natural, emotionally spontaneous, and innocent entered into this thinking as well. As all of these views mingled in the nineteenth century, a gradual and uneven shift occurred in the approach that adults adopted towards teaching children morals and character.[5]

In mid-nineteenth-century America, two educational reformers, Horace Mann in the realm of public education and Horace Bushnell in the realm of religious education, each rejected the doctrine of innate human depravity and shared a belief that parents and teachers could and should provide children with an education in morality. Their efforts helped increase America's desire for its children to receive a moral education. Mann, the champion of the common school movement in America, appealed to the need for moral education for America's children as a primary purpose of the common school movement. According to Mann, "The germs of morality must be planted in the moral nature of children, at an early period of their life."[6] In the second half of the nineteenth century, parents were becoming increasingly concerned not only for the moral education of their own children but also for the moral education of other people's children as well. B. Edward McClellan suggests that many middle-class European Americans began to fear that the rapidly growing immigrant population, as well as African-Americans and Native Americans that were increasingly entering their workforces, would not become moral citizens or a productive working class. This fear also may have motivated the leaders of the public school movement to push for a public school system that would instill values in America's children that would form them into good citizens.[7] By the turn of the century, more and more school districts enforced laws that required children to attend schools, and school

5. See Karen Sánchez-Eppler, *Dependent States: The Child's Part in Nineteenth-Century American Culture* (Chicago: University of Chicago Press, 2005), xvii–xviii, and Steven Mintz, *Huck's Raft: A History of American Childhood* (Cambridge, MA: Harvard University Press, 2004), 75–91.

6. Horace Mann and William Bentley Fowle, *The Common School Journal* 1:1 (November 1831): 14.

7. McClellan, *Moral Education*, 22–3.

lessons increasingly reinforced virtues that factory owners and heads of industry valued such as punctuality, obedience, and hard work.[8]

Also in the nineteenth century, Horace Bushnell was urging parents to reject the view, common amongst revivalists, that they should permit their children to grow up in sin. Bushnell argued against the common belief that prior to salvation children could really do no good on their own anyway. Rather than try to teach children to live morally, writers and clergy sometimes encouraged parents to let their children stew in their sin. They believed that in this way, when children reached the age of accountability, the Holy Spirit would more easily convict them of their sin and lead them to repent, leading to their salvation at a younger age. After this, they believed, children would naturally begin living a moral life through the sanctifying work of the Holy Spirit. Bushnell argued against this approach and instead urged parents to nurture their children's spiritual and moral character.[9] Bushnell's views did not immediately have much impact on the religious education of children, but by the end of the century his views began to have a growing influence in the Church and wider society.

These various factors help explain the increased desire for moral education in America, especially moral education that would help children grow into productive citizens. They still fail to explain, however, why religious educators increasingly began to turn to the stories of the Bible as the source of these moral values.

Controversies in the Sunday School and the public schools may have contributed to this shift in the use of Bible stories with children. James C. Wilhoit argues that in the late 1800s the influential American Sunday School Union changed its curriculum to focus on specific moral virtues in order to continue to serve Churches of a wide range of beliefs. Different doctrinal beliefs regarding salvation caused concerns among some of the Union's ecumenical constituents, and, according to Wilhoit, "The ASSU's solution to crossing this divide was, in the *Union Questions*, through spiritualizing or moralizing the text."[10] Wilhoit explains that "The Union's focus on behaviorally defined character traits, as opposed to a well integrated Christian lifestyle, grows out of their conviction and desire to find a content that transcended denominational differences."[11]

Another factor that contributed to this change arose out of controversy over Bible reading in public schools. Starting with a court case in Cincinnati in 1870, there were several voices calling to ban the Bible from public schools due to the multiple faiths held by their students. Some argued that the Bible was a sectarian book that would cause divisiveness in society if public schools taught it as part

8. Micahel B. Katz, *Class, Bureaucracy, and Schools* (New York: Praeger, 1971), 34–6.

9. Horace Bushnell, *Christian Nurture* (Grand Rapids, MI: Baker Books, 1861, 1979), and Horace Bushnell, *Views of Christian Nurture and Subjects Thereto* (New York: Scholars Facsimiles & Reprints, 1975).

10. James C. Wilhoit, "The Bible Goes to Sunday School: An Historical Response to Pluralism," *Religious Education* 82 (1987): 402.

11. Ibid., 401.

of their curriculum.[12] In order to defend the Bible from these attacks, many politicians and clergy made the case that the Bible was a necessary part of the public school curriculum because it contained timeless values for life that all students needed to learn in order to become good citizens.[13] Bible curriculum and teaching guides, then, began to model an approach to the Bible in which each Bible story was used to teach a specific moral virtue. Furthermore, these virtues tended to be the ones that would best shore up the society and maintain the status quo.

Soon, educators began to use Bible stories to communicate those values. Sometimes the curriculum used Bible stories to teach a basic lesson on good character, such as the importance of being good and not naughty. In the early twentieth century, however, children's Bibles and the religious education curriculum increasingly used Bible stories to pass on the sort of virtues that would lead children to become good citizens and good employees. The widespread desire to pass on such values in educational settings consequently seems to have had a profound effect on the way that authors and clergy, as well as educators, used the Bible not only in public schools but in the church and in the home as well.

Though this style of teaching the Bible was short-lived in the public schools in many regions of the country, it had a long-term effect on how Americans understood and used Bible stories. The children who learned this approach to the Bible daily in their schools would grow up to write Bible curricula and children's Bibles that would pass on this approach to future generations of Americans. A new generation of future Church leaders, Bible study curricula writers, and children's Bible storybook authors grew up learning to read the Bible in order to find the moral to each story, and they passed that approach on to the children who read their materials.

These factors help explain why Sunday School materials and Bible study curricula materials used the Bible to teach citizenry values. Still, these factors alone do not explain why authors started writing and parents started purchasing children's Bibles that used Bible stories in this way. Several factors related to the popularity and use of children's literature provide a clue to the reasons for this shift.

Up until the late 1800s, some Sunday School curricula contained moralistic short non-fiction stories to impress morals on children.[14] Many Christian leaders and educators, however, maintained a prejudice against storybooks in general, and taught American parents to be suspicious of fictional literature of any kind. Fictional tales were, by definition, untruths, and many considered reading stories a form of idleness in which the devil could find a foothold. Several factors helped lead to the reversal of this trend.

---

12. Charles R. Kniker, "New Attitudes and New Curricula: The Changing Role of the Bible in Protestant Education, 1880–1920," in, *The Bible in American Education: From Source Book to Textbook* (Philadelphia, PA: Fortress Press, 1982), 126.

13. Ibid., 126–30.

14. Wilhoit, "Bible Goes to Sunday School," 395.

In 1872, Jacob Abbot, one of America's foremost parenting experts of the day, wrote *Measures in the Management of the Young* in which he argued against teaching children through corporal punishment and argued for teaching children moral values though literature.[15] Partly as a result of this book, both evangelical and liberal parents were soon using extremely moralistic children's literature to help teach their children proper behavior.[16]

Another factor that moved Protestant America to embrace novels and storybooks in the years that followed was the tremendous popularity of Lew Wallace's novel *Ben-Hur: A Tale of the Christ*. Published in 1880, Wallace's story contained partial retellings of scenes from the Bible, and the first section of the book recounting Jesus' birth was actually republished as a children's Bible storybook of sorts itself.[17] The book's story of bravery and its pious evangelistic message led many Protestant clergymen not only to permit but to encourage their flocks to read the fictional story. Largely due to these endorsements, *Ben-Hur* quickly became the best-selling American novel of all time, with the initial editions selling over a million copies. Sales of the book helped revolutionize the bookselling industry in America and the reading habits of American adults and children.[18] Suddenly, it seemed for many Christians that purchasing and reading novels and storybooks was not only an acceptable practice, but could be a pious exercise as well.

In this context, with parents looking for children's literature that they could trust and that taught virtues, it is not surprising to see Americans turn to the stories of the Bible as a source for storybooks that taught children the virtues that would help them be good and productive members of society. Advances in printing technology, along with the great increases in the publication and distribution of books, resulted in a marked increase in the number of children's Bibles and children's books in general at the end of the nineteenth century.

In the late 1800s and early 1900s, then, publishers offered Americans many children's storybooks that emphasized these citizenry virtues. For a while, during the post-World War Two era, many children's Bibles tended to be large-volume or even multi-volume works that contained translations of the Bible or rather exhaustive retellings of Bible stories printed in single columns with many illustrations or photographs. In the late 1970s and 1980s, however, children's Bibles that taught children citizenry virtues were once again very popular.

The resurgence of children's Bibles teaching socially conservative values in the late 1970s, the 1980s, and the years that followed coincided with the growing

---

15. Jacob Abbot, *Gentle Measures in the Management of the Young* (New York: Harper and Brothers, 1872), and the discussion of the book in Bernard Wishy, *The Child and the Republic* (Philadelphia, PA: University of Pennsylvania Press, 1968), 92–104.

16. Mintz, *Huck's Raft*, 82.

17. Lew Wallace, *The Boyhood of Christ* (New York: Harper & Brothers, 1888).

18. For more on the effects of *Ben-Hur* on American popular culture, see Russell W. Dalton, "Introduction," *Ben-Hur: A Tale of the Christ* (New York: Barnes and Noble Books, 2004), xiv–xix.

anxiety many parents and authors felt about the perceived shifts in American culture at the time. Many Americans longed for "traditional" values and joined organizations such as the Moral Majority. As outlined by James Davison Hunter in his books *Culture Wars: The Struggle to Define America*[19] and *The Death of Character: Moral Education in an Age Without Good or Evil*,[20] America's Christian leaders and parents wanted their children to learn traditional "family values."

At the same time, many evangelical churches taught their members that every passage of Scripture had a lesson that could be applied to their daily lives. This hermeneutical approach to the Bible continued to pick up momentum and became perhaps the primary way that religious educators used Bible stories with children in the early twenty-first century. Many children's Sunday School lesson plans briefly recount a Bible story or recite a Bible verse, draw a moral from it, and then continue with an extended lesson on the importance of that moral virtue, whether it be obedience, honesty, courage, or another moral virtue. A survey of shelves of items for children in a twenty-first-century Christian bookstore reveals that this trend continues in resources for the home as well. The children's DVDs and storybooks on the shelves are more likely to be instilling citizenry values such as honesty, friendship, sharing, obedience, and willingness to work than they are to be presenting primarily spiritual and religious lessons on topics such as salvation, prayer, stewardship, forgiveness, or the nature of God.

Given the factors discussed above, it is not surprising to find that children's Bibles increasingly promoted the dominant American culture's social agenda for America's children. Some children's Bibles emphasized the general theme of being a moral person in an immoral society, but more often children's Bibles used Bible stories to highlight particular virtues, such as obedience to God, parents, and all those in authority, and working hard without complaint. Many of these children's Bibles appropriated the popular story of Noah to teach these values in a number of interesting and creative ways.

4.2. Noah as the Good Man in the Midst of Sinners

Many children's Bibles of the late nineteenth and early twentieth centuries were not very complicated in their moral teachings. The basic lesson these children's Bibles extracted from most Bible stories was simply that children should be "good" as opposed to being "bad" or "naughty." As with most moral teaching of children through the past few centuries, parents, teachers, and clergy taught children that if they were good they would be rewarded and if they were bad they would be punished. American children's Bibles have used the story of Noah to offer children at least two perspectives on this theme. First of all, a number

---

19. James Davison Hunter, *Culture Wars: The Struggle to Define America* (New York: Basic Books, 1991).

20. James Davison Hunter, *The Death of Character: Moral Education in an Age Without Good or Evil* (New York: Basic Books, 2000).

of children's Bibles commend Noah for being good and staying good despite the wickedness that surrounded him. Second, some children's Bibles commend Noah not necessarily for being good but for simply *trying* to be good.

4.2.a. Standing apart from society

Throughout American history, some children's Bible authors used the story of Noah and other Bible stories to teach children the basic lesson that people of faith should be people of good character even while living in the midst of a sinful world of unbelievers. Interestingly, many of these stories appear at times when, in retrospect, many historians argue that society was less sinful and more pious. In any case, many children's Bibles and religious education materials made the case that religious children should take a counter-cultural stand by staying pure and unpolluted by the wickedness of the wider society. In actuality, however, these stories usually lifted up the norms and values that the wider society accepted.

The Book of Genesis states that "The Lord saw that the wickedness of humankind was great in the earth, and that every inclination of the thoughts of their hearts was only evil continually" (Gen. 6.5). In contrast, Genesis notes that Noah was morally innocent or "a righteous man" (Gen. 6.9). The Genesis account, however, does not contain any episodes in which Noah is tempted by his neighbors to join them in their wicked ways or in which he privately struggles to stay on the moral path. Contrary to popular belief, Genesis contains no account of any interactions that Noah may have had with any people outside of his own family. Many of these children's Bible authors, however, make effective use of the embellishment of Noah's neighbors mocking him and scorning him as he built the ark. Unlike the examples found in previous chapters, however, these children's Bibles did not use Noah's mocking neighbors to help explain how God could drown so many people or to caution children concerning the risks of waiting too long to accept God's offer of salvation. In these examples, Noah's mocking neighbors serve to underscore the virtue of remaining good and faithful even while those around you are wicked.

Scriptural Stories for Very Young Children, first published in London but reprinted in Philadelphia in 1814, merits an extended examination. It is one of the first children's Bibles published in the United States that emphasized living a life of virtue without the overriding motivation of escaping eternal punishment or death. The book has only sixty-eight pages and included just two plates. One of these plates is an illustration of a smiling Noah welcoming the dove back onto the ark. The anonymous author begins his retelling by contrasting Noah to the people around him, using language young children probably heard from their parents when they misbehaved:

> Almost all the people in the world were naughty; so naughty, that they never thought of God, or recollected to do what he desired them to do; but they did just what they liked themselves, without caring whether God was pleased or displeased. There was one man who was good: his name was Noah. He was

sorry to see so much wickedness, and he tried to make his children good, like himself, and always did what he thought would please God.[21]

The author builds into the story the implicit lesson that one should try to convince others to do good and that one must resist the efforts of others who try to get children to misbehave:

> Though the wicked people laughed at him, and tried to make him do wrong, he would not. He would have been glad to have taught them to behave better, and to be sorry for their faults and sins; but they would not listen to him. So, though he could not make other people good, he took care that they should not make him wicked.[22]

Noah successfully resists the efforts of the wicked to bring him down to their level. According to the story, it was because Noah was good, in sharp contrast to the blatantly wicked lifestyle of others, that God loved him: "When God saw that all the people in the world were wicked, except Noah and his family, he said they should not live any longer then [*sic*] one hundred and twenty years. But God loved Noah, because he tried to be good, and to do what was right."[23] Later in the retelling, in case the point has not been clear enough to his or her young readers, the author explicitly addresses the issue of trying to be good in a wicked world and encourages children to read the Bible with this virtue in mind:

> Do you not think that Noah was very good? Well, then, you must try to be as good as he was; for it is of no use to read about good men, if you do not try to be good like them. That is one reason why the Bible was written by good men, and that we may know that God made us, and all the world; another reason is, that we may try to be good, like the people we read about in that book. Jesus Christ has told us all that [sic] we must do to please God, and to make him love us. We must, therefore, read the Bible, that we may learn what to do. When we read it, we must consider how happy the good people were who are mentioned there. When we read this history about Noah, we should remember that he loved God, though nobody else did; and that he would not do what was naughty, although all the people tried to persuade him to do so.[24]

The author, then, urges children to be good like Noah and encourages them to love God and remember how Noah resisted being naughty, even when others tried to persuade him to do so. The author continues to underscore these points. Even if other people mock them for being good, they should persist, for this is the way to earn the love of good people and the love of God:

21. *Scriptural Stories for Very Young Children* (Philadelphia, PA: Kimber & Conrad, 1814), 23.
22. Ibid.
23. Ibid., 24.
24. Ibid., 33–4.

If you meet with any naughty boys, you should tell them what is right; but if they will not listen to you, but laugh at you, and mock you, come away, and do not play with them any more, for fear you should grow naughty like them. If you cannot make them do what is right, take care to do it yourself. Never mind being laughed at for being good: it is only silly, foolish people, who will laugh at you for doing what you ought to do; and good people will love you, and praise you. Besides, I will tell you what is better still, God will love you.[25]

This retelling, then, offers some benefits for being good. For one, good people will love you. More importantly, being good will earn one the apparently conditional love of God. It is worth noting that authors do not give these lessons to children in the introduction of their children's Bibles or as a summary of lessons to be learned from the Book of Genesis; instead, they integrated these lessons into their retellings of the story of Noah and other Bible stories.

The author of *The Patriarchs; or, Bible Histories for Children*, published by the American Baptist Publication Society in 1852, emphasizes a similar theme. The author begins the story by explaining, "Men had gone from bad to worse."[26] The author continues, "But amid all this wickedness there was one man who feared God, and brought up his children to fear him. This was Noah."[27] Noah warned the people around him to repent, but they did not believe him. According to the book, "Some of them even laughed at Noah because he believed it. But Noah believed what God had said, he would surely do; and so he did not mind them, but kept on and built his ark exactly as God told him he must do."[28] According to the story, then, because Noah had faith in God he persevered in his work despite the fact that others did not believe him. As a matter of fact, he did not even mind people laughing at him.

In *The Illustrated Scripture Alphabet* from around 1855, the letter N stands for Noah. Scripture alphabets are a fascinating and entertaining genre. Each letter of the alphabet denotes a different character or item from the Bible. The task of converting the story into rhyme forces the author to adapt the text and in many cases the result reveals the author's assumptions about what lessons children should learn. According to the page for the letter N,

NOAH, who by faith saw the fierce deluge pour,
Was forty years building his ark for that hour.
Tho' oftentimes mocked, yet his faith stood the shock,
As his ark stood the waves. 'Tis sinful to mock.[29]

---

25. Ibid., 34–5.

26. *The Patriarchs; or, Bible Histories for Children* (Philadelphia, PA: American Baptist Publication Society, 1852), 20.

27. Ibid., 20–1.

28. Ibid., 21–2.

29. *The Illustrated Scripture Alphabet: with prayers and hymns for children* (Boston, MA: J. Buffum, 1855), n.p.

First, the rhyme suggests the positive virtue of enduring ridicule. Noah was often mocked, "yet his faith stood the shock." Second, the author reminds children "'Tis sinful to mock." The author, then, uses the story of Noah's mocking neighbors—an embellishment that is not in the original biblical account—as the basis for both of the lessons that she or he draws from the story of Noah (see Figure 4.1).

The Rev. John Howard's large two-volume *Scripture History for the Young* from 1876 was a popular book that went through many editions and was reprinted by many publishers. Doré's illustration *The Deluge* accompanies the story, and Howard writes, "The same evil spirit that had caused Cain to kill his brother, now spread over the world so much wickedness, that the Divine Being determined to destroy the sons of Adam."[30] According to Howard, however, the tale of Noah teaches us that one can resist the sinfulness of one's surrounding culture: "Noah's righteousness, in the midst of so much sin and depravity, is a proof that we have within us the power to withstand temptation, if we will but exert it. And our being surrounded by crime in all its varied forms should only be an inducement for us to buckle on more tightly the armor of faith."[31] Noah had the power to withstand temptation, and Howard tells his readers that they have the power to resist temptation as well.

In like manner, according to Rev. John Rusk's children's Bible from 1902, *Beautiful Stories that Never Grow Old*, "There were a great many people on the earth at this time and they were all very bad except one man. The good and the bad had mingled until both were pulled down together."[32] Rusk takes a unique approach, interweaving the story of Noah with the story of a young woman who is wearing a white dress and who asks her father why she cannot stay with her "charming" friends. In response, the father takes a pair of tongs covered in charred ashes and asks her if she would take them. She refuses, saying, "One cannot be too careful when they handle charred timber."[33] The father responds, "That is true my daughter, nor can we be too careful in the company we keep."[34] The story then draws a parallel between Noah, who did not allow the bad people of his time to sully his character, and the young woman who needs to be wary of socializing with her charming friends. Noah stood apart from his naughty neighbors, and girls in the present day can stand apart from their neighbors as well.

The story of Noah in *Bible Stories for Children* (1919) offers a similar moral. The book identifies its author only as "A Catholic Teacher." The book veers significantly from the Genesis account in order to emphasize how important it is for one to be honest and good even if others mock you because of it. According to the account,

---

30. John Howard, *The Illustrated Scripture History for the Young* (New York: Virtue and Yorston, 1876), 11.

31. Ibid., 12.

32. John Rusk, *Beautiful Stories that Never Grow Old* (1902), 53. Copyrighted by John Rusk but no place or name of publisher given.

33. Ibid., 55.

34. Ibid.

NOAH, who by faith saw the fierce deluge pour,
Was forty years building his ark for that hour.
Tho' oftentimes mocked, yet his faith stood the shock,
As his ark stood the waves. 'Tis sinful to mock.

Figure 4.1. The letter N from *The Illustrated Scripture Alphabet: with prayers and hymns for children* (Boston, MA: J. Buffum, 1855), n.p.

After a great number of years, so many people became very bad and committed such awful sins that God said: "I will destroy man from the face of the earth."

But among all these sinners there was one good man called Noe … It took Noe many years to build this ark. During all that time, he was trying to make the people sorry for their sins; but they would not listen to him and kept on eating, drinking and making merry in sinful ways.[35]

Here, the author appears to have drawn upon Matthew 24.37-39, which indicates that people were eating and drinking and marrying, linking this with some of the vices of people in Noah's day. The author then interrupts the telling of the story in order to make the lesson explicit for the readers' present-day lives:

Noe feared God; but he did not fear the people who were so wicked. Sometimes little children fear people so much that they will not do what is right. Once in a while you may see a little boy or girl who is ashamed to tell the truth or to be nice to companions, because bad children make fun of them for it. Never do this, dear little ones; pay no attention to such children, but remember God and do what you know pleases Him Who loves you so much.[36]

The "Catholic Teacher" uses Noah's story to tell children, in effect, that they should not allow bad children to pressure them or intimidate them into being bad, but that, instead, the desire to please God and their fear of God should motivate them to be good.

Elsie E. Egermeier also called children to stand apart from their neighbors. Egermeier was an editor for the Gospel Trumpet Publishing Company, the precursor to Warner Press, and was part of the Church of God Reformation Movement. Writing during the roaring '20s, Egermeier often underscored the importance of good character in the midst of a secular, evil world in her stories. In her book *Egermeier's Bible Story Book* from 1923, she said of Noah, "Here was a man who tried to do right regardless of all his wicked surroundings."[37] For Egermeier, many Bible characters were made of stern stuff when it came to their piety, and Noah was no exception.

Miss Bettie's Book of Bible Stories, written by Bettie Burson and published by Wm. B. Eerdmans Publishing in 1939, is a highly moralistic work that lifts up a number of virtues to children and emphasizes the importance of doing good work and standing apart from the wickedness of the world. The remarkable Burson was a young widow who taught at the State Orphans Home in Texas. She had a great impact on her students and often stayed after school hours to tell Bible stories to the children. Burson's story does not reflect a very positive view of humankind. In the passage that follows, she describes God as being "disgusted" with wicked people, and does not shy away from bluntly saying that God is going "to kill all the people":

35. *Bible Stories for Children* (New York: Schwartz, Kirwin & Fauss, 1919), 11–12.

36. Ibid., 12.

37. Elsie E. Egermeier, *Egermeier's Bible Story Book* (Anderson, IN: Warner Press, 1923, 1939), 30.

God became so disgusted with the wicked people that he thought he would drown every one of them with all the live things on earth; but when he looked down into Noah's heart he saw that Noah was not so wicked as the rest of the people; so he talked to Noah saying, "Noah, I am going to kill all the people on the whole earth, except you and your family."[38]

Note that instead of praising Noah's virtue, Burson gives him the faint praise that he is not as wicked as the others.

Burson further reveals her pessimism about human nature when she condemns even Methuselah who many other children's Bibles lift up as a model of righteousness: "Even old Grandpa Methuselah would not pay any attention when Noah kept telling him, that if he did not quit his meanness he was going to be drowned with the rest of the world, while Noah and his family would be safe in the Ark."[39] She uses the embellishments of Noah preaching to the neighbors and their mocking of him to underscore the importance of trying to "do better" in one's moral behavior: "Noah worked away on the boat and preached to the people, telling them that if they did not do better God was going to send a flood of waters all over the whole earth and drown every living creature; but they only laughed at him and did not do any better at all."[40]

Burson uses Noah's work building the ark to make a point about how many people in her day failed to observe the Sabbath properly:

> Noah built this Ark way out on the plains where there was not even a stream of water, so the people had made fun of him and made it hard for him to keep working those hundred and twenty years. You say that you do not see why it was hard for Noah after God had talked to him and told him what to do and how to do it. Well, you try this, God has told us to remember the Sabbath day to keep it holy. Most of the people around you do their own pleasure on God's Holy day. Are you doing as they do, or are you keeping Sunday holy in spite of what they do?[41]

In describing the death of the wicked, Burson alludes to the language of Genesis, writing that "nothing that breathed could find any breath."[42]

Those who have seen cities and towns that have been devastated by floods know how messy the land can be following a flood. Burson, however, gives an optimistic picture of a world cleansed from all its wicked people:

> Can you imagine the nice clean world that greeted the eyes of Noah and his family? Everything had been washed clean by the waters of the flood. Every

---

38. Bettie Burson, *Miss Bettie's Book of Bible Stories* (Grand Rapids, MI: Wm. B. Eerdmans Publishing Company, 1939), 27.

39. Ibid.

40. Ibid.

41. Ibid., 28.

42. Ibid., 29.

wicked thing that man had ever made in the history of the world had been destroyed. It was like a new world, a new world without sin.[43]

Given Burson's distress over the wickedness of so many people, one might sense a new-found optimism for the future of humankind in this new world. Burson's very next lines, however, are, "Oh that it could have remained that way! But it was not to be, for sin was soon to enter it again."[44] In Burson's vision of Noah's world and her own, most people are wicked and one must live life in a very different way from them.

The late 1960s and early 1970s were times of great cultural upheaval in the United States. People began to question and doubt societal institutions, including religious ones. The cover of the April 8, 1966, issue of *Time* magazine asked "Is God Dead?" and exposed the nation to the thought of Friedrich Nietzsche and others. Many religious communities tried to offer an answer. In the decades that followed, some children's Bibles used the story of Noah to impress upon children the need to stay faithful and moral at a time when many were questioning traditional faith and traditional values.

David Daniel's *The Complete Book of Bible Stories for Jewish Children* from 1971 contrasts Noah and his neighbors and commends Noah's righteousness in their midst:

> God's heart was filled with sorrow when He saw how ugly people were making His beautiful world. He became very angry. God was pleased, however, that there was at least one man who was good and kind. That man was Noah. Even though Noah lived in the midst of wicked people, he did not allow their sinfulness to turn him from his good ways.[45]

The story assumes that good people are in danger of letting the wicked people around them turn them from their good ways. Noah, to his credit, did not do so and stood apart from his neighbors and their wicked ways.

Gwen Ellis's *Read and Share Bible* from 2007 makes a similar point. When God tells Noah to build an ark, "Noah started right away. People laughed at Noah because they lived in a desert and there was no water for his boat. Noah just went on building the boat."[46] Steve Smallman's cartoon-style illustration on the page shows Noah's neighbors pointing and laughing and Noah is clearly troubled that he is being mocked. At the bottom of the page, in a box separated from the rest of the text, the reader is asked, "Do you think it is easy to obey when everyone is

---

43. Ibid., 31.

44. Ibid.

45. David Daniel, *The Complete Book of Bible Stories for Jewish Children* (Jersey City, NJ: KTAV Publishing House, Inc., 1971), 19.

46. Gwen Ellis, *Read and Share Bible*, illus. by Steve Smallman (Nashville, TN: Thomas Nelson, 2007), 21.

laughing at you?"[47] Ellis, then, acknowledges to her young readers that standing apart from others and staying true to one's faith can lead to being mocked, but encourages children to do so anyway.

The stories above commend Noah for being someone who takes a counter-cultural stance. It is significant, however, to note how these children's Bibles do this. Their stories do not call upon children to defy any particular values that the majority of Americans accept. Instead, these versions of the story of Noah call upon children to obey God, believe in God, or simply to be good while everyone around them is being wicked.

4.2.b. Standing apart even when others think you are crazy

In the last decades of the twentieth century, when many evangelicals saw themselves in the midst of a cultural war, a small cluster of children's Bibles appeared that used the story of Noah to suggest, among other things, that if they believed God and followed God's commands the world around them might think they are crazy, but that they should remain faithful anyway. These examples use the embellishment of Noah's mocking neighbors, not in Genesis, to underscore this point by having the neighbors call Noah crazy for building the ark.

In Jenny Robinson's *The Encyclopedia of Bible Stories* (1974), not only do Noah's wicked neighbors call him crazy, but there is a danger that his own sons might think he is crazy as well. For Robinson, a native of Scotland who worked as a school social worker, the story is not so much about the morality of living a virtuous life in a wicked world as it is about maintaining one's faith in a world of unbelief. The story makes the case that Noah was not crazy for hearing God's voice and following God's command though the rest of the world might think him mad. To do this, Robinson introduced some imagined conversations between Noah and his sons. As the story begins, Noah's sons are initially alarmed to find him building a boat and ask him what he is doing:

> Noah looked at them with a twinkle in his eyes. "I'm building a boat, sons," he said. "Don't worry, I'm not going mad—though folks are certainly going to think so! God has told me to build a boat."
>
> "Why?" they asked. They weren't surprised that God had spoken directly to their father, nor that Noah was doing exactly what God told him, however strange it seemed, because they knew that Noah and God were very close, almost like friends, in fact, and that Noah always tried to please God in everything.[48]

The narrative carries the implicit message that if one follows God's commands and listens to God's voice, others may think you are crazy. Robinson's story does not

---

47. Ibid.

48. Jenny Robinson, *The Encyclopedia of Bible Stories*, illus. by Gordon King (Philadelphia, PA: A. J. Holman Company, 1974), 18.

make an explicit claim that Noah is sane, but instead uses the characters of Noah's sons to provide reliable commentary attesting to Noah's close relationship with God. Yes, Noah is living his life differently than others, but that does not make him crazy. Robinson next introduces the embellishment of Noah's mocking neighbors: "Many people came to watch. Quietly, Noah went on with his work. He told everyone exactly what God was going to do, but no-one believed him. They laughed at him, and went away, shaking their heads: 'He's gone mad, stark raving mad.'"[49] While Noah's neighbors call him stark raving mad, the way that Noah faithfully talks of God's commands and faithfully carries out his work suggests that it is actually Noah's neighbors that are out of touch with reality because they are out of touch with God.

Sandy Silverthorne's *The Great Bible Adventure* from 1990 also has neighbors who call Noah crazy because he follows God's commands. The book includes illustrations that are full of people and things, similar in style to the "Where's Waldo" books of the time. In Silverthorne's version of the story of Noah, the neighbors are especially mean-spirited in their language, and their mocking of Noah serves to underscore his determined obedience to God's commands. The story begins, "Noah refused to listen to the taunts and jeers of his neighbors. 'Hey, idiot!' they called. 'Why are you building a boat on dry land?' At times, Noah must have wondered if he really *was* crazy. But God had told him to build an ark and he wasn't going to disobey the voice of the Lord."[50] Silverthorne therefore creates a bit of drama by having Noah himself wonder if he is crazy, an idea that could potentially lead children to consider thoughtfully the nature of faith. The indecision is short lived, however, because it is clear that no amount of mocking is going to cause Noah to disobey the voice of God.

In 1998, evangelical authors and speakers Dottie and Josh McDowell released *The Right Choices Bible* in which they retold Bible stories in ways designed to highlight the right or wrong choices that the Bible characters made. Very often, as in the case of Noah, the right choice is one that is counter to the values of the culture that surrounds them. According to the story, Noah is worried that people would laugh at him if he started to build a boat: "Now Noah had a big choice to make. He could say, 'Yes, I'll build the boat. I'll do it even if there is no water and no rain in sight.' Or he could say, 'No, I won't build the boat. Then my neighbors won't laugh at me.'"[51]

The text underscores the irrational nature of building a boat with no water in sight. Joe Boddy's illustration on the facing page shows Noah with a wooden hammer and a plane, pausing from his work to look up to the heavens, while people in the background point at him and laugh. The McDowells then quickly report, "What did Noah do? He got a hammer and wood, and he began to build

49. Ibid., 19–20.

50. Sandy Silverthorne, *The Great Bible Adventure* (Eugene, OR: Harvest House, 1990), n.p. Emphasis in original. For a very similar scenario, see Pat Alexander, *The Children's Story Bible* (Louisville, KY: Westminster John Knox Press, 1991), 9–10.

51. Dottie and Josh McDowell, *The Right Choices Bible*, illus. by Joe Boddy (Wheaton, IL: Tyndale House, Inc., 1998), 20.

the boat."[52] The story of Noah concludes, "God always loved Noah and was glad he had made a good choice."[53] For the McDowells, ignoring the opinions and the scorn of others and following God's commands, even when it might seem irrational, is the right choice.

In 2002's *Focus on the Family Bedtime Bible*, Rick Osborne, Mary Guenther, and K. Christie Bowler title their story of Noah "Crazy or Right?"[54] Like Josh McDowell's ministries, Focus on the Family is an evangelical ministry that has often advocated that Christians should stand apart from and against many of the prevailing values of the wider culture and has prepared those in their ministries for the mocking or misunderstanding they might receive because of their faith. The authors take a creative approach to the story of Noah, retelling it from the perspective of Noah's young son Shem. The story emphasizes the lessons that faith is counter to the culture and that people of faith are often persecuted, yet the faithful are to evangelize their neighbors. Christian readers are meant to identify with Shem, who tries to get his friends to give themselves to God and God's ways: "Shem's heart ached for his friends. He tried to convince them to stop sinning and perhaps God would save them too. But they only laughed at him. 'Yeah, right! Whatever you say, Shem.'"[55] The title and story encourage children to stay true to their faith, in this case demonstrated by telling friends about God and obeying God's commands, even when those around them think they are crazy.

Zondervan's *The Veggie Tales Bible: New International Version* (2009) is a children's study Bible that offers notes that are presented as being told to children by characters from the popular children's video series *Veggie Tales*. The note in a box on the page of the text of Genesis chapter 6 has Junior Asparagus, a talking stalk of asparagus who wears a baseball cap, offer children the following thoughts:

> What would you do if God told you to do something crazy? Ask Noah. He looked pretty crazy to all his friends as he built a gigantic boat, right in the middle of the desert. Real crazy! Silly! Nuts! But he built it. He did what God told him to do, not caring what other people thought. And because Noah did, he saved the lives of his family.[56]

While the text of Scripture is taken directly from the New International Version, the notes are presented in a box right next to the holy writ. In this case, they present a message that people might think you are crazy if you obey God, but you should do it anyway.

52. Ibid., 22.

53. Ibid.

54. Rick Osborne, Mary Guenther, and K. Christie Bowler, *Focus on the Family Bedtime Bible* (Wheaton, IL: Tyndale House, 2002), 39–44.

55. Ibid., 40.

56. *The Veggie Tales Bible: New International Version* (Grand Rapids, MI: Zondervan, 2009), 7.

Many of these authors and publishers of the late twentieth century have quite a high regard for the inspiration and authority of the canonical text, so one might presume that they would be disinclined to add to the Genesis account or to raise doubt about the sanity of a Bible hero. Instead, these authors not only add the embellishment of Noah's mocking neighbors, but use the extra-biblical episode as the source of the lesson they feel children should primarily glean from the story. Furthermore, they tweak the embellishment of Noah's mocking neighbors to have them call him crazy in order to encourage children to remain true to their faith even if their views lead others to question their sanity. The truly faithful, this version of the story seems to imply, will be mocked and even be called crazy.

4.2.c. *"Trying" to do what is right*

According to Genesis, Noah was "a righteous man, blameless in his generation" (Gen. 6.9) and, according to the same account, Noah follows every one of God's commands completely. What, then, accounts for the number of children's Bibles that commend Noah not for being "good" but for "trying" to be good? Unlike much of the moral teaching of children throughout American history, this teaching introduces the role of one's internal motivations, and not just one's external actions, into the moral equation.

Scriptural Stories for Very Young Children, a book initially published in Britain but republished in the United States in 1814, provides an early example of this motif. According to its version of the story, "When God saw that all the people in the world were wicked, except Noah and his family, he said they should not live any longer then [sic] one hundred and twenty years. But God loved Noah, because he tried to be good, and to do what was right."[57] It was because Noah tried to be good, in contrast to the blatantly wicked lifestyle of others, that God loved him.

Another nineteenth-century example of Noah *trying* to do what is right comes from the pen of the prolific English novelist Charlotte Mary Yonge. Yonge was known for her moralistic novels. She made a distinction between books for "the drawing room," for the upper classes, and books for "the cottage," for working-class children, who Yonge felt needed less subtle and more direct lessons in their literature.[58] Yonge specialized in novels for the upper classes and her work was criticized at times for including some of the prejudices and mores of England's social elite.[59] In *Young Folks' Bible History*, published in Boston in 1880, Yonge suggests that the fact that Noah tried to do good was one of the things that saved him:

The reason Noah was saved was because, first he tried to be good, and not do like the bad people around him; and next, because he believed what God said to

57. *Scriptural Stories for Very Young Children* (Philadelphia, PA: Kimber & Conrad, 1814), 24.

58. See Gillian Avery, *Behold the Child: American Children and Their Books 1621–1922* (London: Bodley Head, 1994), 123.

59. Ibid., 155.

him, and went on making the ark, even when he saw no danger. If we wish God to save us, then we must take care that we do just what we are told—not what seems pleasant now, but what is really right.[60]

Yonge emphasizes trying to be good, even when others are being bad, as one of the reasons God saved Noah. To further emphasize the point, Yonge's commentary notes that children should "take care" to follow instructions and obey even when the task seems unpleasant.

Initially published in 1921, *The Wonder Book of Bible Stories* was quite popular, going through at least ten editions. Logan Howard-Smith, a member of St. Paul's Episcopal Church in Philadelphia, wrote the book under his occasional pen name of Logan Marshall. Actually, according to the book, Marshall merely "arranged and edited" the book. The stories contained in the book, however, are clearly not just edited and arranged but completely rewritten. For the story of Noah, for example, Marshall writes that God said, "Everyone must die, because they are all wicked. But you and your family shall be saved, because you alone are trying to do right."[61] Marshall underscores that all the people are wicked and suggests that it is crucial that one put forth an effort to be good. *Trying* to do what is right, the story seems to suggest, is the best that one can do.

Edna B. Rowe wrote *Bible Stories for Little Folk* (1926) with the goal of building the character of children. In her preface, Rowe writes that like the hidden foundations of a building, "The forgotten things build future characters."[62] She adds that, "Noah loved God, and tried always to do what was right. The other people were wicked. They did not care for God."[63] Rowe repeats the motif of *trying* later in the story. God tells Noah, "You shall be saved because you are trying to do what is right."[64] Rowe, then, does not only open her tale by crediting Noah for "trying" to do what was right, but she also suggests that this is the reason God saved Noah.

Eulalie Osgood Grover, whose father was a congregational minister in New England, wrote reading primers including the popular *Sunbonnet Babies Primer*. In 1927, she offered a children's Bible titled *Old Testament Stories*. Grover opens her story of Noah by explaining, "Noah was a good man who tried to obey God's laws, and his sons grew up to be good men like him. But the other men of that

---

60. Charlotte M. Yonge, *Young Folks' Bible History* (Boston, MA: D. Lothrop Company, 1880), 21–2. This exact quote is reproduced, without any credit or citation, in Lindley Smyth, Jr., *Happy Sundays with the Bible, Arranged for the Fifty-two Sundays of the Year; an Interesting Method of Fixing Indelibly Upon the Minds of Young and Old, the Important Truths of the Old Testament and of the New Testament, by Symbols, Pictures and Stories* (Philadelphia, PA: Uplift Publishing Company, 1908), 24.

61. Logan Marshall, ed., *The Wonder Book of Bible Stories* (Philadelphia, PA: John C. Winston Company, 1921), 9.

62. Edna B. Rowe, *Bible Stories for Little Folk*, illus. by Otto Stemler, with copies from the Old Masters (Cincinnati, OH: Standard Publishing Company, 1926), 5.

63. Ibid., 20.

64. Ibid.

time were very wicked."[65] Grover later puts into God's mouth the idea that Noah and his family are *trying* to do what is right. God says to Noah, "Every living thing shall be drowned. But you and your family shall be saved, because you are trying to do right."[66] Grover makes no claim that Noah or his family is morally perfect. They are singled out by God because they are *trying* to do what is right.

It was not only reformed Protestants who carried on this theme in the 1920s. In *A Child's Garden of Religious Stories*, from 1929, Rev. P. Henry Matimore, a Roman Catholic and professor of Education at Loyola University, contrasts Noah with those who lived around him: "Noe was just, kind, and faithful. He tried to do what was right, although all about him were wicked."[67] Matimore not only carries on the theme of *trying* to do what is right, but also underscores the way Noah stood apart from the wicked people around him.

In 1949, Marian M. Schoolland, a member of the Christian Reformed Church of North America and graduate of Calvin College, told the story of Noah in *Marian's Favorite Bible Stories*. Her retelling focuses on the negative side of moral intention. Schoolland not only chides the wicked in Noah's day for their actions, but for their feelings and their lack of effort as well:

> Once upon a time, many years ago, God looked down upon the earth and saw that men were very, very sinful.
>
> God made us, and we ought to serve Him. But in those days men forgot all about God. They just did whatever they wanted to do. They did not love God. They did not even think about Him. They did not try to do what is right.[68]

Schoolland does not detail the wicked people's sinful actions. Instead, the story suggests, they are bad for what is inside their heads and hearts. They are bad because they forgot about God, did not love God or even think about God, and did not *try* to do what is right.

Bedtime Bible Stories, from 1955, titles the story of Noah "The Boat Noah Built."[69] In this story, mocking neighbors antagonize Noah while he works, but they fail to deter him from doing God's will. According to the story, God chose Noah for the job because "Every day he tried to do the things that are right."[70] The phrase "every day" underscores the virtue found in constantly striving to do those things that are right.

What accounts for this use of the term "tried to" be good? Especially curious is the cluster of examples of this phenomenon in the 1920s. Is it just an anomaly,

---

65. Eulalie Osgood Grover, *Old Testament Stories* (Boston, MA: Little, Brown, and Company, 1927), 14.

66. Ibid., 15.

67. Henry Matimore, *A Child's Garden of Religious Stories*, illus. by Carl Michel Boog (New York: Macmillan Company, 1929), 21.

68. Marian M. Schoolland, *Marian's Favorite Bible Stories* (Grand Rapids, MI: Wm. B. Eerdmans Publishing Company, 1949), 19.

69. *Bedtime Bible Stories* (Racine, WI: Whitman Publishing Company, 1955), 14.

70. Ibid.

or does it reflect an early renewed interest, following the events of World War One, in the reformed doctrine of original sin? Reinhold Niebuhr would not publish his influential book *Immoral Man and Moral Society* until 1932,[71] and Christian Realism would only enter the wider Christian consciousness in the years following World War Two. These children's Bibles possibly indicate that some pessimism about Christian progressivism and human perfectibility emerged earlier in the public mind, and perhaps reflect the conservative theology of some of their authors who were reacting to some of the more liberal theology of their time. If this is the case, they could be insisting that the best that sinful humans can do is to *try* to do what is right. On the other hand, this trend could have had more to do with emerging understandings of children and their moral development and moral education. Educators and psychologists were telling parents and teachers that they should not hold children to impossible standards, but instead nurture them in their own emerging moral development. Another possibility is that this trend was simply a sign of secular times. While being surrounded by people who lived the wild lifestyle of the roaring '20s, perhaps some Christian authors hoped that the next generation would at least try to do what is right and to follow God's commands. In any case, this small handful of examples illustrates that not all moral educators expected children to behave in a perfect manner, but they did expect them to *try*.

4.3. Noah as a Model of Obedience

4.3.a. Noah, a man of obedience

From one perspective, commending Noah for obeying God could be seen as another general appeal to children to be good and follow God's commands or as an appeal to a piety in which one completely submits to God's will. The examples from children's Bibles that follow certainly include those perspectives on the virtue of obedience. As the examples progress into the twentieth and twenty-first centuries, however, one also gets the sense that it is the particular virtue of obedience itself, whether that is obedience to God or obedience to other authority figures such as parents, supervisors, or others, that many children's Bibles are commending to their young readers.

The United States is a nation birthed in rebellion against authority, nearly divided by what some called "The Great Rebellion" during the time of the Civil War, a nation that questioned the blind obedience of others in the aftermath of World War Two, and a nation that came to question its own leaders and institutions during the eras of the Vietnam War and the Watergate scandal. Still, America has consistently and persistently taught its children to obey their teachers, parents, and others in positions of authority; many religious educators in particular have

---

71. Reinhold Niebuhr, *Moral Man and Immoral Society* (New York: Charles Scribner's Sons, 1932).

taught children the virtue of complete and unquestioning obedience to the will of God.

Obedience to authority figures, such as God, parents, and other adults, is the virtue that is most often emphasized through the stories in children's Bible storybooks.[72] As a matter of fact, nearly all of the virtues discussed in this chapter could be placed under the umbrella of the virtue of obedience to God and could be framed as part of carrying out God's will.

4.3.b. Using embellishments, commentary, and repetition to underscore Noah's obedience

The fact that children's Bible authors have used the story of Noah to teach children the importance of obedience is not surprising. Commentators such as George J. Wenham have noted that the Genesis account of the flood, in contrast to other ancient flood stories, emphasizes its hero's obedience rather than other virtues.[73] James McKeown notes, "God gives the instructions and does the work that is beyond human capability, but in return the human beings and even the animals must obey."[74] Bill T. Arnold writes that Genesis repeatedly notes Noah's obedience (Gen. 6.22, 7.5, 8.18, 9.18) and observes that it is a quiet obedience since the character of Noah goes about his tasks and does not speak until Genesis 9.25-27, after he has followed all of God's instructions.[75] While the text of Genesis itself, then, provides plenty of fodder for teaching children the virtue of obedience, children's Bible authors have also appropriated previous embellishments, such as Noah's mocking neighbors, in particular ways and created embellishments of their own in order to underscore the virtue of obedience in ways their young readers might understand. They have also used repetition of the word "obey" to make the same point.

Hazel Gillmore Alden's *The Kingdom of Heaven. An Instruction in The Catholic Faith for Children* from 1907 provides a good example of how these embellishments were used to highlight the virtue of obedience. Alden titles the tale of the flood "The Story of Noah: Obedience" and introduces it as one would a fairy tale by writing, "Once upon a time there lived a man by the name of Noah, and a very

72. For example, when the story of Abraham and Isaac is retold for children it is often not Abraham's submission to God but rather Isaac's obedience to Abraham that is emphasized, as in J. H. Willard, *The Boy Who Obeyed: The Story of Isaac* (Philadelphia, PA: Henry Altemus Company, 1905). In these reconstructions, authors suggest that Isaac could have easily escaped his father, but passively allowed himself to be bound because he knew that children should obey their parents no matter what.

73. George J. Wenham, *Word Biblical Commentary: Genesis 1–15* (Waco, TX: Word Books, 1987), 165.

74. James McKeown, *Genesis* (Grand Rapids, MI: William B. Eerdmans Publishing Company, 2008), 57.

75. Bill T. Arnold, *Genesis* (Cambridge: Cambridge University Press, 2009), 99.

good man he was, too, as you will soon see."[76] Alden retells the tale in a way that casts God as a work supervisor of sorts who places unusual demands on a worker and in the process highlights Noah's unquestioning obedience:

> God told Noah to do a strange thing. At least Noah's neighbors thought it strange, because they did not understand it, and people are apt to think things strange which they do not understand. As for Noah, he did not stop to think whether it was strange or not, because he knew it was God's will, and so he set to work at once, on this task that God had given him. It was quite a long task, even in those days, for it took nearly a hundred years, but Noah did not stop, you may be sure, until it was finished.[77]

Alden embellishes the tale with a scene in which other people think he is odd and make fun of him.[78] According to Alden's story, Noah obeys despite all of the factors that might lead a person to disobey a command from someone in authority. In case her readers have missed her point, Alden adds a moral to the end of her story to make it clear:

> There are many things to think about in this story of Noah, and one of the things is his obedience. When God told him to build the Ark, he did not say to himself, "Oh, I guess I won't do it just now, there is plenty of time," and when God told him just how to build it, he did not think he would try some other way. No indeed, and if he had put it off and if he had built it his own way it might not have floated at all![79]

Alden acknowledges the multivalent nature of the biblical narrative, and uses it here not only to commend the virtue of obedience, but to explain that people should do what they are told to do right away and refrain from putting it off until later. This virtue of not only obeying, but obeying right away and without question, is a common theme in many children's Bibles, whether it is describing how one should obey God or one's parents.[80]

In 1960, Dena Korfker, a teacher in Sunday School, Mission Sunday Schools, and in Daily Vacation Bible Schools, also emphasized the virtue of obedience in her retelling of the story of Noah through repeating the word "obey" multiple times. One could argue that the Genesis account does the same thing, repeating several times that Noah did what God asked him to do. Korfker writes of the sinners, "But all the people were sinful. Most of them, like Cain, did not love

76. Hazel Gillmore Alden, *The Kingdom of Heaven. An Instruction in The Catholic Faith for Children* (New York: Church Publishing Company, 1907), 26.

77. Ibid., 27.

78. Ibid.

79. Ibid., 29.

80. See, for example, my article, Russell W. Dalton, "Meek and Mild: American Children's Bibles' Stories of Jesus as a Boy," *Religious Education* 109:1 (2014): 49–53.

God. They would not obey Him."[81] Noah and his family were different, however. According to Korfker, "All eight people in this family loved God. They obeyed Him and served Him."[82] When God speaks to Noah, he says, "The world is very wicked. The people do not obey Me."[83] When God commands Noah to build the ark and gather the animals, Korfker writes, "Noah obeyed God. He began at once to build the ark."[84] Korfker's narrative also emphasizes how long it took for Noah to build the ark:

> But it took a long time to build such a huge boat. It took one hundred and twenty years! And during all those years, while Noah was working on the ark, he preached to the wicked people. He warned them of the great flood that was coming. But the people only laughed. They thought Noah was foolish for building such a huge boat when there was no flood. They did not believe God's word. And they kept on being wicked.[85]

By describing how Noah persisted in his work while other people persisted in their wickedness, Korfker underscores Noah's obedience.

Susan L. Lingo's *My Good Night Bible*, published in 1999, provides questions and lessons after each Bible story. She titles the story of Noah "Noah Obeys God," and includes as a subtitle the verse "*God said, 'Obey me.' Jeremiah 7:23*."[86] By providing these titles, Lingo prepares her readers for the lesson she hopes they will learn from the story. Lingo's retelling points out that people everywhere were disobeying God, and that only Noah loved God. There is no mention of anyone drowning and the story ends by reassuring children, "Drip, drip, drop—God's love will never stop!"[87] After the story, Night-Light the firefly asks children the following questions:

* Why did Noah obey God?
* What did God say?
  "Obey me."
* Who can you obey?[88]

We can presume that the answer to the final question is "God," but the wording of the final question allows children to think of others whom they might obey as

---

81. Dena Korfker, *My Picture Story Bible* (Grand Rapids, MI: Zondervan Publishing House, 1960), 29.

82. Ibid.

83. Ibid.

84. Ibid.

85. Ibid., 29–30.

86. Susan L. Lingo, *My Good Night Bible* (Cincinnati, OH: Standard Publishing, 1999), 29.

87. Ibid., 30.

88. Ibid., 31.

well. The "Sleep Time" section of the story tells children, "Tonight's Bible word is **obey.** Think about how happy you feel when you obey God. Night-Night!"[89] In addition to Lingo's retelling of the story, then, her titles, closing questions, and closing commentary all serve to highlight the virtue of obedience.

Bible Stories for Boys and *Bible Stories for Girls* were published in 2011 by Scholastic Publishing with the American Bible Society logo on the cover. *Bible Stories for Girls* contains stories of biblical women and does not contain a version of the Noah story. In *Bible Stories for Boys*, however, the story of Noah is included and used to teach the virtue of obedience to God.

> God asked Noah to build a boat.
> "Yes! I'll start right away!"
> Whatever God asked of Noah,
> He was quick to obey.[90]

As with children's Bibles of years past, the Bible hero obeys cheerfully and right away.

The examples above are just a few of the many children's Bibles that have, in one way or another, emphasized Noah's obedience. Besides the use of embellishments and repetition, children's Bibles have used a number of different strategies to retell the story of Noah to compel children to be obedient.

4.3.c. Minding Noah

Children's Bible authors use many Bible stories to commend children for obeying their parents or to demonstrate the virtue of obeying or serving those in authority. The story of Noah, however, seems to involve only Noah and God and therefore is used primarily as an example of how people should obey God. A couple of early children's Bibles, however, position Noah as an authority figure of sorts and condemn his neighbors for their failure to obey *him*.

D. P. Kidder's small 1851 book, *Bible Stories for Children*, for example, tells his readers that the wicked people would not obey Noah, or as Kidder explains it to children, "They would not mind."[91] The neighbors, then, are condemned for not minding Noah's instructions, not for their refusal to obey God's commands. Meanwhile, in contrast to those neighbors, the animals were obedient: "All these went into the ark; for God made them gentle and obedient."[92] The phrase "they would not mind" is one that children would find familiar and the image of even the animals being gentle and obedient would likely have made an impression on his young readers as well.

---

89. Ibid. Bold in original.

90. *Bible Stories for Boys* (New York: Scholastic, Inc., 2011), 4.

91. D. P. Kidder, ed., *Bible Stories for Children*, Vol. I (New York: Lane & Scott, 1851), 36.

92. Ibid., 38. A similar motif is found in Faith Latimer, *Dear Old Stories Told Once More* (New York: American Tract Society, 1877), 14–16.

Annie R. White's *Easy Steps for Little Feet*, from 1903, also emphasized the virtue of obedience by explaining that even the animals obeyed God: "All these went into the ark; for God made them gentle and obedient."[93] She proceeds to describe the people of earth as disobedient and, when the flood came, "How the wicked people must have wished they had minded Noah!"[94] Again, the story gives children an example of the consequences of not minding those in authority. After the flood, Noah steps out of the ark and reflects on the new world. According to the text, "Noah saw all the green hills and fields again; but where were all the wicked people? He would never see their faces again."[95] White simply states this stark truth as a fact. She does not tell her readers whether Noah found this fact satisfying or depressing. It simply serves to remind the reader that the disobedient people were all dead and Noah and his family alone were left alive. The phrase "minded Noah," so closely followed by a description of the dire consequences of not doing so, could prompt children to avoid the mistake of the wicked and obey those in authority over them.

4.3.d. The practical benefits of obedience

Children's Bibles written for Generation X also represent the first children's Bibles written by and purchased by adults of America's Baby Boom generation. The Baby Boom generation had items marketed to them that met their needs, and regularly looked for what might be beneficial to their own interests. These generational characteristics may help explain the reason why, beginning in the 1970s, an increasing number of children's Bibles began to commend to children the practical benefits of obeying God. Some go further, not only pointing out that Noah's obedience served his own best interests, but that the disobedience of the wicked had severe, negative consequences for them.

V. Gilbert Beers' *Jesus is My Guide* (1973) titles his story of Noah "Noah Obeys and Makes a Boat." Beers, a former editor at David C. Cook Publishing and *Christianity Today* magazine, writes, "Noah listened to God. He loved God. He wanted to obey God. So Noah began working on the big boat the way God had told him."[96] Beers adds, "For many years Noah worked on the big boat. At last it was done. Noah had obeyed God."[97] The story ends with Noah's little boy and Noah himself underscoring the point of the story:

Then all the bad people were gone.
But the water did not hurt Noah and his family. It did not hurt the animals.

93. Annie R. White, *Easy Steps for Little Feet from Genesis to Revelations* (Los Angeles: Martin Press, 1903), 24.
94. Ibid.
95. Ibid., 28.
96. V. Gilbert Beers, *Jesus is My Guide* (Grand Rapids, MI: Zondervan Publishing House, 1973), n.p.
97. Ibid.

They were all in the boat that Noah had made.
"I am glad we obeyed God," one of Noah's boys whispered.
"We must always do what God tells us," Noah said.[98]

According to the story, then, Noah's son is glad they obeyed God. He whispers this thought. Perhaps he whispers because it is a profound thought. Perhaps he whispers out of fear of God, having seen what God did to those who did not obey him. In any case, Beers' text conveys the idea that obeying God is not only a good thing to do for its own sake. There are glad benefits to obeying God and dire consequences for not obeying God.

Nearly twenty years later, Beers would offer another children's Bible that retells the story of Noah with an emphasis on the same theme of obedience. According to Beers' 1992 book, *The Toddlers Bible*, when Noah sees that he is safe from the flood he is moved to pray. "'Thank You, God,' Noah said. He was glad now that he obeyed God."[99] In Beers' later edition, then, he not only tells children that Noah said we must obey God, but adds that when he had survived the flood, Noah was glad that he obeyed God.

Christine Harder Tangvald focuses on the same theme in *The Big Big Big Boat and Other Bible Stories about Obedience*, published by Chariot Books in 1993. Tangvald subtitles her story of Noah "Noah OBEYS God." According to Tangvald's account, the laughter of Noah's neighbors did not deter him from following God's instructions: "'Ha! Ha! Ha!' said all the other people. 'Look at silly Noah. He is building a silly boat! Ha! Ha! Ha!' But Noah just kept on building. BANG, BANG, BANG! **Hammer, hammer, hammer!** *SAW, SAW, SAW!*"[100] Later, when the people ask Noah why he is putting animals on the boat, Noah replies, "Because God told me to. That's why."[101] Tangvald explains that the flood covered the earth, "But Noah and his family were safe and cozy inside the BIG BIG boat with all of God's animals ... because Noah had OBEYED God."[102] Tangvald makes the point that Noah's obedience is what kept Noah and his family safe from the flood, a fact she emphasizes by placing the word "OBEYED" in all capital letters. Tangvald revisits the theme as she closes her story of Noah:

"Hooray for Noah!
Hooray for God!"
"Good job, Noah," said God.
"Thanks, God," said Noah.

98. Ibid.
99. V. Gilbert Beers, *The Toddlers Bible*, illus. by Carole Boerke (Colorado Springs, CO: Cook Communications Ministry, 1992), 31.
100. Christine Harder Tangvald, *The Big Big Big Boat and Other Bible Stories about Obedience* (Elgin, IL: Chariot Books, 1993), 6. Capital letters, bold type, and italics are all in the original.
101. Ibid., 7.
102. Ibid., 10.

"I'm glad I OBEYED You."
"So am I," said God. "So am I."[103]

The language is light and fun, but the implication is that Noah and his family's fate would have been much worse if he had not obeyed God.

Mary Hollingsworth's 1993 Bible storybook, *My Very First Book of Bible Heroes*, also suggests that Noah was saved because he obeyed: "Noah built the big boat just the way God said. That made God happy. So God saved Noah's family and all the animals from the flood. Noah was a real hero."[104] Hollingsworth does not explicitly say that Noah's obedience led to God saving him, but the language is quite suggestive. Noah builds the boat just the way God said, *so* God saves him. Hollingsworth ends the story with two questions for children, and provides answers, in parentheses, that underscore the point:

1. Why was God pleased with Noah? (Noah obeyed God.)
2. Will God be pleased with you if you obey Him? (Yes.)[105]

Hollingsworth does not emphasize obedience as a duty, or something to do solely out a sense of piety for God's sake. Instead, she suggests that Noah is a hero and God is pleased with him because he obeys, and tells children that God will be pleased with them if they obey God.

Obedience, both to God and other authority figures, is a featured virtue in several children's Bibles authored by Carolyn Larsen. Larsen's stories of Noah also highlight the practical benefits of obeying God and the dire consequences suffered by people who do not obey. In 1994's *My Bedtime Bible* she writes, "Noah was the only man who obeyed God. So God saved Noah and his family. Everyone else was killed in the biggest flood ever. All because people didn't obey God."[106] Larsen notes in quick succession that Noah obeyed God, Noah was saved, everyone else was killed, and unambiguously notes that they were killed because they did not obey God.

In *My Favorite Bible Storybook for Early Readers* from 2005, Larsen titles the story of Noah, "Obeying Pays Off."[107] In similar fashion, Larsen titles the story of Noah in her *Jesus Said Bible Storybook*, from 2003, as "Obeying Saves Noah."[108] According to the latter book, "Only one man still obeyed God. That man was

---

103. Ibid., 12.

104. Mary Hollingsworth, *My Very First Book of Bible Heroes*, illus. by Rick Incrocci (Nashville, TN: Thomas Nelson, 1993), 12.

105. Ibid.

106. Carolyn Larsen, *My Bedtime Bible* (Iowa Falls, IA: World Publishing, 1994), 34.

107. Carolyn Larsen, *My Favorite Bible Storybook for Early Readers* (Franklin, TN: Dalmatian Press, 2005), 30–5.

108. Carolyn Larsen, *Jesus Said Bible Storybook*, illus. by Rick Incrocci (Nashville, TN: Thomas Nelson, 2003), 18.

Noah."[109] Following the story, Larsen describes Noah's unquestioning obedience to God:

> It wasn't raining when God told Noah to build the ark. But Noah was a wise man. He did what God said. He didn't ask God a lot of questions. He didn't argue with God. He just obeyed Him. Noah and his family would have drowned in the flood, just like everyone else, if Noah had not obeyed God's words.
>
> We are wise when we obey God's words, too.[110]

Larsen's closing commentary makes it clear that Noah would have suffered dire personal consequences if he had not obeyed God and tells her readers that they would be wise to obey "God's words" as well, even when those commands do not make sense to them.

Lion Hudson's *365 Bible Stories for Young Hearts* (2006) is a book originating in Britain but widely available in stores in the United States as well. The book is designed so that parents can share the Bible with their children in just 90 seconds per day. The book's section on Noah is titled "Day 8: Noah Obeys Orders."[111] According to the story, "Noah did exactly what God told him"[112] and later, "Noah obeyed God's instructions."[113] To underscore the theme of obedience, the story informs children that obedience is what kept Noah safe, for it was "because Noah and his family had obeyed God's warning, they were safe inside the ark, floating on top of the water."[114]

Gospel Light's 2009 offering, *God's Story for Me: 104 Favorite Bible Stories for Children*, also titles the story "Noah Obeys God."[115] The retelling of the story emphasizes obedience as well as the virtue of work. Two pages with two large illustrations serve to emphasize the way Noah and his family worked hard building the ark: "Noah and his family listened and obeyed! They chopped trees and cut wood. They pounded boards and brushed on tar."[116] It continues, "They worked hard for a long time. They did everything God said to do. Finally, the big boat was finished."[117] At the end of the tale, the author offers the moral, "Obeying God helps us stay away from trouble. Obeying shows we love God."[118] The moral

---

109. Ibid.

110. Ibid., 23.

111. Lion Hudson, *365 Bible Stories for Young Hearts* (Wheaton, IL: Crossway Books, 2006), 22.

112. Ibid.

113. Ibid., 24.

114. Ibid.

115. *God's Story for Me: 104 Favorite Bible Stories for Children* (Ventura, CA: Gospel Light, 2009), 32.

116. Ibid., 34.

117. Ibid., 35.

118. Ibid., 37.

of the story is that a practical benefit of obeying God is that it keeps us out of trouble.

In the 2012 edition of *The Preschooler's Bible*, V. Gilbert Beers teaches his young readers about obedience through repetition. Over the course of the book's six pages on the story of Noah, with each page containing only one to three sentences, Beers repeats some version of the phrase "Noah obeyed God" eight times. He introduces the story of Noah by noting, "Noah always tries to obey God."[119] God tells Noah to build a boat and "Noah obeys God."[120] When God tells Noah how many animals to gather, "Noah does what God says. He obeys God."[121] When God tells Noah to put his family on the ark, "Noah and his family obey God. They do everything God says they should do."[122] When God tells Noah to go onto the boat, "Noah does what God says. Noah always obeys God."[123] Beers' version of the story seems designed to fix the phrase "Noah obeys God" in the minds of the young children and their parents.

As the story continues, Beers suggests the benefits of obeying God or at least the dangers inherent in failing to obey God. When the floodwaters rise higher than the mountains, "Noah is glad now that he obeyed God."[124] During the flood, when Noah and his family find that they are safe on the ark, "Noah is glad that he obeyed God."[125] The relationship between Noah and God is made more intimate with the phrase, "Noah loves God. God loves Noah."[126] The story ends with Tammie Lyon's illustration of Noah praying beside a smiling camel and smiling ram and the words, "Are you glad Noah obeyed God? Are you glad when you obey God?"[127] The story does not simply suggest that children should obey God because it is the right thing to do, but that they should obey God because it will help them be happy and escape from harm.

The virtue of obedience has long held a place of privilege in the moral education of children. Throughout America's history, only the most comprehensive children's Bibles have retold Bible stories in which characters question or defy God such as when Abraham debates God in Genesis 18 or when Moses defies God and stands up for his people in Exodus 32. In contrast, children's Bibles more often retell stories such as Abraham's complete obedience when God asks him to kill his son, the stories of young Isaac and Jephthah's daughter completely obeying and submitting to their fathers even as they realized that those fathers are going to kill them, or invented stories of Jesus as a child happily obeying every single

---

119. V. Gilbert Beers, *The Preschooler's Bible* (Colorado Springs, CO: David C. Cook, 2012), 24.

120. Ibid., 25.

121. Ibid., 26.

122. Ibid.

123. Ibid., 29.

124. Ibid.

125. Ibid., 30.

126. Ibid.

127. Ibid., 31.

command from his parents.[128] The examples of the retellings of the story of Noah provided above demonstrate a number of ways that children's Bibles have used the story of Noah to teach children lessons about obedience. As the rest of the chapter will show, however, obedience is far from the only virtue the story is used to teach.

4.4. Noah, the Hard Worker

After obedience, the virtue of work has been the next most common virtue that has been taught to American children through children's Bibles, in particular the importance of doing hard work without complaining about it.

In her book, *The Bible for Children*, Ruth B. Bottigheimer describes a two-tiered tradition of children's Bibles from 1750 to 1850 in which those written for the poor included hard work as part of their religious agenda while those written for the affluent did not.[129] Bottigheimer notes that in the years that followed 1850 there emerged "single-class" Bible story collections that promoted work and industry as virtues for all readers.[130] Gillian Avery notes in her study of American children's literature that self-reliance and industry were common themes in the second half of the nineteenth century.[131] By working hard and taking advantage of opportunities, children could succeed.

At the end of the nineteenth century and with the dawn of the twentieth century, the American economy needed workers who would join a workforce away from their family farm or family trade. America had a vested interest in forming their children into disciplined, obedient citizens who would understand their work as a vital part of who they were.[132] In this context, many children's Bible authors have been quite explicit in drawing the lessons from Bible stories that children should work hard and not complain, and the story of Noah is no exception.

When it comes to the story of Noah, of course, the virtues of obedience and hard work are quite intertwined. God commands Noah to build the ark and gather the animals and Noah obeys and carries out the work. The children's Bibles that follow do not have an exclusive interest in the virtue of work, but often find subtle ways to highlight the virtue of hard work in the ways they retell the story.

One way in which children's Bibles place a subtle emphasis on the virtue of work is to focus on the amount of work that Noah did, which also serves to under-score the extent to which Noah was willing to obey and trust in God. Gordon

---

128. For more on the stories of the child Jesus' obedience, see my article, Dalton, "Meek and Mild," 49–53.

129. Ruth B. Bottigheimer, The Bible for Children: From the Age of Gutenberg to the Present (New Haven, CT: Yale University Press, 1996), 94–100.

130. Ibid., 91–102.

131. Avery, *Behold the Child*, 6–8.

132. See Michael B. Katz, *Class, Bureaucracy, and Schools* (New York: Praeger, 1971), 11ff.

J. Wenham's commentary on Genesis 1–15, for the *Word Biblical Commentary* series, points out that Genesis repeats the fact that Noah obeyed God throughout its account of the flood story[133] and notes that, as opposed to the Gilgamesh epic's depiction of its flood hero, Utnapishtim, "Genesis plays down Noah's effort, merely mentioning his obedience."[134] Many children's Bibles, however, do emphasize the effort and amount of time Noah worked, and rewrite the story in ways that implicitly or explicitly underscore the effort and time Noah spent building the ark. Sometimes the illustrations that accompany the story of Noah also emphasize the work of Noah and his sons as they built the ark.[135]

One of the first American children's Bibles designed to use Bible characters as role models for virtuous behavior was the Rev. Richard Newton's *Bible Models; or The Shining Lights of Scriptures* from 1896. In the preface to *Bible Models*, Newton writes, "The author of this book has endeavored to place before young readers, in a clear and forcible manner, the admirable traits of character possessed by some of the great men of the Bible. The advantages to be gained by following these 'Bible Models' are plainly shown by many interesting stories drawn from actual life."[136] The book is more a series of lessons on Bible characters than a collection of Bible stories. The chapter on Noah is titled "Noah, the Model Worker,"[137] and it introduces many motifs that later American children's Bibles would include as well, such as the virtue of getting to work quickly, persevering in one's work, and not allowing hard work to be a discouragement. The book does not include any of Gustave Doré's illustrations that depict people in distress during the flood or dead bodies littering the ground after the flood. Instead, the story is accompanied by a Doré's illustration *Noah Building the Ark* that depicts Noah sawing a log while his sons strain to lift a large log and chop wood (see Figure 4.2).[138] According to Newton, no ship like the ark had ever been built, and neither Noah nor his sons were shipbuilders by trade. But Noah did not back down from the job given to him: "And if, for reasons like these, he had begged to be excused, from under-taking a work of so much difficulty, it would not have been at all surprising. But Noah did nothing of the kind. He did not make the slightest objection. Instead of this he went out to work at once."[139] Newton notes that Noah was a ready worker: "And it is always pleasant to see those who follow Noah's example, and do the

133. Wenham, *Word Biblical Commentary*, 165.

134. Ibid., 178.

135. For example, see the illustrations in Harriet T. Comstock, *Bible Stories Retold in Words of One Syllable* (New York: A. L. Burt Company, 1900), 4; Margaret Sangster, *The Story Bible* (New York: Moffatt, Yard & Co., 1905), 44; *Bedtime Bible Stories* (Racine, WI: Whitman Publishing Company, 1955), 15; Patricia Summerlin Martin, *Beautiful Bible Stories* (Nashville, TN: Southwestern Company, 1964), 22.

136. Richard Newton, *Bible Models; or The Shining Lights of Scriptures* (Philadelphia, PA: Charles Foster Publishing Co., 1896), 6.

137. Ibid., 57.

138. Ibid., 59.

139. Ibid., 60.

work they have to do in the same ready way."[140] Furthermore, Noah was a persevering worker:

> How much trouble he must have had, in getting the right kind of wood, with which to build the ark! And when the wood was found, how much trouble he must have had in getting the right sort of workmen, to carry on the building! And how many other difficulties he must have had, of which no account is given! But, notwithstanding all these difficulties, he went patiently on, for a hundred and twenty years, till his work was done. How well we may speak of Noah as a model of perseverance.[141]

Noah, then, kept on working even when he faced the sorts of obstacles many workers face in a day of work. According to Newton, Noah was also a successful worker, for, "You and I owe a debt of gratitude to Noah for his successful work. If it had not been for the way in which he did that work, we never should have lived in this world, and never should have had the opportunity of doing any good here."[142] For Newton, then, Noah was a ready, persevering, and successful worker. These characteristics made him a model of the sort of worker any business owner would be happy to employ.

Harriet T. Comstock was a novelist and author of several children's stories. Her 1900 children's Bible is titled *Bible Stories Retold in Words of One Syllable*,[143] although like many books of its kind it uses hyphens to split up two- or three-syllable words as well. The book retells the story of Noah's ark in a way that places a subtle emphasis on a good work ethic. The story is titled "No-ah trust-ed in God and went to work and built the Ark"[144] and is accompanied by a large engraving from around 1860 by the German painter Julius Schnorr von Carolsfeld (1794–1872) titled *The Prophecy of the Flood*, which shows Noah and his sons hard at work building the ark (see Figure 4.3). The text of the story explains, "Noah trust-ed God and went to work: for in that far off time to do what God had said meant much work and took a long time."[145] Unlike the text of Genesis, then, Comstock emphasizes the amount of work and the length of time it would take to do the work. adding, "I think Noah must have had a hard time while he worked, for no one thought as he did, and yet he nev-er for one mo-ment stopped the task which God had bade him do."[146] Again, the Book of Genesis does not mention the difficulty of Noah's work or whether he ever took a break, but by telling the story

140. Ibid.

141. Ibid., 63.

142. Ibid., 76.

143. This volume was also published the same year and with identical contents and title page, with a cover that bears the title *Bible Heroes in Words of One Syllable*.

144. Harriet T. Comstock, *Bible Stories Retold in Words of One Syllable* (New York: A. L. Burt Company, 1900), 5.

145. Ibid., 4.

146. Ibid.

Figure 4.2. Gustave Doré's *Noah Building the Ark*, included in Richard Newton, *Bible Models; or The Shining Lights of Scriptures* (Philadelphia, PA: Charles Foster Publishing Co., 1896), 59.

in this way Comstock presents Noah as a model employee. He does hard work and does not stop working for a moment.

In Margaret Sangster's *The Story Bible* from 1905, Noah is portrayed as a diligent worker. Sangster was a poet and author who, early in her career, worked for the non-denominational evangelical journal *The Christian at Work*. She was typical of many authors of her time who saw Bible stories as an ideal way to inspire

Figure 4.3. German painter Julius Schnorr von Carolsfeld "The Prophecy of the Flood," included in Harriet T. Comstock, *Bible Stories Retold in Words of One Syllable* (New York: A. L. Burt Company, 1900), 5, and several other nineteenth-century children's Bibles.

children "to live noble lives."[147] Sangster's Bible stories almost always focused on how children should approach work with humble determination. She introduces the story of Noah by explaining that the people of earth "had grown so wicked that they had stopped being ashamed and did not care what they did, or how they offended God, and they were all the worse because among them were giants, strong men and brave, and also beautiful women, but all just as bad as bad could be!"[148] Noah, on the other hand, was a diligent worker. When God had said that he needed to build an ark, Noah went to work and completed the task. As Sangster puts it, "At last the work was done. God had said that the ark was to be built. Noah had believed God, and so he had worked away at the great task when skies were clear and there was no hint of any coming storm."[149] Later, Sangster explains, "Noah was a grand old ship builder and the ark he made was the forerunner of the

147. Margaret Sangster, *The Story Bible* (New York: Moffatt, Yard & Co., 1905), 9.
148. Ibid., 42.
149. Ibid., 44.

fleets and navies of the world."[150] Given Sangster's common and pervasive theme of work, it is perhaps surprising that she does not place even more emphasis on Noah's building of the ark and connecting it to the need for children to work hard.

As mentioned in Chapter 1 of this book, most Jewish children's Bibles either stay very close to the biblical text or openly acknowledge that they are engaging in a form of creative midrash. As historian Penny Schine Gold points out in her book, *Making the Bible Modern: Children's Bibles and Jewish Education in Twentieth Century America*, children's Bibles created for Jewish children from 1915 to 1936 in the United States occasionally made changes to Bible stories in order to teach children certain Jewish and American cultural values.[151]

For some Jewish children's Bible authors, such as Addie Richman Altman, this included teaching Jewish children the value of work. Altman, in the introduction to *The Jewish Child's Bible Stories*, first published in 1915, explains her approach. She states that her goal was "to bring the ethical side of the Bible into equal prominence with religious thoughts. The results were gratifying. I drew no moral, but told the stories in such simple language that very young children could unconsciously deduct their own inferences."[152] Altman acknowledges, however, that "In a few instances I have taken the author's privilege to emphasize the ethical value at a slight expense of accuracy, but I trust no one will take exception to this."[153]

In the story of Noah, Altman seeks to explain God's judgment through the flood by giving children a relatable context: "He must punish them, just like papas and mammas punish their children when they have been naughty."[154] She proceeds to underscore that one of the naughty people's sins was that they were lazy and not good workers by writing, "But these people were not very good, and they were very lazy. They did not want to work, and the only thing they thought about was to have a good time. They forgot all about the good God, and they often did wicked things."[155] Altman, then, places the vices of being lazy and not wanting to work next to those of forgetting about God and doing wicked things. By contrast, according to Altman, Noah and his sons were not afraid of a hard day's work:

> Noah called his three sons, Shem, Ham and Japheth, and the four men went into the forest together. They took heavy axes with them, and cut down some tall, strong trees. They chopped and sawed and hammered, day after day, from

---

150. Ibid., 49.

151. Penny Schine Gold, *Making the Bible Modern: Children's Bibles and Jewish Education in Twentieth Century America* (Ithaca, NY: Cornell University Press, 2004), 117–78.

152. Addie Richman Altman, *The Jewish Child's Bible Stories* (New York: Bloch Publishing Company, 1949), 3.

153. Ibid., 4.

154. Ibid., 20.

155. Ibid.

morning till night. It was very hard work, but, after a long time, the great big boat was finished.[156]

Later, Altman underscores their hard work by inserting the comment, "And just think how long it took to catch so many animals, and to get them all in line ready to go into the ark."[157] Through these subtle additions and points of emphasis, Altman suggests to her readers that being lazy is bad, and working hard is good.

Likewise, according to Laura Merrihew Adams's version of the story of Noah, found in *Old Testament Story-Land* from 1923, Noah was not lazy, but a hard worker:

> Well, now, did Noah say to God, "Oh, I don't think you mean what you say. You surely cannot make rain come down so hard and so long that everyone will be drowned, and so I won't bother about the Ark. It's too much trouble." Did Noah say that? No indeed, he got to work just as soon as God told him to start, and began making that Ark.[158]

While the story is ostensibly about how Noah is obeying God, one also senses that Adams is making a point to children about working hard and not complaining about the difficulty of one's work. Adams continues the story by suggesting, "How the neighbors and people round about mocked and jeered at Noah,"[159] and adds, "But Noah went right on just the same. Day after day, and day after day, he worked with a will until the big Ark was finished."[160] Adams's story, then, implies that neither the difficulty of the work nor the jeering of his neighbors could deter Noah from his work.

In 1956, April Oursler Armstrong wrote an adaptation of her father Fulton Oursler's *The Greatest Book Ever Written* for children, titled *The Book of God: Adventures in the Old Testament*. In it, Armstrong uses the embellishment of the mocking neighbors for two purposes. First of all, it creates the satisfying narrative arc that helps justify the flood by suggesting that it was the mean mocking neighbors who drown and not the whole world. Second, Armstrong's use of these embellishments helped highlight the virtue of hard work by emphasizing that Noah was working hard while his neighbors had disdain for work. Noah's neighbors say to him, "You're always working, as if work were important."[161] Note that Armstrong's text implies that it is not only Noah's particular task that

156. Ibid., 21.

157. Ibid., 23.

158. Laura Merrihew Adams, *Old Testament Story-Land* (Philadelphia, PA: Union Press, 1923), 7.

159. Ibid., 8.

160. Ibid., 7.

161. April Oursler Armstrong, *The Book of God: Adventures from the Old Testament* (Garden City, NY: Garden City Books, 1956), 32. The book was also published as A. Armstrong, *Bible Stories for Young Readers* (Garden City, NY: Junior Deluxe Editions, 1956).

is important, but that contrary to popular opinion work in general is important as well.

As Armstrong describes the wicked, they do not seem to get out in the sun long enough to get a working man's tan: "Their faces in the noonday sun were cruel and sickly pale, twisted with the wickedness of their hearts. 'Who cares about your God?'"[162]

Armstrong highlights that Noah worked hard. A large illustration of Noah and his sons working on the ark spreads over two pages of text. Armstrong writes, "Even for a skilled carpenter like Noah building the ark was no easy task."[163] According to Armstrong, "That would make the ark about half as big as the liner *Queen Mary*, today, and there were only Noah and his three sons to build it, in the time they could spare from their ordinary daily chores."[164] Armstrong writes about the many years they worked on the ark, and notes, "And in all these hard, lonely, tiring years they heard no more the Voice of God."[165] Noah and his sons were "tempted to forget the whole idea of the ark" but "each day they worked again until at last the ark was finished and Noah was six hundred years old."[166] Armstrong's narrative, then, emphasizes the huge size of the job at hand and the long number of years that it took to complete the job. Armstrong does not usually end her stories with an explicit moral, and her retelling of the story of Noah is no exception. While she does not plainly tell her readers that they should work hard as Noah did, her story makes it clear that good Noah and his sons were hard workers while his wicked neighbors did not know the value of a hard day's work.

Mildred L. Jackson takes a similar approach in *Once-Upon-a-Time Bible Stories* from 1959. Jackson was a Methodist who, according to the book flap, was the only grandmother attending Southern Methodist University. She also studied at Perkins School of Theology. Jackson wrote the book while she was co-owner with her three children of the Northeast Louisiana Wholesale Oil and Gas Company, which she served as president. Her retelling of the story of Noah seems to suggest that the American ideals of industry and self-reliance are consistent with faith in God. In other words, God helps those who first help themselves and put in the necessary work. Jackson recounts all of the jobs God gives to Noah, to build the ark and just how big it would be, to gather all the animals and just how many there would be, and to gather enough food for all of them to eat.[167] In the midst of her description of the flood, she seems to infuse her retelling with an American emphasis on self-reliance and a Methodist emphasis on human responsibility:

162. Ibid.

163. Ibid., 33.

164. Ibid.

165. Ibid.

166. Ibid.

167. Mildred L. Jackson, *Once-Upon-a-Time Bible Stories* (New York: Exposition Press, 1959), 25–6.

God caused it to rain for forty days and forty nights. All but those on the Ark with Noah were drowned, but those on the Ark were safe.

You see if you do all you can to help yourself, when you try to do good and you ask God, He will help you if you trust Him. God loves all of His children and we are all His children.[168]

According to Jackson, then, it is the fact that Noah was both willing to help himself and trust in God that saved him. It is both God's work and human endeavor, when we try to do good, that saves us.

In Katherine Fessenden's 1960 collection, *The Old Testament Story: Adam to Jonah*, Noah is commended for working vigorously: "Noah did as the Lord commanded. He and his son labored mightily, and at last the gigantic task was completed."[169] The facing page presents a large black and white reproduction of the Italian Renaissance painter Raphael's *The Building of the Ark*. The caption reads, "Noah directs his sons in the building of the ark according to God's specifications. They are working vigorously, and the enormous craft is beginning to take shape behind them."[170] Fessenden's brief text emphasizes the particularly difficult nature of Noah's work.

In her 1968 book, *Runaway Jonah and Other Tales*, Jan Wahl draws upon several sources to commend Noah and his family for their hard work. Wahl is a well-known American children's book author. She titles her retelling of the story of Noah and the ark "Captain Noah."[171] Like a number of other children's Bibles, Wahl integrates into the story the tradition that Noah tended grapes in a vineyard. In Genesis, Noah does this after the flood. Wahl uses the tradition to suggest that Noah and his family were hard workers even before they began to build the ark: "Nearby lived his three sons, Shem and Ham and Japheth, who'd married three pretty and clever ladies. All of them worked hard picking tender grapes in the vineyards. They knew they mustn't work on the Sabbath. And the sons were very good about visiting their father and mother regularly."[172] Wahl, therefore, establishes that Noah's whole family worked hard in the vineyard and kept the Sabbath. Noah's mocking workers are used by Wahl as a contrast to Noah and his family. Noah and his family know the value of good work, while his neighbors just want to have fun:

Everyone laughed at Noah and his sons and wives being so busy instead of having a good time. However, Noah knew what he was doing.

---

168. Ibid.

169. Katherine Fessenden, *The Old Testament Story: Adam to Jonah* (New York: Henry Z. Walck, Incorporated, 1960), 26.

170. Ibid., 27.

171. Jan Wahl, *Runaway Jonah and Other Tales*, illus. by Uri Shulevitch (New York: Macmillan Company, 1968), 7.

172. Ibid.

Then, when they had a fine Ark, Noah and his sons went out to gather up the fishes, beasts, and fowls. It was not easy. But they worked very hard at it.[173]

The work, then, according to Wahl, was not easy. Many children's Bibles suggest that God miraculously brought the animals to the ark and others suggest that Noah at least did not have to gather any fish. According to Wahl, however, "Now the fish were difficult, that was true. They had to be carried in wooden buckets two by two."[174] Wahl proceeds to further underscore the amount of work that Noah and his family did and provides over a full page of text that details the specific animals Noah needed to gather and how they were brought into the ark. Work, Wahl's story seems to suggest, is a natural part of a life with God.

Hard work was also among the themes of Marianne Radius's retelling of the story of Noah in her book *The Tent of God* from 1968. Radius describes the size of the ark as "about as long as the city block on which I live."[175] She explains the great amount of work that Noah had to do to build such a large boat. According to Radius, "It took Noah a hundred and twenty years to build this boat. At first he worked all alone, cutting down the trees, dragging them to his yard, joining them together carefully, sealing the joints with pitch."[176] Radius interrupts her account of Noah building the ark to suggest, "The long, difficult building of the ark, log by log, was a test of Noah's faith, just as suffering was a test of Job's faith."[177] She notes that even after the ark was built, the animals were loaded into the ark, and the flood came, Noah and his family still had a great deal of work to complete. According to Radius, however, this was a good thing: "There was plenty of work to do, and that helped to keep up their spirits."[178] Radius depicts Noah as a hard worker and her final lines imply that hard work is good for us since it keeps us from becoming depressed due to idleness.

In *The Nelson Children's Bible* from 1981, in a scene highlighted with an illustration by Lyndon Evans, Pat Alexander's text describes the people mocking Noah, and then explains, "But Noah did not let them stop him. He got on with the work and at last was finished."[179] Similar to the stories mentioned above in which Noah must resist the peer pressure of his neighbors, here the embellishment of Noah's mocking neighbors serves primarily to tempt Noah to quit working instead of keeping his nose to the grindstone.

173. Ibid., 8.

174. Ibid., 9, 11. For a similiar emphasis, see Pearl S. Buck, *The Story of the Bible* (New York: Bartholemew House Ltd., 1971), 26–7.

175. Marianne Radius, *The Tent of God: A Journey through the Old Testament*, illus. by Chris Soffel Overvoorde (Grand Rapids, MI: William B. Eerdmans Publishing Company, 1968), 33.

176. Ibid.

177. Ibid., 34.

178. Ibid., 37.

179. Pat Alexander, *The Nelson Children's Bible* (Nashville, TN: Thomas Nelson, 1981), 9–10.

Children's book authors Salley Grindley and Jan Barger's 1998 volume, *Bible Stories for the Young*, emphasizes the virtue of hard work in a number of ways. It is interesting to note that the authors seem to be particularly intent on the painful nature of the work. When Noah and his family receive God's command, "They set to work right away. Noah and his sons went into the forests and cut down the tallest cypress trees. Then, day after day, month after month, they sawed and shaped them until their hands were covered with blisters. They hammered and nailed them until their fingers were black and blue."[180] While the work was painful, Noah and his sons appear to work through the pain. Grindley and Barger divide the labor along gender lines, but note that the women do painful work as well: "Noah's wife and the wives of his sons gathered sack loads of food until they thought their backs would break."[181]

The neighbors are described as mocking Noah, though here again they are used not to make the reader feel better about their eventual demise, but to highlight how Noah keeps working and keeps his faith despite the distraction: "'We are building the ark to save us from the flood,' Noah told everyone who asked. When they laughed and said he was crazy, he kept working, for he trusted in God's word."[182] Also, again, God does not here miraculously gather the animals for Noah. Instead, God gives Noah instructions on gathering the animals, and Noah begins the hard work of gathering them. According to Grindley and Barger, "When God had finished speaking, Noah began his work and started to gather together creatures from every corner of the earth. He collected one male and one female of every kind and brought them to the ark, two by two. From the tiniest leaping flea to the biggest lumbering elephant, they were led to the ark and climbed aboard."[183]

Though the authors do not end their story with an explicit lesson about the value of work, Noah, his wife, his sons, and their wives all serve as positive role models of hard work.

Carolyn Nabors Baker's 1995 book, *The Beginners Bible Tales of Virtue: A Book of Right and Wrong*, assigns one specific virtue to every Bible story it tells. It puts Noah's story under the section titled "Work."[184] As Baker tells the story,

Noah worked every day on the ark. He worked for many years. His sons helped him. Sometimes it was easy. Sometimes it was hard. Sometimes it was fun. Sometimes it was boring. But they knew they were doing God's special work.

180. Sally Grindley and Jan Barger, *Bible Stories for the Young* (Waukesha, WI: Little Tiger Press, 1998), 20.

181. Ibid.

182. Ibid., 21.

183. Ibid., 22.

184. Carolyn Nabors Baker, *The Beginners Bible Tales of Virtue: A Book of Right and Wrong*, illus. by Kelly Pulley and Lisa Reed (New York: Little Moorings, 1995), 77–85.

Noah did everything God told him to do. He was happy because his work made his family strong.[185]

Children who do not enjoy their chores may be skeptical of the story's suggestion that work is sometimes easy and sometimes fun. Still, Baker makes her point that work can be a positive experience and, even when it is hard or boring, it has its own benefits.

As noted above, Carolyn Larsen most often uses the story of Noah to spotlight the virtue of obeying God in her children's Bibles. In Larsen's 2001 book, *Little Boys Bible Storybook for Fathers and Sons*, however, she uses the story of Noah to highlight both the virtue of obedience and the presumably more masculine virtue of doing hard labor. Larsen suggests that it was the virtue of obedience to God that was the reason God chose Noah in the first place: "He obeyed God, that's why God warned him about the flood."[186] Larsen also uses the story to teach boys that they should not be afraid of hard work. When Noah's sons wake up in the morning, Shem moans, "I know it's a good thing that Dad is building the big boat, but it sure is hard work."[187] Shem's words serve to highlight the amount of work Noah and his family have been asked to do. One of Caron Turk's illustrations depicts Noah's sons, looking like young children who are much too young to be married, working on building the ark. The boys happily followed their parents' instructions and did their work on the ark, so much so that, "When the boat was finished, the boys happily went back to their old chores, which seemed pretty easy now."[188] If Larsen's young readers or their fathers were savvy enough, they would get the message that when compared to the hard work of Noah and his sons, they should be happy to do the work that they had to do.

Children's Bibles have used the stories of the Bible repeatedly to teach children the value of work and obedience. It is worth noting that during the nineteenth and early twentieth centuries the stories of the child Samuel and "Namaan's Little Maid" were popular in children's Bibles, providing children with role models of children who were taken from their home but still happily did the work that was forced upon them. During those years and continuing to the present day, stories created about the childhood of Jesus often showed him happily working at home helping Mary or later with Joseph in the carpentry shop and often explicitly comment on what a good worker he was, and that if Jesus was not afraid of hard work children today should not complain about it either.[189] The examples above attest to the variety of ways that the story of Noah has been appropriated to teach the virtue of hard work throughout American history. As the rest of this chapter

185. Ibid., 81.
186. Carolyn Larsen, *Little Boys Bible Storybook for Fathers and Sons* (Grand Rapids, MI: Baker Publishing, 2001), 32.
187. Ibid., 31.
188. Ibid., 33.
189. See Dalton, "Meek and Mild."

illustrates, however, the story of Noah has been used to commend a number of other virtues to children as well.

4.5. Noah, the Man who Cared for Animals and the Environment

4.5.a. Caring for animals

The so-called Benevolent Empire movement of the early 1800s sought to form the United States into a "Christian" nation through philanthropic societies devoted to evangelization, promoting virtue, reducing juvenile delinquency, temperance, and the abolition of slavery.[190] One social agenda of these societies that is sometimes forgotten today is the attempt to abolish cruelty to animals. Several retellings of the story of Noah have given special attention to this theme.

Scriptural Stories for Very Young Children, from 1814, uses a short episode in the story of Noah's ark to teach children a lesson about the humane treatment of animals. The author explains that after Noah and the animals left the ark,

> God blessed Noah and his children; and he told them that they might kill some of the animals for food. But though God gave them leave to eat the flesh of some animals, he did not mean that they were to be cruel and torment the poor beasts. God loves every thing he has made, and will be angry with those people who are cruel to the poor creatures they ought to take care of.[191]

The lesson appears to be that God loves animals, so people can kill them and eat them, as long as they are not cruel to them.

Reverend Mortimer Blake's posthumous book, *Bible Children* from 1886, offers the same lesson from the story of Noah. The book is not technically a children's Bible, but rather a collection of sermons for children that retells select Bible stories about children and offers children lessons on them. Blake, a Congregational minister, departs from the pattern of telling stories of children in order to tell the story of "Noah's Menagerie" in order to "teach you children to be kind to all of God's animals."[192] Blake goes into some detail on how God must have provided for the animals on the ark, even suggesting, "In some way God must have changed the appetites of the lions and the bears and the wolves, and satisfied them to eat grass and vegetables and such other food as Noah could carry and keep sweet and good for a year."[193] He also describes the many ways God provides care for animals in the present day. Blake then offers children his lesson from the story: "Now, I have

190. See Bernard Bailyn et al., *The Great Republic: A History of the American People* (Boston, MA: Little, Brown and Company, 1977), 541–8, for a helpful overview.

191. *Scriptural Stories for Very Young Children* (Philadelphia, PA: Kimber & Conrad, 1814), 31.

192. Mortimer Blake, *Bible Children* (Boston, MA: Congregational Sunday School Publishing Company, 1886), 166.

193. Ibid., 173.

come to the lesson which I especially wish you, children, to learn from God's care of his creatures of all kinds: that is, not to abuse or trouble any of them for which God has expended so much kindly thought and provision."[194]

Blake proceeds to describe the troubling presence of cruelty to animals: "Sometimes children seem to have a natural disposition to abuse God's creatures. Probably it is an ignorant thoughtlessness, and a parent's neglect to teach them better; but it often looks as if some children took a delight in hurting animals, and their parents apparently have no idea of the disposition it is cultivating in their children."[195] He adds, "Don't abuse God's young creatures, because *it is wrong.*"[196] Blake acknowledges that some animals are annoying or harmful, and must be killed, but even then tells children to avoid cruelty: "Still it is wrong to abuse and torment even a bee or a fly. If you must do it, kill him quickly, but don't be cruel and abusive of the little nimble enemies."[197] He also pleads with children to be kind to useful animals such as dogs, horses, and cows that are often abused in the course of their work for people. Blake concludes the story by writing, "Let me say once more that cruelty to animals will make you cruel."[198] For Blake, then, cruelty to animals is not only a vice in and of itself, but also may lead people to become cruel to other people.

In 1911, Harvey Albert Snyder drew a similar lesson about the humane treatment of animals from the story of Noah in his book *Boys and Girls of the Bible*. Snyder titles the story of Noah, "Boys and Girls in Noah's Time."[199] Snyder writes that as Noah was building the ark, "The boys and girls often came and pointed their fingers at this good man and made fun of him because he believed in God."[200] The narrative does not focus on the subsequent deaths in the flood of the mocking children, but instead tells a story of how God and Noah cared for the animals in the ark and how they were safely released back upon the earth after the flood. According to Snyder, "This shows us that God is very careful of all his creatures and everything he has made, and that boys ought not to be cruel to any living animal, but treat it kindly."[201] He tells children that they are not to disturb bird nests or to bother kittens or horses, for "innocent animals often have to suffer because we are thoughtless."[202] Snyder ends his retelling of the story of Noah by summarizing the moral to his story: "Let us be kind to all of God's creatures."[203]

The children's Bibles above use the story of the flood to argue against harming innocent animals. As they do this, they conveniently overlook a problematic

---

194. Ibid., 179.

195. Ibid., 179–80.

196. Ibid., 181. Emphasis in the original.

197. Ibid.

198. Ibid., 183.

199. Harvey Albert Snyder, *Boys and Girls of the Bible* (Washington, DC: W. E. Scull, 1911), 23.

200. Ibid., 24.

201. Ibid., 28.

202. Ibid.

203. Ibid.

aspect of the story—namely that God destroyed millions of presumably innocent animals in the flood.

Lessons teaching children not to be cruel to animals seemed to fade from children's Bibles as America moved into the twentieth century and fewer children lived on farms. The illustrations in some later children's Bible depictions of the story of Noah, however, include images of animals and people living in harmony on the ark that may inspire children to feel warmly towards animals. Some of these illustrations are quite beautiful and realistic and, like a child's visit to a zoo, may inspire children to be more sensitive to the plight of animals. The three-dimensional View-Master scenes of Noah's ark designed by Florence Thomas and the story booklet that came with it, for example, depict Noah's family providing gentle care for the animals in ways that may inspire children to see such care for animals as a virtuous undertaking.[204] In the same way, Yvonne Gilbert's beautiful illustrations of Noah and his wife gently holding and caring for animals on the ark in Miriam Chaikin's *Children's Bible Stories from Genesis to Daniel* (1993) could draw attention to and evoke sympathy for animals and their wellbeing.[205] Still, explicit lessons on animal cruelty in the texts of more recent children's Bibles are rare.

4.5.b. Caring for the environment

In the twenty-first century, while the story of Noah is rarely used to urge children to treat animals kindly, it has occasionally been told in ways that promote care for all of God's creation.

In her 2001 Bible storybook, *The Loving Arms of God*, Anne Elizabeth Stickney frames her stories through a title page and suggested topics for prayer that she offers following the stories. Stickney sets an environmental theme for the story of Noah. She titles the story of Noah and the flood, "God Sustains the Earth,"[206] and after retelling the story she suggests to children, "Thank God for taking care of the world and taking care of you. As you pray, picture in your mind God's strong arms cradling the earth and everything on it."[207] She titles the story of Noah's work after the flood, "God's People Take Care of the Earth," and tells children about the pollution plaguing earth today.[208] After the story of Noah planting a vineyard, a part of the Noah story usually omitted from children's Bible storybooks, she suggests that children "Ask God to help you learn to care for your home, your

---

204. Florence Thomas, *Noah's Ark: Bible Story Series* (New York: GAF View-Master, 1965).

205. Miriam Chaikin, *Children's Bible Stories from Genesis to Daniel*, illus. by Yvonne Gilbert (New York: Dial Books for Young Readers, 1993), 18.

206. Anne Elizabeth Stickney, *The Loving Arms of God* (Grand Rapids, MI: Eerdmans Books for Young Readers, 2001), 16.

207. Ibid., 20.

208. Ibid., 21.

neighborhood, and your world. Ask God to give you a keen mind at school as you learn about God's creation."[209]

Rabbi Sandy Eisenberg Sasso is the first woman to have been ordained a rabbi in the Reconstructionist movement of Judaism and the first rabbi to become a mother. Sasso greatly expands upon the ancient midrash *Genesis Rabbah* to tell the story of *Noah's Wife: The Story of Naamah* in which Naamah is a protagonist who cares for the plants of creation. While several children's Bibles that deal directly with women's roles tend to emphasize a subservient role for women,[210] Sasso tells an empowering tale of a strong, resourceful, and faithful woman. According to the story, published in 2002, God speaks to both Noah and his wife Naamah and asks for their help.[211] God asks Noah to gather animals and says to Naamah, "Walk across the land and gather the seeds of all the flowers and all the trees. Take two of every kind of living plant and bring each one onto the ark. They shall not be for food, but they shall be your garden, to tend and to keep."[212] Sasso emphasizes the extent of God's command and one can picture Naamah walking across the land and taking care to gather every type of seed. According to the story, "Naamah did as God commanded."[213] Sasso's story both acknowledges the role of a woman in the story and speaks to the care for all living things in creation, including plant life.

Tami Lehman-Wilzig, a Jewish English-language copywriter who lives in Israel, devotes her entire 2011 book, *Green Bible Stories for Children*, to retelling nine Hebrew Bible stories in ways that place an emphasis on environmental themes. For the story of Noah, Lehman-Wilzig begins by subtly highlighting God's concern for the whole planet. God looks at planet earth and says, "Everyone is misbehaving. It's time to give the earth a fresh start."[214] God raises concern for global hygiene, stating, "To heal this land I have to wash it out completely."[215] As the story continues, God uses language that suggests concern for endangered species, asking, "Why endanger Noah and all the species I have created?"[216] So God whispers to Noah, "Psst, Noah. I need your help. You and your family are the only good people around. Everyone else has ruined the earth. You can help me heal it and repopulate it."[217] Lehman-Wilzig's text may suggest to those unfamiliar with Genesis that the wickedness of humankind is related to their lack of care for the earth and that Noah must help God heal the earth. In describing Noah's time

---

209. Ibid., 24.

210. As seen in the section on "Fulfilling gender roles" below.

211. Sandy Eisenberg Sasso, *Noah's Wife: The Story of Naamah*, illus. by Bethanne Andersen (Woodstock, VT: Jewish Lights Publishing, 2002), 4.

212. Ibid., 8.

213. Ibid.

214. Tami Lehman-Wilzig, *Green Bible Stories for Children*, illus. by Durga Yael Bernhard (Minneapolis, MN: Kar-Ben Publishing, 2011), 7.

215. Ibid.

216. Ibid.

217. Ibid.

on the ark, Lehman-Wilzig highlights an aspect of the journey rarely touched upon in other children's Bibles. She explains that Noah "set aside separate areas for food and waste matter to safeguard the health of man and beast."[218] When the time came for Noah and his family to leave the ark, Lehman-Wilzig concludes, "Once again, earth was in mankind's hands."[219] While Lehman-Wilzig does not end her story with a moral injunction addressed directly to her readers, her message of humankind's responsibility to care for the environment is implicitly clear. The earth is in humankind's hands.

In the twenty-first century, with concerns about climate change, oil spills, and other environmental issues being brought to prominence, these children's Bible stories represent an attempt by three female authors to get children to become concerned for the environment and to connect that concern to their faith in God. These three examples represent a small but significant group of children's Bibles that appropriate the story of Noah in ways designed to raise children's awareness of environmental concerns and inspire them to care for the planet.

4.6. Noah as a Model of Other Virtues

Especially in more recent decades, Noah has been used as an exemplar of a wide variety of virtues. While none of these virtues are emphasized in as many versions of the story of Noah as are the virtues of obedience or work, the following survey helps to demonstrate the multivalency and malleability of the text and the wide variety of virtues that adults have wanted the children of their times to exhibit. In the examples that follow, the story of Noah is used to teach children virtues such as controlling one's anger, bravery, prayer, patience, trust and trustworthiness, thankfulness, and self-actualization. "Mrs. Noah" is even used as a role model for a virtuous woman who fulfills certain traditional gender roles. If such alternative moral lessons are rare in children's Bibles of the eighteenth and early nineteenth centuries, the emergence of evangelical concerns about teaching children "traditional" morality seems to have brought on a host of retellings that are crafted to teach these moral virtues and more.

4.6.a. Controlling one's anger

Occasional psychological and therapeutic readings of Bible passages emerged with the advent of psychology as a field of study in the early twentieth century. The Rev. Robert Crawford Falconer's 1922 book, *A Child's Ramble through the Bible: The Old Testament*, provides a case in point. His book is a series of reflections on Bible stories arranged in canonical order. Falconer uses the story of the ark as an extended allegory for dealing with one's anger. Falconer talks of the flood formed by one's temper: "It rises most suddenly, and rushes on with a roar like that of a

218. Ibid., 9.
219. Ibid.

great waterfall. Nothing in its path is safe—toys, furniture, dishes, other boys and girls, even grown up people."[220] He even draws an analogy between Noah applying pitch to the ark and counting to ten when one is angry:

> Well, our counting to ten or one hundred today, compares with Noah smearing his pitch many, many years ago. Counting ten or one hundred gives us a chance to think about God, and to have Him with us—to climb into the Ark of Safety which His presence is. Into the Ark our tempers cannot reach. For as we realize how patient, and gentle, and loving God is, we grow ashamed of our tempers.[221]

Falconer provides children with an image of a God who is patient, gentle and loving and talks to them about their anger. While many later psychologists may applaud Rev. Falconer for his attempt to teach children about how they might deal with their anger, they may be troubled by his attempt to shame children for their tempers in this final sentence. Still, Falconer's appropriation of the story of Noah is interesting and rare if not unique, especially for his time. He turns the story of Noah into an extended allegory designed to increase children's emotional intelligence and give them tools for dealing with their anger.

4.6.b. Bravery

In the early 1950s, Ruth S. Gray wrote the Little Folks Picture-Story Series, which included the books *Bible Helpers, Bible Friends, Bible Places* and *Bible Heroes*. Each book included a number of selected Bible stories, each being allotted one page of color illustration and one page of text. Gray includes the story of Noah in *Bible Heroes* from 1950, and titles it "Brave to Obey." The Book of Genesis makes no reference to Noah's courage, but according to Gray, "Noah and his family watched the water creeping higher and higher, but they were not afraid, for they were safe in the ark which God had told them how to build."[222] The very brief summary of the story indeed serves to highlight the virtues of courage and obedience. More often, stories such as David and Goliath or Daniel in the Lion's Den are the ones used in children's Bibles to teach children that they should be brave. Here, Gray makes a rare use of the story of Noah to teach bravery.

4.6.c. Prayer

In the midst of the Cold War, when many Americans reasserted the importance of having a personal relationship with God, E. Jerry Walker highlighted the virtue of prayer in his retelling of the story of Noah's ark in the 1955 book, *Stories from the Bible: Old Testament*. Walker begins his tale by telling children about Noah's

---

220. Robert C. Falconer, *A Child's Ramble through the Bible: The Old Testament* (New York: Fleming H. Revell Company, 1922), 14.

221. Ibid., 14–15.

222. Ruth S. Gray, *Bible Heroes* (Anderson, IN: Warner Press, 1950), n.p.

work in his vineyard, and conjuring an image of prayer as the act of walking and talking with God.

> Noah was a farmer. With his three sons he raised a beautiful garden of grapes. Everyone liked Noah's grapes because they were so big and round and sweet. Noah liked to raise grapes, but there was one thing he liked more—to take long walks across the hills and talk with God.
>   What do we call it when we talk with God?
>   Yes, we call it "prayer."[223]

Instead of indicating that God spoke to Noah in an audible voice, Walker creates scenes in which God speaks to Noah through feelings in Noah's heart:

> Noah would walk into the country and pray. Sometimes when Noah prayed he talked to God. At other times he listened for God to talk to him. God spoke to Noah in many ways: in the sunset and the flowers, in the storms and the stars. Most of all, God spoke to Noah in his heart.
>   One day as Noah looked down from the hillside toward the valley where all the people lived, he felt sad. His heart told him that these people were bad. They did not walk with God. They did not pray. They were not kind to each other. They were selfish and mean and ugly.
>   "I must call these people back to God," Noah said, "for my heart tells me God is not pleased with them."[224]

The wicked people have no sense of the sacred, but when Noah feels the presence of God, Walker describes it as the sort of religious experience that might make the hair stand up on the back of one's neck: "Suddenly, Noah felt chilled. The night was warm, but Noah was cold. He knew it was because he was afraid. It seemed that God was right there on the hilltop with him, and he was afraid."[225] According to Walker's retelling, Noah persists in trying to change his neighbors' minds by inviting them to "pray" as he did and, in a rare embellishment, suggests that they build arks of their own. Walker writes, "'Don't laugh,' Noah said, 'God is angry with people who do evil things. You should go into the hills and walk with God. Then you'll build an ark too!'"[226] According to Walker, Noah "pleaded with them" repeatedly, but they would not listen.[227] Noah, on the other hand, was spared: "Yes, God saved Noah from the flood of waters because Noah was good. He liked to walk and talk with God."[228] While Walker does not come out and say it explicitly,

---

    223. E. Jerry Walker, *Stories from the Bible: Old Testament* (Westwood, NJ: Fleming H. Revell Company, 1955), 14.
    224. Ibid., 14–15.
    225. Ibid., 15.
    226. Ibid.
    227. Ibid., 16.
    228. Ibid., 18.

the juxtaposition of these sentences suggest that it was because of Noah's walking and talking prayers, as well as Noah's goodness, that he was spared.

4.6.d. Positive thinking

In 1973, popular Protestant preacher and author Norman Vincent Peale first released *Bible Stories*. In his introduction, Peale wrote of his hopes for the young readers of the book. Peale hoped that "his mind and imagination will be challenged by fact [sic] that in the Bible narratives are to be found workable answers to his every question. He will see that truly this is the book of life ... notably his life. The Bible shows the young person how to have the best that he wants in life."[229] It is perhaps not surprising that Peale, the author of the 1952 best-selling book *The Power of Positive Thinking* and co-founder of the Horatio Alger Association, frames the story of Noah's ark as the story of a man with an indomitable spirit who was not bound by his limitations, and who endured through hard times because of his unwavering belief in God and his ability to remain hopeful even in the darkest times.

According to Peale's account, Noah was a model of faith:

If ever a man showed blind, unquestioning faith, it was Noah. He lived far inland where floods never came. He knew nothing about the sea, or about boats. The Lord even had to tell him how to make the ark watertight! Now, suddenly, he was told to start building an oceangoing vessel roughly the size of a modern tanker. But he didn't hesitate. He didn't ask questions. He just did what the Lord told him to do.[230]

Peale suggests that in the face of being mocked, Noah and his family were willing to be different from others:

How they must have laughed when he told them that a flood was coming that would drown them all. They must have agreed among themselves that the old man had become senile. No doubt it became a form of neighborhood entertainment to go out and watch as the huge vessel slowly took shape, to ridicule the old man and jeer at his strongly muscled, sunburned sons.[231]

This portion of Peale's story recalls children's Bibles that laud Noah for remaining righteous in the midst of wicked people who try to drag him down to their level. For Peale, however, the focus is not on Noah resisting the temptation to be wicked as much as it is on Noah resisting the temptation to become discouraged. Peale tells of the dove returning with an olive leaf in her mouth, and uses the image to drive home his point for story to his readers:

229. Norman Vincent Peale, *Bible Stories* (New York: Banner Press, Inc., 1978), n.p.
230. Ibid., 27.
231. Ibid.

The scene of the gentle bird retuning and of Noah's joy as he "put forth his hand, and pulled her in unto him into the ark" is one of the most touching and reassuring in the whole Bible. It symbolizes the resurgence of hope after a dark time of difficulty and distress. It means that while floods and dangers and uncertainties occur in every life, the man who trusts God will come through intact. It means, too, that if people will just hang on long enough in times of trouble, God will send a sign, when the testing period is almost over, that good things lie ahead for those who keep the faith and refuse to admit defeat.[232]

Peale's version of the story talks about hope after a dark time of difficulty and surviving the floods and dangers of uncertainty that occur in life. For Peale, faith and hope provided Noah with a way to come through these hard times and, by extension, can help his readers do the same today. Not surprisingly, then, Peale uses Noah as a model for children of positive thinking, self-actualization, and hope in the midst of hard times.

4.6.e. Kindness, peace, and harmony

Patricia Daniels' *Noah's Ark* (1995) depicts Noah as a kind and gentle man. The story begins by explaining, "Noah was a good man, and he and his family lived a peaceful life. They grew grapes and figs in the warmth of the sun and took care of their animals with gentle hands."[233] Most children's Bibles place their description of Noah's care for vineyards after the flood, as does the Book of Genesis. Here, however, Daniels uses Noah's life as a farmer to establish that he and his family lived a pastoral life and were peaceful and gentle people.

In the middle of Daniels' tale, she creates a telling scene on the ark: "Noah felt a light touch on his shoulder. It was a shy white dove, leaning close to him. 'Don't worry, little one,' he said, stroking its neck."[234] Daniels' text and Kathy Rusynyk's illustrations have a synergy that is not always found in children's Bibles. Here, Rusynyk depicts a close-up of Noah as an old white-haired man with a kind face as he gently cuddles a tiny dove on his shoulder. The dove looks like it is cooing with contentment. Later, Daniels describes Noah and his family's care for the animals on the ark in a manner that recalls the ways in which modern readers might care for their pets: "Noah's family fed and bathed them. Shem scratched the pigs' backs when they were itchy. Japheth filed the rhinos' toenails when they got too long."[235] As for Noah and the dove, "The little dove went everywhere on Noah's shoulders."[236] When Noah finally sends the dove out to search for land he says, "Go, little friend," and when the dove returns with an olive leaf in its mouth

---

232. Ibid., 30.
233. Patricia Daniels, *Noah's Ark*, illus. by Kathy Rusynyk (Alexandria, VA: Time Life Kids, 1995).
234. Ibid., n.p.
235. Ibid.
236. Ibid.

Noah says "Bless you, small one."[237] Daniels does not explicitly instruct children to be gentle and kind anywhere in the text, but she highlights Noah's gentleness more than any other virtue. Supporting the text, Rusynyk's illustrations depict both Noah and the animals as docile and gentle creatures. The effect of the entire story, therefore, is to transmit a sense of gentleness and peacefulness in the presence of God, and Noah and his family serve as perfect examples of the virtue of gentleness.

Unsurprisingly, Archbishop Desmond Tutu's *Children of God Storybook Bible* (2010) repeatedly presents children with images of a kind God of love and stories of peace, kindness, and harmony amidst diversity. In his telling of the story of Noah, it is the lack of these virtues that upsets God: "Before long, people started fighting and hurting one another terribly. God wept that they were not enjoying the lovely earth he had made."[238] Tutu highlights the virtue of kindness by noting that in contrast to other people, "one man named Noah was kind and did what was right."[239] According to Tutu, when the animals were together on the ark, "Boy, did it smell inside the ark! And the noise! The *ROAR*ing and the *BAA*ing, the *NEIGH*ing and the *MOO*ing! But—amazingly—everyone got along. Yes, even the lion lay down with the lamb."[240]

Tutu, then, adds a fanciful embellishment to the story in which even the animals embody the virtues of gentleness and harmony in the midst of diversity.

4.6.f. Trust

Suzanne Lieurance emphasizes the virtue of trust by repeating the word throughout her brief retelling of the story of Noah's ark in *5-Minute Bible Stories* (2002). Lieurance's text highlights the point that Noah was a trustworthy person and that he trusted in God: "God knew that Noah and his family would listen to him, so he trusted them with a very serious job."[241] God not only trusted Noah, but "God told Noah to trust him."[242] When Noah's wife gets nervous as she looks at the darkening skies, Noah reassures her: "'God told me to trust him,' Noah said. 'He will protect us.'"[243] This confident trust in God is tested later in the story. In the ark, during the flood, "Noah and his family felt frightened and lost."[244] Still, they maintained their trust in God: "They knew that God would take care of them,

---

237. Ibid.

238. Desmond Tutu, *Children of God Storybook Bible* (Grand Rapids, MI: ZonderKids, 2010), 16.

239. Ibid.

240. Ibid., 17. Capital letters and italics in the original.

241. Suzanne Lieurance, "Noah's Ark," in Brian Conway, Lora Kalkman et al., *5-Minute Bible Stories* (Lincolnwood, IL: Publications International Ltd., 2002), 30.

242. Ibid.

243. Ibid., 33.

244. Ibid., 34.

though, because God had made a promise to Noah."[245] As the story draws to a close, Lieurance explains, "Noah had trusted God. God was so pleased, he decided to make a special promise to Noah. He promised him that he would never bring another great flood."[246] Lieurance's narrative suggests that Noah's trust in God elicits God's pleasure. Throughout her narrative, then, Lieurance repeatedly tells children in a variety of ways that Noah trusted in God throughout the ordeal of the flood. For Lieurance, then, the story of Noah becomes a story that commends Noah's trust in God and calls her readers to have this same trust.

4.6.g. Thankfulness

A significant number of children's Bible address the theme of thankfulness through the story of Noah, especially those that are more comprehensive and retell the story of Noah's sacrifice after the flood. Candy Cane Press's 2005 storybook, *Noah and the Ark: A Story About Being Thankful* (2005), focuses the entire storybook on lessons of thankfulness and hope.[247] The story describes Noah as being thankful while avoiding any graphic description of Noah killing any animals for his sacrifice and in the process avoids distracting children from the message that they should be thankful to God as well.

4.6.h. Patience

In *Miss Bettie's Book of Bible Stories*, published in 1939, Bettie Burson emphasizes the virtue of patience among many other virtues: "Noah was a splendid patient man, and his sons must have been somewhat like him, for they did not even open that window in all those months. No, they simply sat there in that Ark and waited to be sure that it was time to look out."[248] As a teacher at the State Orphans Home in Texas, Miss Bettie was likely familiar with how impatient some children could become, and uses the story of Noah to encourage children to be splendidly patient.

Gwen Ellis titles her story of Noah "Patient Noah" in *Our Together-Time Bible* (2008). Before getting to the story itself, she introduces children to the virtue of patience: "A patient person waits calmly without complaining. How patient are you? Is it hard for you to wait your turn while playing a game or to wait to eat just-baked cookies?"[249] With this introduction, it is safe to assume that nearly all of Ellis's readers have identified themselves as impatient. Ellis then introduces the tale by explaining, "In today's Bible story see how patiently Noah waited in the big

---

245. Ibid.

246. Ibid., 38.

247. *Noah and the Ark: A Story About Being Thankful* (Nashville, TN: Candy Cane Press, 2005).

248. Burson, *Miss Bettie's Book*, 29.

249. Gwen Ellis, *Our Together-Time Bible* (Nashville, TN: Thomas Nelson, 2008), 5.

boat with all those smelly animals."[250] While Noah and the animals are on the ark, Ellis explains, "Everyone and every creature on that ark practiced patience as they waited for the day to come when they could leave the boat."[251] In case the point is still not clear to her readers, in the lessons Ellis supplies at the end of the story, she writes, "Being patient isn't easy, but it is something God wants us to do."[252] The Genesis account of the story of Noah does not explicitly extol the virtue of patiently waiting one's turn or patiently waiting to eat cookies, but like so many others, Ellis finds ways to appropriate the story to speak to the particular virtue that she has in mind.

4.6.i. Fulfilling gender roles

Children's Bible authors have occasionally invented scenes which use Noah's wife in ways that reinforce certain stereotypical gender roles and behaviors. As mentioned above, in *Bible Stories for the Young* (1998), Sally Grindley and Jan Barger have Noah and his sons building the ark while Noah's wife and the wives of his sons gather the food.[253] In Suzanne Lieurance's "Noah's Ark" (2002), Noah's wife gets frightened by the coming storm and needs to be reassured by her husband.[254] In Charles Reasoner's board book, *Inside Noah's Ark* (2002), once on the ark, "Mrs. Noah keeps things clean, On top, below, and in between."[255] These invented scenes are, perhaps, simply added by the authors in passing to lend atmosphere to the story. Nonetheless, they serve to reinforce certain gender roles.

Also, as mentioned in Chapter 1, a host of children's Bibles have been published in the late twentieth and early twenty-first centuries that are designed specifically for girls, with bright pink covers, illustrations of girls in sparkling pink dresses, and titles such as *The Little Girls Bible Storybook for Mothers and Daughters*,[256] *The Princess in Me Storybook Bible*,[257] *My Princess Bible*,[258] and *The Sweetest Story Bible: Sweet Thoughts and Sweet Words for Little Girls*.[259] While some of these children's Bibles do not address the issue of gender roles explicitly, they all clearly affirm certain images of what girls should like and how girls should look.

250. Ibid.

251. Ibid., 6.

252. Ibid., 7.

253. Sally Grindley and Jan Barger, *Bible Stories for the Young* (Waukesha, WI: Little Tiger Press, 1998), 20.

254. Lieurance, "Noah's Ark," 33.

255. Charles Reasoner, *Inside Noah's Ark* (New York: Price Stern Sloan, 2002), n.p.

256. Larsen, *Little Girls*.

257. Sheila Walsh, *The Princess in Me Storybook Bible* (Nashville, TN: Thomas Nelson, 2008). See also Fiona Boon, *My Princess Bible Purse* (Nashville, TN: Thomas Nelson, 2012).

258. Andy Holmes, *My Princess Bible*, illus. by Sergey Eiliseev (Carol Stream, IL: Tyndale House, 2010).

259. Diane Stortz, *The Sweetest Story Bible: Sweet Thoughts and Sweet Words for Little Girls*, illus. by Sheila Bailey (Grand Rapids, MI: Zondervan, 2010).

Carolyn Larsen's books for little boys and little girls are not as subtle in passing on certain gender roles to children. As noted above, her *Little Boys Bible Storybook for Fathers and Sons* has Noah's sons, who look like little boys, working like construction workers building the ark and learning the lesson that they should not be afraid of hard work.[260] In Larsen's Baker Book House offering, *The Little Girls Bible Storybook for Mothers and Daughters* (1998), she uses creative retellings of Bible stories to pass on particular views of women's roles and duties.[261] She ends each story by passing on to girls a characteristic of a "Woman of God." Larsen uses the story of "Mrs. Noah" to teach little girls the lesson that "A Woman of God is Obedient," in this case to her husband as well as to God.[262] The story of Mrs. Noah is titled "Whatever You Say, Dear," and the title page for the story includes a cheerful illustration by Caron Turk of Noah sawing a board while Mrs. Noah is baking bread (see Figure 4.4).[263] When Noah tells his wife about God's command to bring animals onto the ark, she expresses her distress:

> "With us? We're going in the boat with those wild, smelly animals?" Mrs.
>   Noah wondered.
> "We'd better. Flood coming you know."
> Mrs. Noah looked at the lions, bears, and spiders (did there have to be
>   spiders?) She smiled and took Noah's hand, "Whatever you say, dear."[264]

Mrs. Noah takes on the stereotypical role of a woman who does not like smelly animals and is somewhat afraid of spiders, yet she virtuously defers to her husband's will. Significantly, Mrs. Noah is not saying "Whatever you say, God" but "Whatever you say, dear." Later in the retelling we are told, "Mrs. Noah kept busy cleaning up after the animals and keeping her family fed and the clothes cleaned."[265] Again, Mrs. Noah keeps busy carrying out the traditional gender roles of women, doing the cooking and the cleaning and caring for her family. The book was popular enough to merit another version by Larsen in 2014, this one titled *Little Girls Bible Storybook for Fathers and Daughters*. According to this story, "Mrs. Noah shooed out the animals. Quickly sweeping the boat clean, she joined Noah on dry ground."[266] Noah apparently stays outside and waits for his wife while Mrs. Noah finishes up the cleaning.

In 2014, Thomas Nelson publishers offered Jennifer Gerelds' *Brave Girls Bible Stories* with a bright pink cover. The story of Noah's wife is told by a young

---

260. Larsen, *Little Boys*, 31–3.

261. The issues of gender and understanding of gender roles as they are depicted in children's Bibles will be examined further in later chapters.

262. Larsen, *Little Girls*, 29.

263. Ibid., 24.

264. Ibid., 28.

265. Ibid., 32.

266. Carolyn Larsen, *Little Girls Bible Storybook for Fathers and Daughters*, illus. by Caron Turk (Grand Rapids, MI: Baker Book House, 2014), 27.

modern-day girl named Gracie. She begins, "I am sure it was tough for Noah and all ..."[267] but continues, "I think it also had to be rough for Noah's wife. She had to trust that God was able to lead her through her husband, and she had to stand by Noah even when others thought he was nuts. And don't you know the ladies around town whispered when she walked down the street."[268] Some readers may be concerned to see a model wife being depicted as someone who had to be led by God through her husband and who "had" to stand by her man even when others questioned his sanity. Furthermore, the other ladies in town are described as gossips. As the story continues, Gracie informs the reader that Noah's wife "went right into that ark with all those loud and smelly animals without a single recorded temper-tantrum—I know I couldn't have done that. I'm sure I would've had a major fit!"[269] Gracie, like the other narrators in the book, is a sweet, brave girl who fits a certain image of girls who are especially averse to smelly animals and prone to major fits. Noah's wife is commended for enduring these things, while one might suspect that Noah or a young boy narrator would not be portrayed in quite the same way.

In the late twentieth century and early twenty-first century, then, conservative Christian concerns over issues of traditional gender roles seem to be manifest in these children's Bible adaptations of the story of Noah.

Children's Bibles in America, especially those of the twentieth and early twenty-first centuries, have adapted the story of Noah to commend a wide variety of virtues to children. The examples above again demonstrate the multivalency and malleability of the story of Noah and also illustrate the wide variety of virtues that Americans have deemed important to teach to their children. While many of these authors may have well been aware that the story of Noah could be used to teach other virtues, often the effect of their stories upon the reader is that of a fable. The stories are told as though they each exist to teach one moral principle and that moral principle alone. Children and their parents who read these children's Bibles may well get the sense that, even in the original biblical texts, these stories and the Bible in its entirety were created as a series of morality tales to teach people right from wrong. In the process, readers are not only learning about certain virtues that the authors have decided are important, but learning to approach the Bible as a book of virtues, with each story designed to teach a particular lesson.

4.7. The Story of Noah and the Romantic Ideal of the Pure and Innocent Child

As seen in some of the children's Bibles discussed in previous chapters, children in the eighteenth and early nineteenth centuries were often seen as small adults

267. Jennifer Gerelds, *Brave Girls Bible Stories*, illus. by Aleksey and Olga Ivanov (Nashville, TN: Thomas Nelson, 2014), 11.

268. Ibid.

269. Ibid., 14.

Whatever You Say, Dear

Figure 4.4. Illustration by Caron Turk from Carolyn Larsen, *Little Girls Bible Storybook for Mothers and Daughters* (Grand Rapids, MI: Baker Book House, 1998), 24.

who needed to learn the harsh reality of their sinful natures and their own mortality. Furthermore, children were taught that they needed to learn to control their impulses and take responsibility for their behavior. Among the nineteenth-century American urban middle class, however, a new view of childhood began to take hold. Historian Steven Mintz describes it as "a Romantic vision, which viewed children as symbols of purity, spontaneity, and emotional expressiveness, who were free from adult inhibitions and thus required parents who would ensure that their innocence was not corrupted."[270] As the nineteenth century progressed, many Americans considered these characteristics not only as descriptive of childhood, but prescriptive as well. A child's purity, spontaneity, emotional

270. Mintz, *Huck's Raft*, 76.

expressiveness, and lack of inhibitions were seen as virtuous behavior that represented the Romantic ideal and were evidence of admirable parenting on the part of a child's mother and father.

The story of Noah does not initially appear to lend itself well to promoting these virtues. A children's Bible author could, presumably, cast Noah's sons as young children who exhibit these virtues, but this has rarely been done. The virtues do appear, however, in another form. Those children's Bibles that frame their stories as conversations between a parent and child have occasionally cast the child as one who exhibits these Romantic ideals.

The little child in Laurie Loring's *Little Truths for Little Folks; Bible Stories* (1877) serves as an extreme example of the Romantic view of the sweet, innocent little girl that was emerging in American children's literature at the time. The girl's name is Goldlocks (as opposed to Goldilocks) and she exhibits the tender concerns and stylized baby talk that appear to have been considered prized virtues of many of the young heroines in the literature of the time. Goldlocks demonstrates her sweet, sensitive nature by her surprising response to her mother's story of Noah:

> "Mamma," said little Goldlocks, "I guess Noah was a naughty man."
> "What do you mean, child?" asked mamma in surprise. "Why do you think he
>   was naughty?"
> "'Cause he put his dove out of the ark when it was all—all water. I know
>   Downy would feel sorry if I put her out in the rain." Goldlocks held her pet
>   dove closely as she said this, and her eyes were almost tearful.
> "Noah was a good man. He let the dove fly out to see if the waters were dried
>   up. It didn't rain then."[271]

Mamma is surprised by Goldlocks' question, but does not chide her or shame her for suggesting that Noah was naughty, as one might imagine some of the other parents in similarly framed children's Bibles of the nineteenth century may have done. Instead, Mamma patiently answers Goldlocks' question. Meanwhile, Goldlocks is described tenderly petting her dove and being on the verge of tears. This tenderness and emotional vulnerability is not depicted as weakness, but rather as evidence of Goldlocks' good and tender heart.

Mamma then tells Goldlocks that the dove returned to the ark, which leads to the following exchange between Goldlocks and her mother:

> "How did she get into the ark again, mamma?"
> "Noah put out his hand and took her in."
> "That was nice!" cried Goldlocks. "Was she real tired, mamma?"
> "Yes, she was tired; but Noah let her rest a week before he sent her out again."[272]

271. Laurie Loring, *Little Truths for Little Folks; Bible Stories* (Boston, MA: D. Lothrop & Co., 1877), 9.

272. Ibid., 10.

In the exchange, Goldlocks shows concern for the dove and cries out about how happy she is that Noah took the dove back into the ark by hand. The mother does not chide her for her questions or comments that interrupt her story. Instead, mamma uses a term of endearment when she asks her daughter, "Can my little girlie tell what the dove brought back in her mouth?"[273] The term "my little girlie" affirms Goldlocks and her status as a young child as something to be embraced. When Goldlocks finds the answer to mamma's question in her little Bible she cries out joyfully, "An olive leaf! Oh mamma! The trees weren't all dead, were they?"[274] Loring's narrative, then, affirms Goldlocks's status as a sweet, caring, emotional, and impulsive little girl, and Goldlocks's mother models a good parent who affirms these qualities in her daughter.

Even after mamma's patient explanations, it is clear that Goldlocks still has to work through the story by the dream she has that night: "Goldlocks dreamed a funny little dream that night. She thought she was in Noah's ark all alone; and when she cried for her mamma, a flock of beautiful white doves came to the window of the ark to take her home."[275] For Loring, that ends her story of Noah. She leaves the reader with the image of Goldlocks crying out with a nightmare, an act that demonstrates spontaneity, a lack of inhibition, and emotional expressiveness. Again, Loring does not portray these characteristics as vices or weaknesses, but rather as evidence of a young child's sweet and tender nature.

In Gertrude Smith's *Baby Bible Stories*, published in 1904, the author frames her story as a conversation between a mother, who is repeatedly referred to as "precious mamma"[276] or "mamma dear,"[277] and Robbie, a boy who is approximately three or four years old.[278] The retelling of the story of Noah's ark begins with "mamma dear" telling Robbie about toy Noah's arks, a popular toy of the time. Smith then describes the following episode of domestic bliss: "And Robbie clapped his hands and said: 'Oh, I want a toy Noah's ark! I want a Noah's ark, mamma!'" Robbie's father, naturally, responds immediately:

> And dear papa put down his paper and said: "Well, I'll go right down town and buy one, my son."
> And precious mamma laughed, and said: "And will you tell our Robbie a beautiful Bible story to-night about the *truly Noah's* ark?"
> And papa said: "Yes, I'll do my best, mamma, but I can't tell stories as well as you do."

273. Ibid.

274. Ibid.

275. Ibid., 12.

276. Gertrude Smith, *Baby Bible Stories* (Philadelphia, PA: Henry Altemus Company, 1904), 67.

277. Ibid.

278. The character of Robbie would also appear in a collection of Bible stories in the following year. See Gertrude Smith, *Robbie's Bible Stories* (Philadelphia, PA: Henry Altemus Company, 1905).

And Robbie clapped his hands, and said: "But you can tell this story, papa. You can tell me about Noah's ark in my own little gilt-edged Bible."[279]

The passage reveals the role of consumerism in relation to children in some Christian families of the time. It suggests that parents with the means to do so may purchase religious-themed toys and gilt-edged little Bibles for their young children. Also, according to the episode, Robbie is a child who is both seen and heard in the home. When he asks for a toy, he does not receive a stern moralistic lecture about the evils of greed, selfishness, or frivolity. Instead, the father immediately responds that he will purchase the toy that Robbie wants and precious mamma affirms that decision with a laugh. Finally, Robbie himself is the image of a sweet, innocent child who asks for what he wants and claps enthusiastically when told he will get it, demonstrating spontaneity, a lack of inhibition, and emotional expressiveness.

Smith writes that later, "Robbie boy sat on his dear father's knee, and his pretty mamma sat near, and papa told him the story of Noah's ark."[280] When papa tells Robbie that God told Noah to build an ark, a curious Robbie asks a question:

And Robbie boy said: "How did Noah know that God told him, papa; did he hear Him shout it right out of the sky?"

And papa said: "No, Noah knew it was God who made him think that he must build the ark, and build it quick, because it was a good and wise thing to do."

And darling mamma said: "I think Noah felt almost as though God whispered to him, Robbie, just as you do when you think 'I must be good today.' That is God's voice, dear child."[281]

In contrast to some earlier children's Bibles that present Bible stories in the form of conversations between parents and children, Robbie is not chided for asking a question. Robbie's curiosity is affirmed, his question answered, and he is called a "dear child."

Later, Papa tells Robbie that it "rained and rained, and rained and rained,"[282] which leads to the following exchange:

And Robbie said: "Oh, papa, I don't like to have it rain so long, papa!"

And papa laughed and said: "Well, dear old Noah did n't [sic] like to have it rain so long either, but he kept saying, 'The sun *will* come again, and God is Good.'"

And Robbie clapped his hands and said, "That is what precious mamma tells me to say when it rains all day."[283]

279. Smith, *Baby Bible Stories*, 68–9. Emphasis in the original.
280. Ibid., 69.
281. Ibid., 70, 73 (note that pages 71–2 contain an illustration).
282. Ibid., 75.
283. Ibid. Emphasis in the original.

In this exchange, Robbie is told, in effect, to have a happy, optimistic, and sunny outlook on life. Papa then closes his story by reassuring Robbie that Noah and his family "lived happy ever after."[284] The example of Robbie and his parents' responses to him would likely have more of a lasting impression on the readers than the father's story of Noah or any commentary on the sun coming out again after a rain. Robbie models a happy, sweet child who asks his parents questions and asks them to do things for him and the parents respond with happy affirmations. Religious books in America from a half century earlier would seldom if ever have presented readers with this image of a child or of how parents should respond to children.

These stories, then, offer an alternate means of passing on certain values. The authors do not use the story of Noah itself to pass on these Romantic ideals of childhood, but instead use the characters in the sequences that frame their Bible stories to do so.

4.8. The Vices of Noah and Ham: The Curious Case of Drunken, Naked Noah

Children's Bibles rarely retell the curious story of how Noah, after the flood, became drunk on wine and fell asleep naked in his tent (Gen. 9.20-27). According to the Book of Genesis, Noah's son Ham "saw the nakedness of his father, and told his two brothers outside" (Gen. 9.22). Noah's other sons, Shem and Japheth, took a garment and covered Noah's nakedness taking care to avoid looking at him in the process. When Noah realized what had happened, he pronounced a curse on Ham's son Canaan, stating, "Cursed be Canaan; lowest of slaves shall he be to his brothers" (Gen. 9.25). Noah then proclaimed blessings for Shem and Japheth.

Several reasons immediately come to mind as to why this episode in the life of Noah is so rarely told in children's Bibles. First of all, drunkenness and nakedness are often considered inappropriate subject matters for children, and the desire to edit unseemly or inappropriate subject matter out of the Bible is precisely one of the benefits that some children's Bible authors have listed for their books in their introductions. Authors, editors, and publishers also may omit the story simply out of a desire to abridge the story of Noah. The story of Noah, his family, and the animals surviving the flood, Noah giving thanks and God promising no more floods, and God marking the promise with a rainbow provides a natural and satisfying end to the story. Finally, deleting the story of Noah getting drunk and falling asleep naked helps children's Bible authors preserve Noah as a positive role model for children. This erasure is especially helpful for those who wish to use the Bible as a book of virtues. The story of drunken, naked Noah complicates the simple story of a good man who always did what God wanted him to do.

When the story does appear in children's Bibles, it often serves a particular purpose and reflects particular agendas. Martin Luther wrote that the episode of Noah getting drunk and being discovered by Ham was "a silly and altogether

---

284. Ibid., 76.

unprofitable little story."[285] A number of children's Bible authors, however, apparently disagreed and used the episode for a number of reasons, including to teach children about the vice of drunkenness, to explain away concerns they may have regarding Noah's character, to teach children to honor their parents, or even to explain their perspectives on how Noah's curse of Canaan relates to slavery.

4.8.a. Noah's sin of drunkenness

As mentioned above, many American Christians in the 1800s joined societies that collectively are often referred to as the Benevolent Empire. Perhaps the most common of these groups were temperance societies that denounced drunkenness and eventually helped lead to the era of Prohibition in the United States. The Genesis account of Noah getting drunk and falling asleep naked does not pause to criticize Noah's behavior explicitly.[286] As Old Testament scholar Bill T. Arnold comments, "It is most unlikely that this text condemns Noah for drinking wine, and even his drunkenness is not lifted for critique."[287] Given the American context of the 1800s and early 1900s, however, it is not surprising to find that several children's Bibles appropriate the story to teach children about the evils of alcohol and the general sinfulness of humankind.

Some children's Bible authors do not emphasize the sin of drunkenness alone, but use the episode to make the point that all people—even good people like Noah—can fall into sinful behaviors. In the book *Histories from Scripture, for Children*, written by a "Miss Graham" and published in 1839, the character of Momma tells Bible stories to her children Mary and John. The book makes only a cryptic reference to Noah's drunkenness in later life, but is less vague on the wickedness of Noah and Ham's behavior. After the story of the flood has concluded, John asks what happened to Noah after the flood.

> "Did Noah and his sons continue to be good?" asked John.
> "No, my dear; Noah forgot God, in his old age; and one of his sons, Ham, was
>   very wicked: so God blessed Shem and Japheth, but Ham was not blessed,
>   and his children were not happy."[288]

Without getting into the issue of Noah's drunkenness, the exact nature of Ham's sin, or the nature of Noah's curse on Canaan, Miss Graham uses the story to establish the sinfulness of even Noah's family. She also seems to take Noah's one night of drunkenness to mean that he had forgotten God in his old age.

---

285. Martin Luther, *Luther Works*, II. *Lectures on Genesis Chapters 6–14*, ed. By J. Pelican (St. Louis, MO: Concordia Publishing House, 1960), 166.

286. Wenham, however, also suggests that the Hebrew Bible is often brief in its description of shameful acts. See Wenham, *Word Biblical Commentary*, 199–200.

287. Arnold, *Genesis*, 112. See also Wenham, *Word Biblical Commentary*, 199.

288. Miss Graham, *Histories from Scripture, for Children* (New York: John S. Taylor, 1839), 50.

In the late 1800s, Julius Katzenberg wrote several children's Bibles that were used in Jewish homes and schools, including *Biblical History for School and Home: Part I* (1878). Perhaps because Jewish children's Bibles rarely moralized biblical stories, Katzenberg provided readers with his rationale for drawing moral lessons from them:

> Any one at all conversant with the work in our Sabbath-schools, must be aware of the fact that we have been hitherto without any text-book of Biblical History suitable for children of the tender ages of eight, nine, or ten years. Moreover, the study is often nothing more than a mere repetition of the names and facts of a story, without any attempt being made to bring the more important moral lessons therein contained, within the grasp of the child's intellect.[289]

Biblical stories do little good, Katzenberg seems to suggest, if the moral lessons contained in them are not made clear to children.

Katzenberg cleverly integrates both Noah's drunkenness and the shamefulness of Ham's behavior to instruct his readers: "Take care and do not indulge in strong drink, for it injures the health. Drunkenness is shameful. Turn away your eyes, if you should happen to see anything which is not decent and respectable; close your ears, if you hear improper words, and let such speech never escape from your lips. Modesty is a guardian angel which guides us on the path of virtue."[290] Katzenberg does not so much condemn Noah for getting drunk as much as he condemns drunkenness itself as a shameful thing. In contrast to Ham, children should avoid shameful things by trying their best to see no evil and hear no evil.

For "Grandpa" Reuben Prescott, author of *Grand Father's Bible Stories* (1897), Noah's behavior in getting drunk was wicked indeed: "But even Noah, who had been so good before the flood, fell into sin afterwards. Like Adam, he kept a garden, and he also grew vines, from which he made wine, and foolishly and wickedly drank of it too freely, and committed the sin of drunkenness."[291] Prescott acknowledges that Noah was "so good" before the flood, but offers no excuse for Noah's behavior. Drinking too much alcohol was both foolish and wicked.

While most children's Bible stories of drunken, naked Noah were published before the turn of the century, a few twentieth-century children's Bibles use the story as well. Philip Turner was an ordained priest in the Church of England and known for his religious writing, children's books, and his Reverend Septimus Treloar mystery novels. Turner's *The Bible Story*, published by Oxford University Press in Britain, Canada, and the United States in 1968, used the story of the drunken Noah as a confirmation of the inherent sinfulness of all humankind. Turner writes that after the flood God said, "I set my bow in the heavens as a

---

289. Julius Katzenberg, *Biblical History for School and Home: Part I* (New York: Industrial School of the Hebrew Orphan Asylum, 1878), 3.

290. Ibid., 17.

291. Grandpa Reuben Prescott, *Grand Father's Bible Stories* (Chicago: C. W. Stanton Company, 1897), 31.

sign and a promise. While the earth remains I will never again smite every living thing. For the heart of man is twisted and he cannot, without my help, walk in my ways."[292] The story continues, "And that very night, as if to prove the truth of what God had said, old Noah got so terribly drunk with wine that his sons had to put him to bed. And he was the one good man who had been saved from the flood."[293] For Turner, Noah's drunkenness is evidence of the sinfulness of humankind and its need for God.

4.8.b. Redeeming Noah as a role model

Many American children's Bibles throughout history have used biblical characters as role models of moral living and have gone to some lengths to retain them as such.[294] The stories of the Bible itself continually remind their readers that characters of faith, such as Adam, Abraham, Moses, David, and many more, are fallible and detail their acts of sin and disobedience. Children's Bibles that attempt to use these biblical characters as models of moral behavior for children, however, have often avoided these passages or attempted to explain them away.

Since the sins of biblical "heroes" are sometimes sexual or violent in nature, in some cases children's Bible authors may eliminate these scenes because they see them as inappropriate for children. Omitting these unfortunate incidents can also serve to maintain these characters as positive role models in the eyes of children. In the late nineteenth and early twentieth century, Bible characters increasingly transition from being used as shameful examples of how humans sin and disobey God to being presented to children as pristine role models for moral behavior. By deleting episodes of immoral behavior on the part of Bible characters, children's Bible authors are also able to present children with the unambiguous message that good behavior is rewarded while bad behavior is punished.

As seen above, some children's Bible authors that do include the episode of drunken Noah, harshly criticize Noah for his wickedness in getting drunk. Other children's Bible authors, however, go to some length to suggest that Noah was innocent of any wrongdoing. In many of these examples, the authors seem to use the fact that Genesis says that Noah was the first person to plant a vineyard (Gen. 9. 20) to presume that he did not understand that drinking fermented wine would make him drunk.

As *The Child's Book of Bible Stories* (1850), a loose translation of an earlier German children's Bible, suggests, "[Noah] made wine with the grapes; and not knowing the strength of it, he one day took too much of it; and his son Ham

---

292. Philip Turner, *The Bible Story*, illus. by Brian Wildsmith (Oxford: Oxford University Press, 1968), 15.

293. Ibid.

294. For an exploration of the ways in which children's Bibles have retained Jonah as a positive role model for children, despite the events of Jonah 4, see my article, Russell W. Dalton, "Perfect Prophets, Helpful Hippos and Happy Endings: Noah and Jonah in Children's Bible Storybooks in the U.S.," *Religious Education* 102:3 (June 2007), 306–8.

mocked him, which was very wicked."[295] In this case, however, Noah's ignorance of the effects of alcohol not only redeems Noah's character, but serves to make Ham's presumed mockery all the more wicked because it is unjust.

Three children's Bibles by Roman Catholic authors that include the story of Noah becoming drunk, *Bible History; to which is added A Short History of the Church* (1879), *Bible History: A Textbook of Old and New Testaments for Catholic Schools* (1935), and the Maryknoll Sisters' *Crusade: The Story of the Bible Retold for Catholic Children* (1955), all explain to their readers that Noah did not know that the wine would make him drunk.[296] The authors of these books do not enter into an extended defense of Noah's character or discuss whether drinking alcohol in any amount is wicked. They simply suggest that Noah did not know how strong the drink was or that it would make him drunk before they continue with their stories.

In his 1934 volume, *The Story of the Bible*, Episcopal priest Walter Russell Bowie, who later became a professor at Union Theological Seminary in New York, also included the story of Noah getting drunk after the flood. Bowie acknowledges the fact that Noah was drunk and does not excuse it, but asked his readers not to judge Noah too harshly: "[T]his frank and unvarnished picture of Noah, in his badness as well as in his goodness, is a witness to a very significant fact about the Old Testament which needs to be borne in mind. These men in the early days were not completed saints. They must not be judged by the standards of our own times."[297] Bowie notes that people of that time had several wives instead of one, had slaves, and were merciless in war.[298] Noah's drunkenness, then, must be understood in the context of the primitive mores of his time.

The efforts of children's Bible authors to redeem Noah's character find a parallel in many children's Bible retellings of the stories of other Bible characters. Through these explanations, children are able to retain an unblemished view of their Bible heroes, but in the process may lose out on a lesson about the moral frailty and fallibility of all people.

4.8.c. Honor your parents

To the modern reader, Noah's curse can seem to be a severe reaction to a minor offense. Commenting on Genesis 9.22, Bible scholar Gordon J. Wenham notes, "Westerners who are strangers to a world where discretion and filial loyalty are supreme virtues have often felt that there must be something more to Ham's offense

295. *The Child's Book of Bible Stories* (Philadelphia, PA: Henry F. Anners, 1850), 36.

296. See *Bible History; to which is added A Short History of the Church* (New York: P. O'Shea, 1879), 17; George Johnson, Jerome D. Hannan, and M. Dominica, *Bible History: A Textbook of Old and New Testaments for Catholic Schools* (New York: Benziger Brothers, 1935), 21–2; and Maryknoll Sisters, *Crusade: The Story of the Bible Retold for Catholic Children* 3 (Chicago: John J. Crawley & Co., Inc., September 10, 1955), 71.

297. Walter Russell Bowie, *The Story of the Bible* (New York: Abingdon Press, 1934), 37.
298. Ibid.

than appears on the surface."[299] Wenham notes that the attention the passage pays to Shem and Japheth's efforts to discreetly cover their father's nakedness by ingeniously covering it with a robe (Gen. 9.23) confirms the passage's concern with these issues.[300] Several children's Bibles have used this episode to commend the same virtues of modesty and respect for parents. Many of these also include the long-standing embellishment, not mentioned in Genesis, that Ham not only told his brothers about what he saw, but laughed at or mocked his father Noah as well.

According to *The Child's Book of Bible Stories* (1850), Ham's sin of disrespecting his father justified the curse he received. After describing Ham mocking Noah and Noah cursing Canaan, the text suggests, "We must acknowledge that he deserved this fate. The child who can look with contempt upon its father, or treat its mother with disrespect, deserves to be punished by God. God loves the child who respects and obeys its parents, and bears their faults with patience."[301] The curse Noah gives to Canaan, the author suggests, is well deserved, for his father Ham did not show proper respect for his father.

History of the Bible, for the Use of Schools, translated from German by Rev. Theo Noethen and published in 1860, does not mention Noah's drunkenness, but still manages to use the story to teach a lesson about honoring one's parents. According to the book, "The sons of Noah were Shem, Ham, and Japheth. Before his death he blessed Shem and Japheth, but not Ham, because he once mocked him."[302] Then, in smaller letters, the book adds the comment, "It is pleasing to God when children honor their parents, and patiently overlook their faults."[303] Children reading just this retelling of the story would not know that Noah's fault was getting drunk and falling asleep naked; the moral of the story is simply for children to overlook the faults of both their mothers and their fathers in general and never to mock them.

In addition to using the story of Noah to teach children about the shamefulness of drunkenness, in *Biblical History for School and Home* (1878) Julius Katzenberg uses the story to observe, "Dear children, try to be worthy of your parents' blessing. Honor, love, and obey them."[304] Again, the story serves to remind children that they should honor both of their parents.

4.8.d. The curse of Canaan and the rationale for slavery in America

Any discussion of the moral teachings gleaned from the story of Noah's drunkenness and the cursing of Canaan must address the disturbing widespread use

---

299. Wenham, *Word Biblical Commentary*, 200.

300. Ibid.

301. *The Child's Book of Bible Stories*, 37.

302. Theo Noethen, trans., *History of the Bible, for the Use of Schools* (Albany, NY: Weed, Parsons & Company, Printers, 1860), 9.

303. Ibid.

304. Katzenberg, *Biblical History*, 16.

of the passage to rationalize the slavery of African people in eighteenth- and nineteenth-century America.

While most scholars today denounce readings of Genesis 9 that suggest that Ham was black or that Africans were his descendants, almost all nineteenth-century Americans, whether they were supporters of slavery or abolitionists, white or black, assumed that Ham was a black man and the father of the African people. For the majority of Americans at the time, the curse of Ham's son Canaan also had something to do with the slavery of his descendants.[305]

As a matter of fact, in nineteenth-century America, those who argued against the teaching that Ham was a black man and the progenitor of the African race often did so not in order to condemn slavery, but to justify it. In the years following the Civil War, rather than toning down their rhetoric, a number of southern writers became even more adamant and extreme in their theories of black inferiority. Some even made the infamous argument that Ham was not a black man and that "the negro" was present on Noah's ark only as one of the animals, and not as one of the humans in Noah's family.[306]

In this context, the Rev. R. A. Morrisey's insistence that Africans and African-Americans were indeed decedents of Ham is understandable. Morrisey was an African-American scholar—a valedictorian of Livingston College and a Doctor of Divinity—and the pastor of a number of churches in the American South and in Pennsylvania. He wrote *Bible History of the Negro* (1915)[307] and a revised edition of the book titled *Colored People in Bible History* (1925).[308] Morrisey explains that his books were written "not only for the benefit of adults, but also as a source of information to children and young folks."[309] Morrisey's goal is to provide African-American readers with a biblical heritage.

Writing about Ham, Morrisey establishes that he agrees with the prominent view of Ham's descendants held by most nineteenth-century and early twentieth-century Americans: "By leading Bible scholars and also ethnologists, it is now almost universally agreed that springing from Adam (Gen. 2.7) the primitive man, black people, called today the Negro race, descended from Ham, the second son of Noah, and that the white race descended from Shem and Japheth, the other

---

305. Cf. David M. Goldenberg, *The Curse of Ham: Race and Slavery in Early Judaism, Christianity, and Islam* (Princeton, NJ: Princeton University Press, 2009), 142, and Sylvester Johnson, *The Myth of Ham in Nineteenth-Century American Christianity* (New York: Palgrave Macmillan, 2004), 32. See also Josiah Priest's widely circulated book *Slavery as It Relates to the Negro or African Race* (New York: Arno, 1843, 1977).

306. See, for example, Buckner H. Payne ("Ariel"), *The Negro: What is His Ethnographic Status: Is he the progeny of Ham?* (Cincinnati, OH: Published for the Proprietor, 1867), 45, and J. S. Sampley, *A Bible History of the Negro* (Greenville, AL: Greenville Advocate, 1887), 11.

307. R. A. Morrisey, *Bible History of the Negro* (Nashville, TN: National Baptist Publishing Board, 1915).

308. R. A. Morrisey, *Colored People in Bible History* (Hammond, IN: W. B. Conkey Company, 1925).

309. Ibid., 8.

two sons."[310] Morrisey, however, argues against the view still held by many of his time that Noah's curse of Ham explained or justified the enslavement of Africans:

> It has been claimed, and is still by some, that Noah placed a curse upon Ham and his descendants, and therefore the Negro race is a divinely cursed people, doomed always to be mere servants, and inferior to other race groups of men. This theory has been handed down from one generation to another and advocated until in the minds of many has become fixed opinion. Yet the Bible, which has been used as a weapon in the defense of this long standing theory, to the contrary, proves that it is absurd and without true foundation.[311]

To debunk the theory, Morrisey argues that God blessed Noah and his family and that this blessing remains intact, despite the sin that followed:

> The Negro race or Ham descendants had the divine blessings bestowed upon it at the same time and to the same extent the others of Noah's family did in the Covenant which God made with Noah. (Gen. 9:8, 9.) Though subsequently Noah as a sinful being fell into sin, into which his son Ham figured largely by a want of respect which a son should show to a father, yet God did not revoke his covenant blessings upon them.[312]

Furthermore, Morrisey argues, Noah's curse was pronounced while Noah was still under the effects of intoxication and that curse was not even uttered in the name of God or given divine approval.[313] Ham, therefore, though he was sinful, was blessed by God and not cursed by God.

Having established this point, Morrisey tells the stories of Bible characters whom he describes as colored people, such as Caleb, Hagar and Ishmael, Pharaoh's daughter, the Queen of Sheba, Nimrod, Ruth, the Ethiopian Eunuch, the Magi, and others. He also includes an introductory chapter titled "Friendly Relations of White and Colored People," describing David's friendship with Ittai the Gittite and Solomon's friendship with Hiram, king of Tyre.[314]

How, then, have the white authors of children's Bibles in America dealt with the story of Noah's curse of Canaan? One early children's Bible author criticized those who claimed certainty that Noah's curse of Ham turned Ham into a black man. Sarah Hall's *Conversations on the Bible*, published in 1818 in Philadelphia, presented the stories of the Bible through a dialogue between a mother and her children. In Hall's introduction, she confidently explained that there was no need for her to write the book anonymously in order to hide her gender:

310. Ibid., 55.
311. Ibid., 57.
312. Ibid., 56–7.
313. Ibid., 57–8.
314. Ibid., 11–16.

An anonymous work may anticipate candour, because it does nothing to the adventitious weight of reputation. Nor is there, in our liberal times, any hostility to a female pen, to be depreciated. The moral and intellectual sphere of women has been gradually enlarging with the progress of the benignant star of Christianity; but it was reserved for the nineteenth century to honour them beyond the circle of domestic life—to form them into societies, organized, active, and useful in the most excellent pursuits. Still, let them ever remember, that whilst here, they may be permitted to emit one invigorating ray,—there, it is their duty, and their privilege to shine.[315]

Hall does not hesitate to draw her own conclusions on any number of issues related to the story of Noah on which the Book of Genesis is silent, such as the specific date and location on which the ark came to rest after the flood.[316] Regarding the curse of Ham, however, Hall has the character of Mother criticize her son's teacher for going beyond the facts of the Bible itself:

> CHARLES. I have heard one of our professors say, that Ham became black in consequence of the curse pronounced by his father against him. And thus he accounts for the colour of the Africans, his posterity.
> MOTHER. Your professor, my dear, has no authority for his opinion—nor will we undertake to discuss a question irrecoverably lost. Let us confine ourselves chiefly to the letter of Scripture, and if we cannot there discover the causes of difference in the colour of the human family, we can with certainty account for the varieties in language.[317]

Hall uses that final phrase as a means of segueing into the story of the Tower of Babel. Mother's harsh rebuke of the theory that Ham became black because of the curse, going to the extent of criticizing her son's teacher rather than modeling respect for him, illustrates how even this issue was a point of heated debate in early nineteenth-century America.

Helene A. Guerber, the author of several popular history books for children in the late nineteenth century, wrote *The Story of the Chosen People*, published by the American Book Company of New York in 1896. Guerber does not teach that Noah's curse turned Ham's skin black, but she does explicitly pass on the interpretation that Ham's curse led directly to African slavery in the United States: "When Noah came to his senses, he was bitterly ashamed; and when he heard how rude Ham had been, Noah sent him away, and cursed him, saying that his children would be slaves. This prophecy came true, and Ham was the ancestor of the black, or negro, race, who were slaves even in this country half a century ago."[318] Guerber

---

315. Sarah Hall, *Conversations on the Bible* (Philadelphia, PA: Harrison Hall, 1818), viii–xi.

316. Ibid., 337.

317. Ibid., 19.

318. H. A. Guerber, *The Story of the Chosen People* (New York: American Book

does not report this as though she is making a defense of slavery, nor does she say that it is regrettable. Instead, she simply reports it as though it were a fact just like others that would appear in her other history books.

Some children's Bibles of the late nineteenth and early twentieth centuries include the story of Noah's curse of Canaan, but simply report that Ham (or Canaan) was to be a servant to his brothers and do not make any reference to race or ethnicity or go into any detail or speculation about what this might mean for the generations that followed. In *Charming Bible Stories: Written in Simple Language* (1894), minister and historian Henry Davenport Northrop notes that Ham was cursed for his sin, but does not tell his readers what that sin was. He explains, as though it was a matter of course, that Ham and his descendants would become "the servant of servants,"[319] but he makes no mention of Ham's race or ethnicity. In "Grandpa" Reuben Prescott's very brief treatment of the incident in *Grand Father's Bible Stories* (1897), he finds space to include the embellishment that Ham mocked Noah. He also addresses a difficulty with the passage that has confounded commentators for centuries, namely that Ham commits the sin but it is his son Canaan who receives the curse.[320] Prescott provides readers with a rationale as to why Canaan may have received the curse that does not go into higher critical methods such as form criticism and source criticism: "His son Ham saw him in a helpless state in a drunken sleep, and made a mock of him; and for this Noah, when he awoke, cursed Ham and his son Canaan, who had, perhaps, mocked him too, and while he blessed Shem and Japheth, said the others should be the servants of their brethren."[321] Like Northrop, Prescott does not address the issue of race.

The authors of *Bible History: A Textbook of Old and New Testaments for Catholic Schools* (1935) did not address the issue of race either. They suggest that Ham, here spelled Cham, was cursed, but also stop short of explicitly stating that his decedents would be cast as slaves to the whole world for centuries to come. Instead, the text describes the curse, saying "that he would always be the servant of his brothers."[322] These children's Bibles stop short of offering an opinion on Ham's descendants or the origin of the races.

Hendrik Willem van Loon's treatment of the passage in his book *The Story of the Bible* (1923) is a curious one. Van Loon was a well-known author and public figure in his time. In his day, van Loon was considered to be quite progressive in his white Protestant circles, even writing a book entitled *Tolerance* in which he gave an optimistic overview of the struggle for tolerance throughout human history.[323] His views on race, however, are somewhat complex. He seems to have

Company, 1896), 24.

319. Henry Davenport Northrop, *Charming Bible Stories: Written in Simple Language* (1894), 30. No place of publication or publisher provided.

320. Wenham, *Word Biblical Commentary*, 201.

321. Grandpa Reuben Prescott, *Grand Father's*, 31–2.

322. Johnson et al., *Bible History*, 22.

323. Hendrik Willem van Loon, *Tolerance* (New York: Boni and Liveright, 1925).

suggested, for example, that the enslavement of Africans would have worked out fine if advancement in machinery had not led to them being overworked.[324]

Van Loon's underlying views on race lend context to his treatment of the story of Noah's curse of Canaan in *The Story of the Bible*. He write, "It happened that Noah, who possessed a vineyard, had made himself a very pleasant wine, and when he had partaken thereof, more than was wise, he became drunken, and behaved after the fashion of such people."[325] Van Loon does not pause to moralize on the vice of drunkenness, however. Instead, he is more focused on the curse. He included the embellishment that Ham mocked his father, writing that Ham "thought it was a great joke and laughed loudly, and was not nice at all."[326] Van Loon then presents the story of the curse by writing, "When Noah woke up from his sleep, he was exceedingly angry and drove Ham away from his house, and the Jews believed that he went to Africa and became the first ancestor of the Negro race, for which they felt a great and most unjust contempt."[327] Van Loon does not counter the interpretation that Ham was the first ancestor of Africans, and in the process implicitly criticizes "the Jews" for feeling contempt towards them. Van Loon was celebrated as a progressive voice in his day. His adaptation of the story of Noah and Ham, however, when taken with other statements he made, casts him as a man who saw himself as a champion of tolerance and freedom, but who was still a white Protestant man of privilege of his time.

The theory that Ham was the progenitor of the "African races" has had a stubborn resilience in American culture. The theory that the origins of races can be traced to the children of Noah, and that Ham "gave origin to the colored races (Genesis 10.6-20)", was taught to teenagers in the official textbook used in Dallas high schools' "Old Testament" courses from about 1923 into the early 1980s,[328] and several Texas public schools have continued to teach the theory in classes and to test their students over the theory well into the twenty-first century.[329] The way this episode in the story of Noah has been appropriated to teach about race, then, is not just past history. The episode still influences what schoolchildren are learning about the nature of race in the present day.

---

324. Hendrik Willem Van Loon, *The Story of Mankind* (New York: Boni & Liveright, 1921), 422.

325. Hendrik Willem Van Loon, *The Story of the Bible* (New York: Boni & Liveright, 1923), 23.

326. Ibid., 24.

327. Ibid.

328. *Dallas High Schools Bible Study Course: Old Testament* (Dallas, TX: Dallas Independent School District, 1972), 9.

329. Mark A. Chancey, *Reading, Writing & Religion II: Texas Public School Bible Courses in 2011-12* (Austin, TX: Texas Freedom Network Education Fund, 2013), 52-3. The report is available at http://www.tfn.org/site/PageServer?pagename=issues_religious_freedom_Bible_Courses (accessed March 25, 2014).

4.8.e. George Peltz's Grandpa's Stories: *It wasn't Noah's fault, Ham was very wicked, so slavery is a reasonable consequence*

George Peltz was an associate pastor to Russell H. Conwell at Philadelphia's Baptist Temple. In his book *Grandpa's Stories*, Peltz creatively interweaves several of the above motifs into his retelling of the story of drunken, naked Noah. Peltz frames his children's Bible as a conversation between a grandfather, Grandpa Goodwin, and his grandchildren. This allows Peltz to insert comments and explanations along the way.

Peltz has Grandpa Goodwin provide an extended explanation for how such a good man as Noah might ever become drunk. Grandpa adjusts his glasses and provides the following detailed explanation to the children:

> In due time grapes were gathered and the juice was preserved. It was a pleasant and wholesome drink, and they put away some of it for future use. But in time grape-juice will ferment and become intoxicating wine; and this happened with the grape-juice of Noah's vineyard. One day Noah wanted grape-juice, and in drinking it he found its flavor had changed. But it was very pleasant, and, ignorant of its effects, Noah drank on until he became drunk and fell over on his tent-floor in a heavy drunken sleep. Good man that he was—able as he had been to disregard the opinions of all the world for a hundred years and to work at the ark—yet when he drank wine he sank helpless to the ground and lay there in shame, like the commonest drunkard.[330]

Peltz seems to feel the need to make it clear to children that Noah did not knowingly drink fermented wine, for he underscores the point by having the granddaughter Carrie express "sympathy" for Noah and say, "That is too bad."[331] Grandpa agrees: "'That Noah became drunk is very sad,' continued Grandpa. 'But that, I think, was an accident. He did not know the strength of what he drank.'"[332] In Peltz's retelling, then, Noah's character is left intact.

Peltz did not, however, wish to downplay the dangers of alcohol. Reflecting on the story, Grandpa Goodwin tells the children, "Intoxicating drink has spoiled more good men and ruined more happy homes than any other ten causes."[333] Charley agrees, saying, "He ought to have joined our temperance society ... We boys don't mean to lose our wits."[334] Through this dialogue, Peltz manages to strongly condemn drunkenness, put in a good word for temperance societies, and absolve Noah of any wrongdoing all at the same time.

---

330. George A. Peltz, *Grandpa's Stories: or Home Talks out of the Wonderful Book* (Toronto: Best Brothers, 1887), 83.

331. Ibid.

332. Ibid., 84.

333. Ibid.

334. Ibid.

The focus of Peltz's retelling, then, is not on the sin of Noah. That was no sin at all. The focus instead is upon the sin of Ham. Peltz signals this focus by titling the episode "Making Fun of his Father: Or, When Wine is in Wit is Out."[335] According to Grandpa, when Noah's son Ham discovered his father in a drunken stupor, he runs off to tell his brothers, "as though it were a good joke, a thing to laugh at."[336] Charley asks whether Noah's other sons laughed as well: "Did they make fun, too? We boys make fun of drunken men often."[337] Grandpa answers, "Noah was their father and they honored him, even if he was drunk."[338] Grandpa tells the grandchildren that though Noah became drunk by accident, "Ham's conduct was not an accident. It was a base, unworthy act; and God is angry with every child who does not honor his father and his mother."[339] Through the commentary of Grandpa, then, Peltz teaches children that failing to honor one's parents is a base act that makes God angry. The story serves not only as an opportunity to teach children about the evils of drunkenness, but also to teach them the evils of not honoring one's parents

When Noah discovers what happened, he pronounces a curse on Ham's son Canaan, but even here Peltz feels the need to defend Noah's character. Grandpa says, "He spoke some terrible words; but he spoke them, not in anger of his own, but for God, who was angry too."[340] Noah, then, is not even guilty of speaking to his son in anger, for his words were a reflection of God's anger. The sole guilty party, according to Peltz's account, was Ham.

Peltz's character Grandpa also follows the tradition of using the curse upon Canaan as an explanation for the enslavement of Africans:

> "But in what way was Canaan cursed, Grandpa? What harm came to him" asked Carrie.
> "From him descended those nations—the Africans for instance—which have always been the servants and burden-bearers of the world."
> "That seems too bad," said both girls together. "But Ham was a mean, bad man," added Mary, to which Charley added a very solemn "That's so."[341]

The children are suitably somber, seeming to suggest that the enslavement of Africans was regrettable, but disrespecting one's father is so bad that the enslavement of an entire race of people for centuries was justifiable after all.

Peltz's appropriation of the story of Noah's life after the flood serves to excuse Noah of any wrongdoing, warn against the evils of drunkenness, and warn against the evils of dishonoring one's parents. His version of the story also serves as a helpful reminder of America's long-lasting attitudes towards slavery. Peltz, who

335. Ibid.
336. Ibid.
337. Ibid.
338. Ibid.
339. Ibid.
340. Ibid., 85.
341. Ibid., 86.

pastored a relatively progressive northern Baptist church in Philadelphia, known for its stand against slavery, and whose book was published in Canada, is still espousing the curse of Canaan as a rationale for the slavery of Africans at the close of the nineteenth century. His book serves as one example of Northern attitudes towards slavery that remained long after the end of the Civil War.

4.8.f. Concluding remarks on the use of the story of drunken, naked Noah

Americans of the nineteenth and early twentieth centuries had grave concerns over the use of alcohol and children disrespecting their parents, and gave a prominent place to the story of Noah cursing Canaan to construct their understanding of race. Given these factors, the relatively rare use of the story of Noah and his sons in American children's Bibles during this time is perhaps surprising. Whether due to the unseemliness of the subject matter, an attempt to leave children with an unblemished image of Noah as a model of virtue, or simply a desire to avoid controversy, relatively few twentieth-century children's Bibles include the story or comment upon it. That pattern has continued into the twenty-first century. Those children's Bibles that do include the story, however, provide insights into the thinking of Americans in their times and the diverse meanings they have found in the passage.

4.9. Conclusions

The children's Bible adaptations of the story of Noah examined in this chapter lend a number of insights. First of all, they once again help illustrate the multivalency of Bible stories such as the story of Noah. Not only can the story of Noah be used to teach children lessons about moral virtues in addition to lessons about the character of God or how they can and should find salvation in Jesus Christ, but it can also be used to teach them a wide variety of different moral virtues. The cultural location and personal agendas of the authors are often evident in the particular virtues they choose to commend to their young readers.

The practice of reframing these Bible stories as fables that each carry a "moral" to the story and presenting them in a collection as a "Bible" may be quite common, but it also raises concerns among some. Literary critics note concerns over those who commit "the heresy of the paraphrase" by reducing a literary work to just one lesson or interpretation.[342] Religious educators, meanwhile, raise concerns over filling gaps that may be more fruitfully filled by children themselves. Many religious educators have offered models of teaching the Bible to children in which children engage the texts themselves and construct their own meanings based upon their own contexts and experiences, rather than having the stories' meanings chosen for them in advance.[343]

---

342. Cf. Cleanth Brooks, *The Well Wrought Urn* (New York: Harcourt, Brace, 1947).
343. See, for example, Dorothy Jean Furnish, *Experiencing the Bible with Children*

What sort of moral values and moral virtues are taught by these retold stories? Members of progressive religious communities may be concerned about the types of moral virtues drawn from these stories while more conservative or conserving religious communities may celebrate them. In their book *Retelling Stories, Framing Culture*, John Stephens and Robyn McCallum examine the ways in which myths, Bible stories, and fairy tales have been retold for children. They note that these retellings tend to be culturally conservative, passing on the cultural heritage of the past but doing so in ways that reinforce the values of the current culture.[344] Put another way, these retellings tend to pass on virtues that help reinforce the status quo.

The children's Bible accounts of Noah's ark surveyed in this chapter are consistent with these findings. Though children's Bibles were written by people from a variety of communities of faith with a variety of beliefs, the vast majority of the authors and artists were members of the dominant culture and had incentive, consciously or unconsciously, to reinforce values that would help shore up and maintain the status quo. They tend to retell stories in ways that reinforce the values of the current culture and serve the needs of those in privilege and power, while at the same time connecting those values to stories that are part of a longer cultural and religious heritage.

The sort of religious education of children that reinforces the status quo has a long tradition in Britain and the United States. When Robert Rakes founded the Sunday School in England in 1785 to teach working-class children how to read, some feared that, once they were able to read, those children would no longer be content with their lot in life. Perhaps to address those concerns, an early purpose statement for the Sunday School was "To prevent vice, to encourage industry and virtue, to dispel the ignorance of darkness, to diffuse the light of knowledge, to bring men cheerfully to submit to their stations."[345] William Fox, a London draper and Baptist, formed the first organization to promote Sunday Schools and voiced a similar sentiment in order to reassure potential donors who might fear that Sunday Schools might lead to social upheaval: "There is no intention of raising them [the children] above their common level; for in that case how would our manufactories be carried on, our houses erected and our tables furnished?"[346] While these goals were not named explicitly, most American children's Bibles

(Nashville, TN: Abingdon Press, 1990); Jerome W. Berryman, *Godly Play: A Way of Religious Education* (San Francisco: HarperSanFrancisco, 1991); Roger A. Gobbel and Gertrude G. Gobbel, *The Bible: A Child's Playground* (Philadelphia, PA: Fortress Press, 1986); and Pamela Mitchell, "'Why Care About Stories?' A Theory of Narrative Art," *Religious Education* 86 (1991): 30–43.

344. John Stephens and Robyn McCallum, *Retelling Stories, Framing Culture: Traditional Story and Metanarratives in Children's Literature* (New York and London: Garland Publishing, Inc., 1998), 3–5.

345. Robert W. Lynn and Elliot Wright, *The Big Little School: 200 Years of the Sunday School* (Nashville, TN: Abingdon, 1971, 1980), 26.

346. Ibid., 27.

throughout American history have taught children virtues such as obedience and hard work that serve to reinforce the status quo.

That so many children's Bibles use the stories of the Bible to teach children to be good, not naughty, to be obedient, and to work hard without complaining is therefore not surprising. In the case of the story of Noah's ark, the values that are being passed on to children tend to be values that serve those who are in authority. To put it another way, children's Bibles rarely retell Bible stories in ways that call on children to question authority, speak truth to power, or subvert the culture in which they live. While Noah is praised as an individual who is good while the people around him are sinful, few children's Bible authors use the story of the deluge to launch into a cultural critique or as a call to revolution or to protest or subvert the present-day government or culture. Similarly, when children's Bibles retell the story of Moses' infancy, they often omit any mention of the merciful yet subversive actions of the Egyptian midwives, and often describe Moses being found in the bulrushes as a miraculous act of God's providence rather than as a subversive plot on the part of Moses' mother and sister. Retellings and imagined stories of the Jesus as a boy depict him as being completely obedient to his parents and teachers, always working hard without complaint, and being completely content with his station in life among the poor. He is rarely, if ever, portrayed as the sort of boy who might grow up to speak out against injustice and criticize those who abuse power.[347] These stories of Noah, then, are not unique in teaching children conservative social values. Also, unlike previous chapters in which certain trends for retelling the story of Noah emerged in different eras of American history, children's Bibles that use the story of Noah to teach virtues such as obedience and hard work are represented throughout all eras of US history.

A variety of historical and theological factors may have led American parents and Church leaders to call for storybooks that would teach their children virtues and good character and at the same time stories of the Bible. As the following chapter attests, once the publishers, authors, and illustrators of children's Bibles began to rewrite the stories of the Bible in ways that taught children these virtues, they found a robust market for children's Bibles that has continued to the present day.

347. For more, see my article, Dalton, "Meek and Mild."

Chapter 5

THE BIBLE AND AMERICAN CHILDREN'S LITERATURE: THE STORY OF NOAH AS HISTORY AND AMUSEMENT

"The BIBLE is no fit PLAY-THING FOR CHILDREN."[1]

The Children's Bible, 1763

"God has told Noah there will be a great flood," squawked the bluejay. "Nonsense!" snarled the tiger. "There never has been."[2]

Annie North Bedford, *Walt Disney's Noah's Ark*, 1952

"Noah saw two young behemoths lumbering over the hill, and he burst out laughing. God knew many adults would be too tall for the height of each floor. So He was sending mostly young ones of all the large beasts."[3]

Gloria Clanin, *In the Days of Noah*, 1996

Should the stories of the Bible be presented to children as serious, profoundly important historical events or as fun and amusing stories that engage them and entertain them? Children's Bibles in America have not been created in a vacuum. Advancements in printing technology, shifts in the understanding of childhood development, and trends in the children's literature marketplace have all had profound effects on the ways in which children's Bibles have retold Bible stories. This chapter focuses on the tension Americans have felt between presenting children with historical facts and providing them with entertainment and amusement in American children's literature in general and children's Bibles in particular.

---

1. *The Children's Bible* (Philadelphia, PA: Andrew Steuart, 1763), xii. Emphasis in original.

2. Annie North Bedford, *Walt Disney's Noah's Ark* (New York: Simon and Schuster, 1952), n.p.

3. Gloria Clanin, *In the Days of Noah*, illus. by Earl and Bonita Snellenberger (Green Forest, AR: Master Books, 1996), 29.

5.1. America's Critical Attitude toward Fiction and Fairy Tales in Children's Literature

Based upon the sorts of children's books found on twenty-first century bookstore shelves, it would be easy to assume that children's literature in America has always consisted of wildly imaginative stories of fantasy, fairy tales, and fun-loving talking animals. This, however, has certainly not always been the case. Throughout much of the eighteenth and nineteenth centuries, American adults, and religious American adults in particular, were very uneasy about the prospect of their children reading fictional stories, especially those stories that contained fantastical elements or were intended primarily for their readers' amusement. This concern appears to have diminished throughout the twentieth century until, in the twenty-first century, even when it comes to children's Bibles, many authors and illustrators seem to be focused on telling fun and amusing stories.

Early Americans were wary of providing children with books that would simply serve the purpose of amusement. As Gillian Avery notes in her historical review of American children's literature, for Americans of the Puritan era, "The ideal child was certainly not a playful one, but old beyond her years."[4] According to Avery, this attitude was applied to children's reading material throughout much of the eighteenth and nineteenth centuries. She notes that most Americans of that time viewed fairy tales and other works of the imagination as "irrational, and irrelevant to modern needs."[5] In 1814, for example, the unnamed author of the book *False Stories Corrected* warns children about the dangers of fictional stories such as that about "old Santa-claw" that "are told merely for sport or pastime."[6] The author explains to children that such stories were not based on truth and therefore, "This [is] also wicked; it is lying, and of course reprehensible."[7] A companion volume from the same year, *True Stories Related*, warns against frivolous and false stories such as those of Tom Thumb, Gulliver, and Sinbad.[8] Those who did dare to offer children collections of fairy tales often in their introductions provided parents with their rationale for doing so and went to great lengths to explain to children that the stories they were telling were only imaginary and not factual, but still carried good lessons.[9] The fear among adults seemed to be twofold. First of all, children may be led to believe that fantastical tales of talking animals and the like were real. Second, the time children spent reading such non-historical and non-instructional tales was time spent in frivolity. Around the same time,

---

4. Gillian Avery, *Behold the Child: American Children and Their Books 1621–1922* (London: Bodley Head, 1994), 19.

5. Ibid., 65.

6. *False Stories Corrected* (New York: Samuel Wood, 1814), 68.

7. Ibid.

8. *True Stories Related* (New York: Samuel Wood, 1814), iii.

9. See, for example, Samuel G. Goodrich, *Peter Parley's Book of Fables* (Hartford, CT: Silas Andrus, 1846), 5–8, and Sophie May, *Fairy Book* (Boston, MA: Lee and Shepard, 1865), 15.

The American Tract Society was openly waging a battle against fiction, Roman Catholicism, Unitarians, Universalists, Deists, and other "social ills."[10] These attitudes continued in some form even into the twentieth century.

Along with Bible studies and curricula focusing on theological doctrines, the American Tract Society, the American Sunday School Union, and other Christian publishers often printed non-fiction tales of real (or at least presumably real) children that served as object lessons for their readers. Many of these children were models of virtue who always did the right thing, often dying horrible deaths stoically and without complaint.[11] Others were models of vice, who did the wrong thing and suffered the consequences for their misdeeds. By the end of the nineteenth century these publishers did print some fictional stories, but they followed the same pattern. They were historical fictions and highly moralistic tales and certainly not fantasies or fairy tales designed for their young readers' amusement.[12]

This aversion to fiction and amusement helps explain the relative popularity of children's Bibles and other religious publications for children in nineteenth-century America. Not only was the Bible considered historically accurate by most Americans, but it also carried spiritual value and reading its stories was not seen as a trivial amusement. The earliest children's Bibles published in the United States, such as Benjamin Harris's *The Holy Bible in Verse*, published in 1717 in Boston,[13] and John Taylor's *Verbum Sempiternum,* available in the colonies as early as 1750,[14] were far from frivolous and instead often described graphic scenes of death and violence and warned children against God's harsh judgments.

The aversion to childish amusement endured in various forms for quite some time in American religious circles. For example, Mary Stewart arranged a group of Bible stories in the 1909 book titled *Tell Me a True Story*, a title that may reflect the fundamentalist-modernist controversies of the time as well as an enduring Christian aversion to the frivolity of reading fictional literature. According to A. F. Schauffler's introduction, "Children dearly love Bible stories, and these can be made more attractive than the most popular fairy stories, on account of their intrinsic merit, and because they are 'true.' For after all, the child, while it loves the fairy tale, loves the 'true' story still better."[15] Stewart's retellings do not make the case for the historicity of the Bible's stories, but assume it, and the paintings that

10. Cf. Avery, *Behold the Child*, 98.

11. See, for example, S. B. Shaw, *Touching Incidents and Remarkable Answers to Prayer: Children's Edition* (Grand Rapids, MI: Shaw Publishing Company, 1895), which contains no fewer than twenty heart-wrenching stories of children who died bravely and joyfully as they bore faithful witness to Christ to adults and calmly awaited the joys of heaven.

12. Cf. Avery, *Behold the Child*, 93–120.

13. Benjamin Harris, *The Holy Bible in Verse* (Boston, MA: John Allen, 1717), n.p.

14. John Taylor, *Verbum Sempiternum*, 3rd edn (Providence, RI: n.p., 1774), n.p.

15. A. F. Schauffler in Mary Stewart, *Tell Me a True Story* (New York: Fleming H. Revell Company, 1909), 7–8.

are reproduced to accompany various stories—there are none that accompany her retelling of the story of Noah—are realistic in style.

The assumption that the Bible was non-fiction and historical seemed to hold intrinsic value and was another factor that made children's Bibles an appealing option for parents who wanted to purchase books for their children.

5.2. Noah and the Flood Presented as an Historical Event

The historicity of the Bible's stories was most often simply assumed and taken for granted in children's Bibles, and nothing on the subject of historicity is mentioned on either side of the debate. Still, some children's Bibles have explicitly provided dates and times for the flood, implying that the story of Noah was a historic event.

Many children's Bibles of the eighteenth and nineteenth centuries were called a "Scripture History" or "Bible History," but these terms were usually meant to convey that the book was a chronological retelling of the Bible's narratives rather than the text of the Bible itself. In most cases, questions of historicity were not explicitly addressed beyond including the dates of the events, presumably taken from Bishop James Ussher's famous work on the chronology of the Bible from the 1650s.[16] These assumptions are evident in the 1790 Thumb Bible, *The Bible in Miniature*. The book is quite specific in its dating of the story of Noah, and allots quite a bit of space to the matter, considering the small size of the pages. The following review of the story takes up five pages of the book:

> It was in the year of the world 1656, the 600th of Noah's age, and before CHRIST 2348, that God for the sin of man brought the flood upon the earth, which destroyed all that breathed therein, except Noah whom God found righteous before him, his family, and the creatures taken with them into the ark. The space from Noah's entering the ark, according to our account of time, October 29, to his coming forth of it, November 8, the following year, was one year and ten days. Now the life of man was afterwards shortened.[17]

About a decade later, in 1802, the small book *Holy Bible: Abridged*, published in Boston, used slightly different wording in its abridgment of the text as *The Bible in Miniature*, but used the same years for the beginning of the flood and the same specific dates for the end of the flood.[18] Several early nineteenth-century volumes, such as *The History of the Holy Bible, Abridged* and *A History of the Bible* (both published in 1819), begin their sections on Noah by noting that the events occurred 1,656 years after creation and 2,346 years before Christ, with their dates of the flood being their only significant embellishment or addition to the Genesis

---

16. Cf. James Ussher, *The Annals of the World* (Green Forest, AZ: Master Books, 2003).

17. *The Bible in Miniature* (New York: Brower, c. 1790), 34–8.

18. *Holy Bible: Abridged* (Boston, MA: William Norman, 1802), 18–19.

account.[19] The small 16-page chapbook, *Pictures and Stories from the Bible*, from around 1840, also includes the specific dates for Noah entering and exiting the ark by concluding the story, "God then commanded Noah with his family, and the living creatures to come out of the ark, in which they had been shut up, according to our account of the time, from the 29th of October to the 8th of November the following year, that is, one year and ten days."[20] As a matter of fact, the most significant embellishment of some of these early Scripture histories—the one point where they veer from the King James Version of Genesis to add to rather than abridge the text—is to assign dates to the events being related.[21] By doing so, they suggest that the flood was an event that occurred in history and instruct children in what they saw as well-established historical knowledge.

5.2.a. Questioning the Genesis account of a worldwide flood

While most children's Bibles have either ignored the question of the historicity of the flood or affirmed it, a small percentage of children's Bibles published in the United States have openly questioned whether a worldwide flood ever took place.

One such book was George A. Peltz's *Grandpa's Stories: or Home Talks about the Wonderful Book* from 1887. Peltz retold Bible stories in the form of a conversation between a wise and loving grandfather and his grandchildren Mary and Charley. In telling the story of Noah and the flood, Grandpa explains the typography of the region in which Noah lived. He tells the children,

> Men then lived east of the Mediterranean Sea where slight sinking of the ground would permit water to flow from the Black and Caspian Seas on the north, from the Pacific Ocean by way of the Red Sea and Persian Gulf on the south, and from the Mediterranean Sea on the west. By causing the land to sink even a little, this whole country would quickly be under water deep enough to cover every hilltop.[22]

Mary follows Grandpa's point, and asks how that might flood the whole earth:

> "But I don't see, Grandpa, how the sinking of that one part of the earth could make a flood all over the world."
> "I do not suppose there was a flood over all the world, Mary. All the world

19. *The History of the Holy Bible: Abridged* (New Haven, CT: Sidney Press, 1819), 2, and *A History of the Bible* (1819), 12. See also John Howard, *The Illustrated Scripture History for the Young* (New York: Virtue and Yorston, 1876), 11.

20. *Pictures and Stories from the Bible* (Worcester, MA: J. Grout, Jr., c. 1840), 7.

21. See, for example, *The Attributes of God; An Account of the Creation and the Story of Joseph and His Brethren, Taken from Scripture* (New Haven, CT: Sidney's Press, 1818), 16–17.

22. George A. Peltz, *Grandpa's Stories: or Home Talks out of the Wonderful Book* (Toronto: Best Brothers, 1887), 75–6.

inhabited by man was flooded. What need was there of more? What the Bible says applies to this narrower limit just as well as to the entire world. Nor do I suppose all existing animals went into the ark. Why should they? All such as might be destroyed by the flood went in and were saved."

"That's a new idea," exclaimed Mary, "but I must admit it seems to be right."[23]

Through the authoritative character of Grandpa, Peltz makes the case, rarely made in children's Bibles, that the flood did not cover the entire globe. The reliable character of Mary, standing in for the child reader, affirms for children that this explanation makes sense. Unfortunately for young Charley, he does not seem to pick up on the point as quickly as his sister. Charley asks Grandpa,

> "Weren't there lions and tigers in the ark, Grandpa?"
> "Why should there be, my boy? They live far beyond where the flood reached and were in no danger of being blotted out, even though some of them were drowned. I don't believe any wild animals were there, though in this opinion I have against me all the picture-books and Noah's arks of the toy stores."
> "Pshaw! the ark wasn't half as grand, then, as I thought it was."
> "You thought it was a menagerie, didn't you, Charley?" asked Mary, with a laugh. Charley made no answer, but looked cross.[24]

Young Charlie's reasonable assumption that animals from all over the globe were taken on the ark, as was portrayed by many illustrations and toy Noah's arks of the time, is corrected by his Grandpa and mocked by his sister. The reader, then, is left with the impression that Charley's initial understanding of a worldwide flood was not only ill-informed, but one worthy of ridicule as well.

A few children's Bibles from the very beginning of the twentieth century presented the story of Noah as a sort of legend or myth. While not using those terms, they describe the story of Noah as an ancient story that carried meaning even while it might not be an historically accurate account of events. Reverend John Rusk, in *Beautiful Stories that Never Grow Old* from 1902, explains to his young readers, "Some take the account of the flood literally; others treat it as a symbol."[25] Rusk uses the story to contrast the righteous Noah from the wickedness of the world around him: "Noah and his family represented the true life, the remainder of the world represented the false."[26] He ends his story by offering the ark as an analogy for God's provision of safety: "Let us remember that whenever trouble comes God will furnish an ARK for the good, enabling them to dwell in

---

23. Ibid., 75.

24. Ibid., 76.

25. John Rusk, *Beautiful Stories that Never Grow Old* (1902), 55. The book is copyrighted by John Rusk but no place or name of publisher are given.

26. Ibid.

safety."[27] For Rusk, uncertainty about the historicity of the flood does not affect the value of its spiritual message.

With a more critical approach being taken to the subject, books such as Rev. William L. Worcester's *On Holy Ground: Bible Stories with Pictures of Bible Lands* from 1904 took a similar approach to the biblical text. The book contains illustrations and many photographs of people and sites in the Middle East. Worcester represents the story of Noah's ark not as a historical event, but as a story inspired by God that ancient people told as a way of understanding their world:

> It seemed to the few people who still tried to obey the Lord as if the whole beautiful world was being destroyed. They had seen great floods, perhaps upon the banks of the Euphrates, when torrents of rain had been washed away, and the people and the cattle had been drowned. Such dreadful floods seemed to picture to them the way the whole beautiful, happy world was now being destroyed. And when the Lord caused the story of these sad days to be written, it was written as the story of a terrible flood which came over all the earth.[28]

Worcester, then, speculates on the historical and socio-psychological origins of the story of a worldwide flood, and does not hesitate to share his views with his young readers.

In 1909 the Unitarian Sunday-School Society published Mrs. Clara Hathaway Parker's *Stories from the Old Testament*. Consistent with the views of many Unitarians, the preface explains that children should not presume that the Bible is historical, but that they can still learn from the truths contained in it:

> It is good for us to know what they in that far-off time thought about the things which we still think about and wonder over,—the earth, the people and creatures upon it, and the God who made it. We must keep in mind the fact that we are not reading histories, but stories which give us thoughts about things instead of facts about them. We are not to think that all they tell us is true, but read the stories for the truth that is in them.[29]

The preface also suggests that some of the acts described in the Bible may not match the mores of the readers' day: "Sometimes He and His servants do impossible things and things which do not seem to us right or good. This is because the stories come to us from a time when people did not have schools and churches and the same thoughts of what is good and true that we have today."[30] In telling the story of Noah, Parker pauses to explain to children, "Stories of floods were

27. Ibid., 57.
28. William L. Worcester, *On Holy Ground: Bible Stories with Pictures of Bible Lands* (Philadelphia, PA: J. B. Lippincott Company, 1904), 8.
29. Clara Hathaway Parker, *Stories from the Old Testament* (Boston, MA: Unitarian Sunday-School Society, 1909), n.p.
30. Ibid.

common in olden times, and this one was told among the Hebrews. Perhaps the overflowing of some great river gave rise to it."[31] She proceeds to tell the story pretty much as it appears in Genesis, with no compulsion to add to it, moralize from it, or make excuses for it.

These children's Bibles were published at a time when many liberal American Christians were being exposed to more serious criticism of the Bible and the burgeoning awareness of concepts often explored in the present-day fields of comparative religions and myth studies. During the same period, a growing number of other American Christians were becoming committed to belief in the inerrant historicity of the Bible as part of the fundamentals of their faith. It appears, however, that liberal American Christians did not see much value in questioning the historicity of Bible stories in children's Bibles. Apart from a few examples, such as those noted above, the historicity of the Genesis flood is hardly ever questioned in children's Bibles from the rest of the twentieth century or in those from the twenty-first century.

Sister Mary Theola's 1983 story of "Noe" in *The Catholic Children's Bible* is one of the few exceptions to this rule. Theola, a popular Roman Catholic author, adds to the end of her retelling of the story of Noah's ark some reflections on the historicity and reliability of the Bible and openly questions the historical accuracy of the Genesis account: "The writer says the Flood was worldwide. He, no doubt, thought so ... We know the Flood was not worldwide and neither were all the men destroyed except those in the ark. Only the inhabitants in the area of Mesopotamia where the Flood occurred, were drowned."[32] Theola adds that, in her view, the biblical author did not set out to deceive readers, but told the story as he thought it had happened: "He knew about a flood that had really happened and told the story as he knew it. He used the story to teach religious truths. He was not interested in telling about a natural flood. The facts about the Flood may be questioned, but the religious truths, not. They remain."[33] While she questions the historical accuracy of the Bible, then, Theola still affirms the infallibility of its religious messages.

These few children's Bibles question the historicity of the flood, but they are clearly the exceptions that prove the rule. The vast majority of American children's Bibles have either affirmed the historicity of the flood or ignored the issue altogether. Also, even while these examples may question the historicity of the flood, they usually suggest that the story is at least based on some actual regional floods and affirm spiritual messages that can be drawn from the story. In any case, even while they question the story's historicity, they still veer far away from treating the Bible story as a frivolous, entertaining fairy tale that is told primarily to amuse children.

---

31. Ibid. For a similar commentary, see Muriel J. Chalmers, *The Bible Picture Book* (London, Edinburgh, New York, Toronto, and Paris: Thomas Nelson and Sons [1950]), 2.

32. Mary Theola, *The Catholic Children's Bible*, illus. by J. Verleye (New York: Regina Press, 1983, 2008), 39.

33. Ibid.

5.3. Entertaining Children's Literature and Children's Bibles in the Twentieth and Twenty-first Centuries

In the twentieth century, while American children's Bibles did not argue against the historicity of Bible stories, many did begin to use Bible stories as the basis of engaging, entertaining, and even amusing stories to entertain young readers. Gradually, throughout the second half of the twentieth century, efforts to compete with cartoons and animated films and fit in with other children's literature pushed children's Bibles towards becoming less somber religious education texts and more fun and amusing storybooks complete with smiling, colorful, cartoon-like animal friends.

As Leonard S. Marcus notes in his book, *Minders of Make-Believe*, the push to make storybooks for children more entertaining and engaging, rather than primarily educational, was perhaps driven in part by the need for publishers to compete with comic books and animated films such as Walt Disney's *Snow White and the Seven Dwarfs* (1937) that emerged in the late 1930s in America.[34] Around the time of World War Two, advancements in the technology necessary to reproduce affordable color illustrations meant that most children's books no longer had to restrict themselves to black and white illustrations.[35] At the same time, the onset of America's baby boom and an increase in childhood literacy provided a ready-made market for the books. The result was a large increase in the number of picture books published for young children in America.

One publisher that capitalized on these factors was the Little Golden Books. The first of the Little Golden Books went on sale in 1942, less than a year after the bombing of Pearl Harbor, coinciding with the start of the baby boom in America. The incredibly popular line of books featured best-selling titles such as *The Pokey Little Puppy* and *The Little Red Hen* with talking animals and religious titles such as *Prayers for Children* with Romantic and sentimental images of children. At the same time, educators and book publishers were promoting the importance of having books in the home to new parents who never before had money or interest in buying books. According to Marcus, "It was as if Little Golden Books had been made for these new buyers."[36] Much of the materials used for toys were being rationed by the war effort, but these small children's books were affordable and colorful, and became popular gifts for children.[37]

The first Golden Book devoted to retelling the story of Noah's Ark was *Walt Disney's Noah's Ark* (1952), with text by Annie North Bedford and illustrations by the Walt Disney Studio based upon the cartoon short of the same name. It is perhaps not surprising for a Disney production that the animals in the story

---

34. Leonard S. Marcus, *Minders of Make-Believe* (Boston, MA: Houghton Mifflin Company, 2008), 136–7.

35. John Rowe Townsend, *Written for Children*: 3rd rev. edn (New York: J. B. Lippincott, 1987), 304.

36. Marcus, *Minders of Make-Believe*, 168.

37. Ibid., 167–8.

talk and that the story is retold from their point of view. As the story begins, the animals are all abuzz as a magpie tells them the news that Noah was building an ark. The first half of the book is devoted to chronicling the reactions of various smiling animals, including the following exchange:

> "God has told Noah there will be a great flood," squawked the bluejay.
> "Nonsense!" snarled the tiger. "There never has been."[38]

The story makes no explicit mention that any people or animals die in the flood. At the end of the story, when it is time to leave the ark, Bedford writes that a few of the animals decide to stay with Noah. Bedford adds a creative twist to the story by ending her tale with the following explanation for the domestication of animals:

> "We have had good food and a pleasant home," they said. "Let us stay with Noah and his family."
> So the dogs and cats and horses and cows and sheep and pigs stayed with Noah.
> And they have lived with men ever since, right down to this very day.[39]

The storybook does not seem to be designed to pass on a close retelling of the Genesis account, to prepare children for salvation, or to teach them a moral lesson. Instead, it is a colorful, fun, and amusing story designed to entertain children.

In 1969, Golden Books offered a new version of *Noah's Ark*, this time without the participation of Disney Studios. In the 1969 version, Tibor Gergely's whimsical but realistic illustrations show a kindly Noah, always dressed in a blue robe, but Noah's sons and others are often drawn wearing togas made of animal furs, draped over one shoulder, making them look like cavemen. Barbara Shook Hazen's text places value on the family, as she writes, "Noah lived in peace and happiness with his family. God saw this and was pleased. God also saw that other people on earth were selfish and cruel to each other."[40] Gergely provides a panoramic illustration of distressed pairs of animals on the ark while Hazen tells readers that all of the animals were uneasy and making anxious noises appropriate to their kind: "Only the lions did not roar or cry out. But they, too, were afraid. They didn't move or eat or even twitch their tails. Instead, they just trembled."[41] The storybook ends with Hazen's description of, and Gergely's brightly-colored illustration of, Noah building an altar and his family thanking God for saving them from the flood. The story has a point to it, but is fun and entertaining as well.

In the 1960s, Concordia Publishing House of the Lutheran Church-Missouri Synod published a popular series of Bible storybooks known as Arch Books that

---

38. Annie North Bedford, *Walt Disney's Noah's Ark* (New York: Simon and Schuster, 1952), n.p.

39. Ibid.

40. Barbara Shook Hazen, *Noah's Ark*, illus. by Tibor Gergely (Racine, WI: Golden Press, 1969), n.p.

41. Ibid.

were roughly the same size as the Little Golden Books and with similar colorful illustrations, each storybook based on an individual Bible story. These stories, while adopting some of the conventions of contemporary children's storybooks, tended to retell their tales in ways that stayed relatively close to the biblical stories. In 1965, *The Story of Noah's Ark*, for example, retold the story in rhyme, and Sally Matthews' whimsical illustrations of animals depicted them all wearing the hint of a smile on their faces.[42]

By the 1990s, a large number of children's Bibles from Christian publishers followed the model of the *Walt Disney's Noah's Ark* storybook and began to present the story as one featuring cute and cuddly animals. Most of these children's Bibles from the 1990s and early twenty-first century feature the ubiquitous image of Noah and his wife with a host of modern-day zoo animals facing the reader with large grins on their faces while spilling over the edges of a small, overstuffed ark (see Figure 5.1). This image commonly serves as the cover of children's Bible story collections as well as the image on a variety of other products available in Christian stores such as lamps, light switch covers, and wall coverings or border papers for young children's bedrooms.

One of the most dramatic developments in children's Bibles in recent decades is the number written for an increasingly younger and younger readership. Bible picture books became available for children of grade school age and even younger, leading to popular versions from Christian publishers in the 1990s such as *The Toddler's Bible* (1992),[43] *The Preschooler's Bible* (1994),[44] *The Beginners Bible for Toddlers* (1995),[45] *Baby's First Bible* (1996),[46] and *The Baby Bible Storybook* (1994).[47] In almost all of these stories there is absolutely no mention that anyone dies in the flood and no mention that God is the cause of the flood. The story of Noah becomes the story of a fun boat-ride with animal friends who act as cartoon characters. Such a story is fun, exciting, amusing, and it is certainly age appropriate, just like other storybooks for small children on bookstore shelves.

The change in children's literature may have come gradually, in stages—shifting from the suspicion of amusement in the eighteenth and nineteenth centuries to it being embraced in the late twentieth and early twenty-first centuries—but has nonetheless been quite remarkable. That the stories of the Bible for children also

---

42. Jane Latourette, *The Story of Noah's Ark*, illus. by Sally Matthews (St. Louis, MO: Arch Books, 1965), n.p.

43. V. Gilbert Beers, *The Toddler's Bible*, illus. by Carole Boerke (Colorado Springs, CO: Cook Communications Ministry, 1992).

44. V. Gilbert Beers, *The Preschooler's Bible*, illus. by Teresa Walsh (Colorado Springs, CO: Cook Communications Ministry, 1994).

45. Carolyn Nabors Baker and Cindy Helms, *The Beginners Bible for Toddlers*, illus. by Danny Brooks Dalby (Dallas, TX: Word Publishing, 1995).

46. *Baby's First Bible*, illus. by Colin and Moira Maclean (Pleasantville, NY: Reader's Digest Books, 1996).

47. Robin Currie, *The Baby Bible Storybook*, illus. by Cindy Adams (Eastbourne: Chariot Books, 1994).

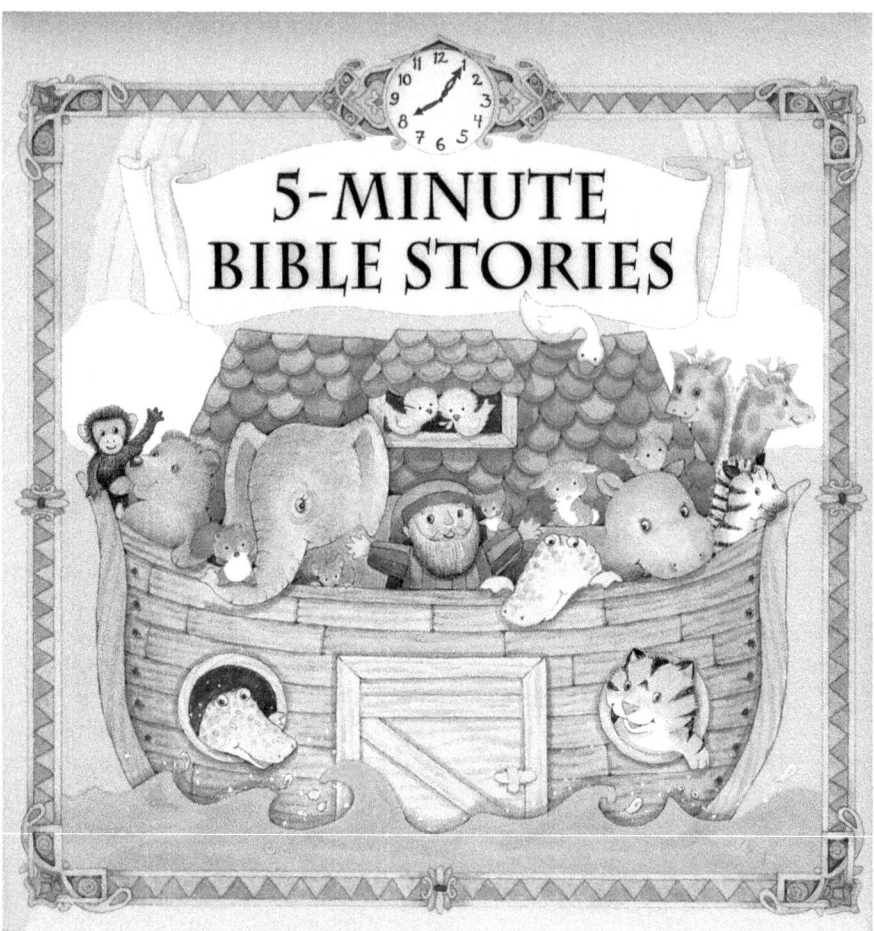

Figure 5.1. Jan Foletta's cover illustration for Brian Conway, Lora Kalkman et al.'s
5-Minute Bible Stories (Lincolnwood, IL: Publications International Ltd., 2002).

follow this pattern may seem especially surprising. Still, the children's Bibles of the nineteenth century fit in quite well with the other American children's literature being published at the time, and the same can be said for many of the children's Bibles of the twenty-first century.

5.3.a. Noah's ark as a fun boat-ride with anthropomorphic animal friends

A significant number of late twentieth-century and early twenty-first century children's Bibles took yet another step further away from depicting the story of the flood as a somber historical event and toward presenting the story as a fun and amusing fantasy. These children's Bibles include textual descriptions and illustrations of cartoon-style, anthropomorphic animals that do things that real animals could not do. Marilyn Lashbrook's *Two by Two: The Story of Noah's Faith*, published in 1987, includes illustrations by Stephanie McFetridge that depict smiling alligators who walk upright, wear necklaces, and carry luggage, while smiling bears and elephants help carry birdcages out of the ark after the flood.[48] In the *God Loves Me Bible* (1993), giraffes, birds, and elephants are seen doing the laundry and hanging it up (see Figure 5.2).[49] In Christine Harder Tangvald's *The Big Big Big Boat and Other Bible Stories about Obedience* from 1993, Mr. Monkey, wearing a top hat and bowtie, and Mrs. Monkey, wearing a pearl necklace, carry a suitcase onto the ark.[50] In *The Preschooler's Bible* (1994), a tiny bear and monkey kneel, close their eyes, and fold their hands in prayer along with Noah and his wife,[51] and in *My Very First Book of Bible Heroes* (1998), a bear, rabbit, and lion smile big smiles and dance for joy on two feet while a little mouse looks on with his hands folded in prayer.[52] In Mack Thomas's *The First Step Bible* from 1994, Noah is shown playing marbles with a cute group of smiling animals, including a rabbit, turtle, bird, and raccoon (see Figure 5.3).[53] In Thomas's earlier book, *The Bible Animal Storybook* from 1990, the animals talk and in one scene, illustrated by Elizabeth Hagler, a giraffe, elephant, and lion argue over who should get to leave the ark first as the dove looks on while holding a leaf in his mouth.[54] In Rhonda Gowler Green's *Noah and the Mighty Ark*, published by ZonderKids in 2014, at the end of the story, as they leave the ark, two pigs, a bear, and a rhinoceros all smile and wave goodbye to Noah.[55] Finally, in Zondervan's 2014 storybook by Laura Sassi, *Goodnight Ark*, on the ark the sheep, wild boars, tigers, and elephants all become frightened by the storm and so crawl into bed with Noah, until the skunks come and release their scent, forcing them all to leave and sleep in the stables.[56] The presence of these anthropomorphic animals is fun, but they effectively move the story of Noah's ark out of the realm of the historical and into the realm of a

48. Marilyn Lashbrook, *Two by Two: The Story of Noah's Faith* (Dallas, TX: Roper Press, 1987), n.p.

49. Susan Elizabeth Beck, *God Loves Me Bible*, illus. by Gloria Oostema (Grand Rapids, MI: Zondervan Publishing House, 1993), 11.

50. Christine Harder Tangvald, *The Big Big Big Boat and Other Bible Stories about Obedience* (Elgin, IL: Chariot Books, 1993), 11.

51. Beers, *The Preschooler's Bible*, 34–5.

52. Mary Hollingsworth, *My Very First Book of Bible Heroes*, illus. by Rick Incrocci (Nashville, TN: Thomas Nelson, 1993), 39.

53. Mack Thomas, *The First Step Bible*, illus. by Joe Stites (Sisters, OR: Gold 'n Honey Books, 1994), 34–5.

54. Mack Thomas, *The Bible Animal Storybook*, illus. by Elizabeth Hagler (Sisters, OR: Questar Publishers, Inc., 1990), 39.

55. Rhonda Gowler Greene, *Noah and the Mighty Ark*, illus. by Margaret Spengler (Grand Rapids, MI: ZonderKids, 2014), n.p.

56. Laura Sassi, *Goodnight Ark*, illus. by Jane Chapman (Grand Rapids, MI: Zondervan, 2014).

fun and silly fantasy world akin to fairy tales in which animals talk and do other things that only humans can do in the real world.

One might suspect that more conservative publishers, those with a primary readership that tends to hold to a serious view of the historical inerrancy and infallibility of Scripture, would want to present their stories as realistically as possible, as historical events that really happened, with quite realistic illustrations and with text that stays as close to the canonical text and events as possible. One might suspect that they would carefully guard against their children's Bibles presenting Bible stories as cartoons, with animals acting in unrealistic ways, and ensure that the children's Bibles are not in danger of trivializing the story as a source of amusement. Meanwhile, one might suspect that secular publishers and religious publishers of more moderate or liberal denominations might feel free to take more liberties with the biblical stories, allowing their authors and artists to use more creative expression than their more conservative counterparts, and not be bound by the desire to depict the events of the story as historical events or by a need to be consistent with the biblical text. The trend, however, seems to be in the opposite direction. The versions of Noah's ark that include anthropomorphic animals tend to come from theologically conservative publishers such as Zondervan, Cook Communications, Thomas Nelson, and Gold 'n Honey Books.

In contrast, secular publishers or those with a wider or more mainstream readership tend to treat the stories as realistic ancient stories with realistic illustrations. Selina Hastings' *Children's Illustrated Bible*, published by Dorling Kindersley (DK) in 1994, for example, retells Bible stories in ways that stay close to the biblical version of events, does not add morals to the stories, and puts historical and cultural annotations in the margin of the book. Accompanying the story of Noah, for example, one note reads, "Noah and his sons would have built the ark by hand. The planks of wood were coated with tar to make the boat watertight. This traditional method of boat building is still practiced in parts of the Middle East today."[57] Eric Thomas's illustrations in the book are also more realistic depictions of animals and people as well, such as an image of Noah offering a sacrifice after the flood (see Figure 5.4). Thomas may be using artistic license by showing zebras, giraffes, lions, the ark, and a rainbow all conveniently placed in the background of the scene, but Noah and the animals are not depicted as amusing, cartoon-style characters.[58] In a similar fashion, Marie-Hélène Delval's *Reader's Digest Bible for Children* from 1995 stays quite close to the events as they are described in the Bible and she does not add morals to the end of the stories. Ulises Wensell's illustrations that accompany the stories are stylized and impressionistic images designed to captivate children, but the images convey a sense of awe and wonder rather than being merely fun or silly.[59]

---

57. Selina Hastings, *The Children's Illustrated Bible*, illus. by Eric Thomas (New York: Dorling Kindersley, 1994), 25.

58. Ibid., 27.

59. Marie-Hélène Delval, *Reader's Digest Bible for Children*, illus. by Ulises Wensell (Pleasantville, NY: Reader's Digest Young Families, 1995).

Figure 5.2. Illustration by Gloria Oostema of the animals helping with the laundry from Susan Elizabeth Beck, *God Loves Me Bible* (Grand Rapids, MI: Zondervan Publishing House, 1993), 11.

This recent development of the story of Noah and the flood being retold as if it was a fun boat-ride with anthropomorphic animal friends still seems quite remarkable when compared to the versions of the story from previous centuries. What might explain this phenomenon? One answer may be the fact that children's Bibles are aimed at a younger and younger readership that is accustomed to books with stories and illustrations of talking animals. Also, if parents in the

Figure 5.3. Illustration by Joe Stites of Noah playing marbles with the animals from Mack Thomas, *The First Step Bible* (Sisters, OR: Gold 'n Honey Books, 1994), 34–5.

Figure 5.4. Illustration by Eric Thomas from Selina Hastings, *The Children's Illustrated Bible* (New York: Dorling Kindersley, 1994), 27.

1930s feared that comic books and movies would distract their children from more noble pursuits, their counterparts in the 1990s and the early twenty-first century are confronted with competition from an increasingly wide array of print, visual, and digital media for their dollars and their children's attention. Children's book publishers realize that in order to compete they need to create stories that are more colorful, more visually engaging, and more entertaining for children. These fun stories of Noah and his animal friends seem to fit the model of popular contemporary children's storybooks, even if they no longer bear much similarity to the story as it is told in the Book of Genesis. The books offered by theologically conservative authors and publishers may, then, reflect an overriding desire to present the Bible and the Christian faith as something that is fun and engaging to the next generation and to introduce them as soon as possible to the stories of the Bible.

5.4. Late Twentieth and Early Twenty-first Century Dinosaurs on the Ark

In the final decade of the twentieth century and first decades of the twenty-first century, for the first time in the history of American children's Bibles, dinosaurs can be found on Noah's ark. For over 200 years, as far as this extensive study has revealed, there had never been a description or illustration of a dinosaur on the ark in a children's Bible published in the United States. At the very end of the twentieth century and the beginning of the twenty-first century, however, with a growing movement of young Earth creationists, several publishers began offering children's books with illustrations of dinosaurs living alongside humans and other animals on Noah's ark.

Mary Hollingsworth's *Bumper the Dinosaur Bible Stories*, published in 1996 by Chariot Family Publishing, which is a division of Cook Communications, contains two stories. One is titled "Bumper and Adam" while the other is titled "Bumper and Noah." Bumper is a cartoonish green dinosaur who is not too coordinated and often bumps into things. In the story of "Bumper and Noah," after Bumper bumps into several things, Whisper the dove tells Bumper that Noah needs his help. According to the next page, "So Bumper bumped the boards into Noah's big boat. BUMP! BUMP! BUMP!"[60] Artist Rick Incrocci's illustration on the following page shows Bumper marching into the ark beside a pink dinosaur and behind pairs of elephants, giraffes, rabbits, bears, and parrots.[61] Children reading the book may dismiss the story of talking animals and a cartoonish bumbling dinosaur as a fantasy, but the author and publisher apparently trust that children, perhaps with the help of their parents, will be able to make the connection between Bumper and historical fact. While *Bumper the Dinosaur Bible Stories* is intended for children ages four to seven, the final page of the book advertises Paul Taylor's *The Great*

---

60. Mary Hollingsworth, *Bumper the Dinosaur Bible Stories*, illus. by Rick Incrocci (Colorado Springs, CO: Chariot Family Publishing, 1996), n.p.

61. Ibid.

Dinosaur Mystery. That book, intended for children ages eight to twelve, explicitly argues the case that dinosaurs were indeed on Noah's ark.[62]

The publisher Master Books has released several titles for children that depict dinosaurs on Noah's ark. According to their website, "Master Books' is the world's largest publisher of creation-based material for all ages including apologetics, homeschool resources, reference titles, and quality children's literature. It is one of New Leaf Publishing Group's three imprints."[63]

Gloria Clanin's *In the Days of Noah*, published in 1996 by Master Books, presents a greatly expanded version of the story of Noah, including episodes in which Shem, Japheth, and Ham are assaulted by a street gang;[64] Noah complains about how the cruel giant Nephilim came from Nod to Noah's city to sell drugs to the young people;[65] Japheth and Shem drag Ham away from the temptations of a drinking establishment;[66] Methuselah officiates at Shem's wedding;[67] and much more. Clanin describes the animals arriving to enter the ark, when, "suddenly out of the trees walked two dragons with three horns to their heads. Then from the other side of the clearing two large tigers strolled. Very quickly there seemed to be animals coming from all directions—giraffes, bears, gazelles, beasts of every kind and description."[68] Soon afterwards, "Noah saw two young behemoths lumbering over the hill, and he burst out laughing. God knew many adults would be too tall for the height of each floor. So He was sending mostly young ones of all the large beasts."[69] The accompanying illustration, by Earl and Bonita Snellenberger, shows two large apatosauruses, which are likely the behemoths that make Noah laugh, and a pair of Triceratops, which may be Clanin's three-horned dragons. The illustration also shows one pair each of velociraptors and pterodactyls among the deer, giraffes, lions, rabbits, wolves, frogs, turtles, and other animals entering the ark.

While on the ark during the flood, Noah and his sons are shown happily feeding the animals: "'We have some especially hearty appetites this morning,' Ham said as he lifted another large forkful of hay up to the mouth of a great beast with an ax-shaped headcrest."[70] The facing page shows Ham feeding a corythosaurus.[71] When the flood is over, the animals leave the ark without incident except for one moment of concern: "Noah turned with alarm when he heard the ramp creaking under the weight of the pair of behemoths. He was afraid the wood

62. Paul Stanley Taylor, *The Great Dinosaur Mystery* (Colorado Springs, CO: Chariot Victor Publishing, 1987), 32–3.

63. "Master Books," http://www.nlpg.com/about-master-books (accessed June 11, 2014).

64. Gloria Clanin, *In the Days of Noah*, illus. by Earl and Bonita Snellenberger (Green Forest, AR: Master Books, 1996), 10–11.

65. Ibid., 9.

66. Ibid., 18–19.

67. Ibid., 24–5.

68. Ibid., 28.

69. Ibid., 29.

70. Ibid., 31.

71. Ibid., 32.

might splinter and injure one of them—but the strong ramp held fast. When these long-necked giants had come aboard, they were no larger than elephants. Now they even towered over the giraffes."[72] The illustration on the page shows the apatosauruses going down the ramp as the other animals are walking away from the ark (see Figure 5.5). The scene not only adds a bit of drama to the narrative, but also provides readers with a rationale for how such large animals could fit on the ark in the first place. It is interesting to note that Clanin never names the dinosaurs as dinosaurs or by their specific genus or species names. Instead, she uses biblical names such as behemoth—a beast described in Job 40.15-24 that some young Earth creationist take to be a description of a dinosaur—and dragons, which are mentioned in the King James Version of Deuteronomy 32.33 and several other passages in the Bible. The appendix at the back of the book is more direct, providing common young Earth creationist answers to questions such as "Were there really dinosaurs aboard the ark?"[73] and "If there were dinosaurs on the ark, why aren't there any around today?"[74]

In his introduction to *The True Story of Noah's Ark*, published by Master Books in 2003, beloved radio host Tom Dooley bemoans fanciful retellings of the story of Noah and claims that his book goes back to the Bible "to get an accurate account."[75] The book, however, seems to carry an agenda that goes beyond what can be learned from Genesis alone. Dooley's description of Noah building the ark is accompanied by a realistic illustration by Bill Looney depicting one of Noah's sons motioning to a beautiful woolly mammoth who is lifting lumber in his tusks to help build the ark.[76] Later, Looney presents a two-page panoramic view of Noah standing with his staff as he watches a majestic procession of animals marching two by two which includes ostriches, mammoths, giraffes, chimpanzees, buffalo, bears, and, in the rear, two apatosauruses.[77] Later in the story, another illustration shows these apatosaureses among the other animals inside the ark, as Dooley's text explains, "The most amazing thing was that they were all able to fit on the Ark with room to spare. It's possible Noah may have been concerned that some might be too large. However, even for the large dinosaurs, God most likely sent average-size young adults."[78] After providing this explanation, the dinosaurs appear in one other illustration, but do not figure in the story's text. The story concludes, as it does in most retellings of the story of Noah, with Noah, his family, and the animals leaving the ark and giving thanks to God.

A parent or grandparent could pick up *The True Story of Noah's Ark* or *In the Days of Noah* from a Christian bookstore shelf, quickly browse through some

72. Ibid., 47.

73. Ibid., 63.

74. Ibid., 64.

75. Tom Dooley, *The True Story of Noah's Ark*, illus. by Bill Looney (Green Forest, AR: Master Books, Inc., 2003), 4.

76. Ibid., 17.

77. Ibid., 30–1.

78. Ibid., 36.

Figure 5.5. Illustration of dinosaurs leaving the ark by Earl and Bonita Snellenberger from Gloria Clanin, *In the Days of Noah* (Green Forest, AR: Master Books, 1996), 47.

of their pages, and purchase them without realizing that they showed dinosaurs living on Noah's ark. Ken Ham's *Dinosaurs of Eden*, however, is much more up-front with its agenda, both in its title and its cover illustrations of a variety of dinosaurs in the garden with Adam and Eve. Ham is the president/CEO and founder of Answers in Genesis–U.S. and the Creation Museum, founded in 2007 in Petersburg, Kentucky, to promote a young Earth creationist view of the origins of life. In *Dinosaurs of Eden*, Ham includes many explanations and presents evidence for dinosaurs living alongside humans but does so in a somewhat random way. The book retells several Bible stories explaining how dinosaurs could have existed at the time. The illustrations, again by Earl and Bonita Snellenberger, place dinosaurs in the Garden of Eden, on a hillside as Cain murders Abel, and so on. Ham covers the story of Noah in two places. In the first retelling, he explains, "Adult dinosaurs would have been too large to fit comfortably on the Ark. It makes sense that God would have sent younger dinosaurs to the Ark."[79] He continues, "There is nothing in the Bible that indicates any of the dinosaur kinds died out before the Flood. It's so obvious, two of every kind of dinosaur, which means probably a hundred dinosaurs at the most, were on Noah's Ark, along with all the other kinds of land animals."[80] Ham writes that after the flood,

79. Ken Ham, *Dinosaurs of Eden: A Biblical Journey through Time*, illus. by Earl and Bonita Snellenberger (Green Forest, AR: Master Books, 2001), 30.
80. Ibid., 31.

Noah's family and all the animals came out of the Ark. This means that two of every dinosaur kind also came out of the Ark, ready to reproduce and spread out across the Earth. Dinosaurs, therefore, must have lived on the Earth after the Flood. People and dinosaurs thus have been living together sometime during the past 4,500 years. Is there any evidence for this?

There's LOTS of evidence.[81]

From this point, Ham provides what he sees as evidence for dinosaurs existing alongside human beings. The pages that follow include several illustrations of humans and dinosaurs living alongside each other, including at the scene of Noah's thanksgiving offering to God[82] and one of people riding saddled dinosaurs at the time of the building of the Tower of Babel.[83] The text of Ham's second retelling of the story of Noah focuses less on the dinosaurs' presence on the ark and more on how the ark "is really a picture of how we can be saved from our sin."[84] The illustration that accompanies the text shows a pair of polacanthuses and a pair of parasaurolophuses entering the ark with other animals.[85] In some ways, these illustrations may have a more lasting effect on children who may retain the images of dinosaurs alongside human beings even if they do not follow Ham's reasoning behind those images.

These children's Bibles, though relatively few in number, are primarily marketed to homeschooling parents and religious educators who desire to teach their children the young Earth view of the history of the world. The books have also effectively found their way onto Christian bookstore shelves alongside other children's Bibles. Through their text and illustrations, these children's Bibles pass on their authors' views of creation to members of the next generation.

5.5. Conclusion

In the eighteenth century and at the beginning of the nineteenth century, children's Bibles would have fit in well with other literature published for American children. Children's literature was non-fiction, instructional, and carried religious or moral messages. Children's books were not intended for children's amusement but for their instruction. By the end of the twentieth century and in the early twenty-first century, many children's Bibles again fit in well with the rest of American children's books in general. This time, however, they fit the general pattern by being brightly colored books for young children full of happy stories and whimsical illustrations of smiling animals and wild adventures.

In their book *Toying with God: The World of Religious Games and Dolls*, authors Nikki Bado-Fralick and Rebecca Sachs Norris note that America is obsessed with

81. Ibid., 35. Emphasis in original.
82. Ibid., 40–1.
83. Ibid., 42.
84. Ibid., 60.
85. Ibid., 60–1.

having fun, even to the point that they feel compelled to market the most somber and serious acts of religious expression as fun and enjoyable activities.[86] The story of a fun boat-ride with animal friends in which no one dies is an engaging story and one that is quite age appropriate by current standards. It is a story, however, that bears only scant resemblance to the story of Noah as it is told in the Book of Genesis or as it was presented in most early nineteenth-century children's Bibles. The presumed goal of many children's Bibles of the past—to pass on an accurate if simplified version of the Bible's stories—no longer seems to be a priority for many children's Bible authors or publishers. Furthermore, the primary goal of some of these versions does not seem to be specifically to pass on certain religious doctrines or to teach children particular virtues. Instead, the goal seems to be to engage and entertain children in a way that creates warm feelings toward God and the Bible and that teaches children that God is a friend and helper to them. In this way, these types of retellings serve the desire of some parents to engage their children with the Bible at a very young age. The goal is not necessarily to pass on the details of the Bible's stories, but to create an early relationship between the child and the Bible, even if the content is adapted in ways that do not closely resemble the stories as they appear in the Bible itself.

86. See Nikki Bado-Fralick and Rebecca Sachs Norris, *Toying with God: The World of Religious Games and Dolls* (Waco, TX: Baylor University Press, 2010), 107–36.

Chapter 6

CONCLUSIONS

6.1. The Remarkable Multivalency and Malleability of Bible Stories and Religion in America

A survey of children's Bibles from throughout American history offers a wide variety of insights. This final chapter offers a few general conclusions and directions for further study.

First of all, this study demonstrates the ongoing significance of the story of Noah for people in the United States. For Americans, the story of Noah and the flood is a story from a faraway place and time. The hundreds of children's Bibles that retell the story, however, attest to the fact that Americans have seen the story of Noah as one of the most significant stories of their faith and have seen it as still relevant to their lives and the lives of their children in the present day. They have repeatedly turned to it as a source of beliefs and values that should be passed on to the next generation.

This study also stands as a testament to the remarkable multivalency and malleability of biblical narrative. The children's Bibles examined in this book demonstrate the ways in which a single ancient story can be appropriated alternatively to warn children about an angry and powerful God who can destroy them in a moment, to assure them that a friendly God loves them and will always keep them safe, to teach children that they can and must find salvation in Jesus Christ, or to inform them that God wants them to work hard without complaining. This study, then, illustrates the ways in which the laconic nature of biblical narratives allows authors and illustrators to adapt, edit, and reframe the story in very diverse ways and to use them as the basis of a wide variety of theological and moral lessons.

These children's Bible versions of the story of Noah also help index America's changing and diverse religious beliefs and values from throughout its history. The fact that the story of Noah *can* be appropriated in such a wide variety of ways stands alongside the fact that the story of Noah *has* been appropriated in such a wide variety of ways. Members of the same faith tradition, and even of the same religious movement or denomination, have approached their faith quite differently at different points in America's history, to the extent that they have felt compelled to change and adapt one of the best-known stories of their Scriptures to reflect the beliefs and values of their times.

Furthermore, these adaptations of the story of Noah offer a unique perspective on American religious history as it was practiced at the grassroots level. Major shifts in laws, denominational structures, and religious scholarship all offer important benchmarks of American religious history. Children's Bibles, however, offer rubber-meets-the-road snapshots of American Christianity and Judaism in practice. They reveal which beliefs and values American Christians and Jews felt were essential to pass on to the next generation and what America's faith looks like when adults try to condense it to its most basic, simple, and understandable forms.

One perhaps surprising finding of this study is that children's Bible authors, whether lay or clergy, male or female, appear to have been less affected by the sectarian views of their particular faith communities than by wider cultural and sociological trends. Writing about Catholic, Protestant, and Jewish children's Bibles in Europe and the Americas over a longer period of time than explored in this study, Ruth Bottigheimer observed, "The notions expressed in children's Bibles have generally incorporated not divisive religious polemic but shared social values, and these Bibles are thus an important part of the transmission of cultural norms and values from one generation to the next."[1] That certainly appears to be the trend when it comes to US children's Bibles' appropriations of the story of Noah. With some notable exceptions, shifts in American culture in general, such as child mortality rates, advances in child development studies, public schooling, the Industrial Revolution, or the general approach to spirituality and faith in the nation, seem to explain the types of adaptations and appropriations made in children's Bibles better than the authors' and illustrators' particular denominational affiliations, their gender, or whether they were clergy or laity, or even Bible scholars. The Bible and its stories are invoked to affirm the beliefs and values shared by most members of society at the time and to teach children to carry those beliefs and values into the future.

Finally, the changing nature of American children's literature, the publishing and marketing of children's books, and changes in the development of printing technology have all played a significant role in how the Bible has been adapted for children. Many children's Bibles have reflected the other children's literature of their time. Once it became affordable and profitable to publish non-religious children's books with colorful, smiling animals, for example, it did not take long for religious book publishers to start creating and selling children's Bibles that fit the same mold.

6.2. Choosing Children's Bibles?

Today's readers may find some of the examples given in this book to be ridiculous or even shocking and offensive. Some of these same readers may be surprised to

---

1. Ruth B. Bottigheimer, *The Bible for Children: From the Age of Gutenberg to the Present* (New Haven: Yale University Press, 1996), xii.

discover that those very same children's Bibles are the very ones that have been given to their own children, are presented to children in their own communities of faith, or are available in their own church or synagogue libraries. Children's Bibles are often chosen simply on the basis of which illustrations seem fun and exciting, and clergy and religious educators often do not attend carefully to the content of the children's Bibles they encourage the children of their faith community to read.

For many parents, the most pragmatic question raised by this study is the question of what sort of Bible one should choose for their children, if any at all. The story of Noah tells the tale of God's judgment upon wickedness, God's recognition of one person's righteousness, God's communication with humankind, God's initiative to preserve human and animal life from the devastation of the flood, and much more. While many adults find value in these and other themes in the story, they are also aware that children may be traumatized by the horrific tale of a God who drowns nearly every adult, child, and animal on earth. How does one faithfully present such a story to children? Four approaches to this dilemma are offered here in no particular order.

6.2.a. Do not use the Bible with children

In his book *Readiness for Religion*, religious education scholar Ronald Goldman writes, "The Bible is the major source book of Christianity for *adults*. It is written by adults for adults and is plainly not a children's book."[2] The Bible has become such a primary curriculum resource for the religious education of Christian and Jewish children in America that many are surprised to learn that the issue of whether or not the Bible is an appropriate resource for the religious education of children has been a controversial one and continues to be so in some religious education circles. Those who oppose the use of the Bible with children have argued either that the violence and sexual content of the Bible are inappropriate for children or that the concepts explored in the Bible are beyond a child's ability to comprehend. One option, then, is simply to have children refrain from reading or studying the Bible until they are older.

While contemporary readers may be shocked by Nathaniel Crouch's *Youth's Divine Pastime*,[3] published in London in 1691, with its sordid Bible stories of sex and violence discussed in Chapter 1 of this book, is the story of drowning of nearly every man, woman, child, and animal on earth considered any more appropriate today? Since the emergence of the Romantic ideal of the sweet and innocent child, and especially since the dawn of child development studies, greater attention has been paid to which sort of stories are appropriate for children. While some children's Bibles edit out stories that they deem too violent or sexual in nature, other adults simply have refrained from presenting the Bible to children at all.

---

2. Ronald Goldman, *Readiness for Religion: A Basis for Developmental Religious Education* (New York: Seabury Press. 1965), 71. Emphasis in the original.

3. Nathaniel Crouch, *Youth's Divine Pastime*, Vol. 1 (London: n.p., 1691).

Others oppose having children read the Bible because they believe that the concepts raised in the Bible are simply beyond their comprehension. In the seventeenth century, John Locke made it clear that, in his opinion, the Bible was not suitable for children. He felt that it did not make a good text to teach reading, since children could not understand what they read. Also, he felt that reading the Bible would only serve to confuse them about religion since the concepts were beyond their understanding.[4] In more recent years, even many religious educators who advocate teaching the Bible to children take quite seriously the question of whether or not the Bible is beyond a child's understanding and experiences.[5]

One option, then, is simply to have children refrain from reading or studying the Bible until they are older. This, however, has been a minority approach in the United States. In the early eighteenth century in the American colonies, for example, the influential New England Puritan minister Cotton Mather urged parents to read the Bible to their children and to teach them to read it for themselves and to do so as soon as possible. In his *A Discourse on the Good Education of Children* from 1708, he wrote, "How early do the children begin to know and do what may be hurtful to them? It is very early that they learn the things condemned in the scriptures. Why should they not as early learn the scriptures themselves?"[6] Throughout American history and even today, many Americans see the Bible as the primary curriculum resource for their children's religious education.

6.2.b. Have children read a full translation of the canonical text of the Bible itself

Another approach that adults have taken is to provide children with translations of the entire Bible itself. For those who believe in the verbal, plenary inspiration of the Bible, any changes to the wording of Scripture itself is suspect. If the Bible itself is the inspired Word of God, they argue, then it should not be changed in any way.

Alternatively, others may prefer this approach because it gives children unfiltered access to the Bible itself, with all of its inspirational stories, oddities, and problematic texts, and therefore children will not grow up with a misleadingly sanitized or watered-down version of the Bible. Still others believe that children can benefit from the laconic nature of the Bible's stories. The Bible provides an excellent example of what reader-response critics refer to as "gaps" in narratives. Narrative and reader-response critics point out that the Hebrew Bible often employs the use of built-in gaps within its stories. These gaps are the parts of

---

4. John Locke, *Some Thoughts Concerning Education* (London: n.p., 1693), 187.

5. See, for example, Goldman, *Readiness for Religion*; Jerome W. Berryman, *Godly Play: A Way of Religious Education* (San Francisco: HarperSanFrancisco, 1991), 136–44; and A. Roger Gobbel and Gertrude G. Gobbel, *The Bible: A Child's Playground* (Philadelphia, PA: Fortress Press, 1986), 5–10.

6. Cotton Mather, *Corderius Americanus: A Discourse on the Good Education of Children* (Boston, MA: Dutton & Wentworth, 1828), 11.

the story that are not filled in by the storyteller, but left to the imagination of the audience. Rather than seeing these gaps as problematic, some see them as beneficial for religious education. These gaps have the advantage of being filled in different ways by different readers.[7] By engaging these gaps, readers participate in the story and can actively find and create meanings relevant to their own contexts and experiences. Experts on educating children in literature note that children are quite adept at interacting with the gaps in stories.[8] Although children may have relatively few life experiences that they can connect to the stories they read, each new story they encounter serves as an experience in itself and can in turn be connected to the next story they read.[9] A number of more recent religious educators favor a similar approach to studying the Bible with children, offering models that allow children to encounter and react to the Bible and fill in gaps in the narratives for themselves.[10] When children's Bible authors fill these gaps for children or offer explanations in an effort to make the Bible's meaning clear to them, they can be seen as denying children the experience of filling in the gaps for themselves and making their own meaning with the text.

For these reasons and more, children and youth editions of full translations of the Bible remain quite popular in the United States. Many American adults who purchase full translations of the entire Bible for their children, however, also provide their children with children's Bibles that retell Bible stories more freely.

6.2.c. Choosing a children's Bible that attempts to stay close to the text of the Bible

Ruth B. Bottigheimer explains the dilemma many people of faith have faced when they have considered how best to present the Bible to children:

> [T]he fact of editing stories from the Bible remains a vexing problem, if as was long believed, the canonical Bible was God's own word. Why should children read edited Bible stories rather than the canonical Bible itself? An easy answer is that young, even adolescent children are simply unready for the cultural and theological complexities of the Bible's narratives. Hence, it is sensible to offer appropriate assistance. At the simplest level of clarification, educators (whether

---

7. Wolfgang Iser, *The Implied Reader: Patterns in Communication in Prose Fiction from Bunyan to Beckett* (Baltimore, MD: Johns Hopkins University Press, 1974), 280–2.

8. Emry Evans, "Readers Recreating Texts," in *Readers, Texts, Teachers* (Upper Montclair, NJ: Boynton/Cook Publishers, Inc., 1987), 33–5.

9. Kathy Short, "Making Connections Across Literature and Life," in *Journeying: Children Responding to Literature* (Portsmouth, NH: Heinemann Press, 1993), 284–6.

10. See, for example, Dorothy Jean Furnish, *Experiencing the Bible with Children* (Nashville, TN: Abingdon Press, 1990); Berryman, *Godly Play*; Gobbel and Gobbel, *The Bible: A Child's Playground*; and Pamela Mitchell, "'Why Care About Stories?' A Theory of Narrative Art," *Religious Education* 86 (1991): 30–43.

in church, in school, or at home) explain unfamiliar words to make God's message understandable.[11]

Those who take this approach may compare the stories as they are found in a number of children's Bibles with the stories as they appear in the text of their Bible and choose one that, in their opinion, stays close to the text of the Bible itself.

Those taking this approach may choose children's Bibles that abridge and edit the text to remove some violent or sexual content and that reword certain passages for simplicity's and clarity's sake, but whose authors still show restraint in veering from the words and events as they appear in the Bible and do not add to the narratives their own commentary or lessons to be learned. They may also note that some people disregard the Bible as adults because, looking back, they remember the Bible to be simply childish fairy tales that were read to them when they were children. Those who take this approach, then, may also reject children's Bibles that illustrate Bible stories in the manner of fun and amusing children's cartoons, choosing instead those that illustrate the stories in a more realistic fashion.

The oversight of people from a variety of faith traditions appears to help moderate or eliminate embellishments to the stories or the insertion of the authors' own personal confessional assumptions or moralizations into the Bible stories. In the second half of the twentieth century, a number of children's Bibles, such as *The Children's Bible* (1962),[12] *The Doubleday Illustrated Children's Bible* (1983),[13] *The Kingfisher Children's Bible* (1993),[14] and *The Children's Illustrated Bible* (1994),[15] were developed with the aid of interfaith editorial boards or consultants comprised of Protestant ministers, Roman Catholic priests, and Jewish rabbis. The stories in these children's Bibles are less likely to veer radically from the canonical text. The illustrations also tend to be more realistic and less fanciful than those in many other children's Bibles and, at least in the more recent editions, they depict Bible characters more accurately as people of Near Eastern descent.

---

11. Ruth B. Bottigheimer, "The Otherness of Children's Bibles in Historical Perspective," in Caroline Vander Stichele and Hugh S. Pyper, eds, *Text, Image, and Otherness in Children's Bibles: What is in the Picture?* Semeia Studies 56 (Atlanta, GA: Society of Biblical Literature, 2012), 321.

12. *The Children's Bible* (New York: Golden Press, 1962).

13. Sandol Stoddard, *The Doubleday Illustrated Children's Bible* (Garden City, NY: Doubleday & Company, 1983). This has been republished as Sandol Stoddard, *The BOMC Illustrated Children's Bible* (New York: Book of the Month Club, 2001).

14. Ann Pilling, *The Kingfisher Children's Bible*, illus. by Kady MacDonald Denton (New York: Kingfisher Books, 1993).

15. Selina Hastings, *The Children's Illustrated Bible*, illus. by Eric Thomas (New York: Dorling Kindersley, 1994).

6.2.d. Choosing a children's Bible that agrees with your theological perspective

Another approach to choosing a children's Bible that one might take is to acknowledge that neutrality is impossible and that any editing or retelling of the stories of the Bible conveys a host of explicit and implicit beliefs and values. Parents, therefore, could simply choose a children's Bible that seems to be consistent with their own approach to their faith. For some socially conservative evangelical Christians, this may mean that they choose evangelical Christian authors and speakers Dottie and Josh McDowell's *The Right Choices Bible*[16] or the *Focus on the Family Bedtime Bible*.[17] More progressive Christians may choose Archbishop Desmond Tutu's *Children of God Storybook Bible*[18] or Norman Vincent Peale's *Bible Stories*.[19] Others may choose Bibles produced by members of their own religious traditions, religious movements, or denominational affiliations. They would do so, however, understanding that no interpretation of the Bible itself is a neutral or objective interpretation, and that their child's children's Bible does not include "objective" retellings of the Bible's stories.

6.3. For Further Study

A study such as this one raises more questions than it answers. It has touched upon some themes only briefly and could benefit from a more thorough analysis by scholars in particular fields of study.

As mentioned above, this research suggests, for example, that the wider cultural issues occurring at the time and place that a children's Bible was written have more bearing on how the story of Noah was appropriated than whether the author was male or female. Based upon children's Bible retellings of the story of Noah, the only clear difference between male and female authors' versions of the story seems to be that female authors tend to produce texts that reflect more age appropriate vocabulary and concepts than those by male authors. This finding is not surprising. Many of the male clergy who wrote children's Bibles in the nineteenth century, after all, probably did not have much direct contact with children that might have given them any intuitive sense of the sort of vocabulary that might have been appropriate for their young readers. This topic is one that would benefit from further analysis, however. Might the gender of children's Bible authors more clearly impact the way the Bible story is adapted when, for example, the Bible story is one that focuses more upon a female protagonist, the

---

16. Dottie and Josh McDowell, *The Right Choices Bible*, illus. by Joe Boddy (Wheaton, IL: Tyndale House Publishers, Inc., 1998).

17. Rick Osborne, Mary Guenther, and K. Christie Bowler, *Focus on the Family Bedtime Bible* (Wheaton, IL: Tyndale House, 2002).

18. Desmond Tutu, *Children of God Storybook Bible* (Grand Rapids, MI: ZonderKids, 2010).

19. Norman Vincent Peale, *Bible Stories* (New York: Banner Press, Inc., 1978).

relationships between parents and children, or relationships between male and female characters?

A study of children's Bible versions of any number of Bible stories other than the story of Noah's ark could be fruitful. For example, children's Bible depictions of the story of creation through the centuries, especially in light of recent efforts by young Earth creationists, could help index popular perspectives on the origin of the earth and life on earth throughout US history. A study of children's Bible versions of the fascinating and somewhat troubling tales from the Book of Judges could reveal any number of trends in the study of the Bible, religious education, and America's understanding of childhood. Others might engage in a thorough study of the implicit or explicit soteriology found in retellings of the story of Jesus' crucifixion in children's Bibles, or reflect on the various ways in which the crucifixion has been illustrated in relation to the view of childhood at the time of publication. Others might track the anti-Semitism found in many children's Bible versions of various stories from the Gospels and how certain prejudices are passed on in subtle and not so subtle ways. In-depth study of these and other Bible stories as they appear in children's Bibles could make significant contributions to religious and historical scholarship and the reception history of the Bible in particular.

This study has focused its analysis upon the printed text and illustrations of children's Bibles, but further analysis could also be made of the reading and writing of children's Bibles. Reader-response scholars could conduct interviews with child readers in order to explore how children read, understand, and experience children's Bibles. What assumptions do they make while reading children's Bibles? Do they make distinctions between what is part of the retelling of the Bible story itself and a children's Bible author's own commentary and revisions to the story? If so, how do they make those distinctions and do they matter to them? While acknowledging the potential danger of committing the intentionality fallacy, interviews with children's Bible authors may lend insights into their processes for composing their Bible stories. Do they have a Bible open in front of them as they write? Do they try to remember how they experienced or understood the Bible when they were children? Do they consult other children's Bibles to give them ideas on how they might approach the story? Do they enter into the task of writing the stories with intentional agendas for using the stories to convey certain doctrinal beliefs or to teach certain virtues? Do they consult with the artists who are illustrating their stories and, if so, how? To what extent are they aware of how they are changing and embellishing the stories or integrating their own confessional assumptions into their stories?

Children's Bibles in America reflect assumptions about what the Bible actually is and how it should be used with children. While today's readers may be amused, outraged, or inspired by some of the ways in which the story of Noah has been appropriated by the creators of children's Bibles in America in the past, a study such as this one leads us to wonder how people 50 years from now might gasp or chuckle at the way we use the Bible's stories today. As David Gunn reminds us, one of the practical benefits of studies in reception history is that by seeing how the

Bible has been used in the past and in other contexts, "we may be led to challenge our own assumptions about the responsible use of religious texts today."[20] This study of children's Bibles, then, is not only relevant to those who work with children. Like any study of the reception history of the Bible, reflection on how people in the past and present have used the Bible can help scholars, clergy, and religious educators today reflect on how they are using the Bible themselves.

20. David Gunn, "Cultural Criticism," in Gale A. Yee, ed., *Judges & Method: New Approaches in Biblical Studies*, 2nd edn (Minneapolis, MN: Fortress Press, 2007), 204.

BIBLIOGRAPHY

Children's Bibles, Bible Storybooks, and Other Bible-related Books for Children

Adams, Laura Merrihew. *Old Testament Story-Land*. Philadelphia, PA: Union Press, 1923.

Alden, Hazel Gillmore. *The Kingdom of Heaven. An Instruction in The Catholic Faith for Children*. New York: Church Publishing Company, 1907.

Aldridge, Betty L. *The Toddler's Activity Bible*. Nashville, TN: Thomas Nelson, 1992.

Alexander, Pat. *The Nelson Children's Bible*. Nashville, TN: Thomas Nelson, 1981.

Alexander, Pat. *The Children's Story Bible*. Illus. by Carolyn Cox. Louisville, KY: Westminster John Knox Press, 1991.

Alexander, Pat. *My First Bible*. Illus. by Leon Baxter. Intercourse, PA: Good Books, 2002.

Allen, J. F., Lane Easterly, Bernice Rich, and Elmer T. Towns. *Nelson's Picture Bible*. Illus. by Carlo Tora. Nashville, TN: Thomas Nelson, 1973.

Altman, Addie Richman. *The Jewish Child's Bible Stories*. New York: Bloch Publishing Company, 1949.

Andrews, Tailer. *Bible Stories for Children*. Illus. by C.W. Kelsey. New York: J. H. Sears & Company, 1927.

Andruss, Bessie Edmond. *Bible Stories as Told to Very Little Children*. Illus. by Olivette. New York: Coward-McCann, Inc., 1932.

Armstrong, April Oursler. *Bible Stories for Young Readers*. Illus. by Jules Gotlieb. Garden City, NY: Junior Deluxe Editions, 1956.

Armstrong, April Oursler. *The Book of God: Adventures from the Old Testament*. Garden City, NY: Garden City Books, 1956.

Arthur, Patti Thisted et al. *Spark Story Bible*. Illus. by Peter Grosshauser and Ed Temple. Minneapolis, MN: Augsburg Fortress, 2009.

Asch, Sholem. *In the Beginning: Stories from the Bible*. Trans. by Caroline Cunningham. New York: Schocken Books, 1935, 1966.

Ashton, Sophia G. *Frankie's Book about Bible Men*. Boston, MA: J. E. Tilton and Company, 1861.

The Attributes of God; An Account of the Creation and the Story of Joseph and His Brethren, Taken from Scripture. New Haven, CT: Sidney's Press, 1818.

Baby Blessings Baby's Bible. Illus. by Mandy Stanley. Norwalk, Connecticut, CT: Standard Publishing, 2004.

Baby's Bible. Illus. by Mandy Stanley. Cincinnati, OH: Standard Publishing, 2003.

Baby's First Bible. Illus. by Colin and Moira Maclean. Pleasantville, NY: Reader's Digest Books, 1996.

Bach, Alice, and J. Cheryl Exum. *Moses' Ark*. Illus. by Leo and Diane Dillon. New York: Delacorte Press, 1989.

Baikie, James. *The Bible Story: A Connected Narrative Retold from Holy Scripture.* New York: Macmillan Company, 1930.

Baker, Carolyn Nabors. *The Beginners Bible Tales of Virtue: A Book of Right and Wrong.* Illus. by Kelly Pulley and Lisa Reed. New York: Little Moorings, 1995.

Baker, Carolyn Nabors, and Cindy Helms. *The Beginners Bible for Toddlers.* Illus. by Danny Brooks Dalby. Dallas, TX: Word Publishing, 1995.

Barnes, Albert. *Questions on the Historical Books of the New Testament*, Vol. 1, *Matthew.* New York: Harper & Brothers, 1830.

Barton, Lucy. *Bible Letters for Children.* London: John Souter, London School Library, 1831.

Beard, Frank et al. *Picture Puzzles or How to Read the Bible by Symbols (Designed Especially for the Boys and Girls to Stimulate a Greater Interest in the Holy Bible).* Naperville, IL: J. L. Nichols & Co., 1899.

Beck, Susan Elizabeth. *God Loves Me Bible.* Illus. by Gloria Oostema. Grand Rapids, MI: Zondervan Publishing House, 1993.

Beck, Susan Elizabeth. *God Loves Me Bible.* Rev. Grand Rapids, MI: Zondervan, 2004.

Bedford, Annie North. *Walt Disney's Noah's Ark.* New York: Simon and Schuster, 1952.

Bedtime Bible Stories. Illus. by Bruno Frost. Racine, WN: Whitman Publishing Company, 1955.

Beers, V. Gilbert. *Jesus is My Guide.* Grand Rapids, MI: Zondervan Publishing House, 1973.

Beers, V. Gilbert. *The Toddler's Bible.* Illus. by Carole Boerke. Colorado Springs, CO: Cook Communications Ministry, 1992.

Beers, V. Gilbert. *The Preschooler's Bible.* Illus. by Teresa Walsh. Colorado Springs. CO: Cook Communications Ministry, 1994.

Beers, V. Gilbert. *The Preschooler's Bible.* Illus. by Tammie Lyon. Colorado Springs, CO: David C. Cook, 2012.

Begbie, Harold. *The Children's Story Bible.* New York: Grolier Society, 1948.

The Beginning Reader's Bible. Comp. by Tama Fortner. Illus. by Marijke ten Cate. Nashville, TN: Thomas Nelson, 2011.

Bible History. Wendell, MA: J. Metcalf, 1828.

Bible History for Schools and the Home. Authorized by the Evangelical Lutheran Augustana Synod. Rock Island, IL: Augustana Book Concern, 1898.

Bible History; to which is added A Short History of the Church. New York: P. O'Shea, 1879.

The Bible in Miniature. New York: Brower [1790].

Bible Stories. Racine, WN: Whitman Publishing Co., 1952.

Bible Stories for Boys. New York: Scholastic, Inc., 2011.

Bible Stories for Children (by A Catholic Teacher). New York: Schwartz, Kirwin & Fauss, 1919.

Bible Stories for Girls. New York: Scholastic, Inc., 2011.

Bible Stories with Engravings. Worcester, MA: Jonathan Grout, Jr. [1840].

Bible Stories and Pictures. New Haven, CT: Sidney Babcock [1850].

Bible Stories with Suitable Pictures. [Worcester, MA]: Dorr & Howland [between 1821 and 1831].

Bible stories, for the use of Sunday Schools and Children. Boston, MA: Charles Gaylord, 1837.

Bible Stories for the Young with Colored Engravings. Worcester, MA: S. A. Howland, 1842.

The Big Picture Interactive Bible Stories for Toddlers from the Old Testament. Nashville, TN: B & H Publishing, 2014.

The Big Picture Interactive Bible Storybook. Nashville, TN: B & H Publishing, 2013.

Blake, Mortimer. *Bible Children*. Boston, MA: Congregational Sunday School Publishing Company, 1886.

Bobb, Ruth Hogue. *A Bible Highway: Charted for Boys and Girls*. Chicago: International Child Evangelism Fellowship, 1941.

Bond, Alvan. *Young People's Illustrated Bible History*. Norwich, CT: n.p., 1878.

Book of Bible Stories. A Present for a Good Scholar. New Haven, CT: S. Babcock, 1842.

The Book of Life, Volume One. Chicago: John Rudin & Company Inc., 1923, 1925, 1927.

Boon, Fiona. *My Princess Bible Purse*. Nashville, TN: Thomas Nelson, 2012.

Bowie, Walter Russell. *The Story of the Bible*. New York: Abingdon Press, 1934.

Brown, Laaren, and Lenny Hart. *The Children's Illustrated Jewish Bible*. New York: DK Publishing, 2007.

Bryant, Lorinda Munson, ed. *Bible Story in Bible Language, The King James Version*. New York: D. Appleton and Company, 1922.

Buck, Pearl S. *The Story of the Bible*. New York: Bartholemew House Ltd., 1971.

Buel, J. W. and T. DeWitt Talmage. *The New Beautiful Story*. Philadelphia, PA: Historical Publishing Company, 1892.

Burnham, Catherine Lydia. *From the Creation to Moses: Nursery Bible stories in words of one syllable*. New York: Geo. A. Leavitt, [1870].

Burson, Bettie. *Miss Bettie's Book of Bible Stories*. Grand Rapids, MI: Wm. B. Eerdmans Publishing Company, 1939.

Byrum, Isabel C. *Beautiful Stories from the Good Old Book*. Moundsville, WV: Gospel Trumpet Company, 1904.

Byrum, Isabel C. *Our Darlings' ABC Book*. Anderson, IN: Gospel Trumpet Co., 1908.

Chaikin, Miriam. *Children's Bible Stories from Genesis to Daniel*. Illus. by Yvonne Gilbert. New York: Dial Books for Young Readers, 1993.

Chalmers, Muriel J. *The Bible Picture Book*. London, Edinburgh, New York, Toronto, and Paris: Thomas Nelson and Sons [1950].

Chessor, James E. *Short Bible Stories: Retold in Simple Language*. Nashville, TN: Gospel Advocate Company, 1924.

Child, Isabella. *The Child's Picture Bible*. Boston, MA: G. W. Cottrell, 1853.

Children of Color Storybook Bible with stories from the International Children's Bible. Illus. by Victor Hogan. Nashville, TN: Thomas Nelson, 2001.

The Children's Bible. [Philadelphia and] London: Andrew Steuart, 1763.

The Children's Bible. New York: Golden Press, 1962.

The Children's Living Bible. Wheaton, IL: Tyndale House, 1972.

The Child's Bible. Philadelphia, PA: Fisher and Brother, 1834.

The Child's Bible. Chicago: L. P. Miller & Company, 1884, 1889.

Child's Book of Bible History: With Engravings. Worcester [MA]: N. Hervey, [1855].

The Child's Book of Bible Stories. Philadelphia, PA: Henry F. Anners, 1850.

The Child's Book of Sunday Reading. Worcester, MA: N. Hervey [1840].

The Child's Book of Sunday Reading. Worcester, MA: G. B. Matthews [1840].

The Child's Instructor: or Stories from the Bible. Boston, MA: William Henshaw, 1842.

The Child's Library of Useful Knowledge. Pittsburgh, PA: Zadok Cramer, 1806.

The Child's Scripture Question Book. Philadelphia, PA: American Sunday-School Union, 1858 (first edition 1836).

Clanin, Gloria. *In the Days of Noah*. Illus. by Earl and Bonita Snellenberger. Green Forest, AR: Master Books, 1996.

Cohen, Lenore. *Bible Tales for Very Young Children*. Cincinnati, OH: Union of American Hebrew Congregations, 1934.

Cohen, Mortimer J. *Pathways through the Bible*. Philadelphia: Jewish Publication Society of America, 1946.

Compact Kids Bible: Green Camo. New York: Thomas Nelson, 2007.

Comstock, Harriet T. *Bible Stories Retold in Words of One Syllable*. New York: A. L. Burt Company, 1900.

Conway, Brian, Lora Kalkman et al. *5-Minute Bible Stories*. Lincolnwood, IL: Publications International Ltd., 2002.

Conwell, Russell H. *Bible Stories for Children*. Philadelphia, PA: W. W. Houston & Co., 1892.

Cotton, John. *Milke for Babes. Drawn Out of the Breasts of both Testaments*. London: F. Coe, 1646.

Crouch, Nathaniel. *Youth's Divine Pastime*. London: n.p., 1691.

A Curious Heiroglyphick Bible; or Select Passages in the Old and New Testaments, Represented with Emblematic Figures for the Amusement of Youth. Worcester, MA: Isaiah Thomas, 1788.

Currie, Robin. *The Baby Bible Storybook*. Illus. by Cindy Adams. Eastbourne: Chariot Books, 1994.

Currie, Robin. *The Baby Bible Storybook for Boys*. Illus. by Gonstaza Basaluzzo. Colorado Springs, CO: David C. Cook, 2008.

Currie, Robin. *The Baby Bible Storybook for Girls*. Illus. by Gonstaza Basaluzzo. Colorado Springs, CO: David C. Cook, 2008.

Dallas High Schools Bible Study Course: Old Testament. Dallas, TX: Dallas Independent School District, 1972.

Daniel, David. *The Complete Book of Bible Stories for Jewish Children*. Illus. by Ben Einhorn. Jersey City, NJ: KTAV Publishing House, Inc., 1971.

Daniels, Patricia. *Noah's Ark*. Illus. by Kathy Rusynyk. Alexandria, VA: Time Life Kids, 1995.

Davidson, Alice Joyce. *The Story of Noah: An Alice in Bibleland Story*. Illus. by Victoria Marshall. Norwalk, CT: C. R. Gibson Company, 1984.

Dawes, Sarah Elizabeth. *Bible Stories for Young People*. New York: Thomas Y. Crowell, 1923.

Dawes, Sarah Elizabeth. *Hours with Mamma*. New York: American Tract Society, 1866.

DeBoer, Rondi, and Christine Tangvald. *My Favorite Bible*. Grand Rapids, MI: Baker Publishing House, 2011.

De La Mare, Walter. *Stories from the Bible*. New York: Alfred A. Knopf, 1961.

Delval, Marie-Hélène. *Reader's Digest Bible for Children*. Illus. by Ulises Wensell. Pleasantville, NY: Reader's Digest Young Families, 1995.

DeVries, Catherine. *Adventure Bible Storybook*. Illus. by Jim Madsen. Grand Rapids, MI: ZonderKids, 2009.

DeVries, Catherine, ed. *The Beginner's Bible: Timeless Bible Stories*. Grand Rapids, MI: Zondervan, 2005.

Dooley, Tom. *The True Story of Noah's Ark*. Illus. by Bill Looney. Green Forest, AR: Master Books, Inc., 2003.

Downey, Roma, with Carolyn Larsen. *Roma Downey's Little Angels Bible Storybook*. Carol Streams, IL: Tyndale House, 2012.

Downing, Julie. *A First Book of Jewish Bible Stories*. London and New York: DK Children, 2002.

Durrant, George D. *Illustrated Stories from the Bible*, Volume 1. Provo, UT: Community Press, 1980.

Eckard, Leslie. *Beginning Bible Stories: Blessings for Baby*. Nashville, TN: Broadman & Holman, 2001.

Egermeier, Elsie E. *Egermeier's Bible Story Book*. Anderson, IN: Warner Press, 1923, 1939.

Ellis, Gwen. *Read and Share Bible*. Illus. by Steve Smallman. Nashville, TN: Thomas Nelson, 2007.

Ellis, Gwen. *Our Together-Time Bible*. Nashville, TN: Thomas Nelson, 2008.

FaiThGirLz! Bible (NIV). Grand Rapids, MI: Zondervan, 2011.

Falconer, Robert C. *A Child's Ramble through the Bible: The Old Testament*. New York: Fleming H. Revell Company, 1922.

False Stories Corrected. New York: Samuel Wood, 1814.

Family Bible: English Standard Version (ESV). Wheaton, IL: Crossway Bibles, 2004.

Farrell, Paul. *Illustrated Stories from the Bible (That They Won't Tell You in Sunday School)*. Austin, TX: American Atheist Press, 2005.

Favourite Bible Stories for the Young. London, Edinburgh and New York: T. Nelson & Sons, 1896.

Fessenden, Katherine. *The Old Testament Story: Adam to Jonah*. New York: Henry Z. Walck, Incorporated, 1960.

A First Bible. New York and London: Oxford University Press, 1934.

Foster, Charles. *The Story of the Bible from Genesis to Revelation Told in Simple Language*. Philadelphia, PA: Charles Foster Publishing, 1873.

Frankel, Ellen. *JPS Illustrated Children's Bible*. Philadelphia, PA: Jewish Publication Society, 2009.

Froeb, Lori C. *Fisher Price Little People: Noah and the Animals*. White Plains, NY: Reader's Digest Children's Books, 2012.

Gallaudet, T. H. *Scripture Biography for the Young, with Critical Illustrations and Practical Remarks*, Vol. 1, *Adam to Jacob*. New York: American Tract Society, 1838.

Gauch, Patricia Lee. *Noah*. Illus. by Jonathan Green. New York: Philomel Books, 1994.

Gellman, Marc. *Does God Have a Big Toe? Stories about Stories in the Bible*. New York: Harper & Row, 1989.

Gerelds, Jennifer. *Brave Girls Bible Stories*. Illus. by Aleksey and Olga Ivanov. Nashville, TN: Thomas Nelson, 2014.

Gerstein, Mordicai. *Noah and the Great Flood*. New York: Simon & Schuster Books, 1999.

Gilder, Joseph B. *The Bible for Young People: Arranged from the King James Version with Twenty-Four Full Page Illustrations from the Masters*. New York: Century Company, 1902.

Gilgamesh, Horus. *The Awkward Moments Children's Bible*. Awkward Moments, 2013.

Gilmour, Richard. *Bible History*. New York: Benzinger Brothers, 1881.

Ginther, Rosamond D. *Bible Stories for the Cradle Roll*. 5 vols. Nashville, TN: Southern Publishing Association, 1933.

Ginther, Rosamond D. *A Treasury of Bible Stories*. New York: Twayne, 1958.

Ginther, Rosamond D. *God's Story for Me: 104 Favorite Bible Stories for Children*. Ventura, CA: Gospel Light, 2009.

Goldin, Hyman E. *Bible and Talmud Stories*, Vol. 1, *From the Beginning to the Death of Moses*. New York: Star Hebrew Book Company, 1931.

Goodrich, Samuel G. *Peter Parley's Book of Bible Stories*. Boston, MA: Lilly, Wait, and Co., 1834.

Goodrich, Samuel G. *Peter Parley's Book of Fables*. Hartford, CT: Silas Andrus, 1846.

Goodspeed, Edgar J., ed. *The Junior Bible: An American Translation*. New York: Macmillan Company, 1936, 1948.

Graham, C. R. *My Mother's Bible Stories*. Philadelphia, PA: Globe Bible Publishing Co., 1896.

Graham, Lorenz. *How God Fix Jonah*. Illus. by Ashley Bryan. Honesdale, Pennsylvania, PA: Boyds Mills Press, 1946, 1974.

Graham, Miss. *Histories from Scripture, for Children*. New York: John S. Taylor, 1839.

Gray, Ruth S. *Bible Heroes*. Anderson, IN: Warner Press, 1950.

Greene, Rhonda Gowler. *Noah and the Mighty Ark*. Illus. by Margaret Spengler. Grand Rapids, MI: ZonderKids, 2014.

Greengard, Alison. *Noah's Ark*. Illus. by Carol Racklin-Siegel. Albany, CA: EKS Publishing Co., 2004.

Grindley, Sally, and Jan Barger. *Bible Stories for the Young*. Waukesha, WI: Little Tiger Press, 1998.

Grive, Mrs. *Half hours with the Bible: or, The Children's Scripture Story-Book*. New York: McLoughlin Brothers [1867].

Grover, Eulalie Osgood. *Old Testament Stories*. Boston, MA: Little, Brown, and Company, 1927.

Guerber, H. A. *The Story of the Chosen People*. New York: American Book Company, 1896.

Hadley, Carolyn. *From Eden to Babylon: Stories of the Prophets Priests and Kings of the Old Testament*. New York: McLoughlin Brothers, c. 1890.

Hall, Newton Marshall. *The Bible Story: Volume One*. Springfield, MA: King-Richardson Company, 1906, 1917.

Hall, Newton Marshall. *The Children's Bible*. New York: Western Publishing, 1981, 1965.

Hall, Sarah. *Conversations on the Bible*. Philadelphia, PA: Harrison Hall, 1818.

Ham, Ken. *Dinosaurs of Eden: A Biblical Journey through Time*. Illus. by Earl and Bonita Snellenberger. Green Forest, AR: Master Books, 2001.

Harrast, Tracy L. *My Baby and Me Story Bible*. Illus. by Gloria Oostema. Grand Rapids, MI: Zondervan Publishing House, 1995.

Harris, Benjamin. *The Holy Bible in Verse*. Boston, MA: John Allen, 1717.

Hastings, Selina. *The Children's Illustrated Bible*. Illus. by Eric Thomas. New York: Dorling Kindersley, 1994.

Hazen, Barbara Shook. *Noah's Ark*. Illus. by Tibor Gergely. Racine, WN: Golden Press, 1969.

Headley, P. C. *Bible Chats with Children*. Philadelphia, PA: John E. Potter and Company, 1895.

Helm, David. *The Big Picture Story Bible*. Illus. by Gail Schoonmaker. Wheaton, IL: Crossway Books, 2004.

Henly, Karyn. *The Beginner's Bible: Timeless Children's Stories*. Illus. by Dennas Davis. Sisters, Oregon: Questar Publishers, Inc., 1989.

The Hieroglyphick Bible: Second Edition. Boston, MA: Buckingham for Thomas, 1814.

A History of the Bible. No place of publication or publisher, 1819.

History of the Holy Bible. Hartford, CT: Cook & Hale [between 1816 and 1819].

The History of the Holy Bible. Abridged. New Haven, CT: Sidney's Press, 1817.

The History of the Holy Bible: Abridged. No place of publication or publisher, 1819.

Hodges, George. *The Garden of Eden: Stories from the First Nine Books of the Old Testament*. Boston, MA: Houghton Mifflin Company, 1909.

Hodges, Turner, and Elizabeth MacLean. *The Bible Story Library*. Vol. 1. New York: American Handbook and Textbook Co., 1963.

Hollender, Betty R. *Bible Stories for Little Children*. New York: Union of American Hebrew Congregations, 1955.

Hollingsworth, Mary. *My Very First Book of Bible Heroes*. Illus. by Rick Incrocci. Nashville, TN: Thomas Nelson, 1993.

Hollingsworth, Mary. *Bumper the Dinosaur Bible Stories*. Illus. by Rick Incrocci. Colorado Springs, CO: Chariot Family Publishing, 1996.

Holmes, Andy. *My Princess Bible*. Illus. by Sergey Eiliseev. Carol Stream, IL: Tyndale House, 2010.

Holy Bible: Abridged. Boston, MA: William Norman, 1802.

Holy Bible: Children's Illustrated Edition: Contemporary English Version. New York: American Bible Society, 2000.

Holy Bible: International Children's Bible: New Century Version. Dallas, TX: Word Publishing, 1983.

Holy Bible: King James Version, Kids Study Bible. Grand Rapids, MI: Hendrickson, 2009.

Houghton, L. S. *The Bible in Picture and Story*. New York: American Tract Society, 1889.

Howard, John. *The Illustrated Scripture History for the Young*. New York: Virtue and Yorston, 1876.

Hudson, Ethel. *Bible Heroes: For Use in the Junior B.Y.P.U.* Nashville, TN: Sunday School Board of the Southern Baptist Convention, 1926.

Hudson, Lion. *365 Bible Stories for Young Hearts*. Wheaton, IL: Crossway Books, 2006.

Hurlbut, Jesse Lyman. *Hurlbut's Story of the Bible: New and Revised*. Chicago: John C. Winston Company, 1932.

The Illustrated Scripture Alphabet: with prayers and hymns for children. Boston, MA: J. Buffum, 1855.

Jackson, Mildred L. *Once-Upon-a-Time Bible Stories*. New York: Exposition Press, 1959.

Jahsmann, Allan Hart. *The Holy Bible for Children: A Simplified Version*. St. Louis, MO: Concordia Publishing House, 1977.

Johnson, George, Jerome D. Hannan, and M. Dominica. *Bible History: A Textbook of Old and New Testaments for Catholic Schools*. New York: Benziger Brothers, 1935.

Juma, Siddiqa. *Nuh (Noah) (Peace be upon him)*. Elmhurst, NY: Tahrike Tarsile Qur'an, Inc., 1998.

Katzenberg, Julius. *Biblical History for School and Home*. Part I. New York: Industrial School of the Hebrew Orphan Asylum, 1878.

Khan, Saniyasnain. *My First Quran Storybook*. Nizamuddin West, New Delhi: Goodword, 2007.

Kidder, D. P., ed. *Bible Stories for Children*, Vol. I. New York: Lane & Scott, 1851.

Kirby, Ralph. *The Bible Story with Living Pictures*. New York: Harper and Brothers, 1960.

The KJV Illustrated Study Bible for Kids. Nashville, TN: Holman Bible Publishers, 2010.

KJV Read to Me Bible for Kids. Nashville, TN: Holman Bible Publishers, 2001.

Knecht, F. J. *The Child's Bible History: Adapted from the Works of J. Schuster and G. Mey*. St. Louis, MO: B. Herder, 1898.

Kolatch, Alfred J. *Classic Bible Stories for Jewish Children*. Middle Village, NY: Jonathan David, 1994.

Korfker, Dena. *My Picture Story Bible*. Grand Rapids, MI: Zondervan Publishing House, 1960.

Krottjer, A. Gertrude. *Fireside Bible Stories: Old Testament. Retold for Children*. Illus. by Joseph Eugene Dash. Chicago: Just Right Books, 1925.

Kynett, A. J. *Sacred Pictures and Their Teachings: Grand Old Stories from the Good Old Book for Young and Old*. Philadelphia, PA: Keystone Publishing Co., 1892.

Larcombe, Jennifer Rees. *Through-the-Bible Storybook*. Illus. by Alan Parry. Grand Rapids, MI: Zondervan, 1992.

Larsen, Carolyn. *My Bedtime Bible*. Iowa Falls, IA: World Publishing, 1994.

Larsen, Carolyn. *Little Girls Bible Storybook for Mothers and Daughters*. Illus. by Caron Turk. Grand Rapids, MI: Baker Book House Company, 1998.

Larsen, Carolyn. *Little Boys Bible Storybook for Fathers and Sons*. Grand Rapids, MI: Baker Publishing, 2001.

Larsen, Carolyn. *Jesus Said Bible Storybook*. Illus. by Rick Incrocci. Nashville, TN: Thomas Nelson, 2003.

Larsen, Carolyn. *My Favorite Bible Storybook for Early Readers*. Illus. by Christopher Grey. Franklin, TN: Dalmatian Press, 2005.

Larsen, Carolyn. *Little Girls Bible Storybook for Fathers and Daughters*. Illus. by Caron Turk. Grand Rapids, MI: Baker Book House, 2014.

Lashbrook, Marilyn. *Two by Two: The Story of Noah's Faith*. Dallas, TX: Roper Press, 1987.

Lathbury, Mary A. *Bible Heroes: Stories from the Bible*. Boston, MA: DeWolfe, Fiske & Co., 1898.

Latimer, Faith. *Dear Old Stories Told Once More*. New York: American Tract Society, 1877.

Latourette, Jane. *The Story of Noah's Ark*. Illus. by Sally Matthews. St. Louis, MO: Arch Books, 1965.

Lehman-Wilzig, Tami. *Green Bible Stories for Children*. Illus. by Durga Yael Bernhard. Minneapolis, MN: Kar-Ben Publishing, 2011.

Lessa, Charlotte F. *The Wonderful World of the Bible*. Illus. by João Luiz Cardozo. Hagerstown, MD: Review and Herald Publishing Association, 2003.

Lingo, Susan L. *My Good Night Bible*. Cincinnati, OH: Standard Publishing, 1999.

Little book of Bible Stories for Children: With Numerous Engravings. Worcester, MA: Dorr, Howland & Co. [1839].

The Little Children's Bible. New York: Macmillan Company, 1924.

Lloyd-Jones, Sally. *The Jesus Storybook Bible: Every Story Whispers His Name*. Grand Rapids, MI: ZonderKids, 2007.

Lloyd-Jones, Sally. *Tiny Bear's Bible*. Grand Rapids, MI: ZonderKids, 2007.

Lloyd-Jones, Sally. *Baby's Hug-a-Bible*. Illus. by Claudine Gévry. New York: HarperFestival, 2010.

Loring, Laurie. *Little Truths for Little Folks; Bible Stories*. Boston, MA: D. Lothrop & Co., 1877.

Lovasik, Lawrence. *New Catholic Picture Bible*. New York: Catholic Book Publishing Company, 1955, 1981.

Lyons, P. J. *Little Lion's Bible*. Illus. by Melanie Mitchell. Grand Rapids, MI: Zondervan Publishing, 2011.

Machowski, Marty. *The Gospel Story Bible: Discovering Jesus in the Old and New Testaments*. Greensboro, NC: New Growth Press, 2011.

Marshall, Logan. *The Wonder Book of Bible Stories*. Philadelphia, PA: John C. Winston Company, 1921.

Martin, Patricia Summerlin. *Beautiful Bible Stories*. Nashville, TN: Southwestern Company, 1964.

Maryknoll Sisters. *Crusade: The Story of the Bible Retold for Catholic Children* 3 (September 10, 1955). Chicago: John J. Crawley & Co., Inc., 71.

Matimore, P. Henry. *A Child's Garden of Religious Stories*. Illus. by Carl Michel Boog. New York: Macmillan Company, 1929.

Maxwell, Arthur S. *The Bible Story*, Vol. 1. Washington, DC: Review and Herald Publishing Association, 1953, 1973, 1975.

May, Sophie. *Fairy Book*. Boston, MA: Lee and Shepard, 1865.

McDowell, Dottie, and Josh McDowell. *The Right Choices Bible*. Illus. by Joe Boddy. Wheaton, IL: Tyndale House, 1998.

McKissack, Patricia, and Fredrick McKissack. *Let My People Go: Bible Stories Told by a Freeman of Color*. Illus. by James E. Ransome. New York: Atheneum Books for Young Readers, 1998.

Meade, Starr. *Mighty Acts of God: A Family Bible Story Book*. Wheaton, IL: Crossway, 2010.

Mendes, F. De Sola. *The Child's First Bible: Mainly in Words of One and Two Syllables, for Younger Children with Questions*. 14th edn. New York: Author, 1915.

Milton, Ralph. *The Family Story Bible*. Illus. by Margaret Kyle. Louisville, KY: Westminster John Knox Press, 1996.

Morrisey, R. A. *Bible History of the Negro*. Nashville, TN: National Baptist Publishing Board, 1915.

Morrisey, R. A. *Colored People in Bible History*. Hammond, IN: W. B. Conkey Company, 1925.

Mortimer, Favell Lee. *Scripture Facts in Simple Language*. [United States]: American Tract Society [1848].

Mortimer, Favell Lee. *Line Upon Line*. Greenfield, MA: L. Merriam. [1860].

Mortimer, Favell Lee. *Line Upon Line*. Philadelphia, PA: Henry Altmus, 1897.

Moses, Montefiore J. *Bible Stories for Jewish Children*. New York: Holt Brothers, 1879.

Murray, Jane Marie, and Eugene S. Geissler. *The Story of Salvation*. Notre Dame, IN: Fides Publishers Association, 1961.

My First Hands-on Bible. Carol Stream, IL: Tyndale House, 2011.

My Holy Bible for African-American Children. Grand Rapids, MI: Zondervan, 2009.

The New England Primer. Boston, MA: Edward Draper, 1777.

A New Hieroglyphical Bible. Boston, MA: Norman [1796].

A New Hieroglyphical Bible. With Four Hundred Embellishments on Wood. 11th edn. New York: American Heritage Press, 1836.

Newton, Richard. *Bible Models; or The Shining Lights of Scriptures*. Philadelphia, PA: Charles Foster Publishing Co., 1896.

NIrV Discoverer's Bible for Early Readers. Grand Rapids, MI: ZonderKidz, 2002.

NIV Adventure Bible. Grand Rapids, MI: Zondervan, 2011.

NIV Boys Bible. Grand Rapids, MI: Zondervan, 2011.

Noah and the Ark: A Story About Being Thankful. Nashville, TN: Candy Cane Press, 2005.

Noah and the flood. Worcester [MA]: H. J. Howland [not before 1835].

The Noah's Ark Bible. Grand Rapids, MI: World Publishing, 1989.

"Noah Saved in the Ark," *Little Bible Lesson Pictures* 18:3 (July 21, 1901).

Noethen, Theo. *History of the Bible, for the Use of Schools*. Albany, NY: Weed, Parsons & Company, 1860.

Northrop, Henry Davenport. *Charming Bible Stories: Written in Simple Language*. Philadelphia, PA: Monarch Books, 1894.

Northrop, Henry Davenport. *From Eden to Calvary; or through the Bible in a Year with our Boys and Girls*. Philadelphia, PA: National Publishing Company, 1900.

Olcott, Frances Jenkins. *Bible Stories to Read and Tell*. Illus. by Willy Pogany. Boston, MA: Houghton Mifflin Company, 1915.

The Older Children's Bible. New York: Macmillan Company, 1924.

Osborne, Rick, Mary Guenther, and K. Christie Bowler. *Focus on the Family Bedtime Bible*. Wheaton, IL: Tyndale House, 2002.

Parker, Clara Hathaway. *Stories from the Old Testament*. Boston, MA: Unitarian Sunday-School Society, 1909.

The Patriarchs; or, Bible Histories for Children. Philadelphia, PA: American Baptist Publication Society, 1852.

Peale, Norman Vincent. *Bible Stories*. New York: Banner Press, Inc., 1978.

Peirce, B. K. *Child's Lesson-Book on the Bible*. New York: Carlton & Porter, 1851.

Peltz, George A. *Grandpa's Stories: or Home Talks out of the Wonderful Book*. Toronto: Best Brothers, 1887.

Petersen, Emma Marr. *Bible Stories for Young Latter-Day Saints*. Salt Lake City, UT: Bookcraft, 1949.

Pictures of Bible History. Northampton, MA: John Metcalf, 1836.

Pictures of Bible History. Northampton, MA: J. H. Butler, 1840.

Pictures of Bible history: with Suitable Descriptions. Wendell, MA: J. Metcalf, 1826.

Pictures and Stories from the Bible. Worcester, MA: J. Grout, Jr. [1840].

Pierson, Helen W. *The Bible Story: In Easy Words for Children*. New York: McLoughlin Brothers, 1900.

Pilling, Ann. *The Kingfisher Children's Bible*. Illus. by Kady MacDonald Denton. New York: Kingfisher Books, 1993.

Piper, David R. *Youth Explore the Bible: A New Story of the World's Most Popular Book*. Illus. by Beatrice Stevens. Boston, MA: W. A. Wilde Company, 1941.

Piper, Sophie. *The Lion Read & Know Bible*. Illus. by Anthony Lewis. Oxford: Lion Childrens, 2008.

Pleasanton, Louise M. *A Nursery Story of the Bible*. New York: Frederick A. Stokes Company, 1920.

Potter, Edward Tuckerman. *Bible Stories in Bible Language*. New York: D. Appleton and Company, 1898.

Precious Moments Children's Bible: Easy-to-Read New Life Version. Grand Rapids, MI: Baker Book House, 1999.

The Precious Princess Bible (NIrV). Grand Rapids, MI: ZonderKidz, 2010.

Prescott, Reuben. *Grand Father's Bible Stories*. Chicago: C. W. Stanton Company, 1897.

The Princess Bible: New King James Version. Nashville, TN: Thomas Nelson, 2008.

Radius, Marianne. *The Tent of God: A Journey through the Old Testament*. Illus. by Chris Soffel Overvoorde. Grand Rapids, MI: William B. Eerdmans Publishing Company, 1968.

Reasoner, Charles. *Inside Noah's Ark*. New York: Price Stern Sloan, 2002.

Reddall, Henry Frederic, ed. *Golden Memories*. New York: Hunt & Eaton, 1890.

Reeve, Joseph. *The history of the Holy bible, comprising the most remarkable events in the Old and New Testaments, interspersed with moral and instructive reflections, chiefly taken from the Holy fathers*. New York: D. & J. Sadler, & Company, 1862.

Remy, Jean S. *Bible Stories for Little Children: In Words of One Syllable*. Philadelphia, PA: Henry Altemus Company, 1909.

Richards, Lawrence O., ed. *The KJV Kids' Study Bible*. Grand Rapids, MI: ZonderKidz, 2001.

Robinson, Jenny. *The Encyclopedia of Bible Stories*. Illus. by Gordon King. Philadelphia, PA, and New York: A. J. Holman Company, 1974.

Rock, Lois. *Five-Minute Bible Stories*. Illus. by Richard Johnson. Minneapolis, MN: Augsburg Books, 2004.

Rowe, Edna B. *Bible Stories for Little Folk*. Illus. by Otto Stemler. Cincinnati, OH: Standard Publishing Company, 1926.

Rusk, John. *Beautiful Stories that Never Grow Old*. [Copyright by John Rusk. No city of publication or publisher provided], 1902.

"The Sabbath Breaker Punished; Or, The Effects of Sabbath-Breaking." *The Youth's Friend* (October 1830): 157–8.

Sanders, Karen N. *A Man Named Noah: The Story of the Great Flood and God's Promise*. Illus. by Marcy Ramsey. St. Louis, MO: Concordia Publishing House, 2007.

Sangster, Margaret. *The Story Bible*. New York: Moffat, Yard, & Company, 1905.

Sassi, Laura. *Goodnight Ark*. Illus. by Jane Chapman. Grand Rapids, MI: Zondervan, 2014.

Sasso, Sandy Eisenberg. *Noah's Wife: The Story of Naamah*. Illus. by Bethanne Andersen. Woodstock, VT: Jewish Lights Publishing, 2002.

Schoolland, Marian M. *Marian's Big Book of Bible Stories*. Illus. by Dirk Gringhuis. Grand Rapids, MI: Wm. B. Eerdmans Publishing Company, 1950.

Schoolland, Marian M. *Marian's Favorite Bible Stories*. Grand Rapids, MI: Wm. B. Eerdmans Publishing Company, 1949.

Scovil, Elisabeth Robinson. *Wee Folks Stories from the Old Testament: In Words of One Syllable*. Philadelphia, PA: Henry Altemus Company, 1920.

Scriptural Stories for Very Young Children. Philadelphia, PA: Kimber & Conrad, 1814.

Scripture History. New York: Wood, 1811.

Scripture History, Abridged. Boston, MA: Lincoln & Edmands, 1819.

Scripture History, or Short Sketches of Characters from the Old Testament. New York: Mahlon Day, 1829.

Scripture Stories. Salt Lake City, UT: Church of Jesus Christ of Latter-day Saints, 1980.

Segal, Lore. *The Book of Adam to Moses*. Illus. by Leonard Baskin. New York: Alred A. Knopf, 1987.

Shaw, S. B. *Touching Incidents and Remarkable Answers to Prayer: Children's Edition*. Grand Rapids, MI: Shaw Publishing Company, 1895.

Sherman, Henry A. and Charles Foster Kent. *The Children's Bible: Selections from the Old and New Testaments*. New York: Charles Scribner's Sons, 1922, 1947.

Sherwood, Mary. *Scripture Prints, with explanations in the form of familiar dialogues*. New York: Pendleton and Hill, 1832.

Shiny Sequin Bible Holy Bible (International Children's Bible). New York: Tommy Nelson, 2011.

A Short History of the Bible and Testament. Hartford, CT: Cooke & Hale, 1817.

A Short History of the Holy Bible: Embellished with numerous colored engravings. Harrisburg, PA: G. S. Peters, 1838.

Silverthorne, Sandy. *The Great Bible Adventure*. Eugene, OR: Harvest House, 1990.

Smith, Angie. *For Such a Time as This. Stories of Women from the Bible, Retold for Girls*. Illus. by Breezy Brookshire. Nashville, TN: B & H Publishing Group, 2014.

Smith, Brendan Powell. *The Brick Bible: A New Spin on the Old Testament*. New York: Skyhorse Publishing, 2011.

Smith, Brendan Powell. *Noah's Ark: The Brick Bible for Kids*. New York: Sky Pony Press, 2012.

Smith, Gertrude. *Baby Bible Stories*. Philadelphia, PA: Henry Altemus Company, 1904.

Smith, Gertrude. *Robbie's Bible Stories*. Philadelphia, PA: Henry Altemus Company, 1905.

Smith, Thomas. *The Sacred Mirror; or Compendious View of Scripture History*. Boston, MA: Samuel H. Parker, 1806.

Smyth, Lindley, Jr. *Happy Sundays with the Bible*. Philadelphia, PA: Uplift Publishing Company, 1908.

Snyder, Harvey Albert. *Boys and Girls of the Bible*. Washington, DC: W.E. Scull, 1911.

Sooy, J. L. *Bible Talks with Children: The Scriptures Simplified for the Little Folk*. New York: Union Publishing House, 1889.

Spalding, Arthur Whitefield. *Golden Treasury of Bible Stories*. Mountain View, CA: Pacific Press Publishing Association, 1954.

Stewart, Mary. *Tell Me a True Story*. New York: Fleming H. Revell Company, 1909.

Stickney, Anne Elizabeth. *The Loving Arms of God*. Grand Rapids, MI: Eerdmans Books for Young Readers, 2001.

Stirling, John, ed. *The Child's Bible*. Indianapolis, IN: Bobbs-Merrill Company, circa. 1920.

Stoddard, Sandol. *The Doubleday Illustrated Children's Bible*. Garden City, NY: Doubleday & Company, 1983.

Stoddard, Sandol. *The BOMC Illustrated Children's Bible*. New York: Book of the Month Club, 2001.

Stories from the Bible. Northampton, MA: E. Turner [1843].

Stories from Scripture for Small Children. New Haven, CT: J. Babcock and Son, 1820.

Stortz, Diane. *The Sweetest Story Bible: Sweet Thoughts and Sweet Words for Little Girls*. Illus. by Sheila Bailey. Grand Rapids, MI: Zondervan, 2010.

Stortz, Diane. *The Sweetest Story Bible for Toddlers*. Illus. by Sheila Bailey. Grand Rapids, MI: Zondervan, 2010.

Stortz, Diane, and Greg Holder. *My Bible Pals Storybook*. Illus. by Jodie McCallum. Cincinnati, OH: Standard Publishing Company, 1996.

Sunday evenings; or, An easy introduction to the reading of the Bible. New York: J. & J. Harper, 1832.

The Super Heroes Bible: The Quest for Good Over Evil (NIrV). Grand Rapids, MI: Zondervan, 2002.

Tallis's Illustrated Scripture History for the Improvement of Youth, Vol. I. London and New York: J. & P. Tallis, 1851.

Tanakh: The Holy Scriptures: The New JPS Translation According to the Traditional Hebrew Text. Philadelphia, PA: Jewish Publication Society, 1988.

Tangvald, Christine Harder. *The Big Big Big Boat and Other Bible Stories about Obedience*. Elgin, IL: Chariot Books, 1993.

Tappan, Eva March. *An Old, Old Story-Book: Compiled from the Old Testament*. Boston, MA, and New York: Houghton Mifflin Company, 1910.

Taylor, John. *Verbum Sempiternum*. 3rd edn. Providence, RI: n.p., 1774.

Taylor, Kenneth N. *My First Bible in Pictures*. Wheaton, IL: Tyndale House, 1989.

Taylor, Kenneth N. *Family-Time Bible*. Wheaton, IL: Tyndale House, 1992.

Taylor, Paul Stanley. *The Great Dinosaur Mystery*. Colorado Springs, CO: Chariot Victor Publishing, 1987.

Theola, Mary. *Catholic Bible Stories*. New York: Regina Press, 1960.

Theola, Mary. *The Catholic Children's Bible*. Illus. by J. Verleye. New York: Regina Press, 1983, 2008.

Thomas, Florence. *Noah's Ark: Bible Story Series*. New York: GAF View-Master, 1965.

Thomas, Mack. *The Bible Animal Storybook*. Illus. by Elizabeth Hagler. Sisters, OR: Questar Publishers, Inc., 1990.

Thomas, Mack. *The First Step Bible*. Illus. by Joe Stites. Sisters, OR: Questar Publishers, Inc., 1994.

Touch-and-See Bible. Illus. by Eileen Hine. Cincinnati, OH: Standard Publishing, 2004.

True Stories Related. New York: Samuel Wood, 1814.

Turner, Philip. *The Bible Story*. Illus. by Brian Wildsmith. Oxford, New York, Toronto: Oxford University Press, 1968.

Turner, William. *An Abstract of the Bible History*. Boston, MA: Bowles & Dearborn, 1828.

Tutu, Desmond. *Children of God Storybook Bible*. Grand Rapids, MI, Zonderkids, 2010.

Tyler, John Williamson. *The Bible Story Newly Told for Young People*. William S. Whiteford, 1901.

Union Questions on Selected Portions of Scripture, Vol. III. Philadelphia, PA: American Sunday School Union, 1830.

Ussher, James. *The Annals of the World*. Green Forest, AZ: Master Books, 2003.

Van Loon, Hendrik Willem. *The Story of the Mankind*. New York: Boni & Liveright, 1921.

Van Loon, Hendrik Willem. *The Story of the Bible*. New York: Boni & Liveright, 1923.

Van Zeller, Dom Hubert. *Old Testament Stories: Scripture Textbooks for Catholic Schools*. Westminster, MD: Newman Press, 1949.

The Veggie Tales Bible: New International Version. Grand Rapids, MI: Zondervan, 2009.

Vos, Catherine F. *Child's Story Bible*. Grand Rapids, MI: William B., Eerdmans, 1934, 1949, 1958.

Wade, Connie Morgan and Diane Stortz. *Rhyme Time Bible Stories: Noah's Ark*. Illus. by Laura Ovresat. Cincinnati, OH: Standard Publishing, 2012.

Wahl, Jan. *Runaway Jonah and Other Tales*. Illus. by Uri Shulevitch. New York: Macmillan Company, 1968.

Walker, E. Jerry. *Stories from the Bible: Old Testament*. Westwood, NJ: Fleming H. Revell Company, 1955.

Wallace Lew. *The Boyhood of Christ*. New York: Harper & Brothers, 1888.

Walsh, Sheila. *The Princess in Me Storybook Bible*. Nashville, TN: Thomas Nelson, 2008.

Waters, Mark. *The Pilgrim Book of Bible Stories*. Illus. by Diana Shimon. Cleveland, OH: Pilgrim Press, 2003.

Watts, Isaac. *Dr. Watts's Plain and Easy Catechisms for children: The Shorter Catechism*. Cambridge: Hillard & Metcalf, 1815.

Watts, Isaac. *Scripture History*. New York and London: George Routledge and Sons, 1820.

White, Annie R. *Bible Story Land: for Home, School and Sunday-School*. Chicago: National Punlishing Co., 1891.

White, Annie R. *Easy Steps for Little Feet from Genesis to Revelations*. Los Angeles: Martin Press, 1903.

Wilder, Charlotte F. *The Child's Own Book*, Vol. 1. Chicago: Howard-Severance Company, 1911.

Willard, J. H. *The Boy Who Obeyed: The Story of Isaac*. Philadelphia, PA: Henry Altemus Company, 1905.

Wolverton, Basil. *The Bible Story*, Vol. I. Pasadena, CA: Ambassador College Press, 1961.

Wolverton, Basil. *The Wolverton Bible*. Seattle, Wash.: Fantagraphics Books, 2009.

Woodhall, Ruth and Shahada Sharelle Abdul Haqq, *Stories of the Prophets in the Holy Qur'an*. Somerset, NJ: Tughra Books, 2008.

Worcester, William L. *On Holy Ground: Bible Stories with Pictures of Bible Lands*. Philadelphia, PA, and London: J. B. Lippincott Company, 1904.

Wright, Sally Ann, and Honor Ayers. *Baby's First Bible*. Lutherville, MD: Anno Domini Publishing, 2012.

Yonge, Charlotte M. *Young Folks' Bible History*. Boston, MA: D. Lothrop Company, 1880.

Young, Sarah. *Jesus Calling Bible Storybook*. Illus. by Carolin Farias. Nashville, TN: Thomas Nelson, 2012.
Young Bible Reader. Cincinnati, OH: William T. Truman [1843].

Other Resources

Abbot, Jacob. *Gentle Measures in the Management of the Young*. New York: Harper and Brothers, 1872.

Adomeit, Ruth Elizabeth. *Three Centuries of Thumb Bibles: A Checklist*. New York: Garland Publishing, Inc., 1980.

Alter, Robert. *Genesis: Translation and Commentary*. New York: W. W. Norton & Company, 1996.

Alter, Robert. *The Five Books of Moses: A Translation with Commentary*. New York: W. W. & Company, 2004.

Amihay, Aryeh. "Noah in Rabbinic Literature," in *Noah and His Book(s)*. Leiden and Boston, MA: Brill, 2010, 193–214.

Armstrong, Herbert W. "At Last! Here is the Bible Story Book." *The Plain Truth* 23:11 (November 1958): 5–20.

Arnold, Bill T. *Genesis*. Cambridge: Cambridge University Press, 2009.

Avery, Gillian. *Behold the Child: American Children and Their Books 1621–1922*. London: Bodley Head, 1994.

Bado-Fralick, Nikki, and Rebecca Sachs Norris. *Toying with God: The World of Religious Games and Dolls*. Waco, TX: Baylor University Press, 2010.

Bailey, Lloyd R. *Noah: The Person and Story in Historical Tradition*. Columbia, SC: University of South Carolina Press, 1989.

Bailyn, Bernard et al. *The Great Republic: A History of the American People*. Boston, MA: Little, Brown and Company, 1977.

Beggs, C. Spencer. "Brick Testament." *Rolling Stone* (October 6, 2005), 98.

Berryman, Jerome W. *Godly Play: A Way of Religious Education*. San Francisco: HarperSanFrancisco, 1991.

Bottigheimer, Ruth B. *The Bible for Children: From the Age of Gutenberg to the Present*. New Haven, CT: Yale University Press, 1996.

Bottigheimer, Ruth B. "The Otherness of Children's Bibles in Historical Perspective," in Caroline Vander Stichele and Hugh S. Pyper, eds, *Text, Image, and Otherness in Children's Bibles: What is in the Picture?* Semeia Studies 56. Atlanta: Society of Biblical Literature, 2012, 321–32.

Boylan, Anne M. *Sunday School: The Formation of an American Institution 1790–1880*. New Haven, CT: Yale University Press, 1988.

Brooks, Cleanth. *The Well-Wrought Urn*. London: Dennis Dobson, 1947, 1968.

Burt, Merlin D. "History of Seventh-day Adventist Views on the Trinity." *Journal of the Adventist Theological Society* 17:1 (Spring 2006): 125–39.

Bushnell, Horace. *Christian Nurture*. New York: Charles Scribner's Sons, 1888, 1916.

Carter, Warren. *Seven Events that Shaped the New Testament World*. Grand Rapids, MI: Baker Academic, 2013.

Chancey, Mark A. *Reading, Writing & Religion II: Texas Public School Bible Courses in 2011–12*. Austin, TX: Texas Freedom Network Education Fund, 2013.

Childs, Brevard S. "Allegory and Typology within Biblical Interpretation," in Christopher

R. Seitz and Kent Harold Richards, eds, *The Bible as Christian Scripture*. Atlanta, GA: Society of Biblical Literature, 2013, 299–311.

Cocks, Neil. "'Scripture Its Own Interpreter': Mary Martha Sherwood, The Bible and Female Autobiography." *Nineteenth-Century Gender Studies* 7:3 (Winter 2011).

Dalton, Russell W. "Perfect Prophets, Helpful Hippos and Happy Endings: Noah and Jonah in Children's Bible Storybooks in the U.S." *Religious Education* 102:3 (June 2007): 298–313.

Dalton, Russell W. "Introduction," in *Ben-Hur: A Tale of the Christ*. New York: Barnes and Noble Books, 2004, xi–xix.

Dalton, Russell W. "Meek and Mild: American Children's Bibles' Stories of Jesus as a Boy." *Religious Education* 109:1 (2014): 45–60.

De Hamel, Christopher. *The Book: A History of the Bible*. New York: Phaidon Press, Inc., 2001.

Dewey, John. "Religious Education as Conditioned by Modern Psychology and Pedagogy." *The Religious Education Association: Proceedings of the First Annual Convention, Chicago, February 10–12*. Chicago: Religious Education Association, 1903.

Edwards, Jonathan. "The Manner in Which Salvation is Sought," in *Sermons of Jonathan Edwards*. Peabody, MA: Hendrickson Publishing, Inc., 2005, 357–75.

Edwards, Jonathan, Henry Rogers, Sereno Edwards Dwight, and Edward Hickman. *The Works of Jonathan Edwards, Vol. II*. London: W. Ball, 1839.

Ephrem the Syrian. "Commentary on Genesis 6.9.2." in *Fathers of the Church: A New Translation*. 91.139. Washington, DC: Catholic University of America Press, 1947.

Erikson, Erik H. *Childhood and Society*. New York: W. W. Norton, 1950.

Evans, Emry. "Readers Recreating Texts," in Bill Corcoran and Emry Evans, eds, *Readers, Texts, Teachers*. Upper Montclair, NJ: Boynton/Cook Publishers, Inc. 1987, 22–40.

Exum, J. Cheryl. "What Does a Child Want? Reflections on Children's Bible Stories," in Caroline Vander Stichele and Hugh S. Pyper, eds, *Text, Image, and Otherness in Children's Bibles: What is in the Picture?* Semeia Studies 56. Atlanta, GA: Society of Biblical Literature, 2012, 333–45.

Fairbairn, Patrick. *The Typology of Scripture*. Philadelphia, PA: Smith and English, 1854.

Feldman, Louis H. "Questions about the Great Flood, as Viewed by Philo, Pseudo-Philo, Josephus, and the Rabbis." *Zeitschrift für die Alttestamentliche Wissenschaft* (ZATW) 115:3 (September 2003): 401–22.

Freud, Sigmund. *Three Contributions to the Sexual Theory*. Trans. A. A. Brill. New York: Journal of Nervous and Mental Disease Publishing Company, 1910.

Furnish, Dorothy Jean. *Experiencing the Bible with Children*. Nashville, TN: Abingdon Press, 1990.

Gadamer, Hans-Georg. *Truth and Method*. Trans. by Garret Barden and John Cumming. New York: Seabury Press, 1975.

Gangel, Kenneth O. and Warren S. Benson. *Christian Education: Its History & Philosophy*. Chicago: Moody Press, 1983.

Giles, Thomas S. "Pick a Bible—Any Bible." *Christianity Today* (October 26, 1992): 26–7.

Gobbel, A. Roger, and Gertrude G. Gobbel. *The Bible: A Child's Playground*. Philadelphia, PA: Fortress Press, 1986.

Gold, Penny Schine. *Making the Bible Modern: Children's Bibles and Jewish Education in Twentieth-Century America*. Ithaca, NY: Cornell University Press, 2004.

Goldenberg, David M. *The Curse of Ham: Race and Slavery in Early Judaism, Christianity, and Islam*. Princeton, NJ: Princeton University Press, 2009.

Goldman, Ronald. *Readiness for Religion: A Basis for Developmental Religious Education.* New York: Seabury Press, 1965.

Gunn, David. "Cultural Criticism," in Gale A. Yee, ed., *Judges & Method: New Approaches in Biblical Studies*, 2nd edn. Minneapolis, MN: Fortress Press, 2007, 202–36.

Gutjahr, Paul C. *An American Bible: A History of the Good Book in the United States, 1777–1880.* Stanford, CA: Stanford University Press, 1999.

Hammond, Gerald. "English Translations of the Bible," in Robert Alter and Frank Kermode, eds, *The Literary Guide to the Bible.* Cambridge: Belknap Press, 1987, 647–66.

Harman, Allan M. "The Impact of Matthew Henry's *Exposition* on Eighteenth-Century Christianity." *Evangelical Quarterly* 82:1 (2010): 3–14.

Haynes, Stephen R. *Noah's Curse: The Biblical Justification of American Slavery.* Oxford: Oxford University Press, 2002.

Henry, Matthew, and Thomas Scott. *Commentary on the Holy Bible: Matthew–Revelation.* Nashville, TN: Royal Publishers, 1979.

Hunter, James Davison. *Culture Wars: The Struggle to Define America.* New York: Basic Books, 1991.

Hunter, James Davison. *The Death of Character: Moral Education in an Age without Good or Evil.* New York: Basic Books, 2000.

Inbody, Tyron. *The Faith of the Christian Church.* Grand Rapids, MI: William B. Eerdmans Publishing Company, 2005.

Iser, Wolfgang. *The Implied Reader: Patterns in Communication in Prose Fiction from Bunyan to Beckett.* Baltimore, MD: Johns Hopkins University Press, 1974.

Isham, G. W. "Mrs. C. F. Wilder." *Woman's Missionary Friend* 49:2. (February 1917): 65–6.

Johnson, Sylvester. *The Myth of Ham in Nineteenth-Century American Christianity.* New York: Palgrave Macmillan, 2004.

Katz, Micahel B. *Class, Bureaucracy, and Schools.* New York: Praeger, 1971.

Kniker, Charles R. "New Attitudes and New Curricula: The Changing Role of the Bible in Protestant Education, 1880–1920," in David L. Barr and Nicholas Piediscalzi, eds, *The Bible in American Education: From Source Book to Textbook.* Philadelphia, PA: Fortress Press, 1982, 121–42.

Laderman, Gary. *The Sacred Remains: American Attitudes Toward Death, 1799–1883.* New Haven, CT, and London: Yale University Press, 1996.

Lankard, Frank Glenn. *A History of the American Sunday School Curriculum.* New York: Abingdon Press, 1927.

Larrick, Nancy. "The All-White World of Children's Books," in Osayimwense Osa, ed., *The All White World of Children's Books & African American Children's Literature.* Trenton, NJ: African World Press, Inc., 1995, 1–12.

Locke, John. *Some Thoughts Concerning Education.* London: n.p., 1693.

Luther Martin. *Luther Works.* II. *Lectures on Genesis Chapters 6–14.* Ed. by J. Pelican. St. Louis, MO: Concordia Publishing House, 1960.

Lynn, Robert W., and Elliott Wright. *The Big Little School.* Rev. edn. Birmingham, AL: Religious Education Press, 1980.

Mann, Horace, and William Bentley Fowle. *The Common School Journal* 1:1 (November 1831).

Marcus, Leonard S. *Minders of Make-Believe.* Boston, MA: Houghton Mifflin Company, 2008.

Mather, Cotton. *Corderius Americanus: A Discourse on the Good Education of Children.* Boston, MA: Dutton & Wentworth, 1828.

Maughan, Shannon. "In the Kids' Corner." *Publishers Weekly* 246:41 (October 11, 1999): 46.

McClellan, B. Edward. *Moral Education in America: Schools and the Shaping of Character from Colonial Times to the Present*. New York: Teachers College Press, 1999.

McKeown, James. *Genesis*. Grand Rapids, MI: William B. Eerdmans Publishing Company, 2008.

Mintz, Steven. *Huck's Raft: A History of American Childhood*. Cambridge, MA: Harvard University Press, 2004.

Mitchell, Pamela. "'Why Care About Stories?' A Theory of Narrative Art." *Religious Education* 86 (1991): 30–43.

Moody, Dwight L. "Day of Rest: Come Thou Into the Ark." *The Aroha News* 4:175 (October 23, 1886): 8.

Murray, David. *Jesus on Every Page: 10 Simple Ways to Seek and Find Christ in the Old Testament*. Nashville, TN: Thomas Nelson, 2013.

Neff, LaVonne. "Bible Stories: Facing a Floodtide." *Publishers Weekly* 248:42 (October 15, 2001): 38.

Neidhart, Walter. "What the Bible Means to Children and Adolescents." *Religious Education* 63 (1968): 112–19.

Niebuhr, Reinhold. *Moral Man and Immoral Society*. New York and London: Charles Scribner's Sons, 1932.

Norris, John. *Spiritual Counsel, or, The Father's Advice to His Children*. London: S. Manship, 1694.

Osa, Osayimwense, ed. *The All-White World of Children's Books and African American Children's Literature*. Trenton, NJ: African World Press, 1995.

Payne, Buckner H. ("Ariel"). *The Negro: What is His Ethnographic Status: Is He the Progeny of Ham?* Cincinnati, OH: Published for the Proprietor, 1867.

Piaget, Jean. *Origins of Intelligence in Children*. Trans. by Margaret Cook. New York: International University Press, 1952.

Preston, Samuel H., and Michael Hains. *Fatal Years. Child Mortality in Late Nineteenth-century America*. Princeton, NJ: Princeton University Press, 1991.

Priest, Josiah. *Slavery as It Relates to the Negro or African Race*. New York: Arno, 1843, 1977.

Priest, Josiah. *Bible Defence of Slavery or, The Origin, History, and Fortunes of the Negro Race*. Louisville, KY: Willis A. Bush, 1851.

Prothero, Stephen. *American Jesus*. New York: Farrar, Straus and Giroux, 2003.

Prothero, Stephen. *Religious Literacy: What Every American Needs to Know – And Doesn't*. San Francisco: HarperSanFrancisco, 2007.

Remy, Jean S. *The Lives of the Presidents Told in Words of One Syllable*. New York: A. L. Burt Company, 1900.

Roberts, Jonathan. "Introduction," in Michael Lieb, Emma Mason, and Jonathan Roberts, eds, *The Oxford Handbook of the Reception History of the Bible*. Oxford: Oxford University Press, 2011, 1–8.

Sampley, J. S. *A Bible History of the Negro*. Greenville, AL: Greenville Advocate, 1887.

Sánchez-Eppler, Karen. *Dependent States: The Child's Part in Nineteenth-Century American Culture*. Chicago: University of Chicago Press, 2005.

Sharon, Nadav, and Moshe Tishel. "Distinctive Traditions about Noah and the Flood in Second Temple Jewish Literature," in Michael E. Stone et al., eds, *Noah and His Book(s)*. Leiden and Boston, MA: Brill, 2010, 143–65.

Short, Kathy. "Making Connections Across Literature and Life," in Kathleen E. Holland, et al., eds, *Journeying: Children Responding to Literature*. Portsmouth, NH: Heinemann Press, 1993, 284–6.

Skinner, John. *A Critical and Exegetical Commentary on Genesis*. New York: Charles Scribner's Sons, 1925.

Smith, Christian, with Melinda Lundquist Denton. *Soul Searching: The Religious and Spiritual Lives of American Teenagers*. Oxford: Oxford University Press, 2005.

Spock, Benjamin. *The Common Sense Book of Baby and Child Care*. New York: Duell, Sloane and Pearce, 1946.

Stannard, David E. *The Puritan Way of Death*. New York: Oxford University Press, 1977.

Stephens, John, and Robyn McCallum. *Retelling Stories, Framing Culture: Traditional Story and Metanarratives in Children's Literature*. New York and London: Garland Publishing, Inc., 1998.

Stout, Harry S. *The Divine Dramatist: George Whitefield and the Rise of Modern Evangelicalism*. Grand Rapids, MI: William B. Eerdmans Publishing Company, 1991.

Tanakh: The Holy Scriptures: The New JPS Translation According to the Traditional Hebrew Text. Philadelphia, PA: Jewish Publication Society, 1988.

Taylor, Edward. *Upon the Types of the Old Testament*, ed. Charles W. Mignon. Lincoln, NE: University of Nebraska Press, 1989.

Thomson, William Hanna. *The Great Argument, or Jesus Christ in the Old Testament*. New York: Harper, 1884.

Townsend, John Rowe. *Written for Children*: 3rd rev. edn. New York: J. B. Lippincott, 1987.

Trent, Kenneth E. *Types of Christ in the Old Testament: A Conservative Approach to Old Testament Typology*. New York: Exposition Press, 1960.

Vander Stichele, Caroline, and Hugh S. Pyper, eds. *Text, Image, and Otherness in Children's Bibles: What is in the Picture?*, Semeia Studies 56. Atlanta, GA: Society of Biblical Literature, 2012.

Van Loon, Hendrick Willem. *Tolerance*. New York: Boni & Liveright, 1925.

Welhausen, Julius. *Prolegomena to the History of Ancient Israel*. New York: Meridian Books, 1957.

Wenham, George J. *Word Biblical Commentary: Genesis 1–15*. Waco, TX: Word Books, 1987.

White, Ellen G. *The Great Controversy; Between Christ and Satan*. Mountain View, CA: Pacific Press Publishing Association, 1888.

White, Ellen G. *The Story of Patriarchs and Prophets*. Mountain View, CA: Pacific Press Publishing Association, 1890, 1913.

White, Ellen G. *Spiritual Gifts*, Vols. III–IV. Washington DC: Review and Herald Publishing, 1945.

Wilhoit, James C. "The Bible Goes to Sunday School: An Historical Response to Pluralism." *Religious Education* 82 (1987): 390–404.

Wishy, Bernard. *The Child and the Republic*. Philadelphia, PA: University of Pennsylvania Press, 1968.

INDEX OF CHILDREN'S BIBLES AND OTHER BIBLE-RELATED BOOKS FOR CHILDREN, SORTED BY ERAS AND LISTED ALPHABETICALLY

INDEX OF REFERENCES

INDEX OF AUTHORS
(EXCLUDING CHILDREN'S BIBLES)